German Modernities from Wilhelm to Weimar

D1610115

German Modernities from Wilhelm to Weimar

A Contest of Futures

Edited by Geoff Eley, Jennifer L. Jenkins, and Tracie Matysik

Bloomsbury Academic
An imprint of Bloomsbury Publishing Plc

B L O O M S B U R Y
LONDON · OXFORD · NEW YORK · NEW DELHI · SYDNEY

Bloomsbury Academic

An imprint of Bloomsbury Publishing Plc

50 Bedford Square	1385 Broadway
London	New York
WC1B 3DP	NY 10018
UK	USA

www.bloomsbury.com

BLOOMSBURY and the Diana logo are trademarks of Bloomsbury Publishing Plc

First published 2016

© Geoff Eley, Jennifer L. Jenkins, Tracie Matysik and Contributors, 2016

British Library Cataloguing-in-Publication Data
A catalogue record for this book is available from the British Library.

ISBN: HB: 978-1-4742-1628-9
PB: 978-1-4742-1627-2
ePDF: 978-1-4742-1629-6
ePub: 978-1-4742-1630-2

Library of Congress Cataloging-in-Publication Data
Names: Eley, Geoff, 1949- | Jenkins, Jennifer, 1966- | Matysik, Tracie.
Title: German modernities from Wilhelm to Weimar : a contest of futures /
edited by Geoff Eley, Jennifer L. Jenkins and Tracie Matysik.
Description: London ; New York : Bloomsbury Academic, an imprint of Bloomsbury
Publishing Plc, 2016. | Includes bibliographical references and index.
Identifiers: LCCN 2015047952 (print) | LCCN 2016011673 (ebook) |
ISBN 9781474216289 (hardback) | ISBN 9781474216272 (paperback) |
ISBN 9781474216296 (PDF) | ISBN 9781474216302 (ePub) | ISBN 9781474216296 (ePDF)
Subjects: LCSH: Germany–History–1871-1918. | Germany–History–1918-1933. |
Social change–Germany–History–19th century. | Social change–Germany–History–
20th century. | Germany–Intellectual life. | Germany–Politics and government–
1871-1933. | Imperialism–Social aspects–Germany–History–19th century. |
Imperialism–Social aspects–Germany–History–20th century. |
BISAC: HISTORY / Europe / Germany. | HISTORY / Modern / 20th Century. |
HISTORY / Modern / 19th Century.
Classification: LCC DD222 .G46 2016 (print) | LCC DD222 (ebook) | DDC 943.08–dc23
LC record available at http://lccn.loc.gov/2015047952

Cover design: Catherine Wood
Cover image © Bildarchiv Preußischer Kulturbesitz/
German History in Documents and Images

Typeset by Integra Software Services Pvt. Ltd.
Printed and bound in India

CONTENTS

LIST OF ILLUSTRATIONS

ACKNOWLEDGMENTS

This book is the result of a long conversation among its contributors and several other valuable interlocutors that took place during five meetings at four institutions. We are consequently grateful for funding support from the many sources that made our work possible: the Joint Initiative in German and European Studies and the Department of History at the University of Toronto; the Canada Research Chairs Program, particularly the Chair in Modern German History at the University of Toronto; the Horace H. Rackham School of Graduate Studies, the Departments of History and of German, Dutch & Scandinavian Studies, the Center for European Studies, and the College of Literature, Science and Arts at the University of Michigan; the Charles Phelps Taft Memorial Fund and the Taft Research Center at the University of Cincinnati; the Institute for Historical Studies, the Center for European Studies, the Departments of History and of Germanic Studies, and the College of Liberal Arts at the University of Texas at Austin. We would like to extend special thanks to the German Academic Exchange Service (DAAD), which provided support for several workshops and discussions. Intellectual contributions from Edward Ross Dickinson, Kathy Pence, Kevin Repp, Mary O'Reilly, Deborah Neill, Roberta Pergher, and Richard Steigmann-Gall were essential to the development of the overall project. They were wonderful interlocutors in the discussions that led to this book. We are especially grateful to Ken Garner for his work in preparing the final manuscript and index.

Chapters from Young-sun Hong and Mark Roseman are reproductions of articles that originally appeared in journals. We thank *Social History* and the *American Historical Review*, respectively, for permission to reprint.

LIST OF CONTRIBUTORS

Manuela Achilles is Associate Director of the Center for German Studies at the University of Virginia. She teaches in the Corcoran Department of History and the Department of Germanic Languages and Literatures and has published at the intersections of history and literature, with a focus on modern Germany. Her edited volume *Environmental Sustainability in Transatlantic Perspective: A Multidisciplinary Approach* (Palgrave Macmillan, 2013) explores the German energy transition (*Energiewende*) within the broader context of transnational partnership and cooperation. She is currently completing a book on constitutional patriotism and the desire for democracy in Weimar Germany.

Kathleen Canning is the Sonya O. Rose Collegiate Professor of History and Arthur F. Thurnau Professor of History, German and Women's Studies at the University of Michigan. She is the author of *Languages of Labor and Gender: Female Factory Work in Germany, 1850–1914* (Cornell University Press, 1996) and *Gender History in Practice: Historical Perspectives on Bodies, Class, and Citizenship* (Cornell University Press, 2006), and co-editor of *Weimar Publics/Weimar Subjects: Rethinking the Political Culture of Germany in the 1920s* (Berghahn, 2010). Her current book project, *Citizenship Effects: Gender and Sexual Crisis in the Aftermath of War and Revolution in Germany*, examines the history of citizenship, gender, and sexuality in Germany during the First World War and the Weimar Republic.

Geoff Eley is Karl Pohrt Distinguished University Professor of Contemporary History and Professor of German Studies at the University of Michigan. His most recent works include *Forging Democracy: The History of the Left in Europe, 1850–2000* (Oxford University Press, 2002); *A Crooked Line: From Cultural History to the History of Society* (University of Michigan Press, 2005); (with Keith Nield) *The Future of Class in History: What's Left of the Social?* (University of Michigan Press, 2007); and *Nazism as Fascism: Violence, Ideology, and the Ground of Consent in Germany, 1930–1945* (Routledge, 2013). He is currently writing a general history of Europe in the twentieth century.

Larry Frohman is Associate Professor of History at the State University of New York at Stony Brook. He is the author of *Poor Relief and Welfare* *in Germany from the Reformation to World War I* (Cambridge University Press, 2008), along with a series of articles on the German welfare state. He is currently working on a study of surveillance, privacy, and the politics of personal information in West Germany.

Young-sun Hong is Professor of History at the State University of New York at Stony Brook. She is the author of *Cold War Germany, the Third World, and the Global Humanitarian Regime* (Cambridge University Press, 2015). She has also published a number of essays on the transnational history of the two German states. Her first book was *Welfare, Modernity, and the Weimar State, 1919–1933* (Princeton University Press, 1998).

Jennifer L. Jenkins is Associate Professor of German and European history at the University of Toronto, where she held a Canada Research Chair in Modern German History. She is the author of *Provincial Modernity: Local Culture and Liberal Politics in Fin-de-Siècle Hamburg* (Cornell University Press, 2003) and is finishing *Weltpolitik on the Persian Frontier: Germany and Iran in the Age of Empire*, an exploration of Germany's involvement in the "Great Game" from the Crimean War to Operation Barbarossa.

Marti Lybeck is Assistant Professor of History at the University of Wisconsin La Crosse. She is the author of *Desiring Emancipation: New Women and Homosexuality in Germany, 1890–1933* (SUNY Press, 2014). Focusing on female homosexuality in Europe between the 1890s and the 1930s, she studies the interconnections between emancipated women's self-constructions and the political issues and affiliations they pursued.

John V. Maciuika is Professor of Art and Architectural history at the City University of New York, Baruch College, and the CUNY Graduate Center. His research interests include the relationship between architecture and cultural identity; shifting narratives of the "modern" over time in architecture and design; the sociology of the design professions; and the cultural politics of architecture in particular national settings. He is the author of *Before the Bauhaus: Architecture, Politics, and the German State, 1890–1920* (Cambridge University Press, 2005).

Tracie Matysik is Associate Professor of History at the University of Texas at Austin. She is the author of *Reforming the Moral Subject: Ethics and Sexuality in Central Europe, 1890–1930* (Cornell University Press, 2008). Currently she is working on a book project provisionally entitled *Spinoza Matters: Pantheism, Materialism, and Alternative Enlightenment Legacies in Nineteenth-Century Europe*.

Mark Roseman is Pat M. Glazer Chair in Jewish Studies and Professor in history at Indiana University. His most recent publications include *A Past* *in Hiding* (Allen Lane, the Penguin Press, 2000); *The Villa, the Lake, the Meeting. The Wannsee Conference and the Final Solution* (Penguin, 2002); and *Jewish Responses to Persecution, 1933–1946: Volume I, 1933–1938* (with Jürgen Matthäus) (AltaMira Press, 2010). His current projects include a critical synthesis of recent work on Nazi perpetrators and a close study of a life-reform and resistance group in Germany between the 1920s and 2000.

Annemarie Sammartino is Associate Professor of History at Oberlin College. She is the author of *The Impossible Border: Germany and the East, 1914–1922* (Cornell University Press, 2010), a study of the First World War and Weimar crisis of sovereignty through the lens of migration. She is currently working on *Freedomland: Co-op City and the Story of New York, 1965–1995*, and an as-yet-untitled project on migration and mobility in East Germany.

Scott Spector is Professor of History, German, and Judaic Studies at the University of Michigan. He is the author of *Prague Territories: National Conflict and Cultural Innovation in Franz Kafka's Fin de Siècle* (University of California Press, 2000) and *Violent Sensations: Sexuality, Crime, and Utopia in Vienna and Berlin, 1860–1914* (University of Chicago Press, 2016), and co-editor of *After the History of Sexuality: German Genealogies with and beyond Foucault* (Berghahn, 2012). The present essay is part of a forthcoming book on German-Jewish subjectivity and historiography tentatively titled *Modernism without Jews? German-Jewish Subjects and Histories*.

Dennis Sweeney is Associate Professor of History at the University of Alberta. He is the author of *Work, Race, and the Emergence of Radical Right Corporatism in Imperial Germany* (University of Michigan Press, 2009) and is currently finishing a book on the German right during the Wilhelmine and Weimar eras, tentatively entitled *Radical Nationalism, Colonial Empire, and the Beginnings of German Fascism, 1890–1924*.

Andrew Zimmerman is Professor of History at the George Washington University. He is the author of *Anthropology and Antihumanism in Imperial Germany* (Chicago, 2001) and *Alabama in Africa: Booker T. Washington, the German Empire, and the Globalization of the New South* (Princeton, 2010). He is also the editor of Karl Marx and Friedrich Engels, *The Civil War in the United States*, a collection forthcoming in 2016 from International Publishers. He is currently writing a history of the American Civil War as part of a transnational revolution against slave labor and wage labor.

1

Introduction:
German Modernities and
the Contest of Futures

Geoff Eley, Jennifer L. Jenkins, and Tracie Matysik

Modernity, among historians no less than social theorists or cultural critics, remains a disputed yet unavoidable term. With its tangle of sociological, political, and aesthetic definitions, it carries highly normative connotations. As an organizing concept for disciplines across the humanities and social sciences, it has a universalizing reach.[1] It refers to developmental sociological and political processes such as industrialization, democratization, secularization, bureaucratization, parliamentarization, even as it invokes their darker sides—colonialism, scientific racism, instrumental rationality, the global spread of capitalism. Aesthetically, it suggests breaks with tradition, the advance of avant-garde experimentation, the cultivation of self and technology.[2] Yet, if once closely identified with a "Western" mode of development, the category of modernity has now become patently a global term. As such, whether historiographically, in the languages of social and cultural theory, or in the common sense of academic discussion, modernity has acquired a range of new complexities. In some uses, it designates a global condition, differentially manifested and experienced depending on local contexts and power relations. In others, it has become truly plural—via the idea of vernacular or alternative modernities—with multiple formations and a built-in critical resistance against normative implications.[3]

This volume considers the long and complex path of modernity as a pivotal category in German history and historiography. It is attentive to the role the category has played in historical developments between 1880 and 1930, to its place in the field since 1945, *and* to the creative potential offered by its most recent formulations. We are dealing here with a two-way street: if "modernity" decisively defined developments in German history and historiography, "Germany" in its turn always informed modernity itself as an analytical category, shaping the efforts at theorizing it across many decades. On this front, discussions of Germany's modernity have focused especially on the rise of National Socialism and the brutalities of the Second World War and the Holocaust. In one long-standing interpretation, where Western European developments of liberal democracy functioned as the "good" version of modernity, Germany became the antithesis. From the 1950s to the 1980s, postwar scholarship expounded an argument on the reasons for Germany's "missed path" to the modern future, namely its lack of modernity. Its industrial strength in the late nineteenth century was said to have outpaced its "normal" political development, creating obstacles to parliamentarization, while its liberal culture and aesthetic progressivism was stifled by a native authoritarianism. The power unleashed by an unrestrained process of economic modernization—absent any matching political and cultural development capable of tempering and directing its force—was seen to have laid the ground for the rise of National Socialism, the drive toward war, the cult of blood and nation and the Holocaust. In short, the Nazi dictatorship and the genocide it pursued were the monstrous results of a modernity lethally out of sync.[4]

A different and later literature, developing since the 1980s, explained the same events with the same term—*modernity*—but with an important twist. This time it was Germany's surfeit of such, rather than its lack, that led to the gas chambers of Auschwitz. In this narrative, bureaucratization, rationalization, and a deep investment in science and medicine, as tools for the engineering of a "therapeutic" modernity, brought governments and professions to embrace projects of population control and improvement, eugenics, and racial hygiene.[5] In this literature, scientific thinking was the seedbed for Nazism, instrumental rationality the fuel. National Socialism was seen as drawing its ideology and instruments from a hypermodernity born from the "spirit of science."[6] It was again modernity, here differently defined—and radically so— that pointed irrevocably forward to an equally dark outcome.

As the decades go by, each of these literatures has grown ever more unwieldy. Seeking to move beyond the polarized claims and counterclaims about modernity in Germany—too much? too little? progressive? reactionary?—this volume adopts a two-pronged approach. Conceptually, it deploys insights from the new thinking about global modernities to shed new light on Germany in the condensed era of its modern formation, roughly from the 1880s to the 1930s. Rather than taking modernity as a given sociological, political, or aesthetic category, already assembled and clear in its meanings, it approaches German modernities as part of an unfinished and uncertainly developing global condition—as multiple, staged, contested, undecided, combative. As an axiomatic condition of *any* approach to this subject, the approach keeps National Socialism and the Holocaust implicitly and avowedly at the forefront of concern. But the new literatures on modernity allow alternative, supplementary perspectives to come into focus: creative and contested formations of citizenship and subjectivities; colonial, transnational, and global dynamics; political—including democratic—experimentation and critique; and the all-pervasive sense distinctive to the earlier twentieth century that state, society, and subject were available for transformation, that they could be shaped and crafted for a future yet to be known, in a process not already set.

In a second direction of our approach, we turn from strictly theoretical questions about modernity to the historical practitioners themselves, those who were actively involved in conceptualizing and shaping—waging battle for and against—German modernity in its most turbulent moments. What did modernity mean for those living through these accelerated decades? How did practitioners use the concept? What did it mean for them to live in a "modern age"? What opportunities and challenges did the modern world offer and what tools were developed for negotiating its complexities? In our understanding, "modernity" in the singular becomes *modernities* in the plural. We seek to capture the competing voices and visions actively shaping debates on state and society between 1880 and 1930. Each essay takes seriously the many meanings "the modern" came to signify, the multiple projects unfurled under its banner.

If one distinctive feature colored the modern experience for contemporaries in and around the German world between 1880 and 1930, our contributors suggest, it was a sense of rivalry in shaping the future. Whether filled with hope and optimism for what was coming or fear of what it promised, whether longing for a return to the past or eager for a break, private and public individuals alike displayed an awareness that the future was open. That being so, it was their job to give it form. If modernities existed in the plural, differently pursued by competing interests, with rival outlooks and needs, debts and visions that clashed or diverged, they came from this common ground. A sense of turbulence, openness, and flux enabled a drive for direction. History would unfold, but not just by its own logic. Nor did the present flow automatically out of the past and into the future. Rather, the common and encompassing sense of modernity inspired different versions of a tangible future—of destinations to be reached and changes to be secured. Contemporaries could battle in the present to take hold of, even master, the time that awaited them. Grasping the future meant actively shaping "the political" and "the social" of the present tense, the ideas of citizen and the subject, their material and intellectual worlds. While political parties campaigned to shape the state and its policies, reform organizations fought to redefine the contours of the social and of national life itself.

This sense of a future within reach but also in question, so widely diffused by the turn of the century among articulate commentators on the age, was linked to perceptions of velocity, of worlds thrown giddily into motion. The nineteenth century's final decades are now commonly seen in this way, as being marked by a sense of general acceleration. Telegraphs, trains, and steamships rapidly sped up both communication and transportation across once vast distances, giving contemporaries an acute awareness of the incessant marching forward of time. One result was a growing nostalgia for a fleeting past. Writers as diverse as Marcel Proust and Sigmund Freud uncovered the present force of past and buried memories. In the interwar years, Walter Benjamin would lament a past consumed as a "homogeneous and empty time," a meaningless passage of past into present into future, countering this vision to one in which the power of the past is revived so as to puncture the continuum and expose revolutionary potential.[7]

If the past was something to revive, the future, too, presented itself both as all too imminent and as open to intervention. Long gone were notions of religious eschatology; long gone, too, were any Enlightenment beliefs in inevitable historical progress. Instead, just over the chronological horizon was both promise and danger. Everywhere in early twentieth-century Germany prognoses of the future abounded. Optimistic perspectives on the future's potential such as Ernst Bloch's revolutionary *Spirit of Utopia* could be matched by anxious projections such as Carl Schmitt's dystopian vision of a technocratic surveillance state or Oswald Spengler's *The Decline of the West*.[8] Life reformers and state bureaucrats alike obsessed over *Bevölkerungspolitik* and the birth rate; military strategists prepared for the next war; Social Democrats debated the inevitability of the coming collapse of capitalism; and national economists planned for its perpetuation. The future was just around the corner, and everybody wanted a hand in shaping it. The language of the future was also the language of "the world" (*Welt*), a term which shot to popularity in the 1890s. Politics became world politics (*Weltpolitik*); the economy was the world economy (*Weltwirtschaft*); culture was also now incipiently global, a world culture (*Weltkultur*). What kind of global presence would Germany have, *should* Germany have, contemporaries wondered? What role would fall to its citizens in domestic and international governance? How might matters as diverse as social welfare, domestic design, and international trade shape the subjects and the social on the horizon? How could one shape the future?

Yet the present volume differs significantly from other studies. Where most "histories of the future" tend to focus on intellectual discourses about a coming time, including attention to evolving techniques in predicting its course, ours attends to those who were actively fighting to *shape* it. If the majority of actors discussed in this book may not have spoken about the future explicitly, their projects for reform and the campaigns they waged were all too geared to the possibility of crafting a desirable tomorrow. They voiced optimism and anxiety. The range of transformation-oriented activities enacted in realms as diverse as philosophy, welfare reform, political aesthetics, and industrial design indicates a population keenly aware of changing times. Equally important, the essays in this volume indicate no *consensus* about that tomorrow, about the fears and aspirations that contemporaries imagined and invested. Rather, as our title suggests, the focus is on the *contest*, the battles in the present to shape the meanings of subject, citizen, social, and state for the coming times. For those living in the 1890s to the 1930s, the future was not to be divined or anticipated so much as crafted—and fought over—in the here and now.

Thus, following Frederick Cooper's discussion of modernity as a "claim-making concept," "German modernities" refers to the plurality of visions and efforts aiming to make claims on the future: to determine which developments would be underway, what kinds of plans made, which of many alternatives pursued, which aspirations endorsed.[9] As German historians, we are all acutely aware of the National Socialist regime that looms large over this period. At the same time, as scholars of Wilhelmine and Weimar Germany, we attend equally to the variety of aspirations and alternatives pursued by contemporaries who were yet uncertain about exactly what they were creating and which particular future would come. The volume as a whole seeks to hold these two perspectives simultaneously in tension.

Amid the profusion of research and publication in the modern German field—in both scale and substance probably more vibrant and challenging than ever before—there is still little that seeks fully to take the measure of these questions. How should we best characterize the vigorously competing claims to Germany's undecided future in the early twentieth century? A number of recent collections, each fascinating in its way, offer generalizing appraisals of the literatures on Imperial Germany and the place of the *Kaiserreich* in German history but they do so without an explicit attention to modernity as such.[10] New histories of the Weimar Republic have also appeared, but without particularly elaborate reflections on the Wilhelmine genealogies and antecedents.[11] A wealth of monographic publication has engaged—perceptively and often quite brilliantly—with particular areas of the early twentieth-century ferment and flux associated with modernity: whether in ethics, sexuality, aesthetics, design, or the diverse areas of cultural practice that went under the heading of life reform (*Lebensreform*)—naturism and cultivation of the body; clothing reform; *Wandervogel* and other youth movements; artists' colonies and communities; *Heimat* ideas; land reform and garden cities; Werkbund ethos and innovation; dance and theater.[12] But none of these works seeks exactly the conceptual departure attempted here. Without abandoning the importance of the older chronologies—such as the major ruptures of 1914/18 and 1933, or the enormity of the First World War—we foreground the impact of movements, developments, and conflicts that carried across those more familiar chronological divisions, often with the most far-reaching of consequences for the future.

That future contained dangers and promises whose meanings moved dramatically across the lives and perceptions of contemporaries, even as they tried to bring the surrounding changes under manageable intellectual, social, and political purview and control. Those contemporary transformations—unexpected, inspiring, troubling—were palpable in their presence and reach. They were anxiety-producing and undecided. How should they best be historicized? *Contest of Futures* is thus a program in two parts. We propose, first, a compelling and overarching coherence to the whole period from the 1890s to the end of the Weimar Republic. But, second, we argue that it was the Wilhelmine era, whose effects reached into the early 1920s, that proved the truly generative time.[13] In freeing the early twentieth century from the determinative thrall of the rise of the Nazis and the catastrophe of 1933, we seek not to displace or dismiss the latter's importance, but rather to bring it freshly into view. By setting such old and important questions temporarily aside, we can return to them with all the greater success.

Larger thematics

In discussions leading to this volume, four central themes characterized the contests over Germany's early twentieth-century futures. The first of these concerned *empire*, *transnationalism*, and *globality*. The second pertained to a new emphasis on *subjectivity* in social life. The *meta-thematics of reform* as a bundle of projects, practices, and desires aimed at transforming the given political, social, and aesthetic frameworks of the German and global world was the third. The last tackled *politics* very broadly conceived. Before we turn to the order of chapters and their contents, these four themes and their relationship to German modernities deserve brief explication.

Empire, transnationalism, globality

Since the later 1990s, in response to both contemporary globalization and a booming historiography of "empire" in Britain, France, and the United States, empire and imperialism have become topics of intense concern in the German field. One impetus came from cultural studies, as the impact of Edward Said's *Orientalism* conjoined with the challenge of postcolonial perspectives to inspire a renewed interest in Germany's overseas colonialism and its effects. In studies of the colonies themselves, older emphases on economic exploitation, military conquest, and colonial administration have given way to studies of colonialism and culture, or what one of Said's commentators called "the ideological invasion of cultural space." Likewise, colonialism's impact inside the metropole is now traced "not only in political debate and economic and foreign policy, but [in] the social fabric, intellectual discourse and the life of the imagination."[14]

The feeding back into German metropolitan settings of ideas and experiences, social relations and cultural practices, political methods and ideological patterns, fantasies and desires produced in the colonial and semi-colonial worlds decisively informs new scholarship. We now possess proliferating accounts of the colonial encounter, recuperating the agency of indigenous peoples and tracking the incursions of missionaries, military adventurers, travelers and explorers, commercial agents, journalists, anthropologists, botanists, and all the other bearers of colonial expertise. To these may be added a growing number of studies of violence, human rights, and colonial genocide, focusing above all on the 1904 Herero and Nama genocide. Finally, calls for a newly "transnational history" have been decentering the nation-state in the histories of political development, subjective affiliations, and state formation, while advancing alternative ideas of imperial sovereignty, imperial social formations, and transnationality.[15]

This new work reshapes how metropolitan modernities need to be understood. Even before the creation of the German national state during 1864–71, the traveling of "Germany" overseas, whether via emigration, Christian missions, mercantile commerce, scientific expeditions, or foreign adventuring, effectively "imperialized" a framework of hopes for the nationhood yet to be created, so that the imagined "boundaries of Germanness" became expansive and far-flung, not confined to contiguous German-speaking Europe alone.[16] Once the national state was fashioned into place, in the era of high imperialism from the 1880s, this became still more palpably the case. Far beyond the tangible incursions of empire into the domestic political arena—most notably, in the naval arms drive underway during 1897–1900, or in the prolonged crisis of German colonial administration that culminated in the so-called Hottentot elections of 1907—a far more generalized impact can now be acknowledged. By 1914, public culture had become entirely suffused with colonial traces and imprints. These ranged from commodified visual representations of consumption and entertainment to the heroics and disasters of colonial expeditions, from the scandals of colonial rule to the fascination of popular writing and reportage. They were present in the multiform ways that colonial knowledge circulated. Once we widen the optic still further to analyze the global rivalry of the "great world empires" and Germany's intended expansion toward the "East," the relevance for German domestic society and politics of this "colonial effect" becomes all the more clear.[17] By 1900, German modernities were always already embedded and framed in these far wider than German terms, taking in the transnational, the imperial and the global.

Subjectivity

Subjectivity has emerged as an acute if elusive site for the complexities and contradictions of German modernities. With regard to the *longue durée*, philosophers have often identified the modern era *tout court* as extending from roughly 1500 to the present and marked by "self-assertion" or the turn to radical humanism.[18] In our own period of focus, individual subjects claimed and exhibited ever new powers even as conceptions of subjectivity-as-agency began undergoing ever new pressures. The democratizing ethos of the era entailed new assertions of citizenship rights, in both legal and sociocultural terms, new emphases on individualizing perspectives, new claims by individual subjects in aspiring to shape the social. Autobiographies circulated as never before; Nietzschean "new women" celebrated their sexual, social, and intellectual autonomy; life-reform movements attended to the newly asserted physical, intellectual, and social needs of individuals. At the same time, intellectual, political, and technological forces were mounting against the very idea of individual autonomy or agency. Materialist science and philosophy from Darwinian evolution to Schopenhauerian pessimism presented individuals as products of social and material forces and impulses, hardly agents of their own destiny let alone intentional shapers of society and politics. Similarly, Nietzsche and Freud unintentionally joined forces to suggest a subject incapable of ever really knowing itself or giving an account of its own actions. Into this mix was then thrown the accelerated process of urbanization underway between 1880 and 1930. For even as the production of the new urban masses deindividuated human subjects, the struggle to survive the alienating city simultaneously compelled individuals into asserting a kind of rabid autonomy.

Politically and socially, these conflicting vectors around subjectivity and individual autonomy played out wherever the individual subject met the apparatus of the state, the mechanics of the market and the sprawling social networks of civil society. The emerging welfare state relied on the developing social sciences such as criminology, sexology, and national economy to manage the body politic and the individual lives from which it was made—a phenomenon as true in continental Germany as it was in its colonies. These institutions sought to understand ever better the inner workings and most intimate details of subjects and citizens, making privacy itself a matter of public concern. In addition, social-reform associations often concentrated on the inner lives of others, whether bourgeois women's organizations concerned to educate workers about "proper" hygiene or family planning or pan-nationalists eager to define and defend a racially pure Germany in a global empire. At the same time, as Young-sun Hong has noted in a challenging essay (included in this volume), those subjects targeted by state and social-reform organizations proved almost impossible for either the state or social-reform groups to manage. Reform projects large and small stumbled when subjects proved incorrigible, immune to discipline. Moreover, as the essays by Kathleen Canning and Marti Lybeck illustrate especially well, the state that might seek to regulate its subjects depended for its very power and legitimacy on the loyalty, investment, and desires of precisely those incalculable subjects. Michel Foucault gave us the helpful categories of "biopower" and "biopolitics," loosely associating the former with the power *over* life that modern states practice and the latter with strategies emanating and accruing from that power.[19] For our purposes, a distinction offered by Michael Hardt and Antonio Negri seems especially useful. They suggest a conception of biopower as power over life and biopolitics as "the power of life to resist and determine an alternative production of subjectivity."[20] As these connotations of the two terms circulate through the essays of this volume, they illuminate both the widespread and multidirectional interest contemporaries had in understanding and controlling the nature of modern subjectivity as well as the persistent elusiveness of subjectivity to categorical definition and to efforts at political and social reform.

Reform

If subjectivity was subject to new pressures at the turn of the century, reform was as well. Discussions of its necessity and its difficulty had a particularly broad scope. One product of the studies on the *Kaiserreich*'s supposedly weak bourgeoisie has been a wave of research into Imperial Germany's vibrant reform milieu. With this new lens on the era, historians—including the authors in this volume—have uncovered new forms of activism, which traversed the political spectrum. Reform campaigns included projects aimed at social welfare, at assessing nature's value, at promoting household aesthetics and modern living styles. They focused on religious and ethical practices, on sexual expression and many other topics besides.[21] Such efforts were neither exclusively social nor cultural. Indeed, as Annemarie Sammartino, John Maciuika, and Marti Lybeck demonstrate, the state itself could be a target for reform even as it was a practitioner of such, an actor interested in the beliefs and life-practices of its subjects. While the literature on global modernity highlights the relationship of the state to its subjects, the German example reveals that state and civil society were not so easily separated. Reformers often moved fluidly between state offices and civil-societal reform associations. Kathleen Canning details how citizenship itself became a category for reform in a variety of legal and cultural ways during the *Kaiserreich*, a problem that arose anew with the shift to democracy under the Weimar state. Recognizing that reform projects traversed a broad cultural and political landscape, one can ask what it meant for contemporaries to understand their world as an intensive work in progress. For it was clear that they believed that—in principle—self, society, state, and culture could all be made anew.

The complexity of reform initiatives presents a far less cohesive context for the topic than the one outlined by Detlev J.K. Peukert and his followers.[22] To be sure, each individual project tended to be highly self-conscious, goal-oriented, and programmatic. Indeed, to be "modern" was to make a claim for particular understandings of self and society, of the sexual, political, and natural order. However, the claims were multiple and conflicted, as reformers struggled over the most basic categories of social and political existence. In a pivotal commentary on the topic, Dennis Sweeney has suggested that we learn most about German modernity and reform if we are attentive to the points of discord, to the ways in which competing reform groups vied with one another to define the social and the state.[23] Reform efforts battled with one another while they simultaneously bled together, the language of the one taking up aspects of another. Modernist design, for example, combined aesthetic concerns with an interest in social welfare. Planning utopias similarly combined social, aesthetic, and hygienic ideas while leavening them with strong amounts of class pedagogy. Reform was not just a middle-class affair. Projects emanated no less ambitiously from the working classes, particularly from the moderate Social Democrats with their hopes of curbing the excesses of capitalism or spreading the virtues of a working-class ethics through the social arena. There were winners and losers over time, to be sure. New discussions on modern reform highlight the stakes and the strategies of the battles as contemporaries experienced them, when their outcomes could not be foretold.

Politics

Coupled with the analytical work of empire, subjectivity, and reform comes a simultaneous revitalization and rethinking of politics in the German context. For many years, the political history of the *Kaiserreich* was approached as a story of entrenched authoritarianism focused primarily on governmental structures and political parties. In that telling, the traditional ruling elites, conceived as "pre-industrial" and aristocratic, preserved the essence of their institutional power by keeping democratizing forces, such as the SPD and the national minorities, at bay. In this reading, a reactionary coalition of protectionist interests ("iron and rye"), represented politically by the National Liberals and the two Conservative parties, sat at the center of governmental politics under Bismarck and most of his successors. They exercised their power in promoting military expansionism and domestic repression. The simultaneous aggression and confusion of Wilhelmine politics, including the naval arms drive—central to any study of the period— were analyzed as manipulative actions undertaken by authoritarian forces aiming to stave off any program of political reform.

Such an approach to the study of political life was long dominant in the German field. It was also unnecessarily narrow, focusing on a highly particular set of continuities between *Kaiserreich* and Third Reich. It relied on a mode of structural analysis from historical sociology and modernization theory, which treated political parties as expressions of socioeconomic interests. This perspective has been superseded of late by a variety of sociocultural approaches to political life, including analyses of political discourse and studies attentive to the importance of gender and sexuality. Such work has produced a far more nuanced picture of the Wilhelmine political system. It is now seen as more parliamentary, more pluralist, more "liberal" in the constitutionalist sense, even more functionally democratic.[24] Recent publications include fully ramified and concrete studies of the electoral system; important studies of liberal influence in the legislative process; case studies in the efficiencies of social administration; and analyses of social policy and governmentality.[25]

This volume pushes toward a new framing of political life in several ways. The contributions broaden the understanding of "the political" as such by expanding the range of ideas, sites, and practices that politics may be taken to include. In this way, the perspective shifts away from parties, interest groups, and elections in order to analyze the informal and everyday places where politics was made. In conjunction, the complicated genealogies of popular ideas are unpacked—such as ideas of local identity (*Heimat*) and the multilayered discussion on nation and community in Germany's different regions—which older literatures saw as straightforwardly reactionary. Early environmental initiatives, for example, and the widespread interest in landscapes and folkways fostered ideas and practices that were simultaneously forward- and backward-looking. This "Janus face" of modernity marked life-reform ideas as well, from natural therapies and nudism (*Freikörperkultur*) to experiments with spiritualism and ethical reform. Germinating in the Wilhelminian period, such ideas flowered in full during the Weimar Republic. In all of these spaces of German life, a real and open-ended complexity was traditionally read by historians in one-sided fashion as belonging to the intellectual origins of Nazism. Against such pre-given interpretations, we stress the salient and enabling diversity and ambivalence inside such practices and programs.

Chapter outline and summaries

While the chapters in this volume cluster variously around the themes of politics, reform, empire, and subjectivity, they are not formally organized by them. Rather, those categories are present and mutually intertwined throughout, illustrating the crossings and overlaps among private, civic, and political life. Political reformers might be equally concerned about matters of subjectivity and empire, just as aestheticians might be consumed with issues of global politics and economy. Accordingly, the volume is structured to display these overlaps, proposing in the process a conception of German modernity that both enables an analytical category and suggests its fruitful indeterminacy, as an invitation to further empirical research. The first three chapters assemble the broader historiographical context, suggesting the challenges and promises posed by the category of German modernity. The second section, comprising four chapters, begins to decenter any overly coherent conception of a singular modernity by approaching the topic from its borders—via transnational, imperial, and comparative perspectives. The seven chapters of the third and largest section each present specific moments of Wilhelmine and Weimar contestation, through which contemporaries explicitly grappled with the challenge of shaping an open future. Finally, the book concludes with a historiographical reflection on the category of modernity in relation to National Socialism.

Appearing originally in *Social History*, Young-sun Hong's opening chapter, "Neither Singular nor Alternative: Narratives of Modernity and Welfare in Germany, 1870–1945," served as one of the starting points for our early discussions. Hong introduces several of the key themes in recent German historiography: reform; biopolitics and the state; society and subjectivity; the private and the public. As she observes, welfare was a primary instrument of intervention for reforming the social and its subjects. It formed a primary interface between individuals and the state. Surveying recent historiography of the welfare state from the *Kaiserreich* through National Socialism, she notes a diversity of interpretations: some find an almost totalizing state reaching deep into the lives of its subjects, while others see the "system" as more confused—an incongruous whole of competing institutional factions whose subjects of control remain always somewhat elusive and hard to discipline. Rather than seeking either a "singular" or an "alternative" character to Germany's modernity, she urges the development of a vocabulary that can capture its "complex, contradictory, and acentric" character.

In "What Was German Modernity and When?" Geoff Eley seeks to reassess the *Kaiserreich* in light of recent theoretical and historiographical developments. He observes efforts to free pre-1914 ideas and movements from earlier teleological narratives linking *Kaiserreich* to Third Reich, giving them a very different and more open-ended set of genealogies and valences instead. He calls on other historiographical departures of the past two decades, including post-Foucauldian understandings of governmentality and the boom in studies of colonialism and empire, which likewise complicate and upset the older assumptions about what constituted "modern" thinking and practice in Germany before 1914. With these developments in hand, Eley articulates a new set of questions for historians of German modernity: How does the conventional periodization based on wars and constitutions (1870–71 … 1914 … 1918–19 … 1933) change once we shake up our understanding of "modernity" and its meanings in the ways outlined above? How might we theorize a common analytical context and interpretive framework for the entire period between the 1890s and 1930s? What were the lines of continuity, and how might they be weighted, freighted, and understood? How far does the sharpness of the revolutionary rupture in 1918–19, with its *political* consequences of constitutional change, institutional innovation, and radical ideological transition, invalidate this argument for reperiodization in the end? How should we see the revalorizing of modernity under the

Kaiserreich in relation to the powerful and contentious conceptions of the modern circulating in the later periods of Weimar and the Third Reich? The essay makes a case for the coherence of the 1890s–1920s in these terms, arguing that the complex of meanings among the *city*, the *nation*, the *local*, and the *global* became sutured together under the aegis of the modern at the turn of the twentieth century in a very potent and particular way.

In an effort to get outside the assumptions of German historiography, Annemarie Sammartino's chapter turns a Russian historiographical lens on the German Empire, finding as a result a modernity filled with failed ambitions. A first instance concerned the nation per se. As historians have long known, much political reform work in Imperial Germany—emanating both from the state and from civil society—pertained to consolidating an idea of German nationhood yet to be fully defined, let alone completed. However, taking a cue from the Russian case, Sammartino highlights how complex and often incomplete the project was. She draws attention to the many rifts between region, language, and religion that interrupted national identification, not to mention the inconsistencies of racial ideologies that created their own fissures. Second, and closely related to the incompleteness of national formation, is the category of failure. Historiography on imperial Russia zeroes in routinely on the failure of reforms to achieve their ends and to ward off revolution. In the German case, Sammartino suggests, many of the biggest national projects also fell flat: for instance, German colonialism itself, as well as the *Kulturkampf*. If German modernity was marked by its optimism about managing society and moving into the future, it found itself as often as not having to give up on its totalizing and sometimes utopian projects. Finally, Sammartino draws attention to chaotic—as opposed to disciplinary—violence. If, as Hong and others point out, disciplinary violence and coercion went hand in hand with the modern administration of state and society, Sammartino suggests that its monopoly on historians' attention has obscured the equally modern if more disruptive chaotic and volatile violence of the Eastern Front during the First World War. In sum, Sammartino suggests a German modernity as much marked by chaos, inconsistency, and unraveling as by administration efficiency or control.

Sammartino's approach to German historiography from the perspective of its Russian neighbor builds a bridge to the second cluster of chapters, all of which situate the German Empire in a broad transnational, colonial, and global context. Scott Spector's "Elsewhere in Central Europe" brings a somewhat sideways approach to the question of German modernity, addressing the matter of subjectivity from the perspectives of Jews in the Habsburg Empire. Discussing what he calls the "Habsburg Myth" and the "Central Europe Effect," Spector's essay draws out the condition of being "elsewhere"—that is, always one or more steps removed from the presumed center of power, culture, meaning. That elsewhere was both spatial and temporal. Spatially, Spector surveys the vast range of the Habsburg Empire on the one hand, where the "Central" of Central Europe was already the periphery in reference to the German Empire. Temporally, he also draws out a unique kind of nostalgia that he suggests is characteristic of the Central Europe Effect. This was a "nostalgia for a nostalgia," or the yearning for a past in which an explicitly identifiable loss could be found as opposed to a present where absence is pervasive and without referent. The Central Europe Effect is a condition Spector finds articulated most explicitly by Jews in the Habsburg Empire, those doubly removed from the center: outsiders in the Habsburg Empire, itself in its last throes, looking on while the neighboring German Empire ascends. But as so often, lessons from the margin pose questions to the seeming center. Was the "elsewhere" sentiment perhaps not more pervasive, a condition of modernity itself, where the centers of power and meaning are always unstable, always on the move? Even in the very process of its inception, modernity was always-already "staged," we have suggested, announcing its arrival as a category of aspiration, often normatively conceived from experiences assumed to be unfolding next door. Such staging of a comparatively derived normativity, Spector's chapter suggests, may have owed less to states at large, or even to segments of civil society, than to the conditions of modern subjectivity per se.

Moving from Eastern Europe to Africa and turning squarely to the matter of politics proper, Andrew Zimmerman examines the specificity of Germany's colonial project. Here, too, the idea of staging and comparison remains central. Zimmerman is interested in depicting how Germany came to serve the role of model colonizer in Africa. In his account, modernity consisted primarily in a fusion between liberal internationalism and capitalism. European colonialism in Africa—of which Germany was the exemplar—derived as a project fundamentally from that fusion. Reform programs in both Europe and the colonies, Zimmerman maintains, were not only consistent with—but even constitutive of—that liberal modernity. Most notably, Zimmerman presents liberal internationalism in counterpoint with democratic configurations of politics that emerged in the trans-Atlantic nineteenth century. Taking a longer perspective, he finds the struggles against slavery and other coercive regimes to be manifestations of a democratic contest against liberal domination. One chief aim of Zimmerman's essay is to remind the reader that the reform projects which appear so central to German modernity were at bottom efforts to sustain and elaborate an *antidemocratic* version of modernity, in reaction against what he identifies as more "primary modernities" associated with the bio-political labor of non-liberal subjects.

As if directly illustrating Zimmerman's case, Dennis Sweeney's contribution approaches the radical-right Pan-German League by negotiating deliberately back and forth between the global, the transnational, and the local. Most historians have treated the Pan-German League primarily in domestic-political terms, Sweeney observes, ascribing it thereby a homegrown, antimodern, agrarian economic and social agenda. By turning the lens to view the Pan-Germans in a context of global capitalism, however,

Sweeney finds something very different: a dynamic nexus between capitalist-industrial *Weltpolitik* (including commitments to colonial expansion, German monopoly of export markets and heavy industry) and bio-political racist-nationalism. In short, Pan-Germanism was not a local, home-focused, antiglobal, or antimodern movement. Rather, it sought as a reform project to mobilize new bio-political conceptions of a population-race (*Volkskörper*), deploying these often inconsistent ideas in an effort to "re-territorialize Germans" inside a global nation-state empire. This move was a response to the perceived "de-territorializing and volatile spatial dynamics of global capitalism," a boldly modernist call from the right to mobilize new bio-political thinking about the nation as *Volkskörper* in order to secure its survival and prosperity under the new conditions of global geopolitical rivalry. If Sammartino suggested the instability of any nationalizing project, Sweeney's work shows the volatile global-capitalist conditions under which such projects were increasingly undertaken.

While Sammartino, Spector, Zimmerman, and Sweeney each highlight the kinds of questions that might be posed about German modernity when seen from the global, transnational, imperial, and borderland perspectives, the next cluster of essays focuses more directly on the local negotiation of modern conditions and possibilities. But in leading with the more explicitly transnational treatments, we are offering a key reminder: that even as they pressed for the most local of social, cultural, and political reforms, historical actors necessarily did so within the economic, technological, and discursive conditions of globality that modernity always-already presented. Whenever debates about citizenship and subjectivity, aesthetics, and social welfare unfolded, imperial and national comparisons were also in play. Actors were well aware of the efforts of their counterparts in neighboring and distant countries, sometimes cooperating and sometimes competing, but rarely considering their own reform efforts in a national or regional vacuum. If some of these next chapters explicitly highlight transnational aspects and others focus more closely on the complexities of local efforts themselves, all see the determinative relevance of the economic, technological, and discursive conditions of global modernity proposed by the more comparative essays.

The imbricating of imperial and local concerns is clearest in the essays from John V. Maciuika and Jennifer L. Jenkins (later in the volume). Maciuika's chapter on the industrialist, National Liberal politician, and Prussian commerce minister Theodor Möller describes a very particular site through which a Wilhelmine imperial imaginary was being engaged. It traces the expansion of Prussian domination of the domestic German political sphere and, using the Deutscher Werkbund as a case study, shows how reforms in the applied arts, commercial policies, and the consumer goods industries came to figure directly in Germany's larger imperial project. It further analyzes the particularity of Wilhelmine modernity in the conjunction of Prussian ministerial reforms, the vision of Germany's leading applied artists, and the subordination of the country's leading applied arts organization to the imperatives of Wilhelmine commercial and imperial expansion. This was a potent brew of modernity indeed. It signified synergy rather than opposition, bringing into dynamic and constructive alignment elements, actors, and tendencies that earlier historiographies more commonly saw apart.

Larry Frohman's essay provides an empirical case study of the modern welfare state, complementing Hong's historiographical discussion. Detailing key developments in infant mortality and tuberculosis prevention, Frohman opens anew many of the central issues raised by Hong's essay: most urgently, the question of individual emancipation versus social control enabled by social welfare programs, the matter of social citizenship inhering in rights and duties of health care, the blurred lines of private and public, and the status of biopolitics in the life of the modern state. Frohman finds that working-class mothers and families rather eagerly invited the welfare programs, and with them the state, into their private domain, rarely evincing a sense of coercion or social control. The sum result is a scene in which the social welfare programs do seem to enhance the individual lives of those they touch, even as they insinuate the state and its knowledge-specialists into the domestic realm of its citizens. Historiographically, Frohman seeks to break from the teleological framework informing so much earlier study of welfare in Germany, in which developments of the *Kaiserreich* are read for their potential to feed into Nazi state practices. By breaking free of the National-Socialist telos, he finds a modernity that implies neither a strict expansion of state powers nor a clear increase in individual autonomy, but rather a complex and nuanced growth of mutual dependency and resulting negotiation between individuals and the state. He calls our attention to the technologies and scientific knowledge production that the vast projects of preventing infant mortality and tuberculosis presupposed.

In her contribution, Tracie Matysik also treats the matter of individual autonomy and its challenges, examining debates about the nature of subjectivity in relationship to secularism and reform. She works with a distinction between "secularization" and "secularism" as different ways to think about modernity. Where secularization was long conceived of as a feature of modernization, part of a unilinear process according to which religion gradually lost its social significance, "secularism" might be thought of as a feature of German modernities in the plural. It is something that individuals and organizations intentionally sought to cultivate, and they came up with competing variations. Where, at the turn of the nineteenth to twentieth centuries, secularization presented itself as a neutral sociological theory, secularism was something reformers actively propagated. Moreover, different secular camps relied on different theories of the secular subject. Theories of secularization had presented the rational-autonomous subject as their counterpart, while secularist camps were consumed with a variety of materialist, socially determined, sometimes irrationalist theories of the subject just as much as they were with the more rational-autonomous variety. In dialogue with more recent theorists of the secular, such as Hans

Blumenberg, Charles Taylor, Talal Asad, Wendy Brown, and others, Matysik examines the activities of the German Society for Ethical Culture with these themes in mind. She finds in the controversies surrounding the ethics reform movement an especially vivid space in which to see the competing claims that cultural reformers made in their active cultivation of secular modernity and with it the modern secular subject.

Working at the intersection of politics, reform, and subjectivity, Kathleen Canning examines the contest to determine women's citizenship as it arose in the upheavals first of war and then revolution. Like Sammartino, she attends to the role of chaos as it figured in German conceptions of citizenship. If Sammartino was especially interested in the ways that German modernity included chaos and the failure of its planned projects, Canning is more attentive to the subjective-political response to chaos and the new political and social formations that arise. Interested here in citizenship not just as a legal category but, more significantly, as a claims-making activity, she depicts the role that "sexual crisis" played in the shaping of women's rights. As their activity became ever more public, crucial to the war effort, women started assuming the rights to increased political participation even as they came under ever greater surveillance by the state. Anxieties circulated about feminine influence, the so-called female surplus (higher proportion of women than men in the general population), and the resulting impact of increased female participation in social and political realms. As a result, debates about reproductive rights, contraception, venereal disease, and war-readiness overlapped with those about women's economic and political rights and activities. In her essay, Canning shows how participants in these debates and activities were simultaneously consumed with matters of immediate urgency, even as they were engaged in a raging battle to define the future—the future of the Weimar state itself and its relationship to its citizens. And it was a battle. Canning's definition of citizenship as a *process* of subjectivity and claims-making activity allows her to move beyond a focus on national or political belonging to indicate instead the antagonistic relationship that citizenship could hold toward the nation-state.

As individuals were involved in shaping citizenship as a process, so too were citizens involved in literally giving form to democracy in the Weimar era. In her essay, Manuela Achilles challenges a long-standing historiographical assumption that the Weimar Republic was lacking in foundational democratic symbols and identifications. She turns to the constitutional debates over the national symbols and their design by the National Keeper of Art (*Reichskunstwart*), a government agency located at the intersections of art and politics. Edwin Redslob, who directed the office from 1920 until Nazi Interior Minister Frick dissolved it in 1933, conceived of his task as a deliberate project of state design (*Formgebung*). A preservationist as well as reformer, the museum director and long-standing Werkbund member worked to create national symbols that engaged the "fantasy of the people," while also refuting both imperial hubris and bureaucratic sterility. In Achilles' interpretation, the republican concern with the invention, production, and use of the Republic's national symbolism shows that Weimar democracy was not, as many historians have claimed, deliberately antiritualistic. On the contrary: officials in the federal and state administrations such as Redslob clearly recognized the political necessity to legitimate the Weimar Republic symbolically. Seeking to render abstract principles such as democratic freedom and justice perceptible to the senses, Weimar republicans engaged in a labor of representation that transcended homogenizing notions of class, religion, or race, thus offering a pluralist alternative to the extremist symbolic politics the interwar years also engendered. Their efforts quite literally to re-form the national symbolism signified an acute break with the country's authoritarian traditions and at the same time aimed to endow the fledgling democracy with the legitimacy derived from historical origins. Negotiating the old and new within the field of Weimar modernity, republican officials with strong roots in the Wilheminian reform milieu (such as Redslob) understood national belonging in terms of values and sentiments that could be created, shaped, and staged. Their attempt to anchor the nation in the democratic form was no less compatible with German national traditions than Nazi ideology. On the contrary, combining a progressive functional style with the selective preservation of national tradition, republican state design drew the symbolic contours of a pluralist mass democracy. It is in this perspective, too, Achilles maintains, that the Republic was the ultimate laboratory of German modernity.

Jennifer L. Jenkins explores the relationships between modernity, Weimar culture, and the state from a different angle than Achilles, raising anew the connections between local actions, imperial contexts, and global aspirations. Starting with the Werkbund exhibition "The New Age," planned for Cologne in 1932, she analyzes Weimar modernism in the transition from the 1920s to the 1930s and the lasting influence of imperialism in these discussions. While the 1932 exhibition is under-researched in studies of the Werkbund, it provides an interesting window onto both the late Weimar Werkbund and the categories that organize its historiography. This includes the vexed conceptual pairs functionalism/organicism, international/national, and *Zivilization/Kultur*, which are joined to the meta-categories of modern and antimodern. As she details, the historical discussion on the 1932 exhibition reveals a complex debate on cultural and political modernity that thwarts the categories traditionally used to read it.

A large part of this complexity was the Werkbund's imperial past and the global aspirations that it generated. The Werkbund occupies a central place in histories of modernist culture, but it is rarely investigated as an imperial institution in itself, a particularly modern combination of industrial, political, and aesthetic forms of power. While Maciuika took up this topic in his focus on the interface between the Werkbund and the Wilhelminian administrative landscape, Jenkins recovers this history by highlighting the life and work of the organizer of the "New Age" exhibition, the Werkbund's business manager Ernst Jäckh. She traces Jäckh's redefinition of the Werkbund after 1912, specifically his effort to embed its work into the government's wartime policies of annexation. She illuminates how its modernist aesthetic was conceptualized as a form of imperialist *Weltkultur*, sign and symbol of a German-dominated *Mitteleuropa*. The roots of the 1932 "New Age" exhibition lay in Jäckh's ideas about German power in the world and in modernist design as an expression of that power. Thus her essay traces a different set of touch points between the Wilhelmine period, the Weimar Republic, and the onset of National Socialism, showing the intertwining of ideas of German culture and global power in the period from 1912 to 1932. Her essay anticipates Roseman's discussion of the 1930s in its evocation of a process through which modernist design, and the category of modernity as such, were gradually emptied of a progressive social vision.

Taking up a line of inquiry complementary to Canning's in particular, Marti Lybeck explores gender and sexual politics in the later Weimar period and, in the process, seeks to invert the conventions of political history. She is interested in the classical problems of individual autonomy and state authority, but approaches them from the angle of subjectivity and desire. With a focus on lesbian writing that embraces the authority of the state, national symbols, and normative morality, she exposes the inner logic of the seemingly contradictory subject-positions that emancipated and same-sex-desiring conservative women appropriated. Her case studies illustrate how women who were seeking a non-normative type of sexual emancipation, breaking from social and institutional norms, often anchored their desires in conservative political identifications and disciplinary moral discourse. If Canning's exploration of sexual crisis during the war and revolution indicates the antagonistic dimensions that could define the relationship between citizen, state, and nation as new futures were being sought, Lybeck's discussion of politically conservative expressions of female desire indicates the unlikely fusions between nation, state, and subjective desire that often demanded very specific conceptions of the past and "traditional" moral authority. What Lybeck's inverted political history reveals most poignantly is how nation, state, tradition, individual autonomy, desire, and disciplinary morality all existed as necessary components of modernity— but as components that could be arranged and mobilized in very diverse and often unpredictable ways depending on the subject-position of any particular individual.

Following explorations of modernity and multiplicity, Mark Roseman's essay sounds a note of disquiet about the term itself. If Hong and Eley assumed modernity to be an appropriate framework for German history in the late nineteenth and early twentieth centuries, Roseman casts a more skeptical eye on its value for the study of National Socialism. That skepticism derives in part from the inversion of assumptions in modernization theory, and their implications for the discussion of modernity, which occurred with particular force during the 1990s. If Nazism was once seen as the vanishing point of modernization, the failure of all of its progressive promise, the regime came to be seen for many in the 1990s as the epitome of a modernity evacuated of progressive elements, as the bearer rather of instrumental reason, technological-scientific planning, and murderous efficiency. The problem with this second understanding of modernity, according to Roseman, is its retention of a generic conception of the "modern." In this generic mode, modernity fails to account for National Socialism's complexity and contradictions—for the historical specificity of the regime, its rise in the unique circumstances of the interwar period alongside regimes that shared many of its aims and techniques but from which it departed in meaningful and disastrous ways. Thus, for Roseman modernity cannot be equated with the gas chamber or biopolitics or the racial state, even as its usefulness as a category must depend on its being able to account for their possibilities. Ultimately, he suggests, a category of "high modernity" might work best for the interwar period and its Nazi product, capturing the "shock of the new" and the experimenting with new political and cultural forms. In that case, National Socialism could appear as one such effort to carve out a new future, drawing on aesthetic modernism while enacting reforms of extreme type with implications for the social, the subjective, and the political. As the last essay in our volume, and following discussions of the varied ways in which modernity was multiple, staged, contested, and debated, Roseman's skepticism appropriately invites further inquiry.

Conclusion

Any treatment of "modernity" today has to reckon with the sheer immensity of the possible approaches to this subject—an unmanageable diversity of the literatures, meanings, and discussion currently available. In the words of Dipesh Chakrabarty, modernity has become a "muddle."[26] Yet for all of the voices recommending jettisoning the concept, others note its necessity. There is a "need to expand and pluralize our definition of modernity," Richard Wolin has stressed, echoing others, for "it remains, after all, a many sided, polyvalent phenomenon."[27] Older theories of modernity and modernization, to be sure, required too linear and direct a relationship between political progress and free enterprise capitalism. They drew too simple a contrast between societies that were "traditional" and societies that were "modern." They also reflected normative understandings of what was thought to have happened in the developmental history of the industrializing world— meaning initially only the north-Atlantic West. Given the weight of this term, and the intensity of the critique levelled against it, it has taken time before a broader and more democratized conceptual vocabulary of "the modern" and "modernization" could shed its older connotations and come back into use in historical analysis.[28] At this point a more flexible, heterogeneous, and differently historicized conception of modernity can be brought once again into play. The lost contingencies, troublesome unevenness, and conjunctural specificities can now be re-engaged.

This is true in general and for German history specifically—a field whose contours have also inevitably changed. Gone in particular is the old negative teleology focused on 1933 and 1941, which cast the earlier German past as an exceptional site of pathology and misdevelopment, while explaining the possibility of Nazism principally by its deeper nineteenth-century origins. Restoring historical contingency to the periods of the Weimar Republic and the *Kaiserreich* allows each to be reevaluated, with the result that other kinds of continuity will soon re-emerge. From our own vantage point, the history of the first half of the twentieth century begins to look very different. Not only "1945," but also the intervening transitions of the 1960s to 1970s and 1989–90 begin to reground and restructure our understanding of that earlier time, making possible overarching interpretations of the course of German history very different than before.

We have explored the ways in which the global discussion on modernity has provided analytical frameworks and languages useful for newly understanding Germany. What can the German case offer to the global historical discussion? If the modern broadly indicates a content and pattern to political and economic development—the transformation of states, the character of public institutions, the importance of political participation, the presence of constitutional frameworks and legal standards, with all of these phenomena defined as diversely as possible—then Germany offered one of the most volatile, innovative, and self-conscious examples. Tempo is important. Indeed the speed and intensity of Germany's industrial transformation are at the very center of one recent discussion. In his magisterial accounting of Germany's long twentieth century, Ulrich Herbert equates "modernity" with "the *exceptional rapidity* of economic, social, and cultural changes" in "the economically advanced countries of Central and Western Europe" during the quarter century before 1914.[29] It resulted from powerfully interarticulated processes of change affecting the lives of "nearly the entire population" of the countries concerned. Those changes included:

advanced industrialization, urbanization, and mass emigration, comprehensive technologization and rationalization of nearly all areas of life, the application of science to all spheres, and especially the triumphal advance of the natural sciences, which competed with religion by dint of their comprehensive model of explaining the universe. Finally, there was the transformative emergence of mass culture and a mass public sphere.

Concentrated in the decades around 1900, this was a transformation of unexampled rapidity and intensity, affecting all human relations and social life, from the gross hierarchies of status and class, the social division of labor, the organization of work and the circulation of goods to the patterns of movement and communication, relations of gender, sexuality and generation, and the experience of religion, entertainment, and general cultural life. With the equivalence of a "shock wave," these years "exposed people to a dynamism of change that was unprecedented in power and scope." The conflict between old and new was exceptionally sharp, and the languages of modernity were tools and weapons in the battle. Political contestation sat at its center. Politics became a "feverish search for adequate responses to the new avalanche of challenges." For Herbert, these changes shaped the twentieth century in an overall formation he calls "advanced" or "high" modernity.[30]

In contrast with older ideas of Germany's pathology, however, we can now see that the dynamism of this advanced modernity was globally instigated rather than generated only inside the nation itself in some primary or exclusive way. As Germany's past is reassessed, it becomes vital to investigate its history in those global contexts that were so fundamental. Germany was one of "the major players in the process of globalization before 1914," as Sebastian Conrad and others have stressed, and it is important that new studies "take into account the global context that reached deep into the German Kaiserreich."[31] This does not flatten out the jagged edges of Germany's transformation or ameliorate the darkness and inhumanity of the Nazi dictatorship, but rather casts these momentous histories into fresh comparative and analytical light. Seeing the global at the core of these questions yields insights for the larger modernity discussion as well, particularly as these discussions begin to fold into one another.[32] If Germany held a particular place in the making of the global order, we are still far from fully knowing that history.

In thinking about the German case as one of multiple modernities, we are greatly indebted to postcolonial studies, whose impact has opened up the category from a singular and largely western focus to one of global variation. Yet it is important to be careful in this venture. An observation from Timothy Mitchell is especially helpful here. Mitchell has argued that modernity was not only something that happened globally and in decentered fashion; it was also something comparative and "staged as representation."[33] That is to say, modernity was something explicitly imagined and crafted in social experiences, what he calls a dualism of image and reality. With each imagining and enacting, he suggests, the very idea of "the West" and the "non-West" was reproduced, and any originary or normative uniqueness to the West's modernity was displaced. If Mitchell's interest is primarily to demonstrate the ways in which colonial settings were part of the ongoing process of representing modernity and creating a bifurcated world, his insight proves valuable for reflecting on the German case too. The contest of futures was very much one of representations that constantly envisioned and displaced any pure or original modernity. At the same time, a caveat is in order that pertains to Germany's status as a colonizing and not a colonized country. Many of our essays illustrate the explicit importance of global and imperial contexts for German stagings of modernity: Zimmerman's essay on colonialism, Sweeney's on Pan-Germanism, and Maciuika's and Jenkins's on two different moments of the Werkbund's imperialist history. But other essays reveal the capacity German reformers had to *forget* the global and imperial contexts in how they were able to envision the modern: Frohman's work on social welfare, Matysik's on secular subjectivity, Canning's and Lybeck's on sexuality. Modernity was being staged in each of these cases; multiple modernities were being explored and produced; and in each one of these gestures, images of an original or pure form of the modern were being contested and displaced. But as inhabitants of a western country not under the colonial rule of another power, German reformers had the freedom to include or not the global context as a referent—a luxury not shared by stagers of modernity in most parts of the world.

Our effort in this book is to understand the multiple modernities that were being produced in the German context—the visions of a modern future that were being crafted. For it was clear that across the realms of imperial interests, reform activism, and experiments in subjectivity, the language of the modern was used in preeminently political ways: to claim territory, to defeat opponents, to enact citizenship, to further one's vision of society—a singular future—over and against another. This process was often highly self-conscious, goal-oriented, and programmatic. It can inform future comparative studies of the making of the modern on a global scale. As we show, to be "modern" was to make a claim for particular understandings of self and society, of citizenship, sexuality, gender, and state. As new relations between organizations and the state were actively forged in the period between 1880 and 1930, and institutions were shaped and reshaped through the war and the interwar period, such contestation was vital to both political processes and their outcomes. A contest over the future belongs to the study of modernity, in both Germany and globally.

Notes

1   Arjun Appadurai refers to modernity as a theory "that both declares and desires universal applicability for itself." In Appadurai, *Modernity at Large: Cultural Dimensions of Globalization* (Minneapolis: University of Minnesota Press, 1996). See also Stuart Hall, David Held, Don Hubert, and Kenneth Thompson (eds.), *Modernity: An Introduction to Modern Societies* (Oxford: Blackwell, 1996); Dipesh Chakrabarty, *Provincializing Europe: Postcolonial Thought and Historical Difference* (Princeton: Princeton University Press, 2000). As these works attest, modernity's meanings are now redistributed across truly global (i.e., non-Western) fronts, diversifying the sites from which the idea can be engaged. But for two omnibus surveys firmly situated in the classic Euro-American mold of thought, each helpfully indicative of the term's capaciously heterogeneous reach, see John Jervis, *Exploring the Modern: Patterns of Western Culture and Civilization* (Oxford: Blackwell, 1998); Vassiliki Kolokotroni, Jane Goldman, and Olga Taxidou (eds.), *Modernism:*

An Anthology of Sources and Documents (Chicago: University of Chicago Press, 1998). Two volumes that respond to the broadening of perspectives would be Julia Hell and Andreas Schönle (eds.), *Ruins of Modernity* (Durham: Duke University Press, 2010); Julia Adams, Elisabeth S. Clements, and Ann Shola Orloff (eds.), *Remaking Modernity: Politics, History, and Sociology* (Durham: Duke University Press, 2005).

2   Seeing modernity as the contemporaneous development of both social modernization and aesthetic modernism was the distinctive contribution of Marshall Berman, *All That Is Solid Melts into Air: The Experience of Modernity* (New York: Simon and Schuster, 1982).

3   See, for example, Dilip Parameshwar Gaonkar (ed.), *Alternative Modernities* (Durham: Duke University Press, 2001); Timothy Mitchell (ed.), *Questions of Modernity* (Minneapolis: University of Minnesota Press, 2000); Dipesh Chakrabarty, *Habitations of Modernity: Essays in the Wake of Subaltern Studies* (Chicago: University of Chicago Press, 2002).

4   David Blackbourn and Geoff Eley roundly criticized this thesis of Germany's *Sonderweg* in *The Peculiarities of German History: Bourgeois Society and Politics in Nineteenth-Century Germany* (Oxford: Oxford University Press, 1984). Research in the present volume works from this ground and reflects the working forward of the discussions on the meanings of modernity initiated via this early intervention.

5   Zygmunt Bauman, *Modernity and the Holocaust* (Ithaca: Cornell University Press, 1989), provides one locus of this discussion, Max Horkheimer and Theodor Adorno, *Dialectic of Enlightenment*, trans. John Cumming (New York: Herder and Herder, 1972), another. For a sampling of the literature, see Frank Bajohr, Werner Johe, and Uwe Lohalm (eds.), *Zivilisation und Barbarei. Die widersprüchlichen Potentiale der Moderne. Detlev Peukert zum Gedenken* (Hamburg: Christians, 1991).

6   Detlev J.K. Peukert, "The Genesis of the 'Final Solution' from the Spirit of Science," in Thomas Childers and Jane Caplan (eds.), *Reevaluating the Third Reich* (New York: Holmes and Meier, 1993), pp. 234–52.

7   Running throughout Benjamin's work, this theme is crystallized especially in his "Über den Begriff der Geschichte," in Walter Benjamin, *Gesammelte Werke*, ed. Hermann Schweppenhäuser and Rolf Tiedemann, vol. 1/2 (Frankfurt: Suhrkamp, 1991), pp. 690–708.

8   Ernst Bloch, *The Spirit of Utopia*, trans. Anthony Nassar (Stanford: Stanford University Press, 2000); Carl Schmitt, "Die Buribunken: Ein geschichtsphilosophischer Versuch," *SUMMA* 1 (1918), pp. 89–106; discussed in Reinhart Koselleck, *The Practice of Conceptual History: Timing History, Spacing Concepts*, trans. Todd Presner et al. (Stanford: Stanford University Press, 2002), esp. pp. 84–99.

9   Frederick Cooper, *Colonialism in Question: Theory, Knowledge, History* (Berkeley: University of California Press, 2005), p. 115.

10 For example, James Retallack (ed.), *The Short Oxford History of Germany: Imperial Germany 1871–1918* (Oxford: Oxford University Press, 2008); Matthew Jefferies, *Contesting the German Empire, 1871–1918* (Oxford:

Blackwell, 2008). Geoff Eley and James Retallack (eds.), *Wilhelminism and Its Legacies: German Modernities, Imperialism, and the Meanings of Reform, 1890–1930* (New York: Berghahn, 2003); Suzanne Marchand and David Lindenfeld (eds.), *Germany at the Fin de Siècle: Culture, Politics, and Ideas* (Baton Rouge: Louisiana State University Press, 2004); Sven Oliver Müller and Cornelius Torp (eds.), *Imperial Germany Revisited: Continuing Debates and New Perspectives* (New York: Berghahn, 2011; orig. German edn, 2008); also Geoff Eley and Jan Palmowski (eds.), *Citizenship and National Identity in Twentieth-Century Germany* (Stanford: Stanford University Press, 2008). For an earlier discussion, see Geoff Eley (ed.), *Society, Culture, and the State in Germany, 1870–1930* (Ann Arbor: University of Michigan Press, 1996).

11 For example, Eric D. Weitz, *Weimar Germany: Promise and Tragedy* (Princeton: Princeton University Press, 2007); Anthony McElligott (ed.), *Weimar Germany* (Oxford: Oxford University Press, 2009); Matthew Stibbe, *Germany, 1914–1933: Politics, Society and Culture* (Harlow: Longman, 2010); Kathleen Canning, Kerstin Barndt, and Kristin McGuire (eds.), *Weimar Publics/Weimar Subjects: Rethinking the Political Culture of Germany in the 1920s* (New York: Berghahn, 2010); McElligott, *Rethinking the Weimar Republic: Authority and Authoritarianism, 1916–1936* (London: Bloomsbury, 2014).

12 This inventory follows the subchapter headings in Matthew Jefferies' discussion of "'Wilhelminism' and Its Discontents," in *Imperial Culture in Germany, 1871–1918* (Houndmills: Palgrave Macmillan, 2003), pp. 123–228.

13 See here the recent *Oxford Handbook in Modern German History*, ed. Helmut Walser Smith (Oxford: Oxford University Press, 2011), which self-consciously constructs a new periodization, only to subsume the distinctiveness of the early twentieth century into a far broader temporal entity of the "nation state" stretching from the 1860s to 1945.

14 Benita Parry, "Overlapping Territories and Intertwined Histories: Edward Said's Postcolonial Cosmopolitanism," in Michael Sprinker (ed.), *Edward Said: A Critical Reader* (Oxford: Blackwell, 1992), p. 24.

15 For the German field, see Sebastian Conrad and Jürgen Osterhammel (eds.), *Das Kaiserreich transnational. Deutschland in der Welt 1871–1914* (Göttingen: Vandenhoeck & Ruprecht, 2004); Gunilla Budde, Sebastian Conrad, and Oliver Janz (eds.), *Transnationale Geschichte. Themen, Tendenzen und Theorien* (Göttingen: Vandenhoeck & Ruprecht, 2006); and the already classic instantiations, Sebastian Conrad, *Globalisation and the Nation in Imperial Germany* (Cambridge: Cambridge University Press, 2010; German edn, 2006); Jürgen Osterhammel, *The Transformation of the World: A Global History of the Nineteenth Century* (Princeton: Princeton University Press, 2014; German edn, 2009).

16 Krista O'Donnell, Renata Bridenthal, and Nancy Reagin (eds.), *The Heimat Abroad: The Boundaries of Germanness* (Ann Arbor: University of Michigan Press, 2005).

17 For an up-to-date overview, see Bradley D. Naranch and Geoff Eley (eds.), *German Colonialism in a Global Age* (Durham: Duke University Press, 2014).

18 See, for instance, Hans Blumenberg, *Legitimacy of the Modern Age*, trans. Robert M. Wallace (Cambridge: MIT Press, 1983); Charles Taylor, *Sources of the Self: The Making of Modern Identity* (Cambridge: Harvard University Press, 1989); Jerrold Seigel, *The Idea of the Self: Thought and Experience in Western Europe since the Seventeenth Century* (New York: Cambridge University Press, 2005).

19 If Foucault did not hold to consistent distinctions, these remain nonetheless discernible patterns. See, for instance, his sustained use of the terms in Mauro Bertani and Alessandro Fontana (eds.), *"Society Must Be Defended": Lectures at the Collège de France*, trans. David Macey (New York: Picador, 2003), pp. 239–64.

20 Michael Hardt and Antonio Negri, *Commonwealth* (Cambridge: Belknap Press, 2009), p. 57.

21 The literature on reform is vast. A few salient examples include Atina Grossman, *Reforming Sex: The German Movement for Birth Control and Abortion Reform, 1920–1950* (New York: Oxford University Press, 1995); Kevin Repp, *Reformers, Critics, and the Paths of German Modernity: Anti-Politics and the Search for Alternatives, 1890–1914* (Cambridge: Harvard University Press, 2000); Jennifer Jenkins, *Provincial Modernity: Local Culture and Liberal Politics in Fin-de-Siècle Hamburg* (Ithaca: Cornell University Press, 2003); Michael Hau, *The Cult of Health and Beauty in Germany: A Social History, 1890–1930* (Chicago: University of Chicago Press, 2003); Jefferies, *Imperial Culture*; Tom Lekan, *Imagining the Nation in Nature: Landscape Preservation and German Identity* (Cambridge: Harvard University Press, 2004); Tracie Matysik, *Reforming the Moral Subject: Ethics and Sexuality in Central Europe, 1890–1930* (Ithaca: Cornell University Press, 2008); Michelle Mouton, *From Nurturing the Nation to Purifying the Volk: Weimar and Nazi Family Policy, 1918–1945* (Cambridge: Cambridge University Press, 2009); Edward Ross Dickinson, *Sex, Freedom, and Power in Imperial Germany, 1880–1914* (Cambridge: Cambridge University Press, 2014).

22 Peukert inaugurated something of a tectonic shift in German historiography when he suggested that many of the murderous practices of the Third Reich had their unwitting origins in Imperial reform movements, that they emerged from the "spirit of science" and out of the social-reform practices of the *Kaiserreich* and Weimar Germany. The studies of reform in this volume, particularly that from Mark Roseman, complicate this picture.

23 Dennis Sweeney, "Reconsidering the Modernity Paradigm: Reform Movements, the Social, and the State in Wilhelmine Germany," *Social History* 31:4 (2006), pp. 405–34.

24 For example, Margaret Lavinia Anderson, *Practicing Democracy: Elections and Political Culture in Imperial Germany* (Princeton: Princeton University Press, 2000).

25 Stanley Suval, *Electoral Politics in Wilhelmine Germany* (Chapel Hill: University of North Carolina Press, 1985); Brett Fairbairn, *Democracy in the Undemocratic State: The German Reichstag Elections of 1898 and 1903* (Toronto: University of Toronto Press, 1997); Jonathan Sperber, *The Kaiser's Voters: Electors and Elections in Imperial Germany* (Cambridge:

Cambridge University Press, 1997); Anderson, *Practicing Democracy*; Holger J. Tober, *Deutscher Liberalismus und Sozialpolitik in der Ära des Wilhelminismus. Anschauungen der liberalen Parteien im parlamentarischen Entscheidungsprozeß und in der öffentlichen Diskussion* (Husum: Matthiessen, 1999); Larry Frohman, *Poor Relief and Welfare in Germany from the Reformation to World War I* (Cambridge: Cambridge University Press, 2008); Jan Palmowski, *Urban Liberalism in Imperial Germany: Frankfurt am Main, 1866–1914* (Oxford: Oxford University Press, 1999); Alastair Thompson, *Left Liberals, the State, and Popular Politics in Wilhelmine Germany* (Oxford: Oxford University Press, 2000).

26 Dipesh Chakrabarty, "The Muddle of Modernity," *The American Historical Review* 116:3 (2011), pp. 663–75.

27 Richard Wolin, "'Modernity': The Peregrinations of a Contested Historiographical Concept," *The American Historical Review* 116:3 (2011), pp. 744–5.

28 Chakrabarty highlights the democratization of the term as it has moved beyond European history, its translation into different historical contexts, and its redefinition in the process.

29 Ulrich Herbert, *Geschichte Deutschlands im 20. Jahrhundert* (Munich: CH Beck, 2014). Emphasis added.

30 Ulrich Herbert, "Europe in High Modernity: Reflections on a Theory of the Twentieth Century," *Journal of Modern European History* 5:1 (2007), pp. 10–11.

31 Sebastian Conrad, "Wilhelmine Nationalism in Global Contexts: Mobility, Race and Global Consciousness," in Sven Oliver Müller and Cornelius Torp (eds.), *Imperial Germany Revisited: Continuing Debates and New Perspectives* (New York: Berghahn, 2011), p. 282.

32 A recent definition of modernity in South Asia—as constituting "a series of historical processes that brought hitherto relatively isolated societies into contact"—echoes descriptions of the globalization process. Sanjay Subrahmanyan, "Hearing Voices: Vignettes of Early Modernity in South Asia," *The American Historical Review* 116:3 (2011), p. 100.

33 Timothy Mitchell, "The Stage of Modernity," in Mitchell, *Questions of Modernity*, p. 16.

FIGURE I.1 *AEG production in Berlin (c. 1900), photo by George Buxenstein & Co.*

FIGURE I.2 *The German Social Security System (1913).*

FIGURE I.3 *A Social Democratic women's meeting in Berlin (c. 1890).*

FIGURE I.4 *"Togo" by Erich Schilling (1922).*

FIGURE I.5 *Poster for the First* Werkbund *Exposition, Cologne (1914).*

2

Neither Singular nor Alternative: Narratives of Modernity and Welfare in Germany, 1870–1945

Young-sun Hong

Introduction

The languages of welfare and social reform have played a central role in scholarly debates on German modernity. However, although the development of social insurance was long regarded as a pivotal element of the country's special, anti-liberal path to the modern world, this account was challenged in the 1980s by an alternative narrative which regarded the culture and society of the *Kaiserreich*, and especially its social institutions, more as paradigmatic for modernity than as a deviation from it. This reversal of scholarly opinion within such a brief period was undoubtedly due in no small part to the influence of poststructuralism and the postmodernist critique of modernity, which has emphasized its pathologies and contradictions rather than its promise. There was, however, always a danger that this revisionist narrative would portray Nazism in an equally simplistic, teleological manner as the unavoidable end product of a precociously modern German

This chapter initially appeared in *Social History* 30:2 (May 2005). Earlier versions were originally presented at the conferences of the German Studies Association and the American Historical Association. I would like to thank Geoff Eley, Larry Frohman, and the participants in these two panels for their constructive comments.

society, and when I began working on this chapter in 2002 my goal was to use discourses on the social from the Wilhelmine era through the Third Reich to problematize the idea that modernity had a single origin and that it developed in a unilinear manner toward a predetermined end of one kind or another. Ultimately, I hoped to make visible the multiple locations of modernity (i.e., places, social actors, political cultures, and visions of the future) and examine the heterogeneous and often competing forms of social practice and cultural production, as well as the ways in which political modernity has been institutionalized in Germany.

* * * * * *

This chapter explores the ways in which the historiography of the German welfare state has been intertwined with our changing conceptions of modernity. This analytical démarche may seem odd or unfamiliar to many readers because, until quite recently, the very idea of German modernity was regarded as something of an oxymoron which was believed to possess about as much reality as "military intelligence" or, to use the German idiom, *hölzernes Eisen*.

The polemical juxtaposition of the German and West European paths to the modern world—of German *Kultur* and the *Zivilisation* of the French Enlightenment and British commerce—was the mainstay of German nationalist historiography at least through the 1960s. Beginning in the 1970s, this positive valorization of German exceptionalism was challenged in an influential series of monographs and syntheses by the leading figures of what came to be known as the Bielefeld school—Hans-Ulrich Wehler, Jürgen Kocka, and Hans-Jürgen Puhle. However, these writers maintained the basic framework of German exceptionalism, while inverting the moral signs. They then proceeded to construct a formidable theoretical apparatus designed to explain the catastrophes of twentieth-century German history as the result of the uneven or incomplete modernization of German society during the Second Empire, the pivotal decades in Germany's transition from an agrarian to an industrial society.[1]

In the classical formulation of sociological modernization theory, which provided the deep structure for the work of the Bielefeld group, economic development was the motor force behind modernization, while a number of other changes, including democratization, urbanization, changes in culture and family structure, the spread of education, and the expansion of social services, were viewed in a circular manner as both the necessary precondition for, and the inevitable consequence of, economic change. For the Bielefelders, the fundamental issue was the disjunction in Imperial Germany between rapid economic modernization, which telescoped the first and second industrial revolutions into a half-century of convulsive change, and the continued hold of traditional elites on the levers of political power: the agrarian nobility, the military caste, the Prussified bureaucracy, and, not least, an emperor who remained unaccountable to the nation. In this modernization-theoretical perspective, the normal path to modernity would have taken the form of a political revolution—a "bourgeois revolution"— which would have made it possible to bring the economic, political, social, cultural, and military spheres back into synchronization with one another and thus create the necessary conditions for the democratic resolution of the manifold problems associated with the coming of the modern world.[2]

The problem was that German political elites failed to either play the democratic game or to succumb to the seemingly irresistible pressures for political change. Instead, from Bismarck onward, traditional German political elites fought a series of rear-guard battles to defend their privileged position against the rising tide of democracy. As Wehler and his colleagues argue, these elites were able to maintain their position by convincing a politically supine middle class—frightened by the specter of social revolution—to buy into the cultural values of the old regime, by engaging in a policy of colonial expansion to distract the working classes from the repressive policies of the regime at home, and by forging a perpetually unstable alliance of agrarians and industrialists against a constantly changing constellation of "enemies of the Empire." For more than a decade, these theories provided the dominant matrix for interpreting the history of the empire, and they inspired a number of extremely important monographs and interpretations of the political system and culture of the empire. Yet, the Bielefelders conclude, the success of these traditional elites was bought at the price of poisoning the political culture of the empire in ways that directly led the nation into the First World War and created the preconditions for the rise of Nazism.

The problem with this comparative analysis of the history of Imperial Germany is that it is based on two problematic assumptions. On the one hand, it relied on an overly idealized view of the rise of the middle classes in Western Europe, which unproblematically equated bourgeois values with political liberalism. On the other hand, it rested on a failure to recognize the extent to which the German middle classes had, in fact, become a bourgeois class which was not all that dissimilar from that to be found in England, France, and elsewhere west of the Rhine. The work which theoretically collapsed both sides of this East–West comparison and won its British authors chairs at prestigious American universities was David Blackbourn and Geoff Eley's *The Peculiarities of German History*.[3] The controversy this set off led to an explosion of research into the German middle classes which shows no sign of abating.[4]

What is most important in the present context is that the evaporation of classical modernization theory (or at least its disappearance as a self-evident and unquestioned paradigm) left a theoretical gap in the literature on Imperial Germany. Perhaps the most urgent task now facing historians of the period is to find new ways of understanding the modernity of Imperial Germany on its own terms by analyzing the forces of change operating in German society, rather than by comparing Germany to a flawed ideal-typical construct. Welfare, social reform, and the general expansion of the capacity of public institutions (though not necessarily of the state bureaucracy itself) to monitor, control, and rationalize the life of its citizens lead directly to the heart of the debates over the modernity of Imperial Germany and the relation of both welfare and modernity to the Nazi regime.

For decades now, if not since the very inception of the Bismarckian social insurance system, our understanding of the novelty and significance of the German welfare state has been intimately linked to our understanding of the modernity of German society or the lack thereof. Originally, the Bismarckian social insurance system was linked positively to the paternalist aspirations of the authoritarian national state and its proud rejection of the norms of West European modernity.[5] For the Bielefeld school, and the large number of historians who have accepted the broad contours of this argument, the precocious establishment of the Bismarckian social insurance system represented yet another strategy designed to guide Germany permanently away from this normal path to modernity by short-circuiting the pressures for democratization. In this schema, social insurance was the carrot that was intended to soften the harshness of the repressive stick provided by the Anti-Socialist Law (1878–90) and the denial of democratic rights, wean the nascent working classes away from the party of revolution, and reconcile them with an authoritarian but paternalistic state.

This Bismarck-centered perspective on the authoritarian, reactionary, or defensive modernity of the German welfare state has been substantially complicated by recent research.[6] But the real issue lies elsewhere, because the most important recent studies of the German welfare system have not so much attacked this interpretation of the Bismarckian welfare state as found it to be not relevant to their critical concerns. These focus on the nature of the social domain, the process of social discipline, and the development of new liberal strategies of governmentality.

If the question was originally framed in terms of modernization theory, since the 1990s the relationship between welfare and modernity has been dominated by the concept of social discipline and by the claim that Nazi welfare and social policies were determined more by modern sciences such as eugenics and regional planning than by an archaizing rejection of modernity. In the literature on the German welfare system from the *Kaiserreich* to the Third Reich, the heart of the issue is that the normative connection between modernity, liberalism, and emancipation, which has defined our understanding of welfare and Enlightenment, has been called into question by those very interpretations which have most advanced our understanding of the Nazi regime.

Over the past decade, historians have increasingly characterized the Nazi regime as a "racial state" whose goal was to recast bourgeois society on the basis of its racial worldview.[7] This new approach has also given us a clearer perspective on the modernity of Nazi social and welfare policies by showing how Nazi policies of discrimination, exclusion, and annihilation can in part be traced back to the same social scientific discourses and administrative practices that were the origin of the German welfare state. This shift is the result of the confluence of two historiographical trends. First, since the 1980s scholars working in the field have argued that Nazi racial ideas were, to a larger degree than had heretofore been recognized, the product of the modern (pseudo-)science of eugenics, rather than traditional religious or social antisemitism. They argue that eugenics exerted a pervasive influence on both Nazi social policies and those university-trained technocrats who eventually assumed prominent positions in the regime. Second, since the 1980s the dispute over the peculiarities of German history and Germany's "special path" (*Sonderweg*) to modernity has given rise to a new wave of research which has clearly established the modernity of German society and economy during the *Kaiserreich* and the Weimar Republic. However, this literature has argued that Progressive social policies were inherently contradictory because their strategies for emancipating the lower classes and improving their way of life often relied on illiberal, coercive means. In turn, this insight gave rise to the claim that, even though the Progressives were often the most important proponents of modernization in Wilhelmine and Weimar Germany, there are important continuities between the authoritarian, technocratic tendencies—some actual and some merely latent—of Progressivism and the social and racial policies of the Nazis. These two lines of argument come together in the notion that the apparently Progressive eugenic measures to promote the health, welfare, and procreation of the racially valuable segments of the population and the Nazi efforts to marginalize and ultimately exterminate asocials, Jews, and other racially inferior and politically suspect groups must be seen as two sides of the same coin. They are, at bottom, simply different manifestations of the fundamental, underlying contradictions of German modernity.[8]

However, this insight has been gained only at the cost of deepening our concern over the potential conflict between modernity and emancipation. The more we understand the continuity between the welfare systems of Wilhelmine and Weimar Germany and those of the Nazis, the more directly we are forced to confront the question of the extent to which the Third Reich can be described as a welfare state. Anyone who writes on race, welfare, and social policy in twentieth-century Germany will have to come to grips with this decentering and complication of the narrative of modernity, and I would like to examine more closely how this connection between modernity and welfare has shaped the recent historiography of the German welfare state.

1

As formulated by Michel Foucault, the social discipline paradigm has focused on the production of the modern subject through disciplining mechanisms designed to provide a more rational—in the sense of being more effective, continuous—form of authority than the awe-inspiring, yet merely sporadic interventions of the early modern sovereign. For Foucault and those who have followed in his footsteps, social discipline represented something very different from the idea of social control, which had itself been articulated to explain how social services had been employed by the governing classes to manipulate, co-opt, and ultimately blunt the potentially revolutionary resentments of the underclasses toward the established social order.

Curiously, scholars employing this new approach have been generally more interested in the poor, the criminal, and the deviant less for themselves than for the light which social interventionist practices throw back upon the norms of the middle classes and for the insights which these practices yield with regard to the changing nature of modern politics. As a result, their works have focused less on the poor as an object of study in their own right or on the recovery of their experiences and have, instead, used them as a mirror for studying the middle classes who defined normality, constructed the discourses through which these fields of social intervention were constituted, and populated the institutions through which these discourses produce their enabling truths. The social discipline paradigm also had a second set of methodological implications, especially with regard to the new social history of the 1970s and 1980s. The study of welfare and the poor helped the new social history make visible the agency of the subaltern groups who were the supposed beneficiaries of public assistance (and the objects of the attendant forms of social control) and rescued these groups from what E.P. Thompson called in another context "the enormous condescension of posterity." At the same time, the concept of social discipline has directed attention away from questions of class and social causality and toward language and the way cultural systems work to produce meaning. The result has been a very French fusion between a Foucaultian analysis of discursive formations and disciplinary practices through which the modern subject was produced and a Derridean deconstructive analysis of both the logic through which these discourses worked and the gaps, limits, blind spots, and contradictions of the identities which are forged through the workings of language and power.

Out of this theoretical conundrum is emerging something which resembles a new historiographical paradigm with welfare and modernity as its master concepts. This link between welfare and modernity was forged as "welfare" became a general term designating not simply the various forms of assistance to the poor, but all forms of public intervention directed toward the production and reproduction of the normal subject within the "social" domain. This model of identity formation which was originally developed for the individual subject is increasingly being applied at the level of the collective, primarily national subject so that welfare, in this broader sense, becomes a privileged medium for studying the formation of national identity. The analytic coupling of welfare, modernity, and violence has become an important theme in recent writing on other societies, such as the Soviet Union and fascist Italy, which have been the object of radical, state-sponsored social engineering.[9]

Following the logic of poststructuralist analysis, the identity of the subject (whether individual or collective) is established through discourses of difference (race, class, gender, ethnicity, nationality). These discourses are constructed through rhetorical strategies whose primary function is to stabilize the identity of the knowing subject by establishing the naturalness of this difference. This is, as Mary Poovey has argued, the "ideological work" of gender and all discourses of difference.[10] Moving from the domain of discourse to social practice, the function of welfare—as disciplinary practice and cultural strategy—is to cultivate those virtues and comportments which are characteristic of the ideal or normal person and which are regarded as necessary for full citizenship and membership in the community. These differential relationships, however, are intrinsically unstable, and the identities they establish are precarious and provisional. At the discursive level, this anxiety leads to the constant refinement and extension of these discourses of difference in the vain and perpetually deferred hope of definitively recouping all potential threats to the coherence and stability of these discourses.

In the realm of social practice, the situation is equally complex. Since all individuals can potentially deviate from the social norm, disciplinary welfare measures acquire a universal applicability and are no longer limited to the poor or otherwise deviant or asocial groups. Here, the ideological labor of welfare pursues several distinct but interrelated strategies: to integrate normal subjects tightly into the community through ever-vigilant efforts to keep them from deviating from the social norm; to reintegrate those persons or groups who are deemed to have the potential to become full-fledged members of the community, but who have failed to do so due to inadequate socialization; and to protect the social body from two groups— reprobates who, although potentially members, have proven themselves to be hopelessly irredeemable, and those persons who, by their very nature, are regarded as incapable of integration into the community and whose difference makes them into real or imaginary threats to its very existence. Of course, the lines dividing these four groups are always only provisional and constantly subject to fundamental revision, just as are the scope, intensity, and nature of the practices of inclusion and exclusion.

These modes of analysis have been developed above all by feminists inspired by poststructuralist approaches to gender and by postcolonial theorists attuned to the impact of empire on the cultures of the metropole.[11] However, there are also obvious similarities between this approach and those works which have characterized Nazi Germany as a "racial state," rather than a form of fascism or totalitarianism. According to this new perspective, the essence of the Nazi regime is to be found in its racial beliefs and in its effort to reconstruct German and European society on the basis of these ideas. Welfare and social policies, it is argued, must be seen as part of a broader racial policy which embraces both positive measures to benefit those deemed to be of value to the community and those negative measures directed against inferior, less valuable persons: policies which range from diminution of welfare benefits and the denial of marriage loans via compulsory sterilization and concentration camp detention to the euthanasia program, the ideological war on the Eastern Front, and genocide. Nazi politics were driven by a powerful dynamic of selection and exclusion or eradication whose continuous radicalization has been explained in a variety of ways: by the liberation of the antisemitic imagination of the leading Nazis from the restraints of law and bourgeois morality during the course of the war (intentionalist accounts); by the force of external circumstances (structuralist accounts); by political rivalries within the state (polycracy theory); and by the totalizing logic of the modern social sciences (Detlev Peukert[12]).

Though it is impossible to address the entire gamut of Nazi racial policies in this chapter or to attempt a general interpretation of the essence of the Nazi regime, we can—without losing sight of the broader framework—focus on the welfare and social policies of the regime. Welfare and social policy have played an increasingly central role in accounts of Nazi Germany in part because this new approach has the potential to provide a more compelling answer to many of the key controversies in the historiography of Nazi Germany. There is, however, a specific set of issues raised by the literature on welfare and social policy.

Much of the recent literature on the German welfare system has noted the role of welfare programs in this process of normalization, selection, and eradication and, on the basis of this insight, postulated that there is an intrinsic connection between modern welfare programs and National Socialism (whether this is conceived of as something *sui generis* or as the German form of fascism). However, these attempts to argue that the same forces which drove the development of the welfare state—which has long been viewed as a vehicle for progress and individual emancipation—could in some essential way also be responsible for something as barbaric as the Nazi regime calls into question that identification of modernity and emancipation which underlies much of the historiography of the modern welfare state—and the welfare state itself. It seems now as *though* we are faced with the choice of either denying the connection between welfare and fascism (for which there is far more than mere *prima facie* evidence) or the modernity of Nazi social policies (a position which seems much more vulnerable to attack) or both. To a certain extent, the analytical constraints surrounding these issues have been loosened by postmodernist critiques, which have uncovered the illiberal potential latent in Western narratives of reason and progress—though only at the price of weakening the normative claims of modernity.

The stakes are high. The main advantage of the new approach to Nazi Germany is that it integrates many aspects of Nazi society which until recently have been approached separately. By putting the symbolic system of racial difference at the heart of the regime's project, we are also able to understand how Germans of this time were able to give meaning to many ideas, institutions, and practices which have heretofore been regarded as irrational or the outcome of a total and barely-comprehensible ideological distortion of reality. Conversely, it will be difficult to speak of Nazi Germany as a racial state which was shaped in essential ways by the modern social sciences if Nazi welfare and social policies are seen either as genuine but atavistic or as measures which were merely intended as ideological diversions to sway a gullible (or terrified) public. I would like to focus on how two interrelated questions have been answered in the literature on the German welfare state in the Weimar and Nazi periods. How modern were Nazi Germany and its welfare policies? And how has our answer to this question been shaped by our understanding of the relationship between modernity and emancipation? As we shall see, understanding the modernity of the German welfare system will require a reconceptualization of both modernity and welfare. However, we will be advised to keep in mind the fact that, even though these new interpretive categories may be based on the German experience, they have a general relevance that is coextensive with that of modernity itself.

2

This postmodern reassessment of the modernist project is a broad intellectual movement drawing its critical energy from literary theory, postmodernist philosophy, feminism, and postcolonial studies. The general disillusionment with Progressive optimism, which has underlain these new methodological departures, has been given a peculiarly German twist by the implication of the welfare system in the Nazi regime. Within the field of German history, much of the impetus for this new departure must be attributed to Detlev Peukert, whose *Limits of Social Discipline* altered in two important ways previous interpretations of the German welfare system.[13] First, he effectively challenged the *Sonderweg* interpretation by showing how the development of the youth welfare system was driven by Progressive efforts to employ modern, social scientific knowledge—backed up by the power of the state—to discipline working-class youth and families by rationalizing their behavior in accordance with middle-class norms. Peukert reinforced this interpretation by situating these methods of welfarist intervention within an overarching theory of modernity drawn from Weber and Habermas. However, and this is the second important point, while Peukert's account of the growth of the German youth welfare system established the modernity of these programs and their emancipatory potential, his claim that fascism represented a pathological possibility latent in the Progressive project (which could be—and which was—realized under specific circumstances) implied that modernity, liberalism, and emancipation could no longer be regarded as coextensive with one another. This double move proved to be extremely fruitful. On the one hand, it established a model for the investigation of modernity in other spheres and, on the other, Peukert's provocative account of the birth of the Final Solution out of the spirit of eugenics and Progressive social engineering has been an important inspiration for subsequent research on welfare, eugenics, and racial policy—even if this research has not endorsed all of Peukert's conclusions.

Over the past decade, an immense amount of literature has appeared on various aspects of the German welfare and insurance systems, especially from the *Kaiserreich* to the Third Reich. Although this literature has fleshed out and modified the overview provided by Sachße and Tennstedt,[14] it has been dominated by Peukert's work and by the question of modernity. Although these publications have qualified his theses in many respects, by and large they continue to work within the basic analytic framework established by him. While Peukert implied the existence of a single, universal process of social discipline and surveillance, Ross Dickinson, David Crew, Dennis Sweeney, Warren Rosenblum, and I have all worked in various ways to complicate this picture, arguing that the process of social discipline was hardly anonymous in the manner depicted in Foucault's *Discipline and Punish*.[15]

As I argued in *Welfare, Modernity, and the Weimar State*, the development of the welfare system in its various aspects can perhaps best be conceptualized as a multidimensional process of competitive rationalization in which the efforts of any one group to establish the terms for the rationalization of the social sphere called forth responses by other groups whose own traditional values were threatened by these measures. The resulting competition led to the rationalization and modernization of traditional reform organizations (especially religious charity organizations) and the mobilization of welfare clientele. The efforts of these groups to insulate themselves from the pressures of pluralism and oversight by the sovereign state contributed in important ways to the paralysis of parliamentary government and the overthrow of the Republic. Even Marcus Gräser, who attempted to refute Peukert by attributing the crisis of the republican welfare system to the resistance of confessional and conservative groups to the pressures of modernization, rather than to a highly modern and equally illiberal response by Progressives disillusioned by their growing sensitivity to the limits of emancipatory social pedagogy, is still working within the categorical framework established by Peukert.[16] Ewald Frie is clearly moving in the right direction when he argues that, in view of the localistic, highly fragmented and intensely contested nature of the German welfare system, our perception of the modernity of this system depends very much on where we look. In his comparative study of welfare policy in Westphalia and Saxony, Frie argues that the contradictions of Progressive modernity identified by Peukert were abundantly evident in Saxony, where welfare policy was influenced by the Progressive-Social Democratic welfare minister Hans Maier, while in Westphalia the more conservative and more politically influential welfare administrators were able to oppose successfully the pressure for Progressive reforms.[17]

More recently, Kevin Repp, building on the work of Daniel Rodgers, has attempted to turn the tables on Peukert and break the link between modernity, Progressivism, social reform, and fascism that was so central to Peukert's own reasoning. However, although Repp succeeds in capturing the positive, emancipatory achievements of German Progressive reformers, he downplays the novel, complicated, and potentially problematic aspects of their work.[18] In his *Making Security Social*, Greg Eghigian has not so much rejected Peukert as turned him on his head. Peukert argued that Progressivism revealed its illiberal potential as reformers and social workers lost sight of the emancipatory ends which the new mechanisms of surveillance and discipline were originally intended to serve. However, in an interesting but largely implicit reversal of Peukert, Eghigian explores the other dimension of this process of social discipline, the dialectics of emancipation (or welfare provision). He suggests that the social entitlement state and its characteristic forms of political life emerged as actual and potential beneficiaries of disability insurance argued—in a language of victimization—for the extension of state intervention in forms which would be more sensitive to their subjective sense of injury and insecurity and which would give expression to the obligations of the state to its citizens. Eghigian's interpretation of the social entitlement state as a secular theodicy of welfarist redemption is to a large degree simply the inversion of the negative theodicy of progressive intervention which underlies Peukert's work.[19]

Collectively, these works have demonstrated that the process of social rationalization described by Peukert was far more contradictory and contested than Peukert originally maintained. However, the end result is a more subtle, yet more compelling picture of the multidimensional modernity of German society and the German welfare system than that originally painted by Peukert. These works show clearly that in Germany modernity was *not* the privileged domain of secular-minded, Progressive reformers. The nonconfessional, humanitarianism of these Progressives was hotly contested by conservative Christian reformers who saw their own confessional ideas as the fulcrum for solving the social question. These groups were also forced to modernize and rationalize their approach to charity and poor relief in order to legitimate their views in the age of social science and public opinion. Even though their modernization may have been unwilling and defensive, it substantially complicates any narrative of the modernity of welfare and social reform. As we can see from the history of the Weimar welfare system, it appears that these groups succeeded to no small degree in turning the tides against the Progressives, whose own liberal credentials have been seriously questioned. In short, it has become problematic to identify the Progressives as the primary protagonist of modernity or to equate Progressivism with liberalism and emancipation. As a result, the idea of a singular, normative path to modernity has become problematic if not untenable.

The debate now centers less on the degree to which the various reform groups deviated from or failed to live up to an ostensible normal path to modernity than on the search for a conceptual vocabulary capable of expressing the emergent view of the complex, contradictory, and acentric modernity of the German welfare system. However, this problem has not been explicitly theorized in the literature on the German welfare state. The best analogy to this problem is the debate over the logical and chronological meaning of the "post" in postcolonial studies. This discussion pivots on the privileged status of European modernity in relation to colonial counter-modernities and raises the same questions as the attempt to understand the relation between the progressive provocation and the competing, heteronomous responses to this rationalizing project. As J. Jorge Klor de Alva has written with regard to postcolonialism in Latin America, the "post" of postcolonial studies denotes as much a chronological succession as a subjectivity of oppositionality in relation to the subject of any imperializing master narrative. As a contestatory or oppositional consciousness, postcoloniality, Klor de Alva argues, "is contained both within colonialism, as a Derridian supplement complementing the meaning of this antecedent condition of dependent, asymmetrical relations, and outside of it, by its questioning of the very norms that establish the inside/outside, oppressor (colonizer)/oppressed (colonized) binaries that are assumed to characterize the colonial condition."[20] In short, we postmodern Germanists seem to be left in a theoretical quandary. On the one hand, we seem to need a teleological, essentialized view of modernity and emancipation in the subject position against which we can define our own critical post- or counter-modernity, as described above. On the other hand, however, as these counterdiscourses decenter this narrative of Progressive modernity by showing that it can exist only as something which has always-already been deconstructed, they at the same time call into question the bases of their own existence and authority. With the authority of both the master narrative of modernity and its postmodernist doubles irrevocably called into question, we find ourselves faced with the quintessentially postmodern task of establishing the legitimacy of our own critical discourse.[21]

To the extent that Peukert's influence is due to the parallels between his work and Foucault's work on social discipline, it is also necessary to note that in recent years totalizing theories of social discipline and concerns for state sovereignty have been partially displaced by neo-Foucaultian theories of (liberal) governmentality.[22] However, it is not clear to what extent this analytical shift will alter our understanding of the modernity of German society. In his later writings, Foucault attempted to construct a genealogy of the modern state. He described the development of the modern state in terms of the successive emergence of the sovereign, the disciplinary and the governmental state. But this succession did not mean the complete supersession of the one by the next. Instead, Foucault seemed to imply that the two later modes of governance emerged out of the need to overcome the limitations of the preceding mode(s) and that, in the present, the two earlier modes continue to coexist in a complex relation to each other and to the new mechanisms of liberal governmentality. The defining characteristic of the disciplinary state of the seventeenth and eighteenth centuries was the use of rudimentary forms of social knowledge and political practices to directly guide and control a growing, but limited, number of spheres of social activity. By contrast, the governmental state began to take form when the desire for direct control was replaced by a new strategy of rule whose central logic was based on structuring the social field so as to shape the possibilities of action and subjectivity, rather than attempting to control them directly.[23]

It is this withdrawal of direct, state involvement in favor of self-government through the internalization of these pedagogical and disciplinary structures that lies behind the pleonastic denomination of this new regime as "liberal" governmentality. However, the liberality of this modern regime of rule is itself intrinsically ambivalent because its perfection depends on the other modes of rule—sovereign and/or disciplinary—to establish and maintain the security mechanisms necessary to cultivate those forms of self-discipline whose internalization is the precondition for the withdrawal of direct, external control. This imparts to modern liberal governmentality a distinctly illiberal dimension. However, this illiberality has no intrinsic affinity with any party-political label, and it appears to reflect a contradiction inherent in every doctrine which claims to educate someone toward an ostensibly truer or more authentic notion of freedom which these persons are believed to be uninterested in or incapable of attaining through their own efforts.

There is also a second contradiction or paradox inherent in liberal governmentality. Although the aim of liberal governmentality is to render itself superfluous by inaugurating the reign of the laws naturally governing the individual spheres of social activity, as David Horn and others have argued, this process of normalization—whether under a disciplinary or governmental regime—is itself intrinsically contradictory. Its very operation denaturalizes those modes of comportment upon whose naturalness its own rationality depends. As a consequence, both disciplinary and (liberal) governmental modes of rule give rise to the constant refinement of social scientific knowledge and the expansion of increasingly sophisticated and invasive apparatuses of state intervention necessary to naturalize the social, normalize behavior, and render itself superfluous (or at least invisible). The realization of perfect self-government thus requires the continuous and total application of disciplinary power from without (or at least the permanent potential for such action). The inevitable failure to leap over their own shadows and escape from the fate of modernity keeps this process of welfarist intervention in perpetually expanding motion.[24]

As Dennis Sweeney has argued, it is important to emphasize the local origins and organization of virtually every imaginable set of disciplinary practices and the role of voluntary organizations and local government in pioneering governmental practices, which were subsequently codified by the sovereign, national state.[25] While this account of the contradictions of governmentality and its relation to disciplinary rule may provide a fairly compelling description of modernity, it also reinforces our sense of the ambiguity between liberalism, illiberalism, and modernity in the welfare state. It seems that it will be harder than ever before to discover within, or impose a unitary telos upon, the rationalization of those arts of government linked to the welfare state. The concept of governmentality may well encourage further studies of welfarist initiatives emanating from actors outside the national state. Although these studies of governmentality may enrich the social discipline paradigm to which they are logically wedded, they are unlikely to overturn or supplant it.

3

All of the questions concerning the modernity of the German welfare system and its meaning have been condensed in the debate over the continuity between the Weimar welfare system and the welfare, social, and racial policies of the Nazi regime, as well as the postwar welfare states in East and West Germany. These debates are, in turn, closely linked to the much more murky question of the modernity of the Nazi regime itself.

This debate regime has gone through at least two distinct phases since the 1960s. In the first phase, Ralf Dahrendorf argued that the Third Reich had unintentionally played a vital role of facilitating the establishment of a liberal, democratic society in the Federal Republic by destroying the vestiges of the old, feudal regime and thus made up in certain ways for the absence of a successful bourgeois revolution in the country. At the same time, other authors, such as David Schoenbaum and Henry Turner, argued that the Nazis had been forced to pursue modernizing policies in the economic, social, and political realms in order to achieve fundamentally antimodern ends.[26]

The second round of the academic debate began in the mid-1980s and has developed along two ultimately convergent tracks, placing welfare and social policies at the center of the discussion. The first major interlocutor here was Peukert, who argued that fascism represented the contingent realization of a pathological potential inherent in the Progressive program for social reform. The second track arose out of the German *Historikerstreit* and the controversies surrounding the normalization of German history since the Holocaust and the role of the memory of the Holocaust and the war in the public culture of the Federal Republic.

The debate here was opened by a frankly apologetic biography of Hitler by Rainer Zitelmann, who portrayed the *Führer* as a fanatic but misunderstood modernizer whose aims were frustrated by war and circumstance. However, Zitelmann's tendentious claims led to the publication of a collection of essays on National Socialism and modernization which attempted to resolve the discrepancy between the ostensibly archaic goals and atavistic character of the Nazi regime and the distinctly modern means which the regime employed to achieve these goals. The contributors identified a number of modern elements that were clearly visible in German society in the 1930s. Prinz argues that these developments did, in fact, represent different facets of a comprehensive Nazi effort to recast German society in a more modern mold, though he concedes the complexity, contradictoriness, and undeniably archaic dimensions of the Nazi regime. However, Prinz's interpretation has been sharply criticized by Hans Mommsen and Norbert Frei. Mommsen and Frei have argued that Prinz's characterization of the modernity of Nazi society conflates several analytical levels and fails to distinguish between the ideology or worldview of the Nazis, the actual policies and programs of the government under Nazi rule and long-term, secular trends which continued across the Third Reich, but which could hardly be attributed to Nazi initiatives. Moreover, they argue that the inability of Zitelmann and Prinz to thematize the exclusion and repression that were the preconditions for the realization of the modernizing vision which they attribute to the Nazis represents such a gross failure of the historical imagination that it fatally undermines their claim to have presented a comprehensive interpretation of Nazi Germany, modern or otherwise.

Mommsen is one of the leading proponents of a structuralist interpretation of the Nazi regime. He argues that the Holocaust was the product of the cumulative radicalization of anti-Jewish measures (driven by a combination of internal rivalries within the regime and external circumstances) and that its essential character—such as it was—is to be found in the vast destructive energies it released. While this interpretive position underpins his trenchant attacks on Zitelmann and Prinz and his denial that the Nazis possessed any constructive social vision, Mommsen's criticisms also apply directly or indirectly to Peukert and the theorists of the racial state: their argument that the essence of the Nazi regime is to be found in its plan to reconstruct German and European society on the basis of its racial ideology; that these plans (or at least the actions of a section of the technocratic elite) were directly inspired by eugenics and other modern social sciences; and that modern, constructive social programs to enhance the welfare of the racially valuable segments of the population must be understood as the counterpart to those programs designed to marginalize the racially inferior, exclude them from the body politic and ultimately eradicate them physically. As Ulrich Herbert noted a decade ago, this linkage of positive welfare, labor, and social policies with the entire gamut of Nazi policies of racial discrimination by means of eugenics and racial hygiene, allowing us to see such apparently unrelated and antithetical programs as integral parts of a single, modern whole, represents one of the most important conceptual advances made since the 1980s.[27]

Hitler and the Nazis viewed racial struggle as the motor of history. All of the welfare, social, and racial policies of the regime focused on the single aim of creating a racial national community (*Volksgemeinschaft*) strong enough to prevail in an eternal struggle for survival, a struggle which they believed could only entail either infinite expansion of the *Volk* or its eventual disappearance. Before the Nazis came to power, they had criticized the Weimar welfare system because they felt that the provision of welfare services on the basis of the individualized determination of need had neutralized the mechanism of natural selection and even harmed the *Volk* by encouraging negative selection and the procreation of inferior classes. After 1933, however, the Nazis retreated from their relentless and shrill attacks on the welfare system and, instead, sought to place welfare on a new foundation by making it "racially conscious" (*artbewußt*).[28] The aim of Nazi welfare, or *Volkspflege*, as they termed it, was to improve systematically the quality of the race and expand the size of the racially superior sections of the *Volk* through a process known as *Aufartung*. This policy combined positive social programs to identify and promote the welfare and procreation of racially valuable, genetically superior segments of the population with negative measures to limit progressively the procreation of inferior and/or alien races and prevent them from contaminating the hereditary substance and the moral and cultural life of the nation.

The Nazi reconstruction of the Weimar welfare system was based on the rejection of the Enlightened belief in the intrinsic equality of all individuals. Instead, they maintained that the relative value of individuals was determined by their genetic heritage. According to Hermann Althaus, the director of the Nazi Party welfare department, Nazi welfare was

> fundamentally based on [the sciences of] hereditary biology and racial hygiene. The principle of the equality of all citizens is no longer valid because we have recognized that heredity insures that all individuals are of different value for the welfare of the whole. Environmental factors do not play a determining role in the development of the individual.[29]

The Nazis insisted instead that this misguided "welfare for the weak (or inferior)" (*Minderwertigenfürsorge*) had to be replaced by a new form of welfare (*Vorsorge*) which would strengthen the *Volk* by providing the greatest assistance to the most valuable members of the community and by implementing discriminatory and exclusionary policies to redress the imbalance in the birth rates between valuable and inferior segments of the population which had so vexed the Weimar eugenics community.

The catch here is that, without the basic legal protections secured by a fundamental belief in the value and rights of all individuals, the internal economy of this differential approach to welfare could be infinitely graduated in accordance with the perceived value of the individual to the *Volk*—or the danger which they were believed to pose.[30] While both progressive and conservative Christian welfare reformers had called for renewed emphasis on discipline and duty to counteract the baneful influence of what they regarded as the hypertrophy of individual rights in the republican welfare state, the Nazis went beyond this and, instead, completely inverted the relationship between the individual and the state. They understood the *Volk* as a collective, biological entity which embraced the succession of generations and all individuals living at every point, and they developed an elaborate casuistry to justify sterilization and other negative "welfare" measures which they believed would benefit the *Volk* even as they disregarded the welfare of its living, individual members. As Erich Hilgenfeldt, the director of the Nazi Party's Central Office for National Welfare, wrote in the inaugural number of *Nationalsozialisticher Volksdienst*,

> The unfit must be liquidated (*ausgemerzt*) mercilessly and without reservation on the basis of the insight of our National Socialist worldview that the right of the individual is inferior to the right of the community and that the right of the individual must be violated when the right of the community demands this.[31]

Despite its biologistic terminology, this eugenic discourse employed by the Nazis was always, and primarily, a discourse on social norms and behavior. The idea of the *Volksgemeinschaft* gained much of its wide popular resonance by virtue of an invidious contrast with both the economic conflicts and cultural pluralism of liberal modernity and those Others against whom the authentic members of the community defined themselves: the asocial, the criminal, shirkers who hoped to live from the work of others, those whose conduct so deviated from prescribed social norms and healthy German morality that one could only assume that their behavior was attributable to some innate, hereditary inferiority, and alien racial groups such as Jews and gypsies, whose radical otherness represented an insuperable obstacle to their assimilation into the community. Those who most merited various social benefits were those who, so to speak, had earned this right through their contributions to the common weal, not those whose material need was a clear sign of both their inability and unwillingness to hold up their end of the social contract or their sociobiological inferiority.

There is a large and still growing literature on all facets of Nazi social policy. This can be loosely grouped into several overlapping themes: (1) industrial relations, scientific management, programs to rationalize the labor market, wage policies, social insurance, and the rationalization of production; (2) policies aimed at defining gender roles, family structures, and patterns of sexuality; and (3) traditional welfare programs, including general assistance, welfare for mothers, infants, and the young, policies toward asocials and the social work profession (including the role of social workers and welfare administrators in enforcing Nazi policies). Since debates over eugenics and racial hygiene weave their way through each of these themes, it is impossible to separate scholarly discussion of these policies from the euthanasia program and Nazi plans for the military reconstruction of Eastern Europe and the Holocaust. Most of this literature shows that the secular rationalization of policy and programs in all of these areas continued apace through the 1930s and 1940s, and describes the competition between traditional economic elites and the architects of the racial state to bend these new, more instrumentally rational means to their respective systems of ultimate ends.

Eugenics and racial hygiene were by no means exclusively German sciences, and the relation between heredity and social deviance had been a major concern throughout Europe and the United States since the last decades of the nineteenth century.[32] Nor was eugenics the only modern social science which influenced Nazi social policies. In conjunction with Susanne Heim and other collaborators, Götz Aly has shown how Nazi schemes for the racial reconstruction of Eastern Europe also drew on a number of modern social and policy sciences, including demography, urban planning, and economics, as well as racial hygiene and on such modern social technologies as the census.[33] Similarly, Ulrich Herbert, Michael Wildt, and Michael Thad Allen have all argued that academic elites with training in medicine, law, administration, and other disciplines eagerly sought out leading positions in the SS and the Nazi Party in hopes of putting into practice the technocratic visions of social reorganization which were the root of their personal and professional identities.[34]

The view of the Nazi regime—pioneered by Peukert and Gisela Bock—as a racial state has become widely accepted over the past decade, and this has had an important impact on our view of the regime. Against this background, we can better understand how the differential welfare, family, and population policies for the racially valuable and the inferior could be seen as modern and rational. However, the question running through the literature is this: In view of the extent to which the progressive welfare and social policies of the Weimar Republic were taken over by the Nazis and refunctioned to serve the substantive ends of their racial worldview, is it possible meaningfully to characterize the Nazi regime as a welfare state?

Although the recent literature follows Peukert in tracing the origins of eugenics and other social scientific discourses of racial difference back to the *Kaiserreich*, most subsequent writers have declined to follow him fully in his account of the birth of German fascism out of either the pathologies of Progressive reform or the technocratic hubris of the modern social sciences. In my own book, I have argued that the eugenic foundations of the Nazi welfare system represented an abandonment of the main principles of the Weimar welfare system, rather than their logical development (though it is important to qualify this point by noting the continuities in social work practice and personnel and the strong affinities between certain strands of conservative Protestantism and the racial ideologies of the Nazis). It was the transformation of these biologistic modes of thought into the official social policy that made the elimination of entire groups of the population appear as a rational solution to the various aspects of the social question. And it was only on the basis of this disqualification of these groups as biological dangers and excess mouths or social ballast—rather than viewing them as the objects of Christian charity or Progressive social pedagogy—that the logic of racial hygienic exclusion described by Peukert and Bock could have been followed to its logical extreme.

In their study of the German welfare system in the 1930s, Christoph Sachße and Florian Tennstedt distinguish between the authoritarian reaction to the individualist excesses of the republican welfare system and the *völkish* welfare state created after 1938. However, their use of the term "welfare state" is not entirely consistent. On the one hand, they argue that Nazi welfare policies represented a regression in comparison with the republican welfare state because these differential policies consciously promoted inequality on the basis of biological determinations of the social value of the recipients. However, they immediately qualify this by noting that all welfare systems—including those that take the promotion of equality as their avowed goal—generate new inequalities. On the other hand, they do regard Nazi regime as one possible form of the modern welfare state, which they characterize as "a cumulatively radicalized and perverted terroristic extreme along a broad spectrum of possible developmental paths towards the modern world taken by industrial societies." But it is not clear how they can characterize the Nazi system as something perverse and yet still regard it as a legitimate or rational response to the problems of modern industrial society.[35]

Other authors have argued that the Nazi regime and its social policies were indeed highly modern, but they stripped away connotations of improvement, progress, and emancipation to such an extent that the concept of modernity and the very idea of Nazi "welfare" verge on losing all meaning.[36] The normative connections between modernity, individual emancipation, and welfare are so strong that it seems unlikely that we will ever be able to describe Nazi Germany as a welfare state in a fully satisfactory manner. *Fürsorge* (the German term for "welfare") is embedded in an entirely different symbolic system than are Nazi *Vorsorge* and "welfare of the *Volk*" (*Volkspflege*), both of which emphasize the priority of the rights of the collective and of future generations over those of existing individuals, and, no matter how finely we parse the word "welfare," it is probably a vain hope to think that in this way we can ever satisfactorily resolve the question.

One important advance to come from the new approach to the Nazi regime as a racial state is that its social, welfare, and racial policies can be seen as a conscious intervention into social relations in order to reshape society and thereby, in theory, resolve the problems of modern, industrial society.

This is one definition of the social, interventionist or welfare state whose applicability—even to the Nazi state—would be hard to reject out of hand. We can also extend this definition to emphasize how these interventions were inspired by an enlightened spirit of rationalist, Progressive social engineering, and how they employed ostensibly scientific and universal criteria to define normality and determine who was to enjoy the rights of citizenship, who was to be the object of betterment, and who was to be excluded from the community. However, such an argument strengthens the connections between welfarist intervention and modernity which we just noted were so problematic under the Nazis. Consequently, the more that we explore the rise of the social domain, the more we are forced to modify our inherited understanding of welfare and the welfare state. In turn, modernity and the social become more intensely intertwined with a postmodern conception of welfare which can no longer with a clear conscience claim individual emancipation as an essential attribute.

* * * * * *

In conclusion, I would like to touch briefly on two points. First, we must accept the fact that the word "welfare" has multiple referents that must be carefully distinguished when speaking of Nazi social policies. And, unless we are willing to dismiss these social policies as irrational, the result of an ideological distortion of common sense, or the product of systematic terror, we have to make an effort to understand how contemporaries could see these social programs as contributing to the common welfare, even if they may not have fully accepted the premises of Nazi policymakers or been willing to follow them to their murderous end. Interpretations of Nazi Germany as a racial state have achieved a high degree of acceptance in recent years, with race and eugenics replacing class and fascism as the dominant theoretical framework. There is less and less perceived need to justify the new paradigm, and more and more people have settled down to doing what Thomas Kuhn called "normal science." An important corollary of this outpouring of work on Nazi Germany is the search for new fields to plow, and, increasingly, younger students are moving backwards to unearth the origins of these later discourses of racial difference in the *Kaiserreich*. In particular, German historians are beginning to borrow from the literature on colonialism and postcolonial theory in hopes of uncovering new connections between imperialism, inner missions to bring middle-class cultural norms to the underclasses at home, the rise of the welfare state, and, in particular, the development of discourses of racial difference. This will be an increasingly important field in the coming years.[37]

Second, I would like to suggest that a new historiographical paradigm is emerging with welfare and modernity as its master concepts. The differential dynamic of Nazi racial policies provides a particularly crass, but also a particularly illustrative, example of that general process of normalization and othering which poststructuralist analysis has argued represents a privileged form of analysis. It is precisely this process that has become the focus of the new cultural history. We can see how this new approach has influenced recent work on imperialism and postcolonial studies. Although the history of German society under Nazi rule has yet to take the cultural turn in a serious way, this is one possibility that has been opened up by our new view of the racial state, and it will be interesting to see how the historiography of Nazi Germany and its social policies evolves over the coming years.

Notes

1   The *Sonderweg* debate has a long history and an equally long bibliography. The most recent contributions include George Steinmetz, "German Exceptionalism and the Origins of Nazism: The Career of a Concept," in Ian Kershaw and Moshe Lewin (eds.), *Stalinism and Nazism: Dictatorships in Comparison* (Cambridge: Cambridge University Press, 1997), pp. 251–84; Reinhard Kühnl, "The German Sonderweg Reconsidered: Continuities and Discontinuities in Modern German History," in Peter Monteath and Reinhard Alter (eds.), *Rewriting the German Past. History and Identity in the New Germany* (Atlantic Highlands, NJ: Humanities Press, 1997), pp. 115–28; Lutz Niethammer, "The German *Sonderweg* after Unification," in Monteath and Alter (eds.), *Rewriting the German Past*, 129–51; and Jonathan Sperber, "German Master Narratives," *Central European History* 29 (1996), pp. 107–49.

2   For an illuminating exposition of the modernization-theoretical premises underlying the work of the Bielefeld school, see Geoff Eley, "German History and the Contradictions of Modernity: The Bourgeoisie, the State, and the Mastery of Reform," in Eley (ed.), *Society, Culture, and the State in Germany, 1870–1930* (Ann Arbor: University of Michigan Press, 1996), pp. 67–103.

3   David Blackbourn and Geoff Eley, *The Pecularities of German History: Bourgeois Society and Politics in Nineteenth-Century Germany* (New York: Oxford University Press, 1984).

4   Jan Palmowski, "Mediating the Nation: Liberalism and the Polity in Nineteenth-Century Germany," *German History* 18:4 (2001), pp. 573–98; and Peter Lundgreen (ed.), *Sozial- und Kulturgeschichte des Bürgertums* (Göttingen: Vandenhoeck & Ruprecht, 2000), provide a good point of entry into this body of literature.

5   For a critical reading of this tradition, see Lothar Machtan (ed.), *Bismarcks Sozialstaat. Beiträge zur Geschichte der Sozialpolitik und zur sozialpolitischen Geschichtsschreibung* (Frankfurt: Campus, 1994).

6   This "carrot and stick" approach to the origins of the German welfare state has been criticized by the editors of the multivolume *Quellensammlung zur Geschichte der deutschen Sozialpolitik 1867–1914* (Stuttgart: Wissenschaftliche Buchgesellschaft, 1993ff.). See Florian Tennstedt, "Der deutsche Weg zum Wohlfahrtsstaat 1871–1881. Anmerkungen zu einem

alten Thema aufgrund neu erschlossener Quellen," in Andreas Wollasch (ed.), *Wohlfahrtspflege in der Region. Westfalen-Lippe während des 19. und 20. Jahrhunderts im historischen Vergleich* (Paderborn: Schöningh, 1997), pp. 255–67, as well as the introductions to the various volumes of the *Quellensammlung*, and E.P. Hennock, "Social Policy under the Empire—Myths and Evidence," *German History* 16:1 (1998), pp. 58–74.

7   The works which have made the most important contribution to the development of this new approach include Gisela Bock, *Zwangssterilisierung im Nationalsozialismus. Studien zur Rassenpolitik und Frauenpolitik* (Opladen: Westdeutscher, 1986); Gisela Bock, "Krankenmord, Judenmord und nationalsozialistische Rassenpolitik: Überlegungen zu einigen neueren Forschungshypothesen," in Frank Bajohr, Werner Johe, and Uwe Lohalm (eds.), *Zivilisation und Barberei. Die widersprüchlichen Potentiale der Moderne* (Hamburg: Christians, 1991), pp. 285–306; Gisela Bock, "Antinatalism, Maternity and Paternity in National Socialist Racism," in David Crew (ed.), *Nazism and German Society, 1933–1945* (London: Routledge, 1994), pp. 110–40; Detlev Peukert, *Inside Nazi Germany: Conformity, Opposition, and Racism in Everyday Life*, trans. Richard Deveson (New Haven: Yale University Press, 1987); Peukert, "The Genesis of the 'Final Solution' from the Spirit of Science," in Crew (ed.), *Nazism and German Society*, pp. 274–99; Michael Burleigh and Wolfgang Wippermann, *The Racial State: Germany 1933–1945* (Cambridge: Cambridge University Press, 1991); Robert Jay Lifton, *Nazi Doctors. Medical Killing and the Psychology of Genocide* (New York: Basic Books, 1986); Hans-Uwe Otto and Heinz Sünker, "Volksgemeinschaft als Formierungsideologie des Nationalsozialismus. Zu Genesis und Geltung von 'Volkspflege,' " in Otto and Sünker (eds.), *Politische Formierung und soziale Erziehung im Nationalsozialismus* (Frankfurt: Suhrkamp, 1991), pp. 50–77; Michael Geyer, "Krieg als Gesellschaftspolitik. Anmerkungen zu neueren Arbeiten über das Dritte Reich im Zweiten Weltkrieg," *Archiv für Sozialgeschichte* 20 (1986), pp. 557–601; Ute Herbert, "Labour and Extermination: Economic Interest and the Primacy of *Weltanschauung* in National Socialism," *Past and Present* 138 (1993), pp. 144–95; and Christoph Sachße and Florian Tennstedt, *Geschichte der Armenfürsorge in Deutschland*, 3 vols (Stuttgart: Kohlhammer, 1980–92), here vol. 3: *Der Wohlfahrtsstaat im Nationalsozialismus* (Stuttgart: Kohlhammer, 1992), as well as Tim Mason, *Social Policy in the Third Reich: The Working Class and the "National Community"* (Providence, RI: Berg, 1993), esp. pp. 275–84.

8   For the influence of eugenics and racial hygiene on welfare policy in particular, see, among others, Young-sun Hong, *Welfare, Modernity, and the Weimar State* (Princeton: Princeton University Press, 1998), p. 239ff.; Johannes Vossen, *Gesundheitsämter im Nationalsozialismus. Rassenhygiene und offene Gesundheitsfürsorge in Westfalen 1900–1950* (Essen: Klartext, 2001); Manfred Kappeler, *Der schreckliche Traum vom vollkommenen Menschen. Rassenhygiene und Eugenik in der Sozialen Arbeit* (Marburg: Schüren, 2000); Sabine Schleiermacher, *Sozialethik im Spannungsfeld von Sozial- und Rassenhygiene. Der Mediziner Hans Harmsen im Centralausschuß für die Innere Mission* (Husum: Matthiesen, 1998); and Sigrid Stöckel, *Säuglingsfürsorge zwischen sozialer Hygiene und Eugenik: Das Beispiel*

Berlins im Kaiserreich und in der Weimarer Republik (Berlin: Walter de Gruyter, 1996).

9   Amir Weiner, *Making Sense of War: The Second World War and the Fate of the Bolshevik Revolution* (Princeton: Princeton University Press, 2001); Amir Weiner (ed.), *Landscaping the Human Garden: 20th-Century Population Management in a Comparative Framework* (Stanford: Stanford University Press, 2003); David Hoffmann, *Stalinist Values: The Cultural Norms of Soviet Modernity, 1917–1941* (Ithaca: Cornell University Press, 2003); Hoffmann and Yanni Kotsonis (eds.), *Russian Modernity: Politics, Knowledge, Practices* (New York: Palgrave Macmillan, 2000), pp. 245–60; James C. Scott, *Seeing Like a State: How Certain Schemes to Improve the Human Condition Have Failed* (New Haven: Yale University Press, 1998); and Stephen Kotkin, *Magnetic Mountain: Stalinism as Civilization* (Berkeley: University of California Press, 1995).

10   Mary Poovey, *Uneven Developments: The Ideological Work of Gender in Mid-Victorian England* (Chicago: University of Chicago Press, 1988).

11   Catherine Hall (ed.), *Cultures of Empire: A Reader: Colonisers in Britain and the Empire of the Nineteenth and Twentieth Centuries* (Manchester: Manchester University Press, 2000); and Ann Laura Stoler, *Race and the Education of Desire: Foucault's History of Sexuality and the Colonial Order of Things* (Durham: Duke University Press, 1995); Ann Laura Stoler, "Sexual Affronts and Racial Frontiers: European Identities and the Cultural Politics of Exclusion in Colonial Southeastern Asia," in Frederick Cooper and Ann Laura Stoler (eds.), *Tensions of Empire: Colonial Cultures in a Bourgeois World* (Berkeley: University of California Press, 1997), pp. 198–237; and Ann LauraStoler, *Carnal Knowledge and Imperial Power. Race and the Intimate in Colonial Rule* (Berkeley: University of California Press, 2002).

12   Peukert, "The Genesis of the 'Final Solution' "; and Detlev Peukert, *Grenzen der Sozialdisziplinierung. Aufstieg und Krise der deutschen Jugendfürsorge, 1878–1929* (Cologne: Bund, 1986).

13   Peukert, *Grenzen*. See the assessment of Peukert's work and of the continuities between child welfare in the Weimar Republic, Nazi Germany and the Federal Republic in Eduard Ross Dickinson, *The Politics of German Child Welfare from the Empire to the Federal Republic* (Cambridge: Harvard University Press, 1996), pp. 286–99; Edward Ross Dickinson, "Biopolitics, Fascism, Democracy: Some Reflections on Our Discourse about 'Modernity,' " *Central European History* 37:1 (March 2004), pp. 1–48; and Hong, "Introduction" in *Welfare, Modernity, and the Weimar State*, pp. 3–43. In the realm of hygiene, this concept of social discipline has been reformulated as medicalization in several influential works: Alfons Labisch, *Homo hygienicus: Gesundheit und Medizin in der Neuzeit* (Frankfurt: Campus, 1992); Alfons Labisch, " 'Hygiene ist Moral—Moral ist Hygiene': Soziale Disziplinierung durch Ärzte und Medizin," in Christoph Sachße and Florian Tennstedt (eds.), *Soziale Sicherheit durch soziale Disziplinierung* (Frankfurt: Suhrkamp, 1986), pp. 265–85; Francisca Loetz, *Vom Kranken zum Patienten. "Medikalisierung" und medizinische Vergesellschaftung am Beispiel Badens 1750–1850* (Stuttgart: Steiner, 1993); Ute Frevert, *Krankheit als politisches Problem*

1770–1880 (Göttingen: Vandenhoeck & Ruprecht, 1984); and Ute Frevert, "Akademische Medizin und soziale Unterschichten. im 19. Jahrhundert: Professionsinteressen—Zivilisationsmission—Sozialpolitik," *Jahrbuch des Instituts für Geschichte der Medizin der Robert-Bosch-Stiftung* 4 (1985), pp. 41–59. The other work which had a seminal influence on the social discipline paradigm is Jacques Donzelot, *The Policing of Families*, trans. R. Hurley (New York: Pantheon, 1979), and he too argues in ways that are complementary to, but not identical with, Peukert that modern approaches to child welfare contained within themselves a fascist potential.

14   Sachße and Tennstedt, *Geschichte der Armenfürsorge in Deutschland.*

15   Dickinson, *Politics of German Child Welfare*; David Crew, *Germans on Welfare 1918–1933: From Weimar to Hitler* (New York: Oxford University Press, 1998); Hong, *Welfare, Modernity, and the Weimar State*; Warren Rosenblum, "Punishment, Welfare, & the Policing of Asocials: Visions of Social Order in Modern Germany" (Ph.D. diss., University of Michigan, 1999); and Dennis Sweeney, *Work, Race, and the Emergence of Radical Right Corporatism in Imperial Germany* (Ann Arbor: University of Michigan Press, 2009). On the modernizing reaction of Catholic charities, see Wilfried Loth, "Die deutschen Sozialkatholiken in der Krise des Fin de Siècle," in Jochen-Christoph Kaiser and Wilfried Loth (eds.), *Soziale Reform im Kaiserreich. Protestantismus, Katholizismus und Sozialpolitik* (Stuttgart: Kohlhammer, 1997), pp. 128–41.

16   Marcus Gräser, *Der blockierte Wohlfahrtsstaat. Unterschichtjugend und Jugendfürsorge in der Weimarer Republik* (Göttingen: Vandenhoeck & Ruprecht, 1995).

17   Ewald Frie, *Wohlfahrtsstaat und Provinz. Fürsorgepolitik des Provinzialverbandes Westfalen und des Landes Sachsen 1880–1930* (Paderborn: Schöningh, 1993), esp. pp. 278–9.

18   Kevin Repp, *Reformers, Critics and the Paths of German Modernity: Anti-Politics and the Search for Alternatives, 1890–1914* (Cambridge: Harvard University Press, 2000); and Daniel Rodgers, *Atlantic Crossings: Social Politics in a Progressive Age* (Cambridge: Belknap Press, 1998).

19   Greg Eghigian, *Making Security Social. Disability, Insurance, and the Birth of the Social Entitlement State in Germany* (Ann Arbor: University of Michigan Press, 2000), pp. 116, 228. Eghigian (p. 20) is also explicitly critical of the more extreme versions of social discipline and its hygienic correlate, medicalization. He argues that biopolitics was not only or even primarily conceptualized in medical terms; he criticizes the notion, implicit in concept of social discipline, that patients were passive objects of this process; and he argues that the active agency of the patients in fact succeeded in transforming the nature of social administration.

20   J. Jorge Klor de Alva, "The Postcolonization of the (Latin) American Experience: A Reconsideration of 'Colonialism,' 'Postcolonialism,' and 'Mestizaje,' " in Gyan Prakash (ed.), *After Colonialism: Imperial Histories and Postcolonial Displacements* (Princeton: Princeton University Press, 1995), pp. 241–75, especially p. 245. See also Stuart Hall, "When Was 'the Post-Colonial'? Thinking at the Limit," in Iain Chambers and Lidia Curti (eds.),

The Postcolonial Question: Common Skies, Divided Horizons (London: Routledge, 1996), pp. 242–60.

21 According to Gyan Prakash in Hall (ed.), *Cultures of Empire*, p. 127, the subaltern refers to that impossible thought, figure, or action without which the dominant discourse cannot exist and which is acknowledged in its subterfuges and stereotypes. This is obviously a complex and important question to which I have no pat answer. One book which has helped me think about the question, though, is David Scott, *Refashioning Futures: Criticism after Postcoloniality* (Princeton: Princeton University Press, 1999).

22 Graham Burchell, Colin Gordon, and Peter Miller (eds.), *The Foucault Effect: Studies in Governmentality* (Chicago: University of Chicago Press, 1991); Patrick Joyce, *The Rule of Freedom: Liberalism and the Modern City* (London: Verso, 2003); Mitchell Dean, "A Genealogy of the Government of Poverty," *Economy and Society* 21:3 (2006), pp. 215–52; Mitchell Dean, *Governmentality: Power and Rule in Modern Society* (London: Sage, 1999); Nicholas Rose, "Governing 'Advanced' Liberal Democracies," in Andrew Barry, Thomas Osborne, and Nikolas Rose (eds.), *Foucault and Political Reason* (Chicago/London: University of Chicago Press/University College London Press, 1996); and Patricia Harris, "Public Welfare and Liberal Governance," in Alan Petersen et al. (ed.), *Poststructuralism, Citizenship and Social Policy* (London: Routledge, 1999), pp. 25–57.

23 Michel Foucault, "Governmentality," in Burchell, Gordon, and Miller, *The Foucault Effect*, pp. 101–3. Foucault charted the extensive growth of both state control over the external comportment of its subjects through its security apparatuses and the simultaneous intensification of what he called its pastoral power over their souls. Rule was most effective and economical, Foucault argued, when political domination had been so completely internalized that it became the second nature of the citizen-subject and bore no trace of heterogeneous authority, that is, where the laws of the heart corresponded to the laws of the state. This tendency in what can only be called the rationalization of modern politics culminates, Foucault suggests, in the virtual absorption of heterogeneous disciplinary apparatuses by political practices in a process that he describes as the governmentalization of the state. Foucault, "Governmentality," *The Foucault Effect*, p. 103.

24 David Horn, *Social Bodies: Science, Reproduction, and Italian Modernity* (Princeton: Princeton University Press, 1994) and Mitchell Dean, *The Constitution of Poverty. Toward a Genealogy of Liberal Governance* (London: Routledge, 1991), pp. 176, 215–16. See also Jacques Derrida's analysis of the concept of nature in Rousseau in *Of Grammatology*, trans. Gayatri Chakravorty Spivak (Baltimore: The Johns Hopkins University Press, 1976). The identity and status of the subject(s) of these normalizing discourses and practices are underdefined and difficult at best to describe.

25 Dennis Sweeney, "Governing the Social in Wilhelmine Germany: Rethinking German Modernity," paper presented at the American Historical Association conference (January 2002). In *Health, Race and German Politics between National Unification and Nazism 1870–1945* (Cambridge: Cambridge University Press, 1989), Weindling describes—though from a different perspective—the nationalization of local welfarist initiatives.

26 Ralf Dahrendorf, *Society and Democracy in Germany* (Garden City, NY: Doubleday, 1976); David Schoenbaum, *Hitler's Social Revolution. Class and Status in Nazi Germany, 1933–1939* (Garden City, NY: Doubleday, 1966); and Henry A. Turner, "Fascism and Modernization," in H.A. Turner (ed.), *Reappraisals of Fascism* (London: Franklin Watts, 1975), pp. 117–39.

27 Rainer Zitelmann, *Hitler. Selbstverständnis eines Revolutionärs*, 3. Aufl. (Hamburg: Berg, 1987); Michael Prinz and Rainer Zitelmann (eds.), *Nationalsozialismus und Modernisierung*, 2. Aufl. (Darmstadt: Wissenschaftliche Buchgesellschaft, 1994); Hans Mommsen, "Noch einmal: Nationalsozialismus und Modernisierung," *Geschichte und Gesellschaft* 21 (1995), pp. 391–402; Hans Mommsen, "Nationalsozialismus als vorgetäuschte Modernisierung," in Hans Mommsen, Lutz Niethammer, and Bernd Weisbrod (eds.), *Der Nationalsozialismus und die deutsche Gesellschaft* (Hamburg: Rowohlt, 1991), pp. 405–27; Norbert Frei, "Wie modern war der Nationalsozialismus?" *Geschichte und Gesellschaft* 19 (1993), pp. 367–87; Mark Roseman, "National Socialism and Modernization," in Richard Bessel (ed.), *Fascist Italy and Nazi Germany: Comparisons and Contrasts* (Cambridge: Cambridge University Press, 1996), pp. 197–229; and Ian Kershaw and Moshe Lewin, "Afterthoughts," in Ian Kershaw and Moshe Lewin (eds.), *Stalinism and Nazism: Dictatorships in Comparison* (Cambridge: Cambridge University Press, 1997), pp. 343–58.

28 Emmy Wagner, *Grundlagen einer artbewußten Fürsorge* (Berlin: Heymann, 1935).

29 Hermann Althaus, *Nationalsozialistische Volkswohlfahrt. Wesen, Aufgaben und Aufbau*, 3. Aufl (Berlin: Junker und Dünnhaupt, 1937), p. 14; and Hans-Uwe Otto and Heinz Sünker, "Nationalsozialismus, Volksgemeinschaftsideologie und soziale Arbeit," in H.-U. Otto and H. Sunker (eds.), *Soziale Arbeit und Faschismus: Volkspflege und Pädagogik im Nationalsozialismus* (Bielefeld: Böllert, 1986), p. 19.

30 Hong, *Welfare, Modernity, and the Weimar State*, p. 252ff.

31 Hilgenfeldt, "Aufgaben der NS_Volkswohlfahrt," *Nationalsozialisticher Volksdienst* 1 (October 1933), pp. 1–6, citation 5.

32 See, among others, Bock, *Zwangssterilisierung*; Hans-Walter Schmuhl, *Rassenhygiene, Nationalsozialismus, Euthanasie. Von der Verhütung zur Vernichtung "lebensunwerten Lebens"* (Göttingen: Vandenhoeck & Ruprecht, 1987); Peter Weingart, Jürgen Kroll, and Kurt Bayertz, *Rasse, Blut, und Gene. Geschichte der Eugenik und Rassenhygiene in Deutschland* (Frankfurt: Suhrkamp, 1988); Michael Schwartz, *Sozialistische Eugenik. Eugenische Sozialtechnologien in Debatten und Politik der deutschen Sozialdemokratie 1890–1933* (Bonn: JHW Dietz, 1995); Weindling, *Health, Race and German Politics*; Richard Soloway, *Demography and Degeneration: Eugenics and the Declining Birth Rate in Twentieth Century Britain* (Chapel Hill: University of North Carolina Press, 1995); William H. Schneider, *Quality and Quantity: The Quest for Biological Regeneration in Twentieth-Century France* (Cambridge: Cambridge University Press, 1990); Gunnar Broberg and Nils Roll-Hansen (eds.), *Eugenics and the Welfare State. Sterilization Policy in Denmark, Sweden, Norway, and Finland* (East Lansing: Michigan State University Press,

1996); and Mark Adams (ed.), *The Wellborn Science: Eugenics in Germany, France, Britain and Russia* (New York: Oxford University Press, 1990).

33 Götz Aly, *"Endlösung." Völkerverschiebung und der Mord an den europäischen Juden* (Frankfurt: Fischer, 1995); Götz Aly and Susanne Heim, *Vordenker der Vernichtung. Auschwitz und die deutschen Pläne für eine neue europäische Ordnung* (Hamburg: Hoffmann und Campe, 1991); Götz Aly, "Bevölkerungspolitische Selektion as Mittel der sozialen 'Neuordnung,'" in Norbert Frei and Hermann Kling (eds.), *Der nationalsozialistische Krieg* (Frankfurt: Campus, 1990), pp. 137–45; Götz Aly, Peter Chroust, and Christian Pross, *Cleansing the Fatherland: Nazi Medicine and Racial Hygiene* (Baltimore: The Johns Hopkins University Press, 1994); Götz Aly and Karl Heinz Roth, *Die restlose Erfassung. Volkszählung, Identifizieren, Aussonderung im Nationalsozialismus* (Berlin: Rotbuch, 1984); and Manfred Berg and Geoffrey Cocks (eds.), *Medicine and Modernity. Public Health and Medical Care in Nineteenth- and Twentieth-Century Germany* (Cambridge: Cambridge University Press, 2002). *Vordenker der Vernichtung* has been translated by AG Blunden as *Architects of Annihilation* (Princeton: Princeton University Press, 2003). For a critique of the economistic tendencies of Aly's work, see Dan Diner, "On Rationality and Rationalization: An Economistic Explanation of the Final Solution," in Dan Diner, *Beyond the Conceivable: Studies on Germany, Nazism, and the Holocaust* (Berkeley: University of California Press, 2000), pp. 138–59.

34 Ulrich Herbert, *Best. Biographische Studien über Radikalismus, Weltanschauung und Vernunft 1903–1989* (Bonn: JHW Dietz, 2001); Michael Wildt, *Generation des Unbedingten. Das Führungskorps des Reichssicherheitshauptamtes* (Hamburg: Hamburger Edition, 2002), and Michael Thad Allen, *The Business of Genocide: The SS, Slave Labor, and the Concentration Camps* (Chapel Hill: University of North Carolina Press, 2002).

35 Sachße and Tennstedt, *Geschichte der Armenfürsorge*, III: p. 273ff., citation 278: "ein kumulativ radikalisiertes und pervertiertes terroristisches Extrem in einem breiten Gesamtspektrum möglicher Entwicklungspfade industriegesellschaftlicher Moderne."

36 *Bericht über die 39. Versammlung deutscher Historiker in Hannover 23. Bis 26. September 1992* (Stuttgart: Klett, 1994).

37 See Matti Bunzl and Glenn Penny (eds.), *Worldly Provincialism: German Anthropology in the Age of Empire* (Ann Arbor: University of Michigan Press, 2003); Lora Wildenthal, *German Women for Empire, 1884–1945* (Durham: Duke University Press, 2001); Andrew Zimmerman, *Anthropology and Antihumanism in Imperial Germany* (Chicago: University of Chicago Press, 2001); H. Glenn Penny, *Objects of Culture: Ethnology and Ethnographic Museums in Imperial Germany* (Chapel Hill: University of North Carolina Press, 2002); Annegret Ehmann, "From Colonial Racism to Nazi Population Policy: The Role of the So-Called Mischlinge," in Michael Berenbaum and Abraham J. Peck (eds.), *The Holocaust and History: The Known, the Unknown, the Disputed, and the Reexamined* (Bloomington: Indiana University Press, 1998), pp. 115–33; and Pascal Grosse, *Kolonialismus, Eugenik und bürgerliche Gesellschaft in Deutschland 1850–1918* (Frankfurt: Campus, 2000).

3

What Was German Modernity and When?

Geoff Eley

I'm sitting in the express train from Berlin to Stuttgart. With tremendous speed the train is racing through the flat countryside ... the rapid change of scenery reinforces the overall image that the big city we have just left has once again impressed on me. The hustle and bustle of the big metropolis is simply breathtaking. Just like on the express train, you don't have the leisure to follow a thought through to the end or to finish looking at something, since your attention is immediately caught up by something else ... To me, this phenomenon seems to lie at the bottom of all that is metropolitan: the constant hurry and running around, everything imposing its attraction onto people, tearing on them and pulling them in different directions, preventing them from finding themselves. No wonder that both physical and moral resistance are on the wane; the entire environment is directed at destroying it ... [T]he city most certainly does not harbor Germany's soul, despite the restless thought and incessant activity that takes place there. The soul of Germany rests in the countryside, in the grace of its rolling hills where man is still part of the land which instills him with the strength to defend himself against the developments of our time that are infringing on our lives.[1]

This quotation comes from an essay composed by a young woman in the mid-1920s presenting her own version of the shock of modernity. It contains, either by direct observation or by various kinds of allusion, most of the themes this essay will presuppose, including not least the heavily *gendered* charge carried by modernity's field of metropolitan meanings as they presented themselves during the early twentieth century. It conveys vividly how contemporaries sought to capture the intensities of encountering the big city at a time when such an experience was still new. The particular qualities of metropolitan living—the excitements and dangers, rewards and entailments—were thought to be creating a new sensibility, a distinctively modern structure of feeling. The whirl and blur of experiencing the city, especially its unprecedented density of buildings, people, and traffic, its machines and electricity, its speed, sensation, and spectacle, seemed to be materializing the future before one's very eyes. But the connotations were not only positive. By invoking "the soul of Germany," the young woman's final sentences spoke of a lack and a loss of authenticity too, appealing to a source of moral strength, virtue, and reliability that she thought was being left behind. This contrast—between the city and the country—was essential to the perceptions concerned. If on the one hand the metropolis spelled newness, immensity, crowdedness, noise, velocity, restlessness, shock, risks, stimulation, thrills, erotics, adventure, and opportunity, then on the other hand it brought hazards, danger, accidents, crime, corruption, decadence, sinfulness, loneliness, and anonymity.

This cultural discourse of modernity, as it developed in Germany in the early twentieth century, is inseparable from both politics and historiography—from the contemporary field of early twentieth-century political disagreements, no less than the main dividing lines of intervening historical interpretation. The very intensity of the debates about modernity, which were always-already imbricated with wider conflicts over Germany's social and political future, during times of virtually unrelieved crisis and upheaval between the *fin de siècle* and the 1920s, called for longer-term narratives and larger frameworks of interpretation, and here the question of Nazism continues exerting its necessary pulls and fascinations. That question continues to inform how modern German historians go about their work, whether in writing or in the classroom, seeking to understand how exactly the Third Reich should be positioned inside the larger setting of the German past. How might the distinctive modernities of the *Kaiserreich* and the Weimar Republic best be historicized? How should we see their relationship to the Nazi era that followed?

German modernities—failed, dark, or contested?

Throughout the 1970s and 1980s, such discussion centered around variants of a strong continuity thesis that derived Nazi origins from the developmental peculiarities of Germany's passage into modernity under the *Kaiserreich*. Some of those arguments focused on the ruling socioeconomic interests at the core of the state. Some focused on a particular institutional complex like militarism or the behavior of the bureaucracy. Another version prioritized the importance of Bismarck and his legacies. These, broadly speaking, are the traditions of inquiry associated with Fritz Fischer and his students and the so-called Kehrites or Bielefeld school.[2] A cognate approach takes in the international dimension by proposing continuities in German imperialism, where the key works were clearly those of Fritz Fischer and Hans-Ulrich Wehler.[3] Another still more popular line of inquiry preferred to emphasize certain enduring sociocultural traits that made Germans different from, say, the British or the French, including the absence of civility, exaggerated respect for authority, a spiritual ideal of national belonging, and the affirming of nonpolitical values inside a general culture of "illiberalism." From city élites down to petty home-town notables, this approach argued, the prevailing "apoliticism" signified an absence of civil courage and civic-mindedness, a culture of passivity and deference, which disastrously arrested the chances for the growth of a vigorous liberalism on the model of what happened in Britain. Here we can mention especially Fritz Stern and George Mosse, but Leonard Krieger, Mack Walker, and James Sheehan all contributed vitally too.[4] For many years, M. Rainer Lepsius's "milieu" thesis provided the most familiar means of anchoring the approach conceptually in a claim about Germany's distinctive social structure.[5] All of these are ways of grounding the origins of Nazism in an argument about the earlier peculiarities of German history. Bequeathing fateful handicaps from deep in the nineteenth century, those peculiarities were taken to explain the distinctive authoritarianism of the *Kaiserreich*'s political culture. This was the so-called *Sonderweg* ("special path") thesis regarding Germany's essential difference from the "West."[6]

The most decisive shifting of perspective subsequently was undoubtedly the one we associate with Detlev Peukert's emblematic essay of the mid-1980s, "The Genesis of the 'Final Solution' from the Spirit of Science," along with his classic treatment of the Weimar Republic and allied writings.[7] Peukert also stands in for a much wider array of convergent departures, which over the longer term have decisively reshaped our understanding of the Third Reich's genealogies. These influences include work on women and gender; histories of social policy and welfare; studies of all aspects of the biomedical sciences; the beginnings of everything gathered beneath the rubric of the "racial state"; new work on the social circumstances of everyday life; studies of enslaved and coerced labor; research into population planning, racialized social policies, and logic of economics behind the Nazi New Order; and last but not least the extraordinary profusion of research on every conceivable aspect of Nazi antisemitism and the Judeocide.[8] In the course of the resulting discussions, accumulating during the later 1980s to a steadily widening consensus, historians of Nazism found themselves struggling not with Nazi backwardness, but with what now seemed the unsettling *modernity* of so much of the Third Reich, notably in areas of large-scale economic planning, welfare initiatives, popular leisure, and public health.

This made for an interesting contrast with the preceding historiographical climate, when *any* linking of Nazism to arguments about "modernization" remained highly controversial as they seemed to foreground the "positive" aspects of social change and social experience under the Third Reich such as to obscure or downplay the regime's violence and its impact on the victims.[9] By calling attention to social histories occurring either independently of Nazi racial and imperialist policies or else as their unintended and indirect effects, such work stressed structural processes beneath and beyond the Nazis' own distinctive purposes.[10] The destructive parts of what the Nazis did—persecution of the Jews, the killing of opponents and quashing of dissent, carceral repression, and the concentration camps, *Lebensraum* and imperialist war, population policies, forced labor, genocide, and all aspects of the racial state—became repositioned as the catastrophic but monstrously contingent distraction from underlying changes that ultimately mattered more and outlasted the Third Reich's demise, continuing into the 1950s. Treatments of "Nazism and modernization" seemed to de-emphasize the ideologically driven violence of Nazi rule in favor of longer-term changes seemingly common to all industrial societies—social mobility, schooling, urban planning and design, public health, work organization, welfare, consumption, leisure, and so forth. So against this earlier set of approaches, Peukert and the other new voices started rethinking what the specific valencies of using the category of "the modern" might be. Radically re-evaluating reform movements under the *Kaiserreich*, Peukert now found in reform a *sinister* rather than a *progressive* set of longer-term meanings. He turned the previous meanings on their head—stressing control, regulation, and disciplinary power in contradistinction to the qualities of improvement and emancipation usually associated with reform, while giving "modernity" a kind of totalizing logic deemed generative for the future possibilities of Nazism.[11]

Once we reconceptualize the meanings of Nazi antisemitism, the "racial state," and "the business of genocide" away from the old generalizations about Nazism's "anti-modern" character, there follow troubling longer-term implications.[12] So far from being an atavism or an antimodernism, or even a chaotic incoherence of disordered polycracy, Nazism brought an intensifying of modernist governmentality—that is, the hubris of early twentieth-century medicalizing, welfarist, and social policy expertise, especially the planning utopias that wanted to remake the entire social order in a new image. Such designs sought to encompass whole populations for purposes of reform and improvement, as both means and goal of their ambitions, acquiring under the Third Reich especially virulent momentum.[13] I mean here the new ways of constructing, imagining, visualizing, quantifying, regulating, policing, improving, reorganizing, comprehensively redesigning, and perhaps transforming "the social" or the social sphere. Processes of medicalization and racialization were already underway during the Weimar Republic, involving eugenics, population politics, welfare initiatives directed at women, family policies, criminology and penal reform, imagined projects of social engineering, and the deployment of science for social goals. But under the Third Reich they now took a radicalized and more concerted direction, powered by the machinery of a centralized and coercive state, freed from the earlier restraints of professional ethics, constitutional democracy, and liberal precepts of the rule of law.

This optic has shifted our perceptions of aspects of the Third Reich that previously seemed the epitome of a modernity-denying backwardness. For the late *Kaiserreich* this makes for an interesting field of historiographical contention: *on the one hand*, an earlier body of thought that specifically disputes the *Kaiserreich*'s modernity while presenting its backwardness as the fertile seedbed for Nazism, pushing the origins deep into the nineteenth century; *on the other hand*, a new body of work that highlights the very dynamism of Imperial Germany's societal development in the 1900s and derives Nazism's possibilities from precisely the hypertrophied forms of scientific, managerial, and technological modernity thereby being produced. Under the auspices of the former, older scholarship insists relentlessly on the epistemological priority of deep-cultural explanations for the German *Sonderweg*—including Jürgen Kocka's primacy of "pre-industrial, pre-capitalist traditions"; Karl Dietrich Bracher's "authoritarian and anti-democratic structures in state and society"; Ralf Dahrendorf's "structural syndrome" of authoritarianism; Fritz Stern's "civic nonage"; and Maria Rainer Lepsius's "social-moral milieus."[14] Such recourse to the deeper nineteenth century diminishes the ideas, conflicts, and departures freshly born from the generative contexts of the Wilhelmine years themselves. By inviting us to reperiodize Nazism into a longer crisis of modernity dating from the early 1900s, by contrast, more recent work makes modernity itself into the problem.

There is a vital comparative dimension too. After 1945, "Germany" acquired special significance for ideas of modernization across the social sciences precisely because of the enormity of the apparent Nazi deviation. To make sense of that anomaly, social scientists sought pathologies of backwardness and traditionalism in Germany's deeper history pre-1914, simply because that kind of break from civilized norms after 1933 *had* to imply sharp divergences from the West earlier on. In those terms, the supposed weakness of pre-1914 liberalism—the absence of a flourishing arena for healthy and progressive civic-mindedness among the German middle classes—was taken to have opened a wide field for reactionary, intolerant, and irrationalist thinking instead. Those social layers that elsewhere sustained liberalism's sturdy self-governing ethos became prey to ideas that favored authority and the political right—racial thought, ideas of rootedness and organicism, social Darwinism, a fundamental credo of inequality, forms of cultural pessimism, an aggressively "Germanic" philosophy. The flight from liberal political engagement became a retreat to the private sphere of family, aesthetic value, and subjective pursuit, bringing not just party politics into disregard, but civic responsibility and the civic life per se.

This syndrome has been called, in one famous formulation, "the political consequences of the unpolitical German."[15] By 1900, moreover, the entry of the masses into politics, as well as the growth of the mass market and the first strong signs of a mass-produced commoditized culture, gave this pulling back from politics an increasingly conservative valence. *This*, it is claimed, was where the line became powerfully drawn: the new materialist civilization became identified with a pattern of social development already occurring in the West, whose particular *modernity* the German middle-class observer thereby refused. According to many historians, an ideology of the superiority of German values over those of the West, with their "arid" rationalism, was then able to flourish, foregrounding "a peculiarly intense relationship to nature and a tendency to prefer the 'organic' to the 'mechanical' society," joined to general "hostility to 'modernity' and a strong leaning toward 'cultural despair.'"[16]

But what if the connections among cultural values, political affiliations, and ideas of what it meant to be "modern" were more mobile, complex, and unpredictable than this? Growing bodies of scholarship now see the sociocultural outlook of the pre-1914 bourgeoisie much differently than before, viewing its histories from beyond the existing frameworks altogether—transcending not only the older *Sonderweg* perspectives but the ones influenced by Peukert too. Movements and bodies of thought claimed for the earlier "antimodernist" paradigm are reemerging as far more ambivalent sites of experiment and reform. They sustained heterogeneous purposes; they tended in multiple political directions; their effects were undecided. Examples included a variety of widely supported cultural enthusiasms, including localist and regionalist interests in landscape and *Heimat*; travel cultures and movements for historical preservation; youth movements such as the *Wandervögel*; and all the disparate elements of *Lebensreform* (life reform).[17] If an older historiography claimed these as symptoms of a distinctively German cultural pattern of resistance or aversion *against* modernity, they were actually the settings where *acceptance* of the modern became negotiated and embraced. Quite aside from the issues and ideas directly involved or the future-oriented changes they reflected, such movements formed a crucible where new, quite specifically and self-consciously modern ways of behaving were in process of being worked out—new stylistics, new affects and forms of bodily comportment, a new relationship to nature and the environment, new sexualities, new subjectivities, and so forth. Each marked out the novel settings for creative activism, where Germans understood themselves to be trying out various ways of entering the modern world.

They also intersected increasingly with movements of *social* reform, invariably drawing on the same energies and cohorts of activists to mobilize convergent hopes for improvement and uplift. Some of the most programmatically forward-looking proposals of that kind focused on producing stronger and more active reciprocities between the "local" and the "national," where the former comprised any of the mundane, pragmatic, and personal contexts of everyday life where identification with the nation increasingly had to occur, including above all the family and the home. All across the political spectrum before 1914, reformers brought together the latest thinking about good taste, innovative design, rationally ordered domestic living spaces and successful families with larger visions of social health and national pedagogy. Such ambitions flowed with particular coherence through the Werkbund, for example, an association formed in 1907 from designers, architects, industrialists, civil servants, and politicians, who sought "to move craft production onto an industrial basis and to change the stylistic norms governing the design and consumption of everyday goods."[18] In practical terms, that meant connecting good taste and rational design in the everyday life of private households to the perceived conditions of national prosperity and survival in the emergent global economy—in a powerful discourse of national security, national health, and national productivity. In the words of the architect Fritz Schumacher, in his keynote address to the Werkbund's founding congress, "art is not only an aesthetic force [*Kraft*], but simultaneously an ethical one too. Together, these forces will eventually lead to the most important power of all: economic strength."[19] As the Werkbund conceived them, aesthetic modernism, social reform, and national pedagogy merged into a common priority, forging a vital unity of home and nation: "the famous slogan of the Werkbund—'*from* sofa cushions *to* city planning'—captured the original goal of the group to design new forms of domestic objects and to reform interior spaces before transferring their gaze outwards to the housing block, the neighborhood street and the entirety of the urban fabric."[20] Animating appeals from the right no less than the left, such languages of reform articulated "a bourgeois and/or scientific 'catalogue of norms,' " embracing "thrift, diligence, inclination toward work, 'appropriate' domestic order and gender differentiation and hierarchy, and the 'rational' management of sexual and reproductive practices." Seeking "to impose [these] on targeted individuals and populations in the interest of social health," they deemed what happened inside the home vital to the public interest.[21]

Analysis of this kind fundamentally questions the developmental "exceptionalizing" of pre-1914 Germany. The force of that questioning seems further confirmed, once we consider the transnational circulation of ideas, particularly between Germany and the English-speaking world, as economists and other academics, journalists, businessmen, civil servants, and social commentators moved so avidly back and forth across the Atlantic and the North Sea. Such contemporaries were certainly alive to the country-by-country variations in political-institutional practices and forms, although these increasingly converged toward common acceptance of liberal constitutionalist principles of order, whose prevalence after the European and North American turbulence of the 1860s had grown increasingly normative. More to the point, it was an equivalence in the social impact of industrial transformation that worked powerfully against seeing Imperial Germany as somehow lagging *behind* the "West." In Daniel Rodgers's words, "what struck those who traversed the industrial regions of the Old and New Worlds was not their difference but their extraordinary sameness."[22] Indeed, whether in the shape and extent of state-society and state-economy relations and the associated ordering of public and private interests, or in the process of creating an integrated national polity, at a time of cross-national retreat from earlier laissez-faire liberalisms, it was rather the United States that seemed trapped in "backwardness" and *not* Germany. Massive urbanization and the spread of big industry were the defining challenges of the age: "Places such as Essen, Manchester, Lille, Pittsburgh, and Osaka were not only similar, they were also part of a rapidly growing, increasingly integrated world market." The challenges also crossed national boundaries: "With that sameness came common problems: scarce or inadequate housing, large-scale migrations of people, structural and cyclical mass unemployment, industrial accidents and sudden indigence, inadequate public transport and utilities, chaotic urban building, pollution, toxins, and the new diseases they generated, as well as massive trusts and monopolies."[23]

Indeed, within a European landscape of 1900, the most visible feature of the German case was surely its thrusting dynamism, turbulent industrialism, and forward-moving energy and momentum—in short, its *modernizing* drive. As other Europeans saw, the *Kaiserreich* was the most compelling example of a modern state yet in existence, a model of "national efficiency," sustained by the most dynamic capitalism of the continent. Its accomplishments in science, technology, engineering, planning, design, architecture, and other applied fields, together with the strength of its cultural institutions, the success of its educational system, and the growth of its public sphere, allow us to speak realistically of bourgeois predominance in society, anchored in the growing structural primacy of industrial production in the capitalist mode. If the bourgeoisie was not the class directly and exclusively in charge of the state—but which bourgeoisie of the time, in this sense of collective political agency, ever *was*?—then it increasingly dominated the social, institutional, and ideological arenas where politics and governance were being conducted, that is, by exercising hegemony in the Gramscian sense. If German society did possess a marked and unusual capacity to generate a number of authoritarian and "illiberal" symptoms before 1914, tending toward a politics that was radical nationalist and antidemocratic, then this was inseparably bound up with its modernities—not as a reaction *against* these, but as an extrusion from their leading edge.

So in the end, German history certainly *did* contain a powerful early twentieth-century dynamic whose complicated effects the rise and success of Nazism would eventually presuppose. But this was not one deeply inscribed in the "primacy of pre-industrial traditions" descending from the earlier nineteenth century and before, from a set of oppositions and resistances *against* modernity—from a peculiarly German antimodernism that idealized the past. Rather, it came from the field of febrile and proliferating differences inside a rapidly modernizing society whose contending forces were passionately focused on the possible terms of a still-to-be-determined future. *This* was where the singularity of Germany's national history in this period was to be found: in the process of successful but conflict-ridden capitalist modernization—and conflict-ridden precisely *because* it was so successful. Contemporary observers elsewhere, envious and fearful of Imperial Germany's passage to a position of a restlessly expanding industrial strength, saw this completely. Both German society's interior conflicts and its foreign expansionism were precisely an expression of its modernity, the effects of a modernizing society pressing against its limits.

Defining modernity

Since the mid-1980s, the steady accumulation of new scholarship has laid the earlier *Sonderweg* thesis decisively to rest. German historians largely accept that post-1848 Germany displayed many of those "modern" features previously found lacking, including a politically influential bourgeoisie and a thriving culture of social reform, indeed a generalized drive for reform that from the 1890s spilled energetically across many different spheres of social practice and material life. As a normative paradigm, "modernization theory" has certainly lost its appeal. Few German historians are any longer persuaded by the reified precepts of that older progressivist model, whether in its integrated causal unities of social, economic, political, and cultural history or the underlying presumption of a singular modernity shaped by the West.[24] How, then, might a different discussion proceed?

On the one hand, post-1871 Germany was a new state where allegiances were being freshly made. From a governing perspective, loyalties needed to be refashioned and reordered. Consciousness of belonging to a nation required refocusing from its earlier objects onto a new encompassing ideal, one commensurate with the complexities of the fledgling national state. On the other hand, this shaping of a national culture proceeded during unprecedented societal change: demographic upheaval, rapid industrialization, large-scale rural flight, massive urbanization, capitalist transformation. The physical landscape was transmuting into a new type of built environment—not everywhere at the same time or speed, but with momentous consequences for social perception and social vision. The larger entity of "Germany," where people imagined their futures, needed to be revisualized. This realignment of affiliations and reimagining of the societal form were accompanied by transformations in technologies and media of communication, by new methods for circulating ideas and images in the public sphere, and by new modalities of publicness and public exchange. The infrastructure for identity formation, whether on a microscopic or a society-wide scale, was being rebuilt.

For Germans at the turn of the twentieth century, these three axes of change in state, society, and public sphere supplied the shifting coordinates of political agency and political subjectivity, structuring their capacity to think and act as citizens of the new national state. Such change interpellated people who lived in Germany as thinking and acting subjects more generally. From inside this general condition of simultaneous belonging and indeterminacy, affiliation and estrangement—of owning an identity whose terms were urgently in flux—the tangle of German modernities could then be observed. As Edward Ross Dickinson says of the contemporary debates over sexuality: "What appears to have been happening...was not the flattening out of difference, not the progressive articulation and imposition of norms and normalcy, but the progressive articulation, organization, and politicization of difference."[25] This proceeded from an underlying logic of pluralization:

> In place of a secure order of values and social positions there is a bewildering variety and fluidity of values, roles, authorities, symbolic resources and social encounters...modernity involves a "pluralization of lifeworlds"...ever more "lifeworlds" are made visible to us, become possible choices of identity...Modernity, then, involves the vertiginous production, display, and interaction of myriad possible ways of life, none of which has indisputable cultural authority or value.[26]

In considering the period between the 1890s and 1920s, it is from precisely this openness of choices and affiliations—this febrile indeterminacy—that we must surely begin. This was the context in which the field of meanings joining the *city*, the *nation*, the *global*, and the *modern* became sutured together in especially powerful ways. With respect to the city, urbanization brought the novel creation of the metropolis as a highly distinctive historical space. Likewise, the terms of national affiliation within territorial Germany were in process of being radically democratized and pluralized, with a new scale and intensity of resulting contestation over the national idea. On a wider-than-European front, the ever-deepening penetration of global markets since the first worldwide capitalist boom of the 1850s and 1860s was intensifying transnational flows and interconnections in ways that effectively "imperialized" the force-field of nationhood for the dynamic capitalist societies of the continent. Once imperialist rivalries intensified during the 1880s and 1890s, perceptions of the differences among nations then became increasingly recast in imperial and colonial terms. As an intellectual-cultural formation in ideas and the arts, finally, modern*ism* took its cues and its drive from each of these other histories. Of course, equally compelling arguments can be made in favor of the epoch of Enlightenment and French Revolution as the generative time for ideas of the modern, and how we judge that question of "origins" depends very much, as always, on the kinds of questions we want to ask.[27] My own preferred starting point is the contemporary cultural commentary beginning in the early 1980s with Marshall Berman's *All That Is Solid Melts into Air: The Experience of Modernity* and the discovery of Walter Benjamin.[28]

Here, modernism was associated with a concentrated period of formal innovation in writing, music, performance, and the visual arts in the early twentieth century, whose effects became translated across far wider fields of intellectual life, journalism, academic exchange, and educated sociocultural commentary. That emergent discourse then underwent dramatically politicized radicalization as a result of the First World War, before becoming extended to the new mass media of film, radio, photography, and advertising and their technologies, and thereby to a general sensibility of publicness, fashion, style, and design. The argument may be further extended to the aesthetic and perceptual consequences of what has been called "time-space compression" in the new urban, industrial, and technological circumstances of the early twentieth-century social world.[29] Sociologically, the metropolis materializes into the crucible of the new sensibility, with a distinctive human condition of fragmentation, lack of bearings, and lonely individuation, figuring as both producer and product of the emergent modernist discourse. Georg Simmel and Walter Benjamin become the classic avatars of this metropolitan moment, while the "modern predicament" becomes quickly canonized into a now-familiar line of artistic and literary achievements.[30]

Marshall Berman noted an endemic tension in the modern condition between the mobility, uncertainty, changeability, and perduring instabilities of the lifeworld (the opportunities for self-remaking amid the excitement and creativity they provide), and the countervailing impulse toward order and regulation coming from the anxieties that inhere in the same condition. This view sees indeterminacy, instability of identity, contingency, fractured and fragmented selves and sensibilities, different regimes of perception, *difference* per se. As Baudelaire said, "Modernity is the ephemeral, the fugitive, the contingent, the half of art whose other half is the eternal and the immutable."[31] Crucially, these features are conceived not as free-floating qualities divorced from social and political contexts of their times, but as arising on the contrary from the social ontologies and distinctive social formations of an emergent metropolitan environment. That metropolis was not only massively expanding demographically, heaping together masses of culturally divided populations (divided by ethnicity, for instance), but was doing so in an imperial or colonial relationship to externalities and other peoples. Incoming populations were divided by a wide array of differences—by language and dialect, geography and hometowns, religion and custom, ethnicity and race—whether concentrated into large-scale migrant districts and neighborhoods (Irish in London or Liverpool, Czechs and Jews in Vienna), or mixed in more intricate residential mosaics, all hailed by the continuous din of the city's public interpellations in the rhetorics of race and nation, familiar and foreign. The metropolis reordered the spatial relations between the private and the public, while remapping the social relations of class, and in the process invented entire visual and written languages for understanding each of these things, invoking the mass, race, gender, and sexuality. It was no accident that a main crucible of "modernity" in this sense was that late imperial capital of Vienna.[32]

There is here some evident convergence with late twentieth-century treatments of *postmodernity*, many of whose terms—fragmentation of experience, indeterminacy and mobility of identity, new subjectivities—were exactly prefigured in this earlier moment of *fin de siècle* Vienna. Indeed, much of the reinvigorated interest in modernism and modernity was actually incited by efforts at proposing a theory of the postmodern during the later 1980s and early 1990s.[33] The relevance of latter-day capitalist restructuring for grounding an account of postmodernity likewise suggests the value of relating the discourse of modernity to earlier capitalist formations distinctive to the high industrialization of the late nineteenth century.[34]

Postmodernist treatments of cultures of consumption in their relationship to identity formation and distinctions of public and private, languages of citizenship and nation, or the construction of gender differences make this especially clear, as those themes were actually materialized in precisely the emergent metropolitan settings where Baudelaire, Simmel, and Benjamin were finding the crucible of the modernist sensibility. If we conceptualize modernity/ism via the excitements and dangers of the city, through the transformations of public space and the public sphere and in the city's visual and perceptual landscape, we quickly arrive, too, at the new languages of the crowd and the mass.[35] Those languages—mass culture, mass society, mass civilization, mass market, rise of the masses—came around 1900 increasingly to organize political thinking. They became linked not only to anxieties about class, but further to fears of degeneration; to the health of the social body; to the confusion of boundaries; to the temptations, corruptions, and moral degradation of the city's profane delights; and to the general disordering of accustomed social positions. In relation to any of these particulars, the new discourses of race, sexuality, and the different natures of women and men then supplied an essential code. The figure of the transgressive woman became emblematic for much of this process of destabilizing change. If European modernisms of the early twentieth century were complicated responses to the major anxiety-producing social transformations registered by the social, cultural, and political life of the metropolis, then in addition to crises of race and nationality and the rise of socialism, the rise of the New Woman acquired a central place. In all of those ways, popular culture became vital to the ground from which modernity became experienced and imagined, especially in its gendered dimensions.[36]

In this cultural complex of meanings, the beginnings of "modernity" become heavily spatialized around very particular metropolitan environs, migrating from mid-nineteenth-century Paris to *fin de siècle* Vienna and Prague and thence to early twentieth-century Berlin. It is above all the Weimar Republic that comes to define our perceptions of modernism in the broadened sociocultural sense. Peukert made this Weimar moment of cultural experimentation, characterized as a crisis-ridden culmination of "classical modernity," into the ground of a general analysis of political and social-historical, as well as the cultural, problems of the early twentieth century. In this argument, the transition to industrialism during the 1890s created the conditions for "the socio-cultural penetration of modernity," from which the series of developments discussed earlier in this essay were held to flow. As Peukert put it, "Since the turn of the century modernity has classically shaped developments in the fields of science and culture, in town planning, in technology, and in medicine, in spiritual reflection, as well as in the everyday world—has rehearsed our present-day way of life, so to speak."[37]

In light of these definitional reflections, what follows for our understanding of Nazism and its placement in Germany's early twentieth-century modernity? Here I will develop four general arguments.

First, it seems helpful to distinguish between modernity as a category of ordinary language, or a descriptive term in "plain speech," and modernity as a category of analysis—one capable of capturing the specificities of change in the actually existing worlds of capitalism and its social formations around 1900. This separates the late nineteenth-century intellectual histories that shaped this particular way of conceptualizing social and cultural change (as the passage into modernity) from the actual pasts—economically, sociologically, culturally, institutionally, politically, spatially, ecologically— to which the concept then brought both coherence and further direction. In that sense, "modernity" was both symptom (as the language generated around a particular set of powerful contemporary occurrences) and diagnosis (as the processes requiring description). Societal changes both constructed talk about modernity and became further constructed by it.

Thus we are dealing with that familiar dialectical reciprocity between, on the one hand, the descriptive and analytical purchase of a particular language of social understanding as it circulates through the precincts of academic and intellectual life, the worlds of politics, and the public sphere as a whole; and, on the other hand, the actually existing phenomena, events, and transformations which that language purports to describe and explain. That is, "modernity" as a coherently formulated socioeconomic, cultural, and political postulate (as a set of powerful and insistent claims about changes in the really existing world) became just as crucial to the condition of modernity as the material existence of "the modern" as a demonstrable social fact (in the new lifeworld of the metropolis). This makes the *ideology*, or the *discourse of modernity*, a more fruitful starting point for analysis than the phenomena themselves in a materialist sense, because it was at this discursive level that the operative purchase of modernity on public understanding became constituted and secured. That applied both to the terms under which particular ideas and policies became admitted into its frame and to the matter of who came to speak in its languages, who set the dominant tone. By the "ideology or discourse of modernity," I mean *both* the insistence on modernity as the organizing reality of the early twentieth-century social world *and* the crystallizing of specific practices, policies, and institutions around that insistence. In other words, the history of modernity became inseparable from the history of the category. "The modern" emerged as a set of discursive claims about the social world seeking aggressively to reorder that world in terms of itself. In that case, its meanings were always-already plural and contested. Likewise, from its very inception as a reservoir of meanings, modernity also became of necessity a ground for the raising of conflicting and programmatic political claims.

Second, this decisively shifts our conventional periodization. The arguments about scientific and technological modernity, the post-Foucauldian claims regarding governmentality, and Peukert's argument about "the spirit of science" each have their far-reaching implications for how we see the genealogies of Nazism. Where does that leave our conventional chronology of 1914/18 and 1933 and its observance of the established politico-constitutional temporalities? How do we create a common interpretive context or analytical framework for understanding the *Kaiserreich* in relation to the later periods of Weimar and Third Reich? Where are the lines of continuity running from the 1890s down to the 1920s, and how should they be weighted and understood? Or does the sharpness of the political rupture of 1918–19 still trump any claims of continuity in this specifically political realm of constitutional change, institutional innovation, and more dramatically disruptive and event-laden ideological transition? Does the importance of the revolutionary political rupture bisecting the period disqualify suggestions that these years might be reperiodized, in the end? In a similar vein, powerful and contentious understandings of "modernity" were circulating in those later periods of Weimar and Third Reich too. So how should we see the relationship between the revalorizing of modernity during the *Kaiserreich* and those later discussions of "the modern"?

My *third* point concerns an area easily bracketed from these reflections, namely, the critical modernism of the Social Democrats, who avowedly embraced Germany's capitalist transformation as the necessary foundation of the future—not as an end in itself, but as the modernizing engine of progress and abundance, whose dynamism would be harnessed for the transition into a new kind of society altogether. Pioneered by Karl Kautsky before 1914, extended by Rudolf Hilferding and others in the 1920s, this vision of industrial capitalism's impending maturity delivered a compelling narrative of progressive social change and its cultural effects. Rising concentration of ownership and control in the economy's leading sectors, the effects of advanced technologies and industrial rationalization, the shaping of labor markets and a national wages policy, the direction of international trade and capital flows—in short, the growing prevalence of "organized capitalism," in Hilferding's notation—all made the economy ripe for planning and central direction in the interests of the common good. Given powerful impetus by the centralized economy and "total mobilization" of the First World War, this supplied the main Social Democratic understanding of the prospects for socialism under Weimar. As capitalist industry and commerce became ever more densely self-organized and interconnected, ever greater coordination would also be required of government, making public ownership and control far easier to envisage. With its centralizing tendencies, logics of regulation, and institutional entailments, argued the SPD strategists, capitalist modernity would both *require* central political management once it reached a certain maximal level of development and simultaneously *enable* democratic accountability.

If this was a conception of modernity based in political economy and capitalist development, its consequences translated across all other spheres of policy and practice too, not least because Marxists presumed such interconnectedness. To take an especially salient illustration from the 1920s, talk of rationalization might *begin* from the immediate concerns in the economy, including mechanization and enlargement of capacity, Taylorism and scientific management and controlling the labor process by deskilling, the production line and shedding of redundant labor. Keenly aware of the postulated relationship between technology, work, and economic success, trade union officials remained anxiously caught between logics of industrial modernization and defense of their members' interests.[38] But whether as a general buzzword for new categories of professional expertise or as a more coherent social paradigm, "social rationalization" had far wider resonance than these immediate applications. It encompassed "an abundance of ideas and movements,...ranging from sexual ethics to family planning, from 'good taste' to proper hygiene, from eugenics to racial policies, from the construction of housing to children's playgrounds, from reform pedagogy to education through the media, and so on."[39] Urban planning, housing policy, architecture, and domestic design emerged for socialists during the 1920s as one of the principal sites of innovative reform and visionary practice, enabled by the SPD's unprecedented strengths in city government. Much of the thinking concerned already went back to the early 1900s.[40] Moving out into the wider social policy domain, socialists deployed varieties of expertise in imagining the good society, whether in the SPD's youth sections, schooling, and educational policy, in sex reform and public health, in the elaborate machinery of the different sectors of social policy and the welfare state, or in cultural politics and the arts. Weimar was a vibrant "laboratory of modernity" in that sense, "especially in terms of its fascination with Fordism, rationalization, modern sex and gender politics, progressive welfare policies, and unparalleled avant-garde cultural achievement."[41] If the language and aspirations of "social engineering" also signified initiatives and thinking avowedly to the right (as in Peukert's arguments presented earlier), then the Left's commitment to rational social planning of these kinds should not be gainsaid.[42] Until the end of the 1920s, this *socialist* understanding of what it meant to be "modern" continued to describe a crucial field of meaning.

Finally, I want to return to the issue of the German Right's relationship to the perceived benefits and dangers of modernity. Here I build on Stefan Breuer's distinction between *conservative* and *postconservative* forms of thought, where the latter properly identifies the "Right" per se.[43] Most saliently, it was precisely the active embrace of technological modernity, ideals of national efficiency, and mass-based forms of political action that decisively separated the Right from any preceding traditionalism. The new core was a commitment to *inequality*, whose particular meanings came to be variously conceived. The overriding principle of societal order derived from belief in the naturally unequal endowment of human populations linked to a theory of elites and the attendant hierarchical ethic of social practice. That became combined more and more with a scientistic approach to the measurement and valuation of human capacities and entitlements, which likewise sustained a generalized philosophy of human nature commonly characterized as social Darwinist. Already a powerful explanation for the social topography of class, the distribution of wealth and attainment, and the perpetuating of poverty, such ideas then became worked into proposals for organizing access to power and participation in the polity too. They also connected with theories of sovereignty, imperialism, and antagonistic relations among states. Given such thought, a range of more specific ideologies now coalesced, taking the master concept of inequality for common orientation. These included various types of nationalism, movements of the arts and aesthetics, bio-political and eugenicist programs, visions of prosperity linked to the national economy and its world-political expansion, geopolitical programs, diverse antisemitisms, and varieties of *völkisch* thought, all invariably tending toward a strongly centered conception of race.

The unifying thread in this world of right-wing ideas, its political hardwiring, was the shared enmity against liberal and democratic calls for individual freedom and equality, not to speak of the still more radical hatred of socialism. It was against these progressivist ideals that the Right's redeployed hierarchical prescriptions for social and political order became so vehemently counterposed. In the minds of many right-wing commentators those hated ideals also inhered in the experience of the West, and to that extent the desire to validate a German *Sonderweg*—the idea that Germany could avoid the social divisiveness and class conflict accompanying the victory of liberalism in Britain and France—was certainly in play. But the German Right's hostility to democracy was not by that virtue *antimodern* in any analytically sensible use of the term. Its commitment to inequality implied no across-the-board or straightforward refusal of what by 1900 were understood to be the main features of the arriving social world of modernity.

Indeed, this emergent Right's most fervent beliefs—in the new technologies of industrial expansion and the imperialist entailments of a powerful economy, for example, or in the new challenges of mass-political action— now presumed that modernity had arrived to stay. This unavoidable location *inside* the very processes of industrial society's creation before 1914 made the Right's distinctive political outlook intelligible, whether ideologically in terms of its salient attitudes and commitments or "objectively" in terms of its sociological profile. The Right's most vigorous organizers and activists as it emerged into the 1900s—including Pan-German ideologues such as Alfred Hugenberg and Heinrich Claβ, leading personalities of the nationalist pressure groups like August Keim or Eduard von Liebert, *völkisch* and antisemitic impresarios like Theodor Fritsch or Friedrich Lange, journalists and pamphleteers like Heinrich Oberwinder or Ernst von Reventlow, and countless minor figures and functionaries—lived and worked inside the distinctively *modern* institutional worlds of the professions and the public sphere. Authentically "modern" forces, including the dynamism of the industrial economy, the romance of science and technology, the drive for imperialist expansion, and the harnessing of national resources, including all aspects of the available reservoir of human population, inspired them to grandiose projects of foreign and domestic policy. If superficially the national fantasy of harmonious community harked back to a chimerical lost age, moreover, that discourse, too, was necessarily shaped by the terms and consequences of Germany's unfolding societal transformation. The postconservative Right's critique of the contemporary world itself presumed the continuing and inescapable pervasiveness of "the modern." It subsisted on the given and unfolding actuality of modern times.

Accordingly, it makes no sense to consider Wilhelmine politics through the lens of "backwardness" or the language of "authoritarian continuities" and "pre-industrial traditions," because those years were the site of far more complex and open-ended innovations. The ensuing conflicts are profoundly distorted by those older narratives of stagnation and rigidity, in which the forces of change became blocked by the forces of tradition and pre-industrial elites perpetuated their power. Stasis of that kind was the *opposite* of what Wilhelmine society promised and contained. "Germany" in the early twentieth century was not just a still-novel political-territorial entity, but also a rapidly transforming societal context and a highly contested cultural imaginary. How should claims to modernity be appraised if we resituate them and revalorize them in these settings? In trying to capture those complexities, the best starting point is the present tense of the period itself, its specificities of social and cultural history and the new forms of politics they spawned. German society was in the midst of full-throttle capitalist transformation between the 1890s and 1914, and under those dramatically new societal circumstances—the startling and spectacular conjuncture of the early twentieth-century German modernity—the only reliable constancy was the unceasing pressure toward change. In any case, "traditions" are only as old as the practices and relations that ground or upset their meanings. In those terms, it was change that supplied the Wilhelmine era's strongest continuity.

Notes

1   S.V., "Grosstadtgetriebe," *Junge Kräfte* (April 1926), pp. 44–5, cited in Katherina von Ankum, "Introduction," in von Ankum (ed.), *Women in the Metropolis: Gender and Modernity in Weimar Culture* (Berkeley: University of California Press, 1997), p. 1.

2   For excellent surveys of *Kaiserreich* historiography as a whole, see Matthew Jefferies, *Contesting the German Empire, 1871–1918* (Oxford: Blackwell, 2008), and Helmut Walser Smith, "Authoritarian State, Dynamic Society, Failed Imperialist Power, 1878–1914," in Smith (ed.), *The Oxford Handbook of Modern German History* (Oxford: Oxford University Press, 2011), pp. 306–35. Fritz Fischer, *From Kaiserreich to Third Reich: Elements of Continuity in German History 1871–1945* (London: Allen & Unwin, 1986), usefully summarizes the arguments of Fischer's two major books, *Germany's Aims in the First World War* (London: Chatto and Windus, 1967) and *War of Illusions: German Policies from 1911 to 1914* (London: Chatto and Windus, 1974). For Eckart Kehr and his influence, see James J. Sheehan, "The Primacy of Domestic Politics: Eckart Kehr's Essays on Modern German History," *Central European History* 1:2 (1968), pp. 166–74. The "Bielefeld school" denotes a stream of social-science history established by Hans-Ulrich Wehler, Jürgen Kocka, and others at the University of Bielefeld between the early 1970s and mid-1990s.

3   See Hans-Ulrich Wehler, *Bismarck und der Imperialismus* (Cologne: Kiepenheuer und Witsch, 1969), whose arguments are summarized in "Bismarck's Imperialism, 1862–1890," *Past and Present* 48 (August 1970), pp. 119–55, and "Industrial Growth and Early German Imperialism," in Roger Owen and Bob Sutcliffe (eds.), *Studies in the Theory of Imperialism* (London: Longman, 1972), pp. 71–92.

4   Fritz Stern, *The Politics of Cultural Despair: A Study in the Rise of the German Ideology* (Berkeley: University of California Press, 1961); George L. Mosse, *The Crisis of German Ideology: Intellectual Origins of the Third Reich* (London: Weidenfeld & Nicolson, 1964); Leonard Krieger, *The German Idea of Freedom: History of a Political Tradition* (Chicago: University of Chicago Press, 1957); Mack Walker, *German Home Towns: Community, State, General Estate, 1648–1971* (Ithaca: Cornell University Press, 1971); James J. Sheehan, *German Liberalism in the Nineteenth Century* (Chicago: University of Chicago Press, 1978).

5   See M. Rainer Lepsius, "Parteiensystem und Sozialstruktur: Zum Problem der Demokratisierung der deutschen Gesellschaft," in Gerhard A. Ritter

(ed.), *Die deutschen Parteien vor 1918* (Cologne: Kiepenheuer & Witsch, 1973), pp. 56–80, and "Demokratie in Deutschland als historisch-soziologisches Problem," in Theodor W. Adorno (ed.), *Spätkapitalismus oder Industriegesellschaft. Im Auftrage der Deutschen Gesellschaft für Soziologie* (Stuttgart: F. Enke, 1969), pp. 197–213. Both essays were republished in M. Rainer Lepsius, *Demokratie in Deutschland. Soziologisch-historische Konstellationsanalysen. Ausgewählte Aufsätze* (Göttingen: Vandenhoeck & Ruprecht, 1993), pp. 25–50, 11–24.

6   The full-scale critique of the *Sonderweg* thesis was launched by David Blackbourn and Geoff Eley, *The Peculiarities of German History: Bourgeois Society and Politics in Nineteenth-Century Germany* (Oxford: Oxford University Press, 1984; earlier German edn, 1981). For a succinct summary of the resulting controversy in the 1970s and 1980s, see Jefferies, *Contesting the German Empire*, pp. 18–37. In a nutshell: Germany produced fascism by failing to become "modern" on the model of Britain and France.

7   Detlev J.K. Peukert, "The Genesis of the 'Final Solution' from the Spirit of Science," in Thomas Childers and Jane Caplan (eds.), *Reevaluating the Third Reich* (New York: Holmes & Meier, 1993), pp. 234–52; also *The Weimar Republic: The Crisis of Classical Modernity* (New York: Hill & Wang, 1992).

8   For critical commentary on the relevant historiography, see Geoff Eley, *Nazism as Fascism: Violence, Ideology, and the Ground of Consent in Germany, 1930–1945* (London: Routledge, 2013), esp. chs. 2–3, pp. 13–90; and Ian Kershaw, *The Nazi Dictatorship: Problems and Perspectives of Interpretation*, 4th edn (London: Arnold, 2000).

9   For a critical overview of such discussions, see Kershaw, *Nazi Dictatorship*, pp. 243–8. The most substantial and constructively provocative of the relevant interventions was Michael Prinz and Rainer Zitelmann (eds.), *Nationalsozialismus und Modernisierung* (Darmstadt: Wissenschaftliche Buchgesellschaft, 1991). The question is addressed directly in Mark Roseman's contribution to this volume.

10   Rainer Zitelmann took this furthest by arguing that Hitler's own thinking was coherently ordered around a program of social and economic transformation for Germany's future, for whose purpose the Nazis' racial program, the ideology of *Lebensraum*, and the wars of conquest were each subordinately harnessed. However brutal and reactionary his means, this outlook made Hitler a forward-looking "modernizer," in Zitelmann's view, and indeed a "social revolutionary." See Rainer Zitelmann, *Hitler: Selbstverständnis eines Revolutionärs* (Hamburg and Leamington Spa: Berg, 1987).

11   See, for instance, Detlev J.K. Peukert, *Grenzen der Sozialdisziplinierung: Aufstieg und Krise der Jugendfürsorge von 1878 bis 1932* (Cologne: Bund, 1986); Peukert, "Der 'Traum der Venunft,' " in Peukert (ed.), *Max Webers Diagnose der Moderne* (Göttingen: Vandenhoeck & Ruprecht, 1989), pp. 55–91.

12   See Michael Burleigh and Wolfgang Wippermann, *The Racial State: Germany, 1933–1945* (Cambridge: Cambridge University Press, 1991); Michael Thad Allen, *The Business of Genocide: The SS, Slave Labor, and the Concentration Camps* (Chapel Hill: University of North Carolina Press, 2002).

13   See here Zygmunt Bauman, *Modernity and the Holocaust* (Ithaca: Cornell University Press, 1989); James C. Scott, *Seeing Like a State: How Certain Schemes to Improve the Human Condition Have Failed* (New Haven: Yale University Press, 1998); Amir Weiner (ed.), *Landscaping the Human Garden: Twentieth-Century Population Management in a Comparative Framework* (Stanford: Stanford University Press, 2003); and especially Stephen Kotkin, "Modern Times: The Soviet Union and the Interwar Conjuncture," *Kritika: Explorations in Russian and Eurasian History* 2:1 (2001), pp. 111–64.

14   See here Jürgen Kocka, "Ursachen des Nationalsozialismus," *Aus Politik und Zeitgeschichte*, June 21, 1980, pp. 9–13; Karl Dietrich Bracher, "The Nazi Takeover," *History of the 20th Century*, 48 (London: Parnell, 1969), p. 1339; Ralf Dahrendorf, *Society and Democracy in Germany* (London: Weidenfeld & Nicolson, 1968), p. 15; Fritz Stern, *The Failure of Illiberalism: Essays on the Political Culture of Modern Germany* (London: George Allen & Unwin, 1972), p. xix; for Lepsius, see note 5 above.

15   See Fritz Stern, "The Political Consequences of the Unpolitical German," in Stern, *Failure of Illiberalism*, pp. 3–25. For a recent iteration, astonishingly impervious to the critical debates surrounding the *Sonderweg* thesis, see Wolf Lepenies, *The Seduction of Culture in German History* (Princeton: Princeton University Press, 2006).

16   For these phrases, in a discussion sharply critical of the *Sonderweg* approach, see David Blackbourn, "The Discreet Charm of the Bourgeoisie: Reappraising German History in the Nineteenth Century," in Blackbourn and Eley, *Peculiarities*, p. 161.

17   For example, see Celia Applegate, *A Nation of Provincials: The German Idea of Heimat* (Berkeley: University of California Press, 1990); Alon Confino, *The Nation as Local Metaphor: Württemberg, Imperial Germany, and National Memory, 1871–1918* (Chapel Hill: University of North Carolina Press, 1997); Thomas M. Lekan, *Imagining the Nation in Nature: Landscape Preservation and German Identity 1885–1945* (Cambridge: Harvard University Press, 2004); William H. Rollins, *A Greener Vision of Home: Cultural Politics and Environmental Reform in the German Heimatschutz Movement, 1904–1918* (Ann Arbor: University of Michigan Press, 1997); Jennifer L. Jenkins, *Provincial Modernity: Local Culture and Liberal Politics in Fin-de-Siècle Hamburg* (Ithaca: Cornell University Press, 2003); Rudy Koshar, *Germany's Transient Pasts: Preservation and National Memory in the Twentieth Century* (Chapel Hill: University of North Carolina Press, 1998), and *German Travel Cultures* (Oxford: Berg, 2000); John A. Williams, *Turning to Nature in Germany: Hiking, Nudism, and Conservation, 1900–1940* (Stanford: Stanford University Press, 2007); Michael Hau, *The Cult of Health and Beauty in Germany: A Social History, 1890–1930* (Chicago: University of Chicago Press, 2003); Edward Ross Dickinson, *Sex, Freedom, and Power in Imperial Germany, 1880–1914* (Cambridge: Cambridge University Press, 2014); Corinna Treitel, *A Science for the Soul: Occultism and the Genesis of the German Modern* (Baltimore: Johns Hopkins University Press, 2004); Tracie Matysik, *Reforming the Moral Subject: Ethics and Sexuality in Central Europe, 1890–1930* (Ithaca: Cornell University Press, 2008); Matthew Jefferies, *Politics and Culture in Wilhelmine Germany: The Case of Industrial*

Architecture (Oxford: Berg, 1995) and *Imperial Culture in Germany, 1871–1918* (Houndmills: Palgrave Macmillan, 2005); Kevin Repp, *Reformers, Critics, and the Paths of German Modernity: Anti-Politics and the Search for Alternatives, 1890–1914* (Cambridge: Harvard University Press, 2000).

18 Jennifer L. Jenkins, "Introduction: Domesticity, Design, and the Shaping of the Social," *German History* 25:4 (2007), pp. 468–9. See especially Jenkins's earlier article, "The Kitsch Collections and *The Spirit in the Furniture*: Cultural Reform and National Culture in Germany," *Social History* 21:2 (1996), pp. 123–41; and Jenkins, *Provincial Modernity*. The argument likewise builds on Jefferies, *Politics and Culture in Imperial Germany*, pp. 101–45, and John V. Maciuika, *Before the Bauhaus: Architecture, Politics, and the German State, 1890–1920* (Cambridge: Cambridge University Press, 2005).

19 Spoken in his inaugural address at the Werkbund's foundation, Munich, October 5–6, 1907, printed in *Der Kunstwart* 21 (1908), pp. 135–8. See Jefferies, *Politics and Culture in Imperial Germany*, p. 103. Schumacher was an adherent of Friedrich Naumann, a key inspiration behind the Werkbund and mentor to the emergent networks of Wilhelmine "reformers," who moved during 1900–20 in fascinatingly divergent political directions. See ibid., pp. 146–79; Repp, *Reformers, Critics, and the Paths of German Modernity*, pp. 19–103.

20 Jenkins, "Introduction," p. 481. Emphasis was added by Jenkins. The phrase was attributed to Hermann Muthesius. See Jefferies, *Politics and Culture in Imperial Germany*, p. 102.

21 Dennis Sweeney, "Reconsidering the Modernity Paradigm: Reform Movements, the Social, and the State in Wilhelmine Germany," *Social History* 31:4 (2006), p. 416.

22 Daniel T. Rodgers, *Atlantic Crossings: Social Politics in a Progressive Age* (Cambridge: Harvard University Press, 1998), p. 44.

23 Erik Grimmer-Solem, "German Social Science, Meiji Conservatism, and the Peculiarities of Japanese History," *Journal of World History* 16:2 (2005), p. 215.

24 Hans-Ulrich Wehler probably remained an exception. An imposing consistency linked the credo in *Modernisierungstheorie und Geschichte* (Göttingen: Vandenhoeck & Ruprecht, 1975) to the later *Deutsche Gesellschaftsgeschichte*, vols 1–5 (Munich: Beck, 1987–2008). Otherwise, by the 1990s arguments for the virtues of modernization theory had become few and far between. One prominent defense had been reduced to measuring the Weimar polity against an ideal type of stable parliamentary representation, an approach that owed nothing to modernization *theory* per se. See Gerald D. Feldman, "The Weimar Republic: A Problem of Modernization?" *Archiv für Sozialgeschichte* 26 (1986), pp. 1–26.

25 Dickinson, *Sex, Freedom, and Power*, p. 305.

26 Don Slater, *Consumer Culture and Modernity* (Cambridge: Polity, 1997), pp. 83–4.

27 See Geoff Eley, "German History and the Contradictions of Modernity: The Bourgeoisie, the State, and the Mastery of Reform," in Eley (ed.), *Society,*

Culture, and the State in Germany, 1870–1930 (Ann Arbor: University of Michigan Press, 1996), pp. 67–103.

28 See Marshall Berman, *All That Is Solid Melts into Air: The Experience of Modernity* (New York: Simon and Schuster, 1982). Interest in Benjamin was presaged in Hannah Arendt's selection of his essays (see Walter Benjamin, *Illuminations* [New York: Schocken, 1969]), building during the 1970s in a major program of translation by New Left Books (now Verso). Among early critical commentaries, see Eugene Lunn, *Marxism and Modernism: A Historical Study of Lukács, Brecht, Benjamin, and Adorno* (Berkeley: University of California Press, 1982), and Susan Buck-Morss, *The Dialectics of Seeing: Walter Benjamin and the Arcades Project* (Cambridge: MIT Press, 1989).

29 See David Harvey, *The Condition of Postmodernity: An Enquiry into the Origins of Cultural Change* (Oxford: Basil Blackwell, 1989), pp. 260–307; Paul Virilio, *Speed and Politics: An Essay on Dromology* (New York: Semiotext(e), 1986); Stephen Kern, *The Culture of Time and Space, 1880–1918* (Cambridge: Harvard University Press, 1983).

30 I am most indebted here to the following: Raymond Williams, *The Politics of Modernism: Against the New Conformists* (London: Verso, 1989); John Berger, *Selected Essays and Articles. The Look of Things* (Harmondsworth: Penguin, 1972), esp. "The Moment of Cubism," pp. 133–62; Roy Pascal, *From Naturalism to Expressionism: German Literature and Society 1880–1918* (London: Weidenfeld & Nicolson, 1973), esp. pp. 124–60; David Frisby, *Fragments of Modernity: Theories of Modernity in the Work of Simmel, Kracauer, and Benjamin* (Cambridge: MIT Press, 1988). For the social and political setting, see Perry Anderson, "Modernity and Revolution," *New Left Review* 144 (March–April 1984), pp. 96–113.

31 Charles Baudelaire, *The Painter of Modern Life and Other Essays* (Oxford: Oxford University Press, 1964), cited by David Frisby, "Georg Simmel, First Sociologist of Modernity," *Theory, Culture, and Society* 2 (1985), p. 49.

32 See classically Carl E. Schorske, *Fin-de-Siècle Vienna: Politics and Culture* (New York: Vintage, 1981) and for critical appraisal Steven Beller (ed.), *Rethinking Vienna 1900* (New York: Berghahn, 2001).

33 See Harvey, *Condition of Postmodernity*; Jean-François Lyotard, *The Postmodern Condition: A Report on Knowledge* (Minneapolis: University of Minnesota Press, 1984); Fredric Jameson, *Postmodernism, or, The Cultural Logic of Late Capitalism* (Durham: Duke University Press, 1991); Perry Anderson, *The Origins of Postmodernity* (London: Verso, 1998).

34 See here Alain Lipietz, *Towards a New Economic Order: Post-Fordism, Ecology, and Democracy* (Cambridge: Polity, 1992); Ash Amin (ed.), *Post-Fordism: A Reader* (Oxford: Blackwell, 1994).

35 See the entry on "Masses" in Raymond Williams, *Keywords: A Vocabulary of Culture and Society*, revised edn (New York: Oxford University Press, 1983), pp. 182–7. For ideas of the crowd, the city, and the dangers of degeneration: Robert A. Nye, *The Origins of Crowd Psychology: Gustave Le Bon and the Crisis of Mass Democracy in the Third Republic* (London: Sage, 1976); Daniel Pick, *Faces of Degeneration: A European Disorder, c. 1848–c. 1918*

(Cambridge: Cambridge University Press, 1989); Jaap van Ginneken, *Crowds, Psychology, and Politics, 1871–1899* (Cambridge: Cambridge University Press, 1992); Susanna Barrows, *Distorting Mirrors: Visions of the Crowd in Late Nineteenth-Century France* (New Haven: Yale University Press, 1981); Ben Singer, "Modernity, Hyperstimulus, and the Rise of Popular Sensationalism," in Leo Charney and Vanessa R. Schwartz (eds.), *Cinema and the Invention of Modern Life* (Berkeley: University of California Press, 1995), pp. 72–99. For brilliant reflections on conceptions of the mass in the 1920s, with attention specifically to Germany: Miriam Hansen, "'A Self-Representation of the Masses': Siegfried Kracauer's Curious Americanism," in Kathleen Canning, Kerstin Barndt, and Kristin McGuire (eds.), *Weimar Publics/Weimar Subjects: Rethinking the Political Culture of Germany in the 1920s* (New York: Berghahn, 2010), pp. 257–78; Stefan Jonsson, "Neither Masses nor Individuals: Representations of the Collective in Interwar German Culture," ibid., pp. 279–301.

36 See Andreas Huyssen, "Mass Culture as Woman: Modernism's Other," in Huyssen, *After the Great Divide: Modernism, Mass Culture, Postmodernism* (Bloomington: Indiana University Press, 1986); Eve Rosenhaft, "Women, Gender, and the Limits of Political History in the Age of 'Mass' Politics," in Larry Jones and James N. Retallack (eds.), *Elections, Mass Politics, and Social Change in Modern Germany: New Perspectives* (Cambridge: Cambridge University Press, 1992), pp. 149–74; von Ankum, *Women in the Metropolis.*

37 Detlev J.K. Peukert, "The Weimar Republic—Old and New Perspectives," *German History* 6 (1988), p. 138. The classic presentation of this perspective may be found in the two-volume anthology, *Jahrhundertwende: Der Aufbruch in die Moderne 1880–1930*, which Peukert edited together with August Nitschke, Gerhard A. Ritter, and Rüdiger vom Bruch (Reinbek bei Hamburg: Rowohlt, 1990).

38 See especially Mary Nolan, *Visions of Modernity: American Business and the Modernization of Germany* (New York: Oxford University Press, 1994).

39 Adelheid von Saldern, "Introduction: The Challenge of Modernity," in von Saldern (ed.), *The Challenge of Modernity: German Social and Cultural Studies, 1890–1960* (Ann Arbor: University of Michigan Press, 2002), pp. 22–3. See here Dagmar Reese, Eve Rosenhaft, Carola Sachse, and Tilla Siegel (eds.), *Rationale Beziehungen? Geschlechterverhältnisse im Rationalisierungsprozeß* (Frankfurt: Suhrkamp, 1993); Atina Grossmann, "Gender and Rationalization: Questions about the German/American Comparison," *Social Politics: International Studies in Gender, State, and Society* 4 (1997), pp. 6–18.

40 See especially von Saldern, *Challenge of Modernity*, pp. 93–114, 134–63.

41 Katherine Pence and Paul Betts, "Introduction," in Pence and Betts (eds.), *Socialist Modern: East German Everyday Culture and Politics* (Ann Arbor: University of Michigan Press, 2008), p. 16.

42 See Benjamin Ziemann, Richard F. Wetzell, Dirk Schumann, and Kerstin Brückweh, "Introduction: The Scientization of the Social in Comparative Perspective," in Kerstin Brückweh et al. (eds.), *Engineering Society: The Role of the Human and Social Sciences in Modern Societies, 1880–1980*

(Houndmills: Palgrave Macmillan, 2012), pp. 1–40; Thomas Etzemüller, *Alvar and Gunnar Myrdal: Social Engineering in the Modern World* (Lanham: Lexington Books, 2014), pp. 7–11.

43 Stefan Breuer, *Ordnungen der Ungleichheit. Die deutsche Rechte im Widerstreit ihrer Ideen 1871–1945* (Darmstadt: Wissenschaftliche Buchgesellschaft, 2001); Breuer, *Die Völkischen in Deutschland. Kaiserreich und Weimarer Republik* (Darmstadt: Wissenschaftliche Buchgesellschaft, 2008), pp. 12–22; also Eley, *Nazism as Fascism*, pp. 5–10.

4

Alternative Modernities: Imperial Germany through the Lens of Russia

Annemarie Sammartino

Scholars have argued for at least the last few decades that Western Europe does not have a monopoly on modernity. Those studying colonialism in Africa and Asia, in particular, have stressed that seemingly far-flung colonial outposts were often laboratories of modern experimentation and modern projects that later wended their way back to the metropole.[1] Along with the "laboratory of modernity" argument, others have argued that there are a proliferation of moderni*ties*, rather than one single Western path to a modern future.[2] Historians and other scholars have insisted on the multidirectional and transnational origins of many of the products and processes of so-called Western modernity.[3] Meanwhile, parallel to these discussions of colonial and non-Western modernities, German historians have themselves been engaged in a debate for the past three decades about the "peculiarity" of Germany's own path to modernity.[4] The controversy unleashed by Geoff Eley and David Blackbourn's book *The Peculiarities of German History* was immensely fruitful; by shattering the seemingly coterminous relationship between liberalism, the middle class, and democracy, Blackbourn and Eley forced German historians to reinvestigate questions long believed to be settled. From studies of the bourgeoisie to analyses of nationalism, historians investigated the relationship between the German encounter with modernity and that of its Western European neighbors and the relative health or sickness of German liberalism. Both postcolonial scholars and critics of the German *Sonderweg* challenged the notion of a single path to modernity, which presumed that the experience of Western Europe was the prototype for a normal, modern society.

Ironically, by focusing on Western models and experiences as comparative models, even as these models are often rejected or nuanced, both of these challenges to a Western-centric modernity have put the focus back on the West. The "classic" empires of Britain and France provided the context for much German postcolonial scholarship, even if recent work insists on the connections between Germany's overseas colonialism and its practices on the continent.[5] Meanwhile, the *Sonderweg* debate resulted from a set of concerns specific to the Cold War context in which it emerged; namely, to what degree was Germany a part of the traditions of Western Europe?[6] Put another way by the *Sonderweg*'s critics, to what degree was the tradition of liberalism responsible for, and thus potentially compromised by, the rise of fascism? Blackbourn and Eley's tome was as much a rethinking of Western European liberalism, particularly of the British variety, as it was a recasting of German historical debates.

Historians of Germany's overseas imperium have often used insights reached by scholars of the French and British empires to explore the meaning of race in the lands of German Southwest and East Africa.[7] German historians and literature scholars have also discovered the Afro-Germans.[8] Here, too, Germanists have fruitfully applied French and British work on those nations' colonial and postcolonial encounters with men and women from outside of Europe, as well as expanded upon the differences from these models that constituted the experiences of Black Germans. However, there are three potential dangers with this approach. Firstly, African colonialism was financially, and most likely psychologically, and socially more important for Germany's Western European neighbors than it was for Germany itself. Similarly, while Germany has become a more multinational state in the past fifty years (although it never was as ethnically monolithic as German historians have often imagined), major groups of foreigners in Germany today—the Turks and the Russians—raise questions that are distinct from the post-colonial legacies that dominate the social and discursive encounters in France and Britain. In other words, there is a limit to the usefulness of Western European models for understanding German experience, and if we only ask the same questions as French and British historians, there is a real risk that German historiography falls into a pale imitation of their work. Along these lines, David Blackbourn asks us to consider that the German India or Algeria "was not Cameroon. It was Central Europe [Mitteleuropa]."[9] But even more to the point, the German encounter with other peoples in Central Europe was distinct from that of either the British in India or the French in Algeria, and the model of colonizer and colonized maps only imperfectly onto the terrain of Central and Eastern Europe.

As historians have recognized, Germany's peculiar status as both a colonial power abroad and a multinational empire in Europe means that a discussion of Germany's empire necessarily includes an investigation of its eastern borderlands. The *Kaiserreich* was, from the moment of its inception in 1871 and well before it had any overseas colonies to speak of, a *Vielvölkerreich*. As Philipp Ther provocatively puts it, "[T]he German Empire was built on the continuous partition of one of its neighbors…Viewed from Breslau, Poznan or Warsaw, the so-called [German] unification looked more like a continuous expansion."[10] Within the new German Empire itself, self-identified Germans were in the majority (unlike in Austria-Hungary) but they shared a state with Poles, Frenchmen, and Danes. Throughout the 1870s and 1880s, separatist parties had a significant presence in the Reichstag. Here it might also be mentioned that the importance of the new German state in non-Prussian territories (in Württemberg, for example, to say nothing of Bavaria) was also not a given in the imperial period. Rather, as many historians have explored, the forging of a German nation to match the German state was an ongoing project that lasted at least up until 1914.[11] This fact does not make Germany atypical. Rather, a brief examination of the English in Scotland, Wales, and Ireland, the French in the Pyrenees or Brittany, or the Italians in the *Mezzogiorno* reveals that no nation-state was truly the homogenous realm that nationalists may have dreamed of.[12] However, the degree of heterogeneity and indeterminacy within the German Empire, especially in its eastern borderlands, may have brought it closer to the Austro-Hungarian or Russian empires than many Germans of the time or historians today would like to admit.

In the past, comparisons between the histories of Russia/the Soviet Union and Germany have focused primarily on their respective mid-twentieth-century dictatorships.[13] The *Historikerstreit* of the 1980s focused attention on the supposed causal links between the Soviet Gulag and the Nazi death camp.[14] Over the past decade and a half, historians have paid an increasing amount of attention to Germany's imperial goals in the East. Vejas Liulevicius's *War Land on the Eastern Front* demonstrates the distinctive nature of Germany's Eastern Front during the First World War, an arena that featured open spaces and German conquest in contrast to the stalemate and cramped quarters on the Western Front.[15] Historians have also investigated the Second World War and a lively debate has ensued about the degree to which the Nazis' goals and conduct can be seen as related to either Germany's earlier colonial history or its past aims and practices in Eastern Europe.[16] It is no surprise that this debate has been cast as a kind of *Sonderweg* redux by more than one historian; quite often the terms "colonial" and "modern" are closely—albeit complicatedly—related. More recently, historians have begun to consider the entangled nature of Russian and German history, especially during the tumultuous period between the world wars.[17]

Rather than relitigating the debate about whether or not Germany had a colonial relationship with its Eastern European "other," questioning whether Germany's relationship to the East was reinvented in the twentieth century or built upon longer term antecedents, or comparing Russian and German dictatorships, this essay examines the history of Imperial Germany through the categories of Russian imperial historiography. In other words, I ask what happens when we think of Germany as an Eastern European rather than Western European empire. While work on the German Empire generally focuses on modernity as a series of Foucauldian projects of discipline, order, and categorization, Russian historiography paints a substantially different picture, one marked primarily by disorder and failure. Taking work on the Russian Empire seriously as it might pertain to German experiences unsettles the explicit and implicit Foucauldian assumptions about the German path to modernity, forcing us to consider indeterminacy, chaos, and weakness as emotive and experiential components of German modernity.

The ambiguities of Russification and Germanization

The Russification literature offers an interesting vantage point to reconsider both German policies toward its frontier minorities and the constitution of the empire as a whole. Binary divides are often central to any imperial project; after all, without the ability to distinguish between "self" and "other," the rationale for empire becomes difficult to sustain. Historians of empire often remind us of the constantly shifting and contradictory categories of difference used by imperialists trying to distinguish between even such seemingly dissimilar populations as Europeans and Africans. Drawing a dividing line between self and other is even more difficult in the mixed and fluid populations that lived in the East Central European space occupied by both the German and Russian empires. Deciding who was Russian, who was Belorussian, and who was Polish was a difficult and often doomed enterprise. Similarly, German nationalists often despaired when confronted with groups like the Silesians, who spoke a Germano-Polish dialect that would eventually place them at the crossroads of the nationalist conflict between those two groups. Considering how Russian historians look at such heterogeneity and the Russian Empire's attempts to control it may, therefore, have a lot to offer German historians.

The nationalities policies of the Czars became a subject of academic study comparatively late.[18] However, with the lifting of both taboos and archival restrictions that accompanied the end of the USSR in the 1990s, historians of Russia and of the newly independent republics began to explore this subject. While no single "Russification" policy as such existed and while a Western idea of nationalism had a hard time penetrating an empire dominated by a multiethnic imperial elite, it is still clear that the Russian Empire promoted the Russian language, Orthodox religion, and the Czarist state, especially in the late nineteenth and early twentieth centuries. As the somewhat tortured syntax of the previous sentence indicates, for Russian historians, Russification is not a given but rather is a problematic notion that is a jumping off point for historical debate. In Russia's western borderlands, more specifically, Andreas Kappeler identifies three schools of thought with regard to Russification: (1) Polish historians who see Russian activities after 1830 as clear evidence of Russification; (2) historians of other nationalities in the region (such as Lithuanians or Ukrainians) who see these activities as de-Polonization, which had the ambiguous legacy of often allowing for their own national development; (3) Russian historians who emphasize the conflicted and uneven nature of attempts at Russification in the region.[19] Today, the history of the Russian imperial project has become one of the most robust fields in modern Russian historiography.[20]

Up until the middle of the nineteenth century, in its northwest borderlands, the Russian Czars generally ruled through local elites and paid little attention to the language, religion, or cultural habits of their subjects, believing that loyalty to the Czar trumped all else.[21] However, this policy began to change in Poland after the 1830–31 uprising, when the Russians closed the Polish University of Vilna, secularized church lands, and banned the study of the Polish language. After a period of liberalization, the height of the Russification policy in the region is often dated to the period 1863–68 in the aftermath of the January uprising.[22] Even during the period of high Russification, Russian officials aimed to defang Polish nationalists, but were less concerned with the language and practices of the peasantry.[23] Furthermore, while Poles may have thought of themselves as nationalists, Russian officials often did not ascribe nationalist motives to their rebellious activity; instead, policymakers saw the Pole as "an ideological subversive and religious 'fanatic,' a product of the social degeneration of the aristocracy, or even a victim of abnormally great female influence on politics."[24] Given that they did not necessarily recognize their opponents in national terms, it is not surprising that their reaction itself did not conform to what we traditionally think of as nationalist. Moreover, since the Polish rebellions followed hard on the heels of the emancipation of the peasantry in 1861, it is also unsurprising that this colored the actions of Russian officials, some of whom believed that their anti-Polish measures were a means of liberating the peasantry from Polish domination.[25]

Religion was central to Russification in the late nineteenth century. Becoming Russian was often literally a matter of conversion. In many cases, converts to Orthodoxy received privileges reserved for Russians regardless of what language they spoke.[26] Although, even here, Russian policy was not so clear-cut, as some efforts were made to hold Catholic services in Russian.[27] Some historians have argued that these Russian Catholic services aimed to separate Catholic and Polish identity, thus echoing "a modern ethnic and linguistic definition of nationality."[28] But nonetheless, the very fact that the medium for the communication of Russian identity was a *church* service makes it at least somewhat distinct from the secular nationalisms that dominated Western Europe, which arose out of a liberal distrust of the church and its accompanying superstition. The Russian Empire was, instead, an empire that classed its subjects according to religion, and famously the 1897 census had no category for "atheist." Religion was crucial to the Russian state and thus to Russification.

The second pillar of Russification policies was language. However, in the multilingual world of the Russian western borderlands, measuring linguistic assimilation was, at best, difficult and often misleading.[29] Furthermore, language was itself a fraught category and one inseparable from religion. Mikhail Katkov said in the context of the attempts to create a Russian Catholic service: "A Pole is not a person who loves or can speak Polish. Otherwise, we would have to call many Russians Frenchmen because they speak French more than they speak Russian. The essence of the question is not who usually speaks what language, but what language serves as the necessary organ in matters of religion."[30] Speaking to the peculiar (to Western European eyes) relationship between the state and religion, for Katkov it was only the liturgical language that counted.[31] During the height of the early "Russification" period, that is, 1863–68, the Polish language was banned, but was required to be written in Cyrillic rather than Western letters (and as such was even encouraged). This policy can be seen in two ways: on the one hand, as a method of Russifying the Lithuanians, but also as a means of diminishing Polish influence and thus safeguarding a measure of Lithuanian autonomy.[32] Clearly, as this example reveals, "Russification" is more complicated than any simple label suggests. An ever-present theme of Russian historiography is the complex, contradictory, and unintended objects and consequences of Russian imperial policy. Indeed, as often as not, confusion and ambivalence characterized the motives, implementation, and results of just about everything attempted by Russian officials in this arena. Nonetheless, as Western ideas of nationalism began to penetrate Russia and as, in particular, Russians came into conflict with more nationalist subject populations, more Western categories of ethnicity began to accompany, if not necessarily supplant, the older distinctions based on religion or language.[33]

Furthermore, unlike their ambiguous behavior in the northwest, Russians used more clearly racist language to describe their subjects in the Caucasus from a much earlier date.[34] Michael Khordokovsky notes descriptions of Caucasians from the mid-sixteenth century onward that depict them as savage brutes, vastly inferior to their civilized Russian overlords. According to Khordokovsky, the Caucasians consistently provided "a gauge against which they judged their rising power, their identity as conquerors, and increasingly, their 'civilization.'"[35] That said, others have argued that a full-fledged orientalist discourse of the Caucasus only emerged in the mid-nineteenth century.[36] During the 1860s (in other words, at the same time as the height of the Russification policies in the northwest), Russian authorities carried out a brutal policy of resettlement and exile targeted at rebellious Caucasians, matching orientalist language with imperialist practice.[37] Even in the Caucasus, however, it was never obvious that the Russian Empire was interested in simultaneously being a Russian nation, or that nationalism was the primary identity of Russia's colonizers. Indeed, Christianity and "European civilization" were more important to the self-identity of Russians in the Caucasus than was Russian nationality per se.[38]

At first glance, there are several features of Russian nationalities policies that should not be so foreign to the Germanist. After all, if the Russian language and the Orthodox religion were crucial to Russification, what about *hochdeutsch* and Lutheranism? As Russian officials denied the separateness of the Ukrainians, so too did German (i.e., Prussian) bureaucrats deny that of the Bavarians. What was the *Kulturkampf* if not an imperial project of radical assimilation?[39] Nevertheless, there are some notable differences in the historiography, particularly in the role accorded to nationalism as imperial policy. While Germanists tend to assume nationalism as a motivating factor, Russian historians are much more cautious in their ascription of nationalism to either ordinary people or the state.

One key distinction between the Russian and German empires was the degree to which the ordinary population was schooled in nationalist polemics. By the time of the First World War, residents of the German Empire had learned to speak the language of nationalism. In nationally mixed areas such as Silesia this often led to confusion, but nevertheless people had some idea of what nationalism was and what it meant to be a national subject.[40] As Vejas Liulevicius reminds us, this was not necessarily the case in the territories under Czarist control. In *War Land on the Eastern Front*, he describes the confusion a German soldier felt when confronted with a Schmidt, who was a Catholic and Polish nationalist, a Kowalski, who was an Orthodox Russian, and a Kusnjetzow, who spoke German and worshipped in a Lutheran church. He was even more confused to find out that they were all related.[41] This is not to say that Russian officials were comfortable with the cultural, religious, and national ambiguity of its northwestern hinterlands (or elsewhere). Running throughout Czarist documents of the period is the search for a guiding principle to lead them out of this morass. The difference was that while Germans may have (at least for the most part) found this principle—that is, nationalism—the triumph of a nationalist viewpoint in either official policy or popular self-conception was far from clear in the Russian case.[42]

In the late nineteenth century, German nationalists debated whether German identity was an innate characteristic or something potentially acquirable through assimilation.[43] The Pan-Germans articulated an increasingly racialized sense of German identity that ultimately found its way into the German Citizenship Law of 1913.[44] But at the same time, the Eastern Marches Association used language as the primary marker of German identity, accepting Jews as members of the German community.[45] German policy in its Polish borderlands embodied these differences as contradictions. On the one hand, punitive education policies assumed that Polish children educated in German schools would become German. On the other hand, the aggressive promotion of German settlement in Posen and Westpreussen rested on the assumption that the national struggle in the region was a numbers game and that the Poles would not be easily converted (if at all) to Germandom.

Russian imperial practice may have had its own contradictions, but this was not one of them. Rather, Russification was a policy of assimilation. Whether this assimilation was to be cultural, linguistic, or religious was an open question, but western ideas of race found little expression in Russian policies toward its western borderlands or even in the Caucasus.[46] The Russians' apparent lack of interest in a racial approach to its nationalities question provides a fresh perspective on the complicated role race played in German conceptions of various "selves" and "others." At times race appears as a given—in dealing with Africans, for example—at times as a controversial category—with respect to the Poles—and at times, hardly invoked at all—when looking at Thuringians versus Swabians, for instance. Why and when was race perceived as a useful category of analysis?

Ironically, the very ambivalence of Russians (and Russianists) toward nationalism offers a necessary corrective to what is too often a Pollyannaish view of cosmopolitanism among German historians. Among Germanists, the word "transnational" or "cosmopolitan" can sometimes be used to celebrate the porousness and irrelevance of the nation.[47] But as the Russification literature makes clear, even though they were on some level transnational, the policies pursued in the name of religious or linguistic homogeneity could be just as damaging as those pursued in the name of nation. Furthermore, while the Russian state was more than willing to encourage immigration, this "attract and hold" policy derived from the state's sheer vastness and perceived emptiness was fully compatible with the state's autocratic population policies.[48] When Germans choose to see a group as assimiliable rather than irredeemably racially other, this may be seen as a sign of tolerance. But considering the violence that lay behind the Russians' attempts to assimilate its subject peoples, it is far from clear that assimilation should always be viewed in such a benign light. Eschewing exclusionary nationalism is not the equivalence of tolerance.[49]

Furthermore, many regions of Eastern and Central Europe did not fit easily into the maps of nationalists (as was discovered over and over again, most notably in 1848 and 1919), and even the homogenizers themselves were often of dubious, or at least complex, backgrounds. After all, one of the leaders of a "Russification" campaign in the northwest provinces had the last name "Kaufmann."[50] Western fantasies of a homogenous national space did not even necessarily fit the identities or self-conceptions of even so-called Russian nationalists. It is also not altogether clear that homogeneity was necessarily the goal so much as (in the case of the northwestern territories at least) suppressing political rebellion. I wonder if we might learn from Russian historians to look for the same diversity of motives in our appreciation of German "nationalists." Perhaps German historians impute or assume nationalist motives in cases when the actual discourses were often much more multivalent.

German historians tend to assume that unity in German history means *national* unity while laying a claim to being "German" is to evince a cultural identity.[51] In a 2004 review article, Nancy Reagin wrote:

> In recent historiography, Germanness indeed consists of almost an overabundance of influences or foci for loyalty or identity: the regional state; the *Heimat*; particular dynastic figures; confession; class identities and structures; tribal identity; gender; mythic history, as symbolized by such figures as Arminius; Germans as the "people of music" or culture; and the patriotic public sphere.[52]

It is striking that the German national state does not appear in this list (even as the regional state does). But was every Bismarck Turm necessarily a sign of devotion to the German nation or was it instead (or additionally) a sign of devotion to the imperial state?[53] A distinction between national and imperial sentiments was common in a Russia in which the imperial project was taken more seriously than the national one, and I wonder if there might be any way of thinking about this in a German context in which both the contemporary discourse and the historiography has been more infused by the rhetoric of nationality. As the *Kaiserreich* moved toward its end in 1918, there may have been less and less of a place for an articulation of the German state as anything other than a nation-state. But even the 1913 citizenship law included a provision by which fighting in the German army was a path toward German citizenship (Article 8), and the debates leading up to the law included many expressions of a statist perspective that didn't find its way into the final version of the law.[54] Nationalism in a multinational Germany was not the cultural accompaniment of the political structures of the Reich; similarly, the German state did not function merely as the political expression of nationalist sentiment. Have we privileged the nation at the expense of taking the state seriously as a (dis)unifying force and a focus for identity in its own right? Did state actors feel they were acting on behalf of Germany or in the interests of Germans? There was an ambiguity in the relationship between state and nation that is all too often forgotten when Germanists study nationalist discourse.

This last point finally brings us back to the Poles. In the story of Russification, the Poles play a crucial role as a highly nationalized people whose political rebellions act to spur on Russification. It was through the Polish mirror that Russians to some degree figured out what it meant to be Russian. The Poles played a similar role in nineteenth-century Germany, both before and after German unification.[55] Furthermore, as German, Austrian, or Russian subjects, Polish loyalties to each of their imperial masters were complex. The Poles, then, provide an interesting test case for thinking about the disjuncture between state and nation (and of state patriotism and nationalism) during this period.[56] Poland was the site of aggressive Germanization policies from the 1886 *Ansiedlungskommission* onwards. At the same time, it was also in Poland that the anti-Polish *Ostmarkenverein* largely accepted Jews.[57] Anti-Polish beliefs and activities may have been a constant in the East, but what this meant for evolving notions of the German state and/or nation remained ambiguous. This ambivalence was far from benign. Rather, when viewed in their *longue durée*, the Polish lands were a site of continual violence (interspersed with comparatively brief periods of calm) from the early modern period up through the 1940s. This was a highly instable area, one in which identities may have been fluid, but state borders were set, repeatedly and provisionally, by force of arms.[58] The violent experience of Germany's frontiers is the second point at which German historians may have something to learn from their Russian counterparts.

Chaotic violence

For a historian of Western or Central Europe, the history of Russia appears as one of excess. The spaces are vast; the personalities are grand; the alcohol prodigious; the poverty extreme; the violence unimaginable. From the "Time of Troubles" in the sixteenth century to the revolutions and world wars of the twentieth century, the scale and chaos of violence in Russia is daunting, to the say the least. There are recurring periods in which violence literally *was* the substance of politics in Russia, and not merely a means of carrying out political decisions made elsewhere and by cooler heads.[59] With certain major exceptions (the Thirty Years' War, the Second World War), this seems to dwarf the chaos and violence of the German lands. But I'm not sure this means Germanists don't have something to learn from it. German historians are much more comfortable talking about coercive violence than they are about chaotic violence. For example, they remain less attuned than they should be to the chaotic nature of the violence of the Eastern Front in the First World War. Liulevicius is persuasive that German military authorities viewed Ober Ost as potential colonial territory and that their experiences and activities there were quite different from what happened in the trenches of Belgium and France. Yet even Liulevicius's book is more interested in the steps that German officials took to combat chaos than in their encounter with and contribution to that chaos itself. For Liulevicius, as for German historians more generally, violence is usually analyzed as a tool of policy. If we look at the First World War from the perspective of the disintegrating Russian Empire, we see a very different story.

Peter Gatrell writes about the immense refugee problem in the Russia of the First World War. He concludes by looking at how the chaos of the First World War allowed for the development of national organizations and a national identity among refugees. Yet, while the bulk of Liulevicius's book is devoted to the management of disorder, in Gatrell's book, such management was usually tentative, often counterproductive, and always dwarfed by the disorder it was intended to manage.[60] Also examining migrants, but this time looking at both civilian and military population movements, Joshua Sanborn argues that it is important to "[treat] the Russian battle zones of World War I as a social and temporal space of 'violent migrations,'" maintaining that these "violent migrations progressively unsettled the Russian Empire."[61] For Sanborn, the political importance of violence lies in its disintegrative rather than coercive force. The state was not capable of managing these violent migrations, but rather is depicted as a contributory actor toward their horror.[62] Along these lines, Peter Holquist argues that chaotic violence marks a continuum linking Russian and Soviet history across the revolutionary divide.[63] Historians of violence in late imperial Russia have noted that violence often began in the frontier regions, and that these borderlands functioned as harbingers of the convulsions that were to come for the empire as a whole. Both rebellion and its repression in the frontiers taught lessons that would then be applied when revolution came to Mother Russia itself.[64] This might provide an interesting twist on both the Arendt theory of colonial anticipation of totalitarianism and the postcolonial theory in which the colonies serve as laboratories for the metropole. Here, rather than totalitarian order being what is previewed, it is disorder.

Violence not only marked a temporal continuum but a spatial one as well. The battle lines of the Eastern Front of the First World War were almost all located in what Timothy Snyder has termed the "Bloodlands," or as Sanborn describes, the "colonized spaces of Eastern Europe, in places where the population felt itself under the domination of a foreign power. Indeed, Eastern Front battlefield tourists today need hardly bother with visas to Russia, Austria, Hungary, or Germany. Those sites now lie mainly in Poland, Ukraine, Belarus, Lithuania, Latvia…"[65] On the one hand, the colonial nature of the eastern war contributed to the suspicion military officials harbored toward civilian populations.[66] But it also contributed to the sense of this as an arena of utopian possibility.[67] For all of the major combatants, but perhaps especially for the Germans who knew the least about the region, the areas of conflict and conquest were a once and future colonial space in which utopia, chaos, and violence were inextricably intertwined. David Bell has argued that total war evolved as a counterpart to the Enlightenment drive for perfection: the only thing that justified total war was that it might create a world of everlasting peace.[68] Bell is surely not the first person to note the intimate connection of violence and utopia. Germanists, used to looking at Nazism and Communism, tend to associate utopianism (and, for that matter, violence) with control.

I wonder, however, if we might benefit from thinking more about the relationship between violence, utopia, and chaos, particularly in Germany's imperial holdings, be they in Poland or Africa, and especially during the crucible of war. In my own work, I have seen how the failure to control population mobility during Germany's First World War military occupation encouraged the growth of utopian expectations for a future when such ventures would be manageable. Similarly, the Freikorps' failed paramilitary campaign in the war's aftermath led to a radicalization of its veterans in terms of both their plans for the future and their violence in the present. In both cases, failure, violence, and utopianism became inseparable.[69]

Failure

As these examples suggest, thinking about chaos doesn't merely mean thinking about utopias. It also means thinking seriously about failure. Nazism still casts a certain shadow over the study of German history, so much so that German historians still more often see Imperial Germany as too strong rather than too weak. For the remaining defenders of a *Sonderweg* perspective, in particular, Germany's crises almost always resulted in a more authoritarian state and society.[70] Anti-*Sonderweg* historians offer as a counterargument to Wehler et al., a picture of a robust and rapidly maturing German public sphere and the relative health of democracy within the *Kaiserreich*. Today, historians of Imperial Germany often ignore the imperial state altogether; in part, this is both a cause and result of the emphasis on the nation discussed above.[71] However much historians may continue to disagree about whether Germany was on an increasingly authoritarian or an increasingly democratic path (and however much it may have been riven by divisions or crises), an almost unspoken assumption on the part of Wilhelmine historians is of its strength. It is for this reason that Foucault has found such purchase among German historians looking for a way to theorize discipline and the projection of governmental power. By contrast, the lodestar of Russian history remains the Russian Revolutions of 1917, and the historiography of the decades leading up to those epochal events is one that is preoccupied with weakness. The Russian state may have been autocratic, but it was also incompetent.[72] Russian historians are unsparing regarding the failures of would-be Russifiers. See, for example, Dolbilov's scathing conclusions:

> Examined as part of a bureaucratic routine and as links in a complex chain of decision-making, the principal Russification projects turn out to have been poorly coordinated and devoid of a clear sense of pragmatic logic. They resulted from an abnormal fixation on a single, arbitrarily and fancifully (and sometimes *accidentally*) chosen aspect of Russian identity; this could be the alphabet, the language of church sermons, or even matters of bureaucratic discipline and subordination. The choice of this or that criterion was, to a high degree, subject to the bureaucracy's concern about the symbolic representation of the ruled as a homogeneous,

loyal, static mass. As a result, the Russifiers applied to the Northwestern region an esoteric and shifting notion of Russianness, while its ethnic dimension remained obscure, as it had been under Nicholas I's doctrine of Official Nationality.[73]

One would be hard put to find German historians equally willing to say the same about the German state before the First World War.[74] But why not? If you are looking for it, you can find a *Kaiserreich* that is riddled with failures. Even if Germans were clearer than Russians about the importance of the nation as the central category for understanding belonging, they still vacillated between attempts at assimilation and strategies of repression and/or expulsion. Their goals aside, many of these policies still failed. The *Kulturkampf* did not work, unless its hidden goal was to encourage the formation of a Catholic social and cultural bloc.[75] Germany's policies toward its Polish minority could hardly be categorized as a success.[76] In both cases, these policies largely succeeded merely in rousing the ire of the suppressed population. The German Empire abroad was arguably a failure too. Economically, it remained a drain on German resources until its ignominious end after the First World War. Geopolitically, it never challenged the preeminence of the British or the French. It never even fulfilled the more modest dreams of German nationalists who hoped that it would act to attract potential emigrants away from other overseas destinations. If we take Fritz Fischer's conclusions seriously, the failure of Germany overseas may have been the greatest legacy of empire— leading the Wilhelmine state's leadership to look to fulfill imperial goals on the continent and thus, ultimately, to the First World War.[77] Beyond the weakness of specific projects, it may be useful to think about how these failures impacted our larger-scale narratives of the *Kaiserreich* and, particularly, the role that failures and the humiliations, fears, and opportunities that accompanied them played even before 1918, as doing so may help German historians to ask different questions. Germany, like Russia, ruled over a multinational empire. Germany, like Russia, experienced a revolution at the end of the First World War, a war that both of them lost. There is perhaps much to be gained by comparing their respective histories of empire and its loss.

For Russian historians of the late nineteenth and early twentieth centuries, modernity means chaos, uncertainty, and failure—terms that find little place in the historiography of the *Kaiserreich*. However, this essay has sought to demonstrate that reading German history from the perspective of these categories can be a useful exercise highlighting the uncertainties, failures, and ambiguities that marked both German modernity and that of the behemoth to its East. Just as the comparison with Western Europe opened up a fruitful debate about the nature of Germany's path into the modern world, so, too, the comparison with the Russian Empire can illuminate different, but no less constitutive, elements of this journey.

Notes

1 The number of books that make this argument are legion, but see, for example, Gwendolyn Wright, *The Politics of Design in French Colonial Urbanism* (Chicago: University of Chicago Press, 1991); Paul Rabinow, *French Modern: Norms and Forms of the Social Environment* (Berkeley: University of California Press, 1989); Timothy Mitchell, *Colonizing Egypt* (Berkeley: University of California Press, 1991); Nicholas Dirks, *Colonialism and Culture* (Ann Arbor: University of Michigan Press, 1991); Ann Laura Stoler, *Race and the Education of Desire: Foucault's History of Sexuality and the Colonial Order of Things* (Durham: Duke University Press, 1995); Frederick Cooper, *Tensions of Empire: Colonial Cultures in a Bourgeois World* (Berkeley: University of California Press, 1997).

2 Dipesh Chakrabarty, *Provincializing Europe* (Princeton: Princeton University Press, 2000). More recently, see Frederick Cooper's articulation of similar arguments in *Colonialism in Question: Theory, Knowledge and Practice* (Berkeley: University of California Press, 2005).

3 George Steinmetz, *The Devil's Handwriting: Precoloniality and the German Colonial State in Qingdao, Samoa, and Southwest Africa* (Chicago: University of Chicago Press, 2007); Andrew Zimmerman, *Alabama in Africa: Booker T. Washington, the German Empire, and the Globalization of the New South* (Princeton: Princeton University Press, 2010); Sebastian Conrad, *Globalisierung und Nation im deutschen Kaiserreich* (Munich: CH Beck, 2006).

4 It is noteworthy that Wehler only talks about the colonies in the context of social imperialism, that is, as a distraction from the "real" politics in the metropole. Recently historians such as Dennis Sweeney and Bradley Naranch have begun to revisit the questions from the social imperialism debates in the context of new literature on transnationalism. In another context, Isabel Hull has used the "laboratory of modernity" argument to examine the relationship between violence in the colonies and the metropole and in doing so has reopened questions of the *Sonderweg* debate from a different perspective. Isabel Hull, *Absolute Destruction: Military Culture and the Practices of War in Imperial Germany* (Ithaca: Cornell University Press, 2006).

5 Conrad connects the development of a German idea of the nation to the simultaneous encounters with Polish labor migrations and labor in the colonies. Conrad, *Globalisierung und Nation im deutschen Kaiserreich*. See also Kristin Kopp's work on the importation of German colonial narratives and tropes to understand the German relationship with Poland. Kristin Kopp, *Germany's Wild East: Constructing Poland as Colonial Space* (Ann Arbor: University of Michigan Press, 2012).

6 See, for example, Heinrich August Winkler, *Der lange Weg nach Western*, 2 vols (Munich: Beck, 2000).

7 Sara Lennox and Susanne Zantop (eds.), *The Imperialist Imagination: German Colonialism and Its Legacy* (Ann Arbor: University of Michigan Press, 1998); Lora Wildenthal, *German Women for Empire, 1884–1945* (Durham: Duke University Press, 2001); Eric Ames, Lora Wildenthal, and Marcia Klotz, *Germany's Colonial Pasts* (Lincoln: University of Nebraska Press, 2005);

Sandra Maß, *Weisse Helden, Schwarze Krieger: Zur Geschichte kolonialer Männlichkeit in Deutschland, 1918–1964* (Cologne: Böhlau, 2006); David Ciarlo, *Advertising Empire: Race and Visual Culture in Imperial Germany* (Cambridge: Harvard University Press, 2011).

8   Tina Campt, *Other Germans: Black Germans and the Politics of Race, Gender, and Memory in the Third Reich* (Ann Arbor: University of Michigan Press, 2004) and *Image Matters: Archive, Photography, and the African Diaspora in Europe* (Durham: Duke University Press, 2012); Clarence Lusane, *Hitler's Black Victims: The Historical Experiences of Afro-Germans, European Blacks, Africans, and African Americans in the Nazi Era* (New York: Routledge, 2002); Heide Fehrenbach, *Race after Hitler: Black Occupation Children in Postwar Germany and America* (Princeton: Princeton University Press, 2005); Eve Rosenhaft and Robbie Aitkin, *Black Germany: The Making and Unmaking of a Diaspora Community, 1886–1960* (New York: Cambridge University Press, 2013).

9   David Blackbourn, "Das Kaiserreich transnational. Eine Skizze," in Sebastian Conrad and Jürgen Osterhammel (eds.), *Das Kaiserreich transnational. Deutschland in der Welt, 1871–1914* (Göttingen: Vandenhoeck & Ruprecht, 2004), p. 322.

10 Philipp Ther, "Beyond the Nation: The Relational Basis of a Comparative History of Germany and Europe," *Central European History* 31:1 (Spring 2003), p. 53. Ther uses this fact to then argue that Germany, Russia, and Austria-Hungary's shared suspicion of democracy stemmed from their fears about their national minorities. Ther, p. 54.

11 On the diversity of Imperial Germany, see Dieter Langewiesche, "Föderative Nationalismus als Erbe der deutsche Reichsnation: Über Föderalismus und Zentralismus in der Deutschen Nationalgeschichte," in Dieter Langewische and Georg Schmidt (eds.), *Föderative Nation: Deutschlandkonzepte von der Reformation bis zum ersten Weltkrieg* (Munich: CH Beck, 2000), pp. 215–44. On the relationship between the regions and the state, see Celia Applegate, *A Nation of Provincials: The German Idea of Heimat* (Berkeley: University of California Press, 1990); Alon Confino, *The Nation as Local Metaphor: Württemberg, Imperial Germany, and National Memory, 1871–1918* (Chapel Hill: University of North Carolina Press, 1997); Jennifer L. Jenkins, *Provincial Modernity: Local Culture and Liberal Politics in fin-de-siècle Hamburg* (Ithaca: Cornell University Press, 2003); Abigail Green, *Fatherlands: State Building and Nationhood in Nineteenth-Century Germany* (Cambridge: Cambridge University Press, 2001).

12 On the blurriness of national identity between Catalan, Spanish, and French in the Pyrenees, see Peter Sahlins, *Boundaries: The Making of France and Spain in the Pyrenees* (Berkeley: University of California Press, 1991). On creating a modern nation in Britain, see Linda Colley, *Britons: Forging the Nation, 1707–1837* (New Haven: Yale University Press, 1992). On the *Mezzogiorno*, Nelson Moe, *The View from Vesuvius: Italian Culture and the Southern Question* (Berkeley: University of California Press, 2002).

13 On the balance of the study of totalitarianism in the twentieth century, see Eckhard Jesse (ed.), *Totalitarismus im 20. Jahrhundert* (Bonn: Bundeszentrale

für politische Forschung, 1996). For recent attempts to come to terms with totalitarianism as an organizing concept, see Ian Kershaw and Moshe Lewin (eds.), *Stalinism and Nazism: Dictatorships in Comparison* (Cambridge: Cambridge University Press, 1997); Michael Geyer and Sheila Fitzpatrick (eds.), *Beyond Totalitarianism: Stalinism and Nazism Compared* (New York: Cambridge University Press, 2009).

14 For a good overview, see Peter Baldwin (ed.), *Reworking the Past: Hitler, the Holocaust and the Historians Debate* (Boston: Beacon Press, 1990) and Charles Maier, *The Unmasterable Past: History, the Holocaust and German National Identity* (New York: Cambridge University Press, 1988). The comparative history of Russia and Germany prior to the First World War has received considerably less attention. Lew Kopelew and Gerd Koenen's project on German-Russian interactions provides a noteworthy exception that examines the *longue durée* of Russo-German interactions and images. *West-östliche Spiegelungen: Russen und Russland aus deutscher Sicht und Deutsche und Deutschland aus russischer Sicht. Von den Anfängen bis zum 20. Jahrhundert*, Series A: 5 vols, Series B: 4 vols, New Series: 2 vols (Munich: Wilhelm Fink, 1992–2006).

15 Vejas Liulevicius, *War Land on the Eastern Front: Culture, National Identity, and German Occupation in World War I* (New York: Cambridge University Press, 2001).

16 Matthew Fitzpatrick, "The Prehistory of the Holocaust? The Sonderweg and Historikorstreit and the Abject Colonial Past," *German History* 41:3 (2008), pp. 477–503; Benjamin Madley, "From Africa to Auschwitz: How German South West Africa Incubated Ideas and Methods Adopted and Developed by the Nazis in Eastern Europe," *European History Quarterly* 35:3 (2005), pp. 429–64; Jürgen Zimmerer, "The Best of the Ostland out of the Spirit of Colonialism: A Postcolonial Perspective on the Nazi Policy of Conquest and Extermination," *Patterns of Prejudice* 39:2 (2005), pp. 192–219; Mark Mazower, *Hitler's Empire: How the Nazis Rules Europe* (Penguin: New York, 2009); Shelley Baranowski, *Nazi Empire: German Colonialism and Imperialism from Bismarck to Hitler* (New York: Cambridge University Press, 2010); Vejas Liulevicius, *The German Myth of the East: 1800 to the Present* (New York: Oxford University Press, 2011); Winson Chu, Jesse Kauffman, and Michael Meng, "A Sonderweg through Eastern Europe? The Varieties of German Rule in Poland during the Two World Wars," *German History* 31:3 (2013), pp. 318–44; Kopp, *Germany's Wild East*.

17 The literature here is generally of high quality but too numerous to mention. A 2009 special issue of *Kritika* on entangled Russian and German history is a model here: *Kritika* 10:3 (2009). See also Timothy Snyder, *Bloodlands: Europe between Hitler and Stalin* (New York: Basic Books, 2010); Susan Solomon, *Doing Medicine Together: Germany and Russian between the Wars* (Toronto: University of Toronto Press, 2006). See also Gerd Koenen, *Der Russland-Komplex: die Deutschen und der Osten, 1900–1945* (Munich: Beck, 2005). Karl Schlögel, *Ostbahnhof Berlin: Russen und Deutsche in ihrem Jahrhundert* (Munich: Beck, 1998) and *Die mitte liegt ostwärts* (Munich: Beck, 1998), Michel David-Fox's work on Western visitors to the Soviet Union is yet another excellent example of *histoire croisée*. Michael David-Fox, *Showcasing*

the Great Experiment: Cultural Diplomacy and Western Visitors to the Soviet Union, 1921–1941 (New York: Oxford University Press, 2012).

18   For some of the earliest works on Russification, see Edward C. Thaden, *Russia's Western Borderlands, 1710–1870*, with the collaboration of Marianna Forster Thaden (Princeton: Princeton University Press, 1984); Edward C. Thaden (ed.), *Russification in the Baltic Provinces and Finland, 1855–1914* (Princeton: Princeton University Press, 1981).

19   Andreas Kappeler, "The Ambiguities of Russification," *Kritika* 5:2 (Spring 2004), p. 296.

20   Andreas Kappeler, *Russland als Vielvölkerreich: Entstehung, Geschichte, Zerfall* (Munich: Beck, 1992), published in English as *The Russian Empire: A Multiethnic History*, trans. Alfred Clayton (Harlow: Longman, 2001), marks the beginning of the "imperial turn" in Russian historiography. But see also Theodore R. Weeks, *Nation and State in Late Imperial Russia: Nationalism and Russification on the Western Frontier, 1863–1914* (De Kalb: Northern Illinois University Press, 1996); Witold Rodkiewicz, *Russian Nationality Policy in the Western Provinces of the Empire (1863–1905)* (Lublin: Scientific Society of Lublin, 1998); Daniel R. Brower and Edward J. Lazzerini (eds.), *Russia's Orient: Imperial Borderlands and Peoples, 1700–1917* (Bloomington: Indiana University Press, 1997); Jane Burbank and David Ransel (eds.), *Imperial Russia: New Histories for the Empire* (Bloomington: Indiana University Press, 1998); Robert P. Geraci, *Window on the East: National and Imperial Identity in Late Tsarist Russia* (Ithaca: Cornell University Press, 2001); Robert P. Geraci and Michael Khodarkovsky (eds.), *Of Religion and Empire: Missions, Conversion, and Tolerance in Tsarist Russia* (Ithaca: Cornell University Press, 2001). G.M. Hamburg, "Imperial Entanglements: Two New Histories of Russia's Western and Southern Borderlands," *Kritika* 9:2 (Spring 2009), pp. 407–31, offers a useful chronology of the scholarly attention to the Russian borderlands among historians from the former USSR as well as the West.

21   It is important to make a distinction between Russian policy toward Byelorussians and Ukrainians and that toward other ethnic groups. Russian officials denied the separateness of Byelorussians and Ukrainians, and as a result policy toward them was substantially different than policy toward recognizably separate national groups such as the Poles or Baltic nationalities. Theodore Weeks, "'Us' or 'Them'? Belarusians and Official Russia, 1863–1914," *Nationalities Papers* 31:2 (June 2003), pp. 211–24. See Kappeler and Thaden on the first half of the nineteenth century. The ultimate example of this co-option of native elites might be the Baltic Germans, who were so ensconced in the higher ranks of the "Russian" establishment that there was a telling but apocryphal story of a Russian general whose greatest aspiration was to be promoted to the rank of "German." Robert C. Williams, *Culture in Exile: Russian Émigrés in Germany, 1881–1941* (Ithaca: Cornell University Press, 1972), p. 12.

22   Darius Staliunas, "Did the Government Seek to Russify Lithuanians and Poles in the Northwest Region after the Uprising of 1863–64?" *Kritika* 5:2 (Spring 2004), pp. 276–7.

23   Theodore R. Weeks, "Russification and the Lithuanians, 1863–1905," *Slavic Review* 60:1 (2001), p. 97. This was so much the case that Russian officials used "Pole" only to refer to Catholics who were *not* of the peasant class. Darius Staliunas, "'The Pole' in the Policy of the Russian Government: Semantics and Praxis in the Mid-Nineteenth Century," *Lithuanian Historical Studies* 5 (2000), pp. 45–67.

24   Mikhail Dolbilov, "Russification and the Bureaucratic Mindset in the Russian Empire's Northwest Region in the 1860s," *Kritika* 5:2 (Spring 2004), p. 246.

25   Ibid., p. 247.

26   Ibid., pp. 280–1. This is not to say that converts weren't viewed with suspicion but even those who were suspicious still saw the children of converts, who would be raised in the Orthodox church, as members of the Russian community. Of course, this was the case for Catholics; Jews were regarded as distinct regardless of whether or not they converted.

27   Ibid., pp. 250–8. See also Theodore R. Weeks, "Religion and Russification: Russian Language in the Catholic Churches of the 'Northwest Provinces' after 1863," *Kritika* 2:1 (2001), pp. 87–110.

28   Weeks, "Religion and Russification," p. 104, quoted in Dolbilov, "Russification," p. 250.

29   Kappeler, "The Ambiguities of Russification," p. 293.

30   Katkov quoted in Dolbilov, "Russification," p. 251.

31   Unsurprisingly, Katkov's argument was not universally accepted, and some other Russian officials objected that banning Polish services would still allow the language to flourish in secular settings and thus hardly undermine it. Dolbilov, "Russification," p. 251. Nonetheless, the fact that Katkov could even present such an argument and have it gain some acceptance is pretty remarkable.

32   Staliunas, "Did the Government Seek to Russify Lithuanians and Poles," pp. 284–5. There were also no fewer than ten university scholarships for people bilingual in Russian and Lithuanian.

33   Charles Steinwedel, "To Make a Difference: The Category of Ethnicity in Late Imperial Russian Politics, 1861–1917," in David L. Hoffmann and Yanni Kotsonis (eds.), *Russian Modernity: Politics, Knowledge, Practices* (Houndmills and New York: Macmillan/St. Martin's, 2000), pp. 67–86; and Andreas Kappeler, "Mazepintsy, Malorossy, Khokhly: Ukrainians in the Ethnic Hierarchy of the Russian Empire," in Andreas Kappeler et al. (eds.), *Culture, Nation, and Identity: The Ukrainian–Russian Encounter (1600–1945)* (Edmonton: Canadian Institute of Ukrainian Studies Press, 2003), pp. 162–81.

34   Keziban Acar, "An Examination of Russian Imperialism: Russian Military and Intellectual Descriptions of the Caucasians during the Russo-Turkish War of 1877–1878," *Nationalities Papers* 32:1 (March 2004), pp. 7–21.

35   Jeff Sahadeo, "Conquest, Colonialism, and Nomadism on the Eurasian Steppe," *Kritika* 4:4 (Fall 2003), p. 944.

36   Sara Dickinson, "Russia's First 'Orient': Characterizing the Crimea in 1787," *Kritika* 3:1 (Winter 2002), p. 3.

37   Edward C. Thaden, *Conservative Nationalism in Nineteenth-Century Russia* (Seattle: University of Washington Press, 1964), p. 299.

38   Michael Khordokovsky, *Russia's Steppe Frontier: The Making of a Colonial Empire 1500–1800* (Bloomington: Indiana University Press, 2002). On the importance of European identity in the African colonies, see also Deborah Neill, *Networks in Tropical Medicine: Internationalism, Colonialism and the Rise of a Medical Specialty* (Stanford: Stanford University Press, 2012).

39   For more on the anti-Polish character, in particular, of *Kulturkampf* legislation, see Helmut Walser Smith, *German Nationalism and Religious Conflict: Culture, Ideology, Politics, 1870–1914* (Princeton: Princeton University Press, 1995); Michael Gross, *The War against Catholicism: Liberalism and the Anti-Catholic Imaginary in Nineteenth-Century Germany* (Ann Arbor: University of Michigan Press, 2004); Róisín Healy, *The Jesuit Specter in Imperial Germany* (Boston: Brill, 2003). For a similar treatment in a canonical survey, see Thomas Nipperdey, *Deutsche Geschichte 1866–1918* Bd. 2 (Munich: Beck, 1992), pp. 270–1.

40   James Bjork, "A Polish *Mitteleuropa*: Upper Silesia's Conciliationists and the Prospect of German Victory," *Nationalities Papers* 29:3 (2001), pp. 477–92. See also Caitlin Murdock, *Changing Places: Society, Culture and Territory in the Saxon-Bohemian Borderlands, 1870–1946* (Ann Arbor: University of Michigan Press, 2010).

41   Schmidt, Kowalski, and Kusnjetzow all mean Smith.

42   On the belated development of nationalism in Russia, see the debate "Was the Development of Russian National Identity Merely a Historical Accident?" *Nationalities Papers* 39:1 (January 2011), pp. 135–40.

43   For the contours of this debate among Austrian Germans, see Pieter Judson, "Frontiers, Islands, Forests, Stones: Mapping the Geography of a German Identity in the Habsburg Monarchy, 1848–1900," in Patricia Yeager (ed.), *The Geography of Identity* (Ann Arbor: University of Michigan Press, 1996), pp. 382–406. Judson argues that the success of the Iron Ring coalition at the expense of German liberals in 1879 caused German nationalists to begin to focus on the immutable qualities of German identity (and its immutable German landscape) rather than assimilation.

44   Roger Chickering, *We Men Who Feel Most German: A Cultural Study of the Pan-German League, 1886–1914* (Boston: Allen & Unwin, 1984). For an African perspective on citizenship law and German identity, see Lora Wildenthal, "Race, Gender, and Citizenship in the German Empire," in Ann Stoler and Frederick Cooper (eds.), *Tensions of Empire: Colonial Cultures in a Bourgeois World* (Berkeley: University of California Press, 1997), pp. 263–83. Of course, even if the 1913 citizenship law did rest on a notion of ethnocultural citizenship, the debates leading up to that law witnessed a much more multifaceted set of approaches to understanding German belonging. Dieter Gosewinkel, *Einbürgern und Ausschliessen* (Göttingen: Vandenhoeck & Ruprecht, 2001).

45   Elizabeth Drummond, "On the Borders of the Nation: Jews and the German-Polish National Conflict in Poznania, 1886–1914," *Nationalities Papers* 29:3 (2001), pp. 459–75.

46 Staliunas, "Did the Government Seek to Russify Lithuanians and Poles," pp. 278–9.

47 All too often, transnational and national perspectives are contrasted (usually as a means toward valorizing the transnational) rather than seeing in a more dynamic and dialectical relationship. Ute Frevert, for example, in her recent essay on "Europeanizing Germany's Twentieth Century" contrasts the "petulance and chauvinism" of Europe's post–First World War nationalists with good, "forward-thinking politicians and businessmen" who espoused transnationalism. And yet, were not these nationalists themselves often migrants or minorities, themselves participants in the currents of transnationalism? Ute Frevert, "Europeanizing Germany's Twentieth Century," *History and Memory* 17:1 (2005), p. 97. Aside from a brief and unpersuasive account of the European rhetoric and reality of Nazi Germany, the entire piece is characterized by this sort of celebration of perceived cosmopolitanism.

48 Eric Lohr, *Russian Citizenship: From Empire to Soviet Union* (Cambridge: Harvard University Press, 2012).

49 A similar argument is made by Theodore Weeks, "Religious Toleration in the Russian Provinces," *Kritika* 14:4 (Fall 2013), pp. 876–84.

50 For more on General Konstantin Petrovich von Kaufman, see Dolbilov, "Russification."

51 This is to a degree a legacy of Benedict Anderson, for whom community was national community, perhaps because of his background studying anticolonial nationalisms in Asia. Benedict Anderson, *Imagined Communities: Reflections on the Origins and Spread of Nationalism* (New York: Verso, 1991 revised edn).

52 Nancy Reagin, "Recent Work on German National Identity: Regional? Imperial? Gendered? Imaginary?" *Central European History* 37:2 (2004), p. 289.

53 For obvious reasons, Austro-Hungarian historians have been more interested than Germanists in thinking about this kind of imperial identity. See Jeremy King, "The Nationalization of East Central Europe: Ethnicism, Ethnicity and Beyond," in Maria Bucur and Nancy M. Wingfield (eds.), *Staging the Past: The Politics of Commemoration in Habsburg Central Europe, 1848 to the Present* (West Lafayette: Purdue University Press, 2001), pp. 112–52; Maureen Healy, *Vienna and the Fall of the Habsburg Empire: Total War and Everyday Life in World War I* (Cambridge: Cambridge University Press, 2004).

54 See Gosewinkel, *Einbürgern und Ausschliessen*, pp. 278–327.

55 Ther, "Beyond the Nation," p. 55. It could be argued that the Danes served a similar role in the 1860s.

56 See, for example, Bjork, "A Polish *Mitteleuropa?*" Bjork depicts a scenario in which a wide variety of potential affiliations between Poles and the German state were considered up until the last days of the First World War.

57 Drummond, "On the Borders of the Nation," pp. 468–9.

58 Alfred J. Rieber, "Struggle over the Borderlands," in S. Frederick Starr (ed.), *The Legacy of History in Russia and the New States of Eurasia* (Armonk, NY: ME Sharpe, 1994), pp. 61–90.

59 See the forum on violence in Russian history in *Kritika* 4:3 (Summer 2003).

60 Peter Gatrell, *A Whole Empire Walking: Refugees in Russia during World War One* (Bloomington: Indiana University Press, 1999).

61 Joshua Sanborn, "Unsettling the Empire: Violent Migrations and Social Disaster in Russia during World War I," *Journal of Modern History* 77 (2005), p. 292.

62 Joshua Sanborn, *Imperial Apocalypse: The Great War and the Destruction of the Russian Empire* (New York: Oxford University Press, 2014).

63 Peter Holquist, "Violent Russia, Deadly Marxism? Russia in the Epoch of Violence, 1905–1921," *Kritika* 4:3 (Summer 2003), pp. 627–52.

64 Alfred J. Rieber, "Civil Wars in the Soviet Union," *Kritika* 4:1 (Winter 2003), pp. 129–62. See also Holquist, "Violent Russia, Deadly Marxism?" p. 432.

65 Sanborn, "Unsettling the Empire," p. 302; Snyder, *Bloodlands*.

66 Sanborn, "Unsettling the Empire," makes this point explicitly, p. 303. See also Liulevicius, *War Land*, for details on how this functioned.

67 See Liulevicius's discussion in *War Land* of *Raum* and *Verkehr* on this point. See also Annemarie Sammartino, *Frustration and Utopia: Migration and Germany, 1914–1922*, chs. 2 and 3 (book manuscript, in progress).

68 David A. Bell, *The First Total War: Napoleon's Europe and the Birth of Warfare as We Know It* (New York: Houghton Mifflin, 2007).

69 Annemarie Sammartino, *The Impossible Border: Germany and the East* (Ithaca: Cornell University Press, 2010), chs. 1 and 2.

70 Fritz Fischer's description of a desperate German state grasping at war to escape domestic deadlock in 1914 would seem to be the exception that proves the rule here.

71 Unlike Volker Berghahn, I do not think this necessarily represents the demise of German nineteenth-century history, nor do I believe the roots of the First World War are the only acceptable subject of study for historians of this period. Volker Berghahn, "The German Empire 1871–1914: Reflections on the Direction of Recent Research," *Central European History* 35 (2002), pp. 75–81.

72 Eric Lohr suggests that the image of autocracy was itself a cover for a situation in which it was "brittle, divided, and even close to collapse." Eric Lohr, "Patriotic Violence and the State: The Moscow Riots of 1915," *Kritika* 4:3 (Summer 2003), p. 626.

73 Dolbilov, "Russification," p. 271.

74 By contrast, it remains quite difficult to find historians of Weimar who look at it as a success story in any but narrowly cultural terms. For a history of Weimar that challenges this narrative of failure, see Peter Fritzsche, "Did Weimar Fail?" *Journal of Modern History* 68:3 (1996), pp. 629–56. See also Manuela Achilles' essay in this volume.

75 Ronald Ross, *The Failure of Bismarck's Kulturkampf: Catholicism and State Power in Imperial Germany, 1871–1887* (Washington: Catholic University of America Press, 1998). Ross's conclusions themselves tend toward a view

of the *Kaiserreich* as a "weak" state, unable to forcefully push through its anti-Catholic policies. See also Oded Heilbronner, "From Ghetto to Ghetto: The Place of German Catholic Society in Recent Historiography," *Journal of Modern History* 72:2 (June 2000), pp. 453–95.

76 On the comparative weakness of the *Ostmarkenverein* as well, see Sabine Grabowski, *Deutscher und polnischer Nationalismus: Der Deutsche Ostmarken-Verein und die polnische Straz, 1894–1914* (Marburg: Verlag Herder Institut, 1998).

77 Fritz Fischer, *Germany's Aims in the First World War* (New York: Norton, 1967).

5

Elsewhere in Central Europe: Jewish Literature in the Austro-Hungarian Monarchy between "Habsburg Myth" and "Central Europe Effect"

Scott Spector

Fourteen years after Prussia's defeat of Austria at the Battle of Königgrätz, the newly minted German *Kaiserreich* to the north certainly seemed to any observer to be the bearer of the Central European future. Reform movements, the development of regions of heavy industry, imperial railways, and other stunning infrastructural innovations notwithstanding, the formerly dominant Austrian Empire seemed as burdened by its own unwieldy traditions as it was by the irrepressible economic and social challenges of the modern world. It is in this sense not surprising that in identifying the sites of "German modernities," the modernization projects of the Habsburg Empire would seem somewhere else. One might protest that hallmarks of the modern—of *modernism*—from psychoanalysis to the philosophy of language and from literary innovation to sexology had their roots in this soil. Yet, even to this demonstrable claim, another might respond that this metaphor of "roots" was at odds with some of the ways in which this empire to the south and east of the German one saw itself. Modern historiography cannot but relate this condition to the so-called nationalities problem of the late Habsburg Empire. While in the context of late Austria-Hungary this term referred to the challenge to the imperial political order posed by nationalist movements, in hindsight it may seem that it was the Habsburg monarchy's stubborn refusal to participate in the modern order of European nation-states that was the problem in question. Out of step in this and in many different senses, subjects of the Habsburg Empire were in a position to experience the relationship of past to future in different ways from their fellow German-speaking Europeans.

I am telling a story about the East European Jewish contribution to German modernism that shifts our focus from the *Kaiserreich* to the late Habsburg Empire, and yet that contribution has its roots in "Reich-German" soil. As in traditional narratives of modernity, the story is most sensibly told beginning with the Enlightenment. Here both the most telltale example and the most towering figure is Salomon Maimon (1753–1800), born into a Jewish family in Polish Lithuania, who became an important voice in both the Jewish Haskalah and the German Enlightenment. In the 1790s, Maimon's major philosophical works appeared, written in German, and deeply in dialogue with the budding traditions of German Idealism led by Immanuel Kant (Kant professed that Maimon was his most perspicacious critic) and Enlightenment thought more generally, especially that of the German Jew Moses Mendelssohn, who had taken Maimon in as a sort of protégé. Should we think of Maimon's philosophical interventions as émigré literature, writings of a displaced foreigner composed while in residence in German-speaking lands? In all events, Maimon's writing (his bombastic autobiography as much as the critical philosophy) is a paradigmatic instance of the East European Jewish intervention into modern German thought. Even more than was the case with Moses Mendelssohn himself, Maimon represented the confrontation and amalgamation of traditional Jewish and European rationalist thinking, bringing the powerful influence of Maimonides to bear on the new critical practices of Enlightenment. He was regarded by the German enlightened community as an East European Jewish outsider whose raw genius and critical acumen served as both challenge to and ultimate evidence of the universalism of Enlightenment precepts.

Maimon can in so many senses be seen as the flip side of the coin whose head bore the face of Moses Mendelssohn, the representative figure of assimilationism—or at least of a claim to stand on the same ground as the majority culture.[1] He produced a modern theory of the state, of the distinctions of civil, confessional, and national identities and, along with these, a way of living in the modern world as a Jew and a Central European. But the legacy of Maimon—the outsider who intervened in modern, European culture, but was always out of sorts within it—this legacy seems to have been carried on into the late nineteenth and early twentieth centuries in the Habsburg Empire.

The questions of the national, the modern, and the Central European converge on literature perhaps most poignantly in Joseph Roth's *Radetzkymarsch*.[2] It is a piece written after the dismemberment of the Habsburg Empire, by a Jew from Galicia who learned German as a foreign language, and taking off from a work by the very differently Austrian Grillparzer a century earlier. Roth's example is hence a peculiar and nonetheless excellent choice to begin an inquiry into Central European literature and culture although he cannot be called *representative*—his position is in fact too complex to actually *represent* anything fixed. Roth's homage to the Slovene field marshal does not so much ground a place for a supranational Habsburg identity as much as it articulates Roth's own *dis*placement—the Galician Jew writing in German language from the tiny rump remaining of the Habsburg Empire after its dissolution. Whether we try to think of this literary moment in terms of time or space, language or history or politics, Roth seems free-floating, unanchored, always "elsewhere."

In this contribution, I will be focusing on German-language Jewish writers from the Habsburg and post-Habsburg realm, but this ought to shed light on the broad questions of Central European cultural history and the fraught category of "modernity" raised in this volume. This is so because the very displacement Roth represents, this eternal elsewhere, is intimately connected to a *mystique* at the heart of the problem of locating Central European literature and culture, that of the Habsburg Empire in particular. What is the connection of the Central European to the "national" and to the "modern"? How are we to place it spatially and temporally? Even asking this question raises specters of the Habsburg imperial problematic that haunt the literatures that emerged in late nineteenth- and early twentieth-century Central Europe as well as the histories of them that we write. As a state of multiple nations in an age of nation-states, the empire was living on borrowed time, so the argument goes. An old-fashioned continental empire neurotically burdening itself with the unbearable baggage of its own history, it could not move forward with modernity, like the lithe and nimble German or West European capitalist empires. The "central," in the case of Europe, is "peripheral."

On the other hand, we have the facts of the contributions to the cultures of *modernism* that emerged from this realm, from literary modernism in, say, Kafka, to modernism as a critical category in Hermann Bahr, to its particular brands of *Jugendstil*, to music, to psychoanalysis. This sounds enough like a citation of Carl Schorske to point to another truism of studies of Central European culture: the anachronism of Habsburg politics must have been directly, if inversely, linked to the innovations of Central European culture. (Hence, the "peripheral" becomes "central" to the modernist project.)

Writing from post-Habsburg Trieste, Claudio Magris reads Roth as a paradigmatic voice, to be sure, but he does not take that voice at its word. He instead identified it as embodying what he famously called the "Habsburg Myth." According to this interpretation, Roth's forever tenuous position is in this moment a concentrated version of the overall displacement of Central European identity, and his fantasy production of a grounded Central European identity and patriotism is a kind of defense mechanism. Further, and here Magris's interpretation is particularly compelling, the nostalgia for a place that did not exist represented by this Austrian interwar literature harkened back to a powerful nineteenth century myth of Habsburg dynastic history which had been produced in order to resist the centrifugal force of national movements after 1848. This is why the *Radetzky March* embodies the myth so well, so literally. What Magris's contribution does so brilliantly is to allow us to think of German-language Central European literature (Central Europe in this, the classic, definition, excluding the lands that would be joined in the German *Kaiserreich*) in terms other than but comparable to discussions of "national" cultures proper. The Habsburg Myth thesis allows us to see a unity in Central European literature from 1806 on, but not through the ascription of an essentialist thesis of national essence, but rather ideological necessity.

A different and arguably simpler solution to the problem of placing Central European culture is Maria Todorova's.[3] She has steadfastly asserted that there never was any Central Europe in a culturo-historical sense, but this term only emerged as an ideological instrument of relatively recent vintage, and one that should be rapidly and unapologetically purged from the historiography. This line of argument may be seductive as an antidote to idyllic constructions of Central Europe such as, most famously or notoriously, Milan Kundera's in the often republished essay "The Tragedy of Central Europe," but on the other hand "Central Europe" as term or as problem is not simply of Cold War vintage. Todorova is right in reminding us that the placement of Central European culture is, and has perhaps consistently been, a problem of ideology, while it was engaged by subjects at the time as well as in our own critical and historical literatures. Rather than discarding that complex, it is I think worth trying to capture, and to do so we must take the construct of "Central Europe" seriously on some level.

One thing we are not trying to capture, at any rate, is a unitary Central European experience, or in the particular case under review in this essay, a unitary experience of "Habsburg Jewry." The actual social and cultural experience of Jews in the monarchy—their everyday lives, their social interactions, the bodies of knowledge they commanded or had access to, what they read and could read, the languages they spoke and understood, the food they ate—varied as widely within the empire as it was in various cases apparently identical to lives of Jews in other nations and empires. These differences were not occluded in the period, but rather often discussed. Most evidently, while Jews in Vienna, Czernowitz, Prague, Lemberg, and Trieste might have identified as Habsburg Jews or even as Austrians, they retained a critical distinction of Eastern and Western Europe, and were aware that their empire embraced Jews of both of these not only distinct but perhaps even oppositional realms. None of this belies the reality of a cultural entity, or even an imaginary, that could be called "Central Europe." To the contrary, the displacement I am describing—the lack of a clear territorial, sociocultural integrity (or, again, the fantasy of one)—is precisely what defined this Central European culture for many of its inhabitants. This sense of displacement—

territorial as well as temporal—lent Central Europe its peculiar mystique. A crucial element Magris missed is the way that the literary historiography of Habsburg modernism, including his own, takes on this myth in its own way. The ungrounded, illusory, and displaced position of the Habsburg writer puts her in a privileged position vis-à-vis the modern. Modernism is itself a notoriously slippery category, but whether critics decide to define it by its pervasive sense of self-reflection and self-consciousness, its self-irony and ironic stance toward the outside world, its moods of alienation, neurosis, or paranoia, or its play with the very category of language, Central Europe is suddenly "central" once again. That is, the Habsburg writers have privileged access to the hallmarks of modernism by virtue of the story they tell themselves about the place of Central Europe in the modern world. This historiographical circle is not broken, if you thought it might be, by the much-announced passage from the modern to the so-called postmodern. Witness Stefan Jonnson's insightful book on Robert Musil, *Subject Without Nation*, where the conventional historiography on the Habsburg nationality conflict merges seamlessly with anti-foundationalist philosophy's critique of the existence of a modern self.[4]

Where, then, is Central Europe, where is the "there there"? Where, if its spokespersons and its histories are merely echoes of nonexistent imaginaries, themselves echoing fantasy histories, always displaced, forever elsewhere? Is it not possible that this system of echo chambers is the phantom country we call Central Europe? It is for this reason only that I would even consider burdening an already overburdened terminological historiography with another category, or rather metacategory, and that is what I would like to call the *Central Europe Effect*. For some time now, structuralist (and, in their wake, poststructuralist) thinkers have identified author-functions, author-effects, subject-effects, etc., where authors used to be, replacing models of intention, message-coding, and reception with complex, controlled but not controllable operations of meaning. A starting point of these theoretical investigations has often been that objects that had been taken for granted as essential, immutable, natural, and so forth (author, subject, self, what have you) have particular and sometimes quite short histories. The same must be held of the category of Central Europe, of course, and this model of metacriticism may be useful to bring into the discussion of culture from this diverse region, not at all to expose any general category of Central European literature as a sham, but to give us insight into how all such discussions are structured to operate. Another parallel is the scientific problem, or that of the ethnologist, of gauging and accounting for the effect of the presence of an observer on the processes or subjects being observed. I am hence proposing the Central Europe Effect as a category to contextualize our own discussion historically, critically, and conceptually.

In every instantiation of this effect—wherever a location of Central Europe has been identified in its dislocation, an "idea of Austria" in the need to define an "idea of Austria," etc.—the Jews seem to have played a *paradigmatic* function. In its most literal form, this appears as the assertion that the Jews, in their nationlessness and their status as minority par excellence, in their motility and their adaptivity, in their negative doubling as elastically assimilatory and rigidly unassimiliable, were the monarchy's most loyal subjects, or only true patriots. This truism was indigenous to the period as well as a commonplace of the historiography. Beyond the question of allegiance to the monarchy, what the assertions equating the Jews with the Habsburg monarchy do is reflect the twin symbolic function not of Jewish communities or individuals and Habsburg state actions or positions, but of the *Jews* and *Central Europe* as *figures*.

This figurative similarity, as you will guess from my argumentation so far, was not lost on subjects in the period. One example of this analogic correspondence is found in the Prague Zionist weekly *Selbstwehr*, where an editorialist does the good etymological work of relating the practices of translation or cultural mediation and the geographical centrality of Central Europe: he describes a Habsburg future where the Jews flourish in the empire's mosaic of nations, a confederation of peoples stretching from Hamburg to the Persian Gulf. To reach this progressive and attractive end, the empire will depend on the Jews, their key to *Mitteleuropa*, the means (*Mittel/Mittler*) to unite East and West, their mediators (*Vermittler*): "for this reason the maxim on which the future of Austria *and* the Jewish *Volk* depend must be: Eastward and Forward!"

In the historiographical imagination, the special function of Central Europe and that of the Jews is conflated, particularly as these converge on the modern. We do not have to go to Steven Beller's 1989 standard work of cultural history, *Vienna and the Jews*, to find the thesis that the Vienna Modern and Jewry coincide, and coincide with modernism *tout court*. Vienna Jewish contemporaries like Stefan Zweig and George Steiner in more immediate retrospect made similar gestures in the most extreme terms. Zweig, in a startlingly precise exaggeration, attributed nine-tenths of nineteenth century Viennese culture to have been the property of Jews, whereas Steiner went further to claim that "most of the innovations" of the twentieth century were creations of Viennese of Jewish extraction. I needn't remind the readers that the metonymic correspondence of Central European Jews and modernism came in handy, indeed was indispensable, to the *völkisch* antisemitic and then the Nazi critiques of both.

Let me move on to a term more recent than the Habsburg Myth, and widely influential. "Cultural hybridity" is a term that has been deployed by theorists of colonialism to describe the ambivalent effects of the identities produced by the colonial processes. While the stage for these investigations has typically been the developing world, it is ironic that the model Bhabha and others have used has been that of the Central European Jew between the Enlightenment and the Holocaust. This complex ambivalence is spelled out in Bhabha's essays in *The Location of Culture*, and it is fair to say that the intervention has been misappropriated by those who understand it as an acceptance of a genus or category of the "hybrid" that is then celebrated for subverting the original, pure, colonizing species.[5] In an analysis informed by psychoanalytic sources, Bhabha usually avoids denoting a type ("the hybrid") who acts in certain ways under colonial conditions, but instead refers to hybridity as either a *process* or a *sign* of processes of domination and resistance.[6] It is specifically not "a third term that resolves the tension between two cultures," a description in which we more than faintly recognize the image many have painted of certain groups of Habsburg Jews in the period of nationalist conflict, such as the German-speaking Jews of East-Central Europe. Central Europe, and, paradigmatically, its Jewry, is hence seen not as a *sign* of a (post) colonial *hybrid* representing a *process* of hegemony, but as an *actual cross* of two or more worlds, capable of mediating among them. Even more interesting than this widespread historiographical misreading is the discovery of its presence among the historical subjects themselves; at least in many very different cases, the historian of Habsburg Jews may unearth a self-recognition of an inheritance, the positioning within East and West, past and future, Europe and its Other, and on and on. My current favorite example of this self-referential claim of hybridity is Franz Kafka's fragment "A Hybrid," written in 1917 and included in the posthumous collection *Beim Bau der Chinesischen Mauer.* Readers who know the piece will remember it is the uncanny description of an unusual pet, half-kitten and half-lamb (with something doggish about it), that the narrator has received as inheritance from his father; a fascinating, loving, and also somehow pathetic creature, uncomfortable in its own skin, for whom the narrator knows the butcher's blade would perhaps be the appropriate "solution," but one that he cannot provide. I am not going to join with the many critical voices who have taken this to be Kafka's clear allegorical statement about the status of German-Jewish life in diaspora, or in Central Europe in particular. Rather, that very interpretation is inscribed in the story; hybridity is in this tale what I have elsewhere called a "trap," compelling an allegorical interpretation that is itself part of the narrative.[7] Here as elsewhere, it seems to me, Kafka is appropriating his own appropriation, thematizing the "hybridity" of a German author born in a conflicted Central Europe to Jewish parents. For what is this piece, if not the "purest" of moments of German literary modernism? And the hybrid, the half-breed, the "cross" and the "crossing" of this fragment—is it Jewish or Christian, animal or man, is it European or simply human? I do not think this figure of the hybrid is coincidentally thematized by Kafka, but rather that this is evidence that the discourse of hybridity is more native than it would seem, and that here we must have another case where Kafka adopts a problematic contemporary discourse wholesale and pushes it to an aesthetic extreme, at which point it is unusable as an instrument of hegemony, but an instrument of pure aesthetics. Kafka, so to speak, was a hitchhiker or stowaway on the Central Europe Effect.

I will leave Prague aside temporarily, in part because it is a special case of Central European Habsburg Jewish identity dynamics, and mainly because I cannot claim to be an impartial observer of these dynamics (I will return to it later for just this reason). First, let us look at some other historical examples of Habsburg Jews to see if this peculiar *operation*, rather than *character*, can be detected. Out of Bohemia's neighboring Moravia hailed a great many "Jewish writers of German tongue," as Max Brod referred to himself.[8] An important if also idiosyncratic exemplar is Alexander Friedrich Roda Roda (1872–1945), whose early work has been characterized as emblematic of the "Habsburg spirit." He was born in Drnowitz Moravia in 1872, but his family soon moved to Zdenci in Slavonia, the furthest eastern province of today's Croatia. Roda Roda's Central Europe ranged into German Austria and Germany itself, where he became famous as a satirist and cabarettist, rubbing elbows with leading literati and political writers of the age. This life and career stunningly fits a certain familiar image of "central Europe": peripatetic, highly cultured, and yet distanced and sardonic, a figure that is at once perennially an insider and a hapless outsider—eternally displaced and at home in this displacement—in a word, "hybrid." It is Gregor von Rezzori, that latter-day, profoundly Habsburg-identified writer, who sees in Roda Roda this paradigmatically Central European essence that Rezzori himself emulates.

Jews from the eastern reaches of Cisleithania, particularly Galicia, with its very large Polish-Jewish population, were less likely to contribute to German literature. The Habsburg character of the region was strong, and the population in several areas quite mixed, including German-speaking aristocrats and other German speakers, among them assimilating Jews. But the vast majority of Jews in these areas lived within a strong Yiddish-speaking cultural environment, and while some at the time thought of Yiddish (or "Jargon" as it was commonly called) as a dialect of German and not a language in its own right at all, neither did Yiddish authors consider themselves to be contributing to a German literary tradition nor is their literary production today considered to be a part of it. Several Galician Jews, however, did make significant contributions to German literature.

Two very important examples to name would be men whose background as East European Jews cannot be considered incidental to the content of their contributions. Martin Buber (1879–1965), born in Vienna but raised in Lvov/Lviv/Lemberg, presented mediations of Hasidic tradition to a German audience that were obviously linked to this background, as was his crucial journal *Der Jude* and even his philosophical writing, or so one could argue. One could ask the provocative question, in sum, is it the historian's—let me say *my* fantasy of the mediating, rational-spiritual, "Central European" that construes in Buber a "hybrid" of German Romanticism and Galician Jewish spiritualism, or *his*?

We have already been discussing Joseph Roth, who was born in eastern Galicia and became an important Austrian writer, and indeed a modern author whose great significance is sometimes overlooked, perhaps because the great literary tradition out of which he emerged and which he paradigmatically represented—the Central European—was doomed to failure. At any rate, the argument is sometimes made that the likes of Roth and Musil are robbed of the reception given to a Proust, a Joyce, or a Woolf because of the demise of the Central European idea. If instead of Central Europe as idea we return to Magris's diagnosis of the Habsburg Myth, there is of course a place for Roth reserved for none other—as I've indicated at the beginning, his *Radetzky March* is the classic of a Central European nostalgia for a Central European nostalgia. But if we leave it at this—as though our role in this myth is nothing except for possibly its debunkers—we miss the complicity of contemporary interpretations of Central European culture— including our own—we miss the rich *effects* of the *operations produced* by this discourse. We miss the Central Europe Effect.

If the itinerant Galician Roth is the swansong of this Habsburg-anchored Central Europe in the twentieth century, an important early exponent was another, Karl Emil Franzos (1848–1904). This novelist, essayist, and poet was a fierce German nationalist and an important contributor to the nineteenth-century German "orientalist" image of Eastern Europe and its Jews (this last especially through several volumes of "cultural vignettes from Half-Asia").[9] Franzos was one of the most popular German-Jewish writers of his generation, and the consideration of him as a prime exemplar of the phenomenon of "Jewish self-hatred" is complicated. Yet, I do not think it can be seen as coincidence that this particular "orientalism," which would have such sway in the German perception of Eastern Europe in the half century of Franzos's life and the further half-century after his death (and longer) hailed from a Jewish writer from that world, rather than a resident of the German Empire proper. "Hybridity," you see, does not necessarily yield sympathy as such. Yet, there is in the very exoticism of Franzos's descriptions, as in the very different and yet kin ones of the fellow Galician Leopold von Sacher-Masoch, for example, a homely familiarity. Franzos's childhood was shared by Galicia and the heavily Germanized Bukovina to its south (discussed below); in his mental topography, a city like Czernowitz was clearly European, whereas all of Galicia was mired within "Half-Asia."

Franzos and Roth both made their German-language literary contributions after their moves out of Galicia: after their emigration, as it were, to German-speaking lands beyond the invisible boundary of Eastern Europe. This path was not unusual for a certain tier of Galician Jewish society, who took German to be the language of higher culture and education and had their children schooled in it, even if as a second, third, or fourth language (after Yiddish, Polish, scholarly Hebrew, and sometimes Ukrainian). Such was the path of writers Manès Sperber (1905–84), Soma Morgenstern (1890–1976), Salamon Dembitzer (1888–1964), W.H. Katz, the scholar Nahum Glatzer (1903–90), and psychoanalytic writers such as Sigmund Biran. Most made their path over Vienna, many studied or worked in Germany.

This relationship of Jewish residents to German-language culture was historically quite different from the neighboring Cisleithanian province of the Bukovina.[10] Bukovina was the northeastern corner of what was considered Romania and was the part of Romania under Austrian control. Jews were present in substantial numbers in Romanian lands ruled by the Hungarian half of the Habsburg monarchy, but did not tend to identify with German speakers. Transylvanian Jews acculturated to the politico-culturally dominant Hungarian population rather than its Romanian and German cohabitants, and other Romanian Jews identified strongly with the Romanian majority. Bukovina, by contrast, had a long history of mixed populations, had been under the sovereignty of various kingdoms, principalities, and empires in every direction (including the Ottoman Empire, the Kingdom of Hungary, Rus, Moldau, the Habsburg monarchy, and later Romania and Ukraine). Hence Bukovina was considered by the German leaders of the Habsburg Empire to be a key strategic site for Germanization since the reign of Joseph II, whose campaign included the settlement of many Germans from the West as well as the active Germanization of some local populations, including especially Bukovina's Jews. German-language education was formally required of them in various ways (as prerequisites of Talmudic study or marriage, for instance), and by the nineteenth century the Jews of its many country towns and especially its capital, Czernowitz, were largely German-speaking and strong supporters of the monarchy. The region continued to attract Yiddish-speaking Jewish immigrants from surrounding areas, however. In the early twentieth century, Jews made up nearly half of the population of Czernowitz and well over a tenth of a population of nearly one million where no ethnic group commanded a majority. It is in the twentieth century that the German poetry of this region blossomed due to the extraordinary creativity of Bukovina's Jews.

The most important of the German poetry written by Jews in Bukovina was created in the twentieth century, especially after the First World War and the succession of the region to Romania. Here the most apt comparison may be made to the German literature produced by Jews in Prague earlier in the century. The disproportionate contribution can be thought of in the context of "minority cultures," where the hegemonic status of German language had already been superseded by other national claims, so that the previously privileged language of culture was now a minority culture maintained and promulgated largely by German-acculturated Jews. In both Bukovina and Bohemia, contemporaries and scholars have argued that the disproportionate literary talent might be linked to the isolation of these "language islands" and perpetuation of a high-cultural tradition from centuries past. But these sites were hardly considered language islands before the onset of the national movements that would create them as such, and the assumption that isolation from working-class elements or dialects is salutory seems transparently ideological. It is true that the Jews of Bukovina cherished a high cultural European heritage that seemed old-fashioned to many residents of both the surrounding Slavic and Romanian populations, and to those of most of German-speaking Europe as well. Another important influence is said to have been played by the so-called Ethical Seminar at the University of Czernowitz, where some Jewish students, notably Rose Ausländer (1901–88), were steeped in a German neo-idealist philosophical tradition. The poetry of German-Jewish Bukovina is perhaps best known as Holocaust literature, although the greatest contributions clearly begin in the interwar period. Many and perhaps even most of the writers emigrated or spent substantial time in Germany, Austria, France, England, the United States, or Israel. Some of the most important, in addition to Ausländer and Celan, include Alfred Margul-Sperber (1898–1967), Klara Blum (1904–71), Alfred Kittner (1906–91), Alfred Gong (Alfred M. Liquornik, 1920–81), Selma Meerbaum-Eisinger (1924–42), Moses Rosenkranz (1904–2003), and Immanuel Weissglas (1920–79), to name only the best known of many authors. Women writers were probably more strongly represented in this group than in any other contemporary German literary setting. This was specifically not the case for German writers in other areas of Central Europe, so I hesitate to claim it as an ancillary effect of "hybridity"—but something about the peculiar cultural milieu of this extraordinary place and time played a role in the facilitation of spaces in which women's artistic voices could flourish and be appreciated.

Bukovina and Czernowitz in particular are certainly privileged sites for the phenomenon framing my discussion of Habsburg Jews, and that is namely the power of a mystique of displacement, of uprootedness or of lack of synchronicity, of dual or multiple or elastic identities, or of untimeliness. Part of the attractiveness of this mystique lies in the fantasy of something being salvaged in such an idiosyncratic environment that has been lost to more grounded national territories, cultures, and literatures.

Consider the case of the insane locksmith Karl Piehowicz, interned in the Czernowitz nerve clinic, whose brilliance as a poet is "discovered" by Alfred Margul Sperber, who in turn sends the inmate's work to Karl Kraus. In 1928, the poet is lauded by Kraus in the *Fackel* in these emphatic terms: "The greatest poet working in German today, perhaps the only great one, and one of the greatest that have ever lived, is a locksmith living in the insane asylum at Czernowitz."[11] The end of this story is as important to tell as this crescendo moment: the monomaniac locksmith was actually simply repeating on an endless loop a great number of poems he had memorized as a way of wiling away the time in the foreign legion. Of course, the last thing one wants to imply is that there is something inherently *fraudulent* about Central European modernism. It is simply that its greatness has always been wrapped up in a complex of assumptions about the origin of Central European creativity, and that these sometimes unspoken assumptions are continued in historiographical discourse.

To return to my book on Prague writers, and in particular my discussion of the Czech-to-German translators, I argued that, rather than "hybrids," these particular Central European Jews could be conceived as a "middle nation" (again, from *Mitteleuropa*): their poetry was a new sort of "national literature," grounding an alternative to "nations" in the ordinary sense of the word. To the degree this can be said to be true, it is important to recall that such a literature was not a "Jewish literature," and that such a nation—"Middle Nation"—was not Zion. It functioned, so my argument went, as an alternative—and, yes, a subversive one—to the ideological complex binding essential peoples to eternal literatures and sovereign territories.

What I would like to confess here—and it is emphatically not a disavowal of that thesis—is that the sketch I drew of the ideological dilemma of German-speaking Jews in Prague was a subspecies of the more general genus I am calling the Central European Effect. A special attention to all moments of displacement—spatial, temporal, and ideological—and to the extraordinary outcomes of this sense of displacement establishes the overall architecture of *Prague Territories*. Think of the voyages to eastern Galicia of Jiří Langer and of Hugo Bergman, among others; the fantasy Hebraism melded with socialism in the "untimely" Rudolf Fuchs (central treatment given to his poem "Unzeit"); the work of him and the other Czech-to-German translators, and on and on. What's more, observers at the time, and the Praguers themselves, shared in these self-descriptions. There is no doubt that particular conditions helped bring forth what must be considered an extraordinary literary contribution from a very small demographic group. Yet, at the same time, it must be recognized that a significant component of the cultural phenomenon of Prague German writing was the excitement generated in Germany about this language island, this eccentric and displaced corner of Central Europe. The very particular circumstances surrounding the Prague Circle cannot be generalized throughout Central Europe at all—the particularity and exceptionality of the case was a principal point of the book. It is, however, in another way a special case of a Central European literary topography that we have been outlining; one that is generously proportioned to accommodate so many different spirits, including Habsburg Jewish writers of both Eastern and Western Europe, and above all those hard to fit within these increasingly hardening categories. I have left out of the discussion the tremendous and important literary production of those Habsburg Jews who wrote in other languages than German, notably Yiddish and Hebrew. Their writings arguably inscribe another and different kind of territory. Among non-Jewish identified German speakers and those writing in Slavic languages, Hungarian, Romanian, there may be many other examples that fit this model—but it was not my intention to produce an alternative catalog to that provided by Magris or Kundera. Those visions, along with those of modernist canonists, belong, as I've been arguing, to the same world. They do not so much describe or analyze as much as *perform* the place, if it is one, called Central Europe.

Notes

1   See Michael P. Steinberg, "Mendelssohn and Judaism," in Peter Mercer-Taylor (ed.), *The Cambridge Companion to Mendelssohn* (Cambridge: Cambridge University Press, 2004).

2   Joseph Roth, *Radetzkymarsch* (Berlin: Gustav Kiepenheuer, 1932).

3   Maria Todorova, *Imagining the Balkans* (Oxford: Oxford University Press, 1997), pp. 140–60, and "Isn't Central Europe Dead? A Response to Iver Neumann's 'Forgetting the Central Europe of the 1980s,'" in Christopher Lord (ed.), *Central Europe: Core or Periphery?* (Lanham, MD: Lexington Books, 2012), pp. 219–34.

4   Stefan Jonnson, *Subject without Nation: Robert Musil and the History of Modern Identity* (Durham: Duke University Press, 2000).

5   Homi K. Bhabha, *The Location of Culture* (London: Routledge, 1994), p. 162ff.

6   Ibid., see esp. pp. 112–15.

7   See Scott Spector, "From Big Daddy to Small Literature: On Taking Kafka at His Word," in Linda E. Feldman and Diana Orendi (eds.), *Evolving Jewish Identities in German Culture: Borders and Crossings* (Westport, CT: Praeger, 2000), pp. 79–93.

8   Max Brod, "Der jüdische Dichter deutscher Zunge," in Verein jüdischer Hochschüler Bar Kochba in Prag (eds.), *Vom Judentum: Ein Sammelbuch* (Leipzig: Kurt Wolff, 1914), pp. 261–6.

9   Karl Emil Franzos, *Aus Halb-Asien. Kulturbilder aus Galizien, der Bukovina, Südrußland und Rumänien* (Leipzig, 1876), *Vom Don zur Donau. Neue Kulturbilder aus Halb-Asien* (1877), and *Aus der großen Ebene: Neue Kulturbilder aus Halb-Asien* (Stuttgart: A. Bonz, 1888).

10 See Amy Colin and Alfred Kittner (eds.), *Versunkene Dichtung der Bukowina* (Munich: W. Fink, 1994); Cécile Cordon and Helmut Kusdat (eds.), *An der Zeiten Ränder. Czernowitz und die Bukowina. Geschichte, Literatur, Verfolgung, Exil* (Vienna: Theodor Kramer Gesellschaft, 2002).

11 Karl Kraus, *Die Fackel*, nos. 781–6 (1928), p. 91.

6

Communism and Colonialism in the Red and Black Atlantic: Toward a Transnational Narrative of German Modernity

Andrew Zimmerman

The history of Germany and the history of imperialism have long served as stark reminders that modernity is not always a process of growing enlightenment and emancipation. Once, both modern German history and overseas colonialism could be dismissed as the result of feudal holdovers, for example, in the work of Ralph Dahrendorf on Germany and Joseph Schumpeter on imperialism.[1] Today modern German history and the history of imperialism have become exemplars of modernity, but a modernity of a decidedly authoritarian and dystopian type. Paul Rabinow, for example, has termed colonies "laboratories of modernity," while Detlev Peukert has found the "spirit of science" at work even in the Holocaust.[2] German and colonial history no longer trouble the concept of modernity but rather constitute exemplars of a modernity that is itself troubling.

Given the separate significance of the histories of imperialism and of Germany for our understanding of modernity, it should perhaps come as no surprise that the German colonial empire itself played a central, and contradictory, role in the construction of a modernity that we today recognize as liberal internationalism. Before the First World War, European colonial thinkers, the greatest liberal internationalists of their day, looked to Germany with envy and admiration for its modernizing (or *kulturbestrebend*), colonial policy.[3] After the war, these same European colonial powers cast Germany as an unfit colonizer whose brutal behavior overseas virtually demanded that the victorious powers seize its colonies as part of a "sacred trust of civilization" under the League of Nations.

The modernity of German colonialism hardly forces us to cast modernity itself as essentially dystopian. It is common to talk about good and bad, emancipatory and oppressive, utopian and dystopian sides to modernity. This essay, however, rejects an image of modernity as a coin, with two sides, and rather posits two distinct modernities defined by their class basis and nature: a bourgeois modernity and a proletarian modernity. Bourgeois and proletarian modernity are not two aspects of a single modernity, nor are they independent parallel inventions. Their relation is rather part of a broader class relation between bourgeoisie and proletariat as expressed in the theory of value formulated by Marx: the proletariat creates; the bourgeoisie expropriates. The techniques of bourgeois expropriation shape the processes of proletarian creation to a greater or lesser extent to facilitate the valorization of capital, but capital, like bourgeois modernity is, finally, and fundamentally, a reaction to, an appropriation of, and an attempt to suppress a primary, proletarian modernity.[4]

The dialectic of bourgeois and proletarian modernity emerges in their two characteristic forms of internationalism: colonialism for the bourgeoisie and for the proletariat, communism. (This is a diverse small c-communism that exceeds—but also includes—the variety of big-C Communisms of historical parties and states.) If the great geopolitical achievement of international liberalism in the nineteenth century was the division and redivision of Africa among European states, the great geopolitical achievement of this primary democratic modernity was the production of common lands around the Atlantic.[5] The widespread assumption that the democratic modernity of the common was traditional or primitive—that is, not modern at all—is one of the basic ideological gestures of bourgeois counterrevolution, whether in the colonial images of primitive culture or more recent dismissals of various forms of anti-capitalism and anti-liberalism as backward-looking.[6] The common does not predate capitalism and liberal internationalism, but rather precedes and accompanies it as necessarily as possession does theft. Modernity as a complex of liberalism and capitalism emerged as a secondary form to the commons that it appropriated. The common, then, reasserted and reconstituted itself in utopian settlements, communist movements, and maroon communities, to name just a few instances. This sequence, this back-and-forth—what Polanyi would call this "double movement"—is how I propose narrating colonial modernity, particularly German colonial modernity.[7] I follow Elizabeth Povinelli in seeking to go beyond an analysis of liberalism (or neoliberalism) and focusing instead on the forms of life on which liberalism has both preyed and depended.[8]

This essay will thus add a transnational dimension to the class analysis of modernity offered by Geoff Eley. In his contribution to the *Peculiarities of German History*, Eley demonstrated that any authoritarian aspects one might attribute to German modernity emerged from its bourgeois character, rather than, as writers from Dahrendorf to Hans-Ulrich Wehler had maintained, its lack of a bourgeois character.[9] In this the modernity of the German nation corresponded in its basic features to that of other European bourgeois revolutions. More recently, Eley has offered a genealogy of a proletarian modernity that has presented a more empirically verifiable support for democracy than the bourgeois liberalism praised by Dahrendorf and others.[10] (Dahrendorf rejected such proletarian democracy, from his own Hayekian perspective, as "totalitarian.") There are thus at least two, class-specific modernizing revolutions: bourgeois and proletarian, and only the latter has a plausible claim to being democratic. This has important consequences for how we conceive of colonial modernity, especially of the German variant.

Taking a transnational perspective on German colonial modernity requires breaking with the concept of social imperialism as developed by Hans-Ulrich Wehler and employed in virtually all colonial studies focused on the metropole.[11] As defined by Wehler, social imperialism refers to the process by which manipulative conservative elites redirected pressures for domestic reforms outward, toward overseas expansion. Demands for democracy and social welfare made by left liberals and Social Democrats could thus be offered substitute satisfactions in the material, and especially nationalist psychic, gains from colonial expansion, thus preserving Germany's allegedly backward political and social structure. Wehler's understanding of social imperialism preserved the primacy of internal, national politics even in the face of massive overseas entanglement. Such methodological nationalism remained central to social history in the Federal Republic at the time and was also a *sine qua non* of classical modernization theory.

Wehler's definition of social imperialism, however, as Eley has argued, functioned less well as an explanation of the history of Wilhelmine Germany than the original, Social Democratic use of the term did. For Social Democrats, social imperialism, like its synonyms "social patriotism" and "social chauvinism," described the perspective of party members who embraced nationalism and reformism over internationalism and revolutionary socialism. Wehler, Eley noted, never showed that social imperialism had the psychological effect he claimed it did, in part because he scarcely looked beyond policy documents authored by elites. Moreover, the Social Democrats, apart from their revisionist wing—those criticized by their comrades as "social imperialists"—rejected colonialism, whether as a substitute for domestic reform or as anything else.[12] As Eley explains, the elite classes of Wilhelmine Germany faced a double problem: the threat to their status posed by the swiftly growing Social Democratic Party and the separate strategic and economic imperative they felt to acquire overseas colonies. These two imperatives overlapped in those social imperialist sectors of the German Social Democratic Party (SPD), but they did not proceed from a single, elite social imperialism. By disaggregating—without entirely separating—the two problems, domestic reform and overseas expansions, Eley makes it possible to reject the liberal modernization theory inherent in Wehler's domestic-policy-centered approach to imperialism and reveals more complex articulation among capital, class, nation, and imperialism.[13]

We can perhaps reintegrate the twin problems of extending state and capital power overseas, on the one hand, and of maintaining class hegemony over workers, on the other, by following the recent imperative of colonial studies to, in the words of Fredrick Cooper and Ann Laura Stoler, "treat metropole and colony in a single analytic field."[14] There were, after all, workers overseas also, and they, as much as German workers, presented opportunities for exploitation as well as challenges to the power of the state and capital. The question of dominating workers, as in Wehler's understanding of social imperialism, ceases to be one of playing psychological tricks on German workers and becomes instead a problem of dominating a broad spectrum of workers domestically and overseas. Returning to the original definition of social imperialism, as Eley recommends, thus pushes us productively beyond the revisionist and trade unionist focus on white male wage earners toward a more analytically useful concept of the proletariat.[15] This requires defining the "single analytic field" containing colony and metropole more broadly than a tight figure eight around a colonial territory and the European state that claimed sovereignty over it. This figure eight, after all, is the colonizers' geography: the homogeneity of bourgeois nationalism and the bilateralism of colonial imagination, finally Eurocentric despite itself. The "single analytic field" relevant to German imperialism, and indeed to much of the conquest of Africa carried out in the three decades before the First World War, is an Atlantic world crisscrossed by workers and revolutionaries, enslaved and free, white and black—the Atlantic depicted in Peter Linebaugh and Marcus Rediker's *Many-Headed Hydra*.[16] This field I term the *red and black Atlantic*, borrowing from a wide-ranging literature emphasizing its original and creative democratic modernity.[17]

The colonial power of state and capital emerged as a parasite upon, and a reaction to, the primary modernity of the red and black Atlantic. Beginning an analysis of colonialism with the red and black Atlantic promises a less Eurocentric account of imperial modernity than the otherwise excellent literature on liberalism and imperialism.[18] Through an intense reading of liberal legal and political theory, scholars of liberalism and imperialism have probed the deficiencies in liberal self-understandings while leaving relatively unexplored the nature of the enemies against which liberalism forged itself. The others constitutively excluded by liberalism, however, had political and intellectual lives that are worthy of reconstruction not only because they reveal how incorrect and oppressive liberalism has been, but also, and more importantly for the present essay, because liberalism formed itself in struggle against the original form of modernity created by these others. Liberalism emerged as a secondary modernity out of bourgeois efforts to subvert, redirect, and exploit this primary, and, in the broadest sense, proletarian modernity. White liberalism did not simply exclude and suppress the multiracial working-class democracy of the red and black Atlantic but rather built itself as a reaction formation against this democracy. To understand German imperialism, therefore, we must begin with the revolutions against which German imperialism emerged. These revolutions also had important German origins, beginning in the period of the French Revolution.

A worldwide revolution of unfree labor that partially coincided with the French Revolution not only helped radicalize the process of revolution inside France, but also had important political consequences from Central Europe to the Americas. While rebellions against confinement began as early as the seventeenth century, these later uprising had particularly importance consequences for the history of empires.[19] In Prussia and other German states, unfree peasants used the presence of approaching French armies either to rebel directly against their bondage or, more commonly, to allow French armies to abolish hereditary servitude. The Prussian general Gerhard Scharnhorst was among the first to identify the strategic importance of the politics of unfree peasants in his 1797 diagnosis of the "General Causes for the good fortune of the French in the wars of the Revolution." For Scharnhorst, the French Revolutionary armies received support inside Germany from those who have an "excitable feeling for the rights and for the suffering of the unfortunate classes of people." Opposed to the revolution were, Scharnhorst explained, "that class that had no feeling for the happiness of other human beings." Common people in Prussia and other states that the French invaded thus had little incentive either to defend their states or to support their own armies. Scharnhorst noted that civilians would not provide winter quarter even to their own wounded soldiers, unless compelled to do so.[20]

The 1807 Prussian October Edict sought, in part, to win the allegiance of Prussian peasants against the French occupiers by promising freedom from hereditary servitude even while preserving the coerced labor essential to manorial estates. The idea, in the words of Prussian reformer Prince Karl August von Hardenberg, was to end "hereditary unfreedom" (*Erbuntertänigkeit*) without "repealing the system of forced labor [*Fronverfassung*]."[21] Like the emancipation proclaimed in the United States later in the century, the point here was to win the military participation of unfree workers by promising them freedom, even while seeking to ensure that this freedom had as little an impact as possible on postwar rural class hierarchies. In 1813, the Prussian monarch issued an edict calling on peasants to employ their agricultural implements in a violent uprising against French occupiers. Many officers rejected the compromise with rural insurrection represented by this so-called *Landsturm* edict. As one wrote, it represented "one of the most remarkable documents of fanaticism in recent times," and compared it to the revolution in Haiti: "France has fought wars in all four corners of the world, but—apart from the savages of St. Domingue [Haiti]—it never occurred to any government to openly make assassination, poisoning, and other unspeakable crimes the law for its subjects."[22]

Those who planned the Landsturm seem to have been at least partly aware of the similarities between the Prussian peasants they enlisted and insurgent slaves. Those Landsturm members found guilty of cowardice or abandoning their posts would have, the edict specified, their "usual dues and services" doubled. That is, their serfdom would be intensified. "Who shows the sensibilities of a slave," the relevant paragraph explained, "will be treated as a slave." The paragraph seemed to suggest that the normal labor duties of bonded laborers were like slavery and that serving in the Landsturm was akin to a rebellion against slavery.[23] This was obviously not the intention of Prussian authorities when they employed the vocabulary of slave insurgency, but they had to work with what they had.

Prussian officers succeeded partly in incorporating peasant insurrection into their war against France, but always recognized, in the words of Scharnhorst's protégée, Prussian general Carl von Clausewitz, that "war by means of popular uprisings" introduced "a state of legalized anarchy that is as much a threat to the social order at home as it is to the enemy."[24] The edicts freeing and mobilizing Prussian peasants during the wars of the French Revolution were parts of a long back-and-forth between rural insurgency and state attempts to channel and subvert these revolutionary agrarian energies. It continued through the revolutions of 1848–49, the SPD Rural Agitation after 1891, the 1918 November Revolution, and the 1945–46 land reforms carried out under Soviet auspices.[25]

The Haitian Revolution had similarly important consequences for unfree labor in Africa and the Americas. While historians once thought of this revolution as an echo of the nearly contemporaneous French Revolution, many now recognize the important political and military knowledge that the enslaved, the majority of whom had been born in Africa, brought to the French sugar colony.[26] These included a powerful explanation of slavery as social death that existed prior to its appropriation by G.W.F. Hegel and subsequent scholars of slavery.[27] In the Bight of Benin, as well as in Haiti, where individuals born in the Bight of Benin made up around a quarter of the population, slaves were sometimes imagined as stolen corpses reanimated by a sorcerer whom they were then forced to serve—and who sometimes sold them into slavery. In Haiti, moreover, Jean Zombi was also the name of a particularly committed and violent revolutionary in the final years of the fight against slavery and French colonialism. (Jean Zombi is still today honored as a Loa, or spirit, in Vodou.)[28] The philosopher Susan Buck-Morss, building on the work of Pierre-Franklin Tavares, has established that when Hegel composed his famous dialectic of lord and bondsman or master and slave (*Herr und Knecht*), he was familiar with sympathetic accounts of the Haitian Revolution published in the periodical *Minerva*.[29] For Buck-Morss, the Haitian Revolution helped universalize Hegel's universal history. Instead, we might see how Hegel, living in the midst of Central European peasant insurgencies, also reshaped analyses of Atlantic slavery made by slaves themselves into an intensely partisan account of the class conflict between lord and bondsman that stretched from Haiti to Central Europe.[30] Numerous writers and activists, most famously Karl Marx and Friedrich Engels, developed this Hegelian account of lord and bondsman into a powerful critique of the system of wage labor emerging on both sides of the Atlantic in the nineteenth century.

The two struggles, that of workers and that of slaves, had at least three similarities that made them natural partners and would facilitate various forms of solidarity. First, both slavery and wage labor are what Hegel's greatest follower, Karl Marx, who was also perhaps the sharpest contemporary European observer of both struggles, termed "alienated labor". Both slavery and wage labor, that is, are forms of work performed under the control, and for the profit, of another. Second, it is at least plausible that Marx's critique of private property as a form of oppression (and not just, as in Proudhon's formulation—which Marx rejected—as a form of theft) was inspired by struggles against slavery in which the claim of property (in slaves) stood most explicitly against human emancipation. Indeed, Marx and Engels may have borrowed from anti-slavery the language that they used in the *Communist Manifesto* of the "emancipation" (*Befreiung*) of labor and the "abolition" (*Abschaffung*—not *Aufhebung*) of bourgeois property.[31] Third, both slavery and wage labor emerged from private appropriation of a common, and their particular forms were at least partly determined by the nature of the common particular to Europe and to Africa. In Europe, people were plenty and land was scarce, so that elite appropriation of land through enclosures transformed populations into that "'free' and outlawed [*vogelfreie*] proletariat" that Marx described in his chapter on primitive accumulation in *Capital*.[32] In West Africa, by contrast, land was plentiful in relation to people, so elite, privately appropriated wealth was in people rather than in land. To create the same abandonment of workers to elites that occurred in Europe through the seizure of land required in Africa the seizure of people.[33]

The political heirs of the revolutions against bonded labor in Europe and the Americas collaborated directly for the first time in the American Civil War of 1861–65.[34] A full 10 percent of the Union Army had been born in one of the German states. While only a minority of German Americans were communists, many were part of an international German communist exile community that had fled the continent after the failed revolutions of 1848–49. Like Marx and Engels, who had relocated to England, many had learned from the hard experience of the French June Days and the similarly antirevolutionary Frankfurt Parliament that alliances with the bourgeoisie held few of the strategic advantages promised in the *Communist Manifesto*, written in 1847. Learning from black and white anti-slavery militants in the United States, these transatlantic revolutionaries played a central, though underappreciated, role in the military defeat of the Confederacy. They celebrated a great victory with the end of slavery in the United States and became a much more self-conscious international political community in the course of the Civil War and in the founding of the First International Working Men's Association in 1864, as well as in the subsequent socialist and communist internationals.

As the revolutionary self-emancipation of US slaves played a central role in the political establishment of international communism, the counterrevolution of sharecropping and segregation by US elites, the basis of the so-called New South, became paradigmatic for international liberalism. The New South emerged from what W.E.B. Du Bois has described as a "counterrevolution of property" that reduced to a bare minimum the emancipation won by African Americans in the course of what he identified as their Civil War era "general strike."[35] Economic boosters began describing the former Confederacy as the "New South" in the period after the federal government ended Reconstruction in 1877. They presented the racial order of disfranchisement, segregation, and superexploitation that they had created as a proud achievement of their region and one that promised great political and economic advantage to colonial regions in Africa and elsewhere. While European desires for sources of high-grade cotton outside the United States prompted some of the colonial imitations of the American New South, its more basic racial political economy was the most important factor.

One of the most important contributions of the German Empire to the repertoire of European imperialism was its pioneering efforts to render the American New South a model for politics and economics in colonial Africa.[36] Indeed, the German colony of Togo would gain its good reputation among other colonial powers by modeling itself on the American New South. Yet, as one of the regimes that sought to undermine, and channel the energies of, the emancipatory struggles of people of enslaved, enserfed, and otherwise unfree workers, the New South was already one of the colonial counterrevolutions aimed at the primary democratic modernity created in the red and black Atlantic. From the seizure of Sierra Leone and Liberia as outposts of anti-slavery and settlements of manumitted slaves to the British bombardment and seizure of Lagos in 1861, through the European Scramble for Africa of 1884–1914, capitalist states utilized the political efforts of the enslaved against slavery to seize territory, project their power into Africa, and manage the end of slavery as a transition to capitalism rather than a transition to democracy. The double role of Germany as brutal colonizer and model colonizer rests on the contrary political and economic imperatives of this phase of European imperialism, which fought emancipation in the name of emancipation and wrecked a primary democratic modernity in the name of a secondary, liberal capitalist modernity.

Germans brought some of the specific political economic regimes of the postslavery United States to their colony of Togo in collaboration with the individual whom they, like much of the world, believed most responsible for the allegedly docile and subordinate black workers of the New South. This was the African American educator and principal of Tuskegee Institute,

Booker T. Washington. Washington had founded Tuskegee Institute in 1881 to train African American teachers for the public school system that first came to many southern states to satisfy black demands for public education. Washington initially pursued an agenda that challenged white elites in many respects, even while he couched his efforts in a language of black accommodation to white supremacy. Washington's engagement with German and, later, other colonial projects emphasized the conservative and accommodationist character of his work, for which it has since been admired by some, reviled by others. Washington came to the attention of the world with an 1895 speech that W.E.B. Du Bois years later dubbed the "Atlanta Compromise." Speaking as a representative of black southerners to his white listeners, Washington proclaimed: "In all things that are purely social, we can be as separate as the fingers, yet one as the hand in all things essential to mutual progress."

The agricultural attaché to the German embassy in the United States was likely in the audience during Washington's "Atlanta Compromise" speech, and, in 1900, he persuaded Washington to send an expedition of Tuskegee graduates, led by a Tuskegee faculty member, to the German colony of Togo in West Africa. As Booker T. Washington's German publisher, also the most important publisher of colonial works in Germany, later remarked, the words of the Atlanta compromise "are also true for us in Africa."[37] The agricultural and the political economic results of the Tuskegee cotton program established Togo as a German *Musterkolonie*, a model colony.[38] Colonial thinkers ranging from Congo Reformer E.D. Morel to his arch-nemesis King Leopold of Belgium praised German colonialism and Tuskegee Institute. Colonial reformers and colonial cotton organizations followed the German example in employing the American South, and particularly Tuskegee Institute, as a colonial model. Yet the attempt to reproduce the New South in Togo, like its American original, did not simply introduce modernity from the outside. It was rather a diversion, and a reaction against, a regional variant of a primary democratic modernity that preceded colonial capital and state formation.

Between the decline of the Atlantic slave trade and the onset of German colonial rule, the Ewe, the largest population in Southern Togo, created a free-labor economy resistant to many forms of domination, including colonial capitalism. The territory that would become the German colony had been a no-man's land between the slave-trading kingdoms of Asante to the west and Dahomey to the east (today in the republics of Ghana and Benin). The Ewe developed a system of autonomous households that carried on mixed agriculture and petty manufacturing for subsistence and trade. This not only made the Ewe as a whole resistant to outside control, but also gave Ewe men and women a level of individual autonomy unusual in the Atlantic world at that time. Several Ewe women shared a single husband and could each possess their own households and fields, which were linked to those of their husbands through gift and market exchange. Missionaries and colonial officials would later remark, mostly with dismay, upon the unusual independence of Ewe women. Ewe households could also hold slaves, although the scale of production made this a society with slaves rather than a slave society. The growing world demand for palm oil, as well as the conditions of production of this crop, meant that individual producers could prosper much as large plantation owners could. Oil palms grow freely in much of West Africa, and, while they can be improved by cultivation, oil can also be collected and processed by individuals from wild palms. Palm oil had a wide variety of uses in Africa and in Europe. Palm oil was also a central ingredient in the West African diet, so producers could choose to consume palm oil themselves if they did not wish to market it locally or sell it to European merchants. Ewe society afforded many of its members a greater degree of political and economic autonomy than existed in slave economies of the Atlantic or, arguably, in the free labor economies of Europe.

Economic historian Anthony Hopkins noted the particular modernity of the small-scale production that emerged in West Africa during the period preceding European colonial rule. "In so far as firms of this size and type are the basis of the export economies of most West African states today," Hopkins wrote in 1973, "it can be said that modernity dates not from the imposition of colonial rule, as used to be thought, but from the early nineteenth century."[39] We can take Hopkins's point even further: worker autonomy had long been the goal of enslaved and free workers across the Atlantic, and female political and economic autonomy had more recently become the goal of the most progressive political movements of the region; the Ewe, as well as other societies in West Africa, achieved this broader political and economic modernity relatively early, certainly well before the societies colonizing them did. The colonial state worked against this modernity, finally seeking to bury it in an imagined primitivism.

The cotton project did not modernize Togolese production but, rather, exemplified what later theorists described as the "development of underdevelopment."[40] To make farmers in Togo grow cotton as a raw material for European industry, German colonial officials attacked a well-established local textile industry, acknowledged by all to produce higher quality, if more expensive, cloth than that imported from Europe. They also destroyed a local pottery industry that exported earthenware regionally, and they forced many Togolese to grow cotton instead of harvesting profitable commodities, like palm oil, or carrying out subsistence farming and other household production. Forcing Ewe to grow cotton as a raw material for European industry, moreover, attacked the diffuse and diverse household economies that had afforded Ewe men and women significant economic autonomy and enabled early resistance to German colonial control.

The cotton project also engaged directly with narratives of modernity local to the Ewe. In 1904, the head of the Tuskegee Expedition, John W. Robinson, founded a three-year cotton school in Notsé, Togo. Officials compelled young men from all over the colony to attend this school.

Locating the school in Notsé attacked Ewe history and Ewe modernity. The Ewe traced their present politically and economically dispersed and autonomous households and polities—their primary modernity—to a sixteenth-century exodus from a walled city at Notsé ruled by the despotic King Agokoli. Germans were well aware of this historical narrative by the turn of the century. Ewe historical memory ran counter to the despotism of state formation, capital accumulation, and patriarchal monogamy. Forcing Ewe to learn to grow cotton in Notsé was something akin to forcing Jews to learn to make bricks in Egypt. The German colonial state sent Ewe back to Notsé not only to train them to grow cotton, but also to undo their emancipatory history of modernity and subject them to a new Agokoli of capitalism.

Liberal admirers of German colonialism and other forms of secondary, reactive modernity found themselves in the contradictory position of heralding as modern a form of oppression and exploitation aimed, in the first place, at undoing a prior, democratic modernity.[41] The centerpiece of their ideological work lay in producing a narrative that reversed temporality, so that the primary, interracial modernity of Atlantic commoning was rewritten as a nonwhite primitivism. This narrative figured wrecking the modern Ewe common as a modernizing step rather than an antimodernizing counterrevolution.

Colonialism thus produced prehistories for and about itself that depict colonized societies as lacking modernity when, in fact, it was precisely the modernity of these societies that colonialism attacked. George Steinmetz, in his analysis of what he calls precoloniality, has shown persuasively how variations in these imagined precolonial conditions influenced subsequent colonial policy.[42] The series of binary pairs structuring the various colonial imaginaries of the precolonial are, nonetheless, similar enough, and so familiar by now, that they hardly need elaboration here: primitive/modern; local/international; etc. These imagined precolonial conditions were not simply lies unconnected to history, but rather each articulated with a diverse set of real historical developments in which colonial conquest and rule was but an episode. This colonial temporality has been fundamental to the creation of the modernization theory that both German history and the history of imperialism have, each in their own way, as well as in combination, both built upon and undermined.

In both its origin and structure, colonial temporality is not "European" or "Western" or even proper to one nation or another. Rather, colonial temporality should be specified in class terms as bourgeois. Marx's early comments on British rule in India display a disappointingly Eurocentric— although hardly uncritical—understanding of colonial modernity.[43] In *Capital*, however, a text whose development Marx himself connected to his own observations and extended discussions of the revolution against slavery in the Civil War, Marx presented a more acute understanding.[44] Marx recognized the primitive as a kind of fairy tale, one that goes like this: "In times long gone by there were two sorts of people; one, the diligent, intelligent, and, above all, frugal elite; the other, lazy rascals, spending their substance, and more, in riotous living."[45] Marx refers specifically to a fairy-tale version of the enclosures that displaced so many from the land in Britain. His account of primitive accumulation, with which he proposed to replace this fairy tale, has since been generalized, applied by Rosa Luxemburg to colonialism and by many other theorists to capitalism more broadly.[46] Indeed, one of the most interesting Marxist political discussions today concerns the struggles over the last vestiges of our common: our forms of communication and intimacy, our genes, our air and water.

The false memories of the precolonial, like the fairy-tale version of primitive accumulation, were deployed strategically by the European bourgeoisie to win a set of class wars and bio-political struggles, and then to consolidate this victory by repressing the memory of those struggles. Identifying the precolonial as a primitive object of colonialism further posits the poverty and degradation caused by the counterrevolution of colonialism as a condition that existed prior to colonialism. It even suggests that colonialism was a solution to, rather than one of the causes of, global poverty. The real story, as Marx writes of the seizures of the common, is "written in the annals of mankind in letters of blood and fire." It includes the violence of slave capture and slave rebellion, of factory discipline and worker rebellion, of bio-political regulation around categories of race and the countervailing polymorphous perversity available to all. It also includes revolutionary Atlantic modernity and the colonial countermodernity that opposed it.

At least as paradigmatic as German colonialism as a form of bourgeois countermodernity was German communism and social democracy as a form of primary modernity from below. Some recent historians have followed Lenin, in my view incorrectly, in painting the prewar SPD as at least partly sympathetic to imperialism.[47] Karl Kautsky, the most important theorist in the party, clearly "treat[ed] metropole and colony in a single analytic field" in his critique of capitalism, colonial modernization, and state authoritarianism. In his 1907 *Socialism and Colonial Policy*, Kautsky rejected "the right of peoples of higher culture to 'exercise tutelage' over peoples of lower culture" since that was precisely the "right" that the bourgeoisie claimed justified its own political and economic power in Europe. Ironically, Kautsky explained, the poverty that capitalism brought to Europe and the rest of the world gave the domination of those few who profited from this system, the bourgeoisie, "the appearance of the rule of culture over barbarism [*Unkultur*]." The bourgeoisie could thus claim that "they do not exploit the proletariat for their personal advantage, nor for the sake of profit: they exercise tutelage over it in the general social interest." This was the same logic used in overseas colonization. The proletariat could not, Kautsky wrote, endorse the colonial civilizing mission "without sanctioning its own exploitation and disavowing its own struggle for emancipation." Cultural and economic progress of subordinate groups, Kautsky reminded his readers, "has always occurred *against* and not *through* the upper classes."[48] Kautsky, like many other Social Democrats—and unlike virtually every liberal critic of imperialism—understood colonialism as part of a counterrevolution against allied struggles to overthrow slavery, capitalism, imperialism, and state power.

The liberal internationalism of the League of Nations, for which German colonial countermodernity would prove to be so important, was also, like earlier variants of imperialism, a reaction formation. As Gordon Levin and Arno Mayer established long ago, the Wilsonian internationalism and respect for national self-determination was in part a cooptation of prior Bolshevik calls for the same thing.[49] Unlike the Bolshevik original, however, liberal internationalism explicitly rejected the right of nonwhites to self-determination.[50] If Soviet internationalism was a model and competitor for Wilsonian liberal internationalism, then Germany and its colonies functioned as its excluded other, a constituent exception. Despite Lenin's pronouncements to the contrary, the Bolsheviks and the Comintern continued earlier Social Democratic criticisms of colonialism, including Kautsky's.[51]

The image of Germany as "backward" and illiberal justified its exclusion from, and control by, the League of Nations. The administration of Germany and its former colonies gave international liberalism a new political form and historical role. The League of Nations turned over Germany's colonies to Britain and France—not as the legitimate spoils of a war (which had long precedent in international law), but rather as part of a "a sacred trust of civilization" to be administered by states acting as "mandatories" on behalf of the League of Nations, as laid out in Article 22 of the Versailles Treaty. Soon the concept of the mandate, as well as Germany's unfitness to carry out that mandate, came retroactively to justify all European colonialism, above all as expressed in the writing of Frederick Lugard.[52] There would have been no Article 22 had there not been German, as well as Ottoman, colonies to divide up among powers that had also to formally disavow conquest. Article 22 rested on the assumption that Germany was not a colonizer fit for this new era of humanity and thus that its colonies should be taken as "mandates" of the League and wards of "civilization."

Germans who opposed the negative characterization of their overseas empire referred to a colonial *Schuldluge*, or "guilt lie." German responses to this *Schuldluge* contained two elements, each, in its own way, correct: first, colonialism is inherently violent, and no foreign power thought it desirable to rule in Africa without recourse to the whip and other practices subsequently denounced as German atrocities by the self-appointed trustees of civilization;[53] second, German colonial practices had long been admired and imitated by other colonial powers, who conveniently forgot all they had learned after German defeat in 1918 in order to justify taking Germany's colonies for themselves.[54]

Given the importance of the seizure of the German colonies for the consolidation of the Eurocentric international community after the First World War, it is hardly surprising that the German rightist, and later fascist, legal scholar Carl Schmitt offered a second profound and insightful critique of the international order of liberalism. For Schmitt, the League of Nations represented an attempt to make "humanity," rather than the state or any other specific grouping, into a political subject. Doing so not only disguised the role of the individual states that exercised sovereignty through the League, but also allowed them to claim to act on behalf of humanity, and thus with greater violence and impunity. Writing in 1932, Schmitt described a new type of war that appeared to proceed not from the state or nation but from a self-styled international community: "War is condemned but executions, sanctions, punitive expeditions, pacifications, protection of treaties, international police, and measures to assure peace remain. The adversary is thus no longer called an enemy but a disturber of peace and is thereby designated to be an outlaw of humanity."[55] Wars for humanity thus became especially inhumane. Schmitt himself was less offended by such internationally sanctioned brutality against non-European territories than he was by the treatment of, to take the title of one his early works on the topic, the *Rhineland as Object of International Policy*.[56] Still, Schmitt's description of the politics of internationalism serves as an accurate description—and devastating critique—of liberal imperialism from the "scramble for Africa" until today. For Schmitt, internationalism did not end colonial rule but rather amplified and obscured it. Schmitt had little interest in modernity, and, like many current critics of liberalism and imperialism, offers an immanent critique of forms of European sovereignty without considering in any extended manner their proletarian others.

At least since 1884–85, when European powers met in Otto von Bismarck's Berlin residence to work out the terms by which they would colonize Africa, Germany has played a leading role in the development of colonial modernity, first as an example to be followed and then as a counterexample that justified non-German "white" powers to, nonetheless, continue these projects. This double role of German colonialism reflects a broader, class-contradiction in the concept of modernity, which, perhaps like every concept, has a class dimension so irreducible that there can be no master term that would comprise all its variants. This essay has identified just two class-specific international modernities: a proletarian and a bourgeois modernity. It has given priority to a proletarian modernity, defined as democratic, creative of various commons, multiracial, and revolutionary. Bourgeois modernity was a reaction by propertied elites against this primary modernity that used liberal notions of limited, representative government and a right to private property to combat the democracy of the commons. The idea that the commons were somehow primitive, prior to, and earlier than, capitalist modernity was part of the ideological work of bourgeois modernity, which presented its attack on modernity, paradoxically, as a first act of modernity. Understanding modernity through irreducible class difference allows—indeed requires—historians to go beyond Eurocentric treatments—whether critical or laudatory—of modernity and its others to reconstruct a more dynamic history of class and other struggles whose primary arena and basis is not the state, capital, or even "the economy," but rather the enormously diverse and creative forms of politics fashioned by the commoning multitude over the past centuries.

Notes

1   Ralf Dahrendorf, *Society and Democracy in Germany* (Garden City, NY: Doubleday, 1967); Joseph Schumpeter, *Imperialism and Social Classes* (New York: A.M. Kelly, 1951).

2   Paul Rabinow, *French Modern: Norms and Forms of the Social Environment* (Cambridge, MA: MIT Press, 1989); Detlev J.K. Peukert, "The Genesis of the 'Final Solution' from the Spirit of Science," in David Crew (ed.), *Nazism and German Society, 1933–1945* (London: Routledge, 1994), pp. 274–99. See also Peukert, *The Weimar Republic: The Crisis of Classical Modernity*, trans. Richard Deveson (1987; New York: Hill and Wang, 1993).

3   On the German concept of *Kulturbestrebungen*, see Andrew Zimmerman, "Ruling Africa: Science as Sovereignty in the German Colonial Empire and Its Aftermath," in Geoff Eley and Bradley Naranch (eds.), *German Colonialism in a Global Age* (Durham: Duke University Press, 2014), pp. 93–108.

4   The primacy of labor over capital has been emphasized by Italian Marxists of the workerist (Operaismo) or autonomist tradition, beginning with Mario Tronti and including such thinkers as Paolo Virno and, perhaps best known in the United States, Michael Hardt and Antonio Negri. See Mario Tronti, "Our Operaismo," *New Left Review* 73 (February 2012), pp. 119–39; Paolo Virno, *A Grammar of the Multitude: For an Analysis of Contemporary Forms of Life* (Cambridge: Semiotext (e), 2003); Michael Hardt and Antonio Negri, *Empire* (Cambridge: Harvard University Press, 2000); Michael Hardt and Antonio Negri, *Multitude: War and Democracy in the Age of Empire* (New York: The Penguin Press, 2004); Michael Hardt and Antonio Negri, *Commonwealth* (Cambridge: Harvard University Press, 2009).

5   The commons has become central to much democratic theory recently. Especially helpful for the present essay have been Hardt and Negri, *Commonwealth* and Peter Linebaugh, *The Magna Carta Manifesto: Liberties and Commons for All* (Berkeley: University of California Press, 2008). For an excellent survey, see Tine De Moor, "What Do We Have in Common? A Comparative Framework for Old and New Literature on the Commons," *International Review of Social History* 57 (2012), pp. 269–90.

6   I develop this argument in Andrew Zimmerman, "Primitive Art, Primitive Accumulation, and the Origin of the Work of Art in German New Guinea," *History of the Present* 1 (2011), pp. 5–30.

7   Karl Polanyi, *The Great Transformation*, 2nd edn (1944; Boston: Beacon Press, 2001).

8   Elizabeth A. Povinelli, *Economies of Abandonment: Social Belonging and Endurance in Late Liberalism* (Durham: Duke University Press, 2011). On this shift in the study of liberalism, see Johanna Bockman, "The Political Projects of Neoliberalism," *Social Anthropology* 20 (2012), pp. 310–17.

9   David Blackbourn and Geoff Eley, *The Peculiarities of German History: Bourgeois Society and Politics in Nineteenth-Century Germany* (New York: Oxford University Press, 1984).

10   Geoff Eley, *Forging Democracy: The History of the Left in Europe, 1850–2000* (New York: Oxford University Press, 2002).

11   Hans Ulrich Wehler, *Bismarck und der Imperialismus* (Cologne: Kiepenheuer und Witsch, 1969). For a short, English version, see Hans-Ulrich Wehler, "Bismarck's Imperialism 1862–1890," *Past & Present* 48 (1970), pp. 119–55.

12   See the important article by Jens-Uwe Guettel, "The Myth of the Pro-Colonialist SPD: German Social Democracy and Imperialism before World War I," *Central European History* 45:3 (2012), pp. 452–84.

13   Geoff Eley, "Defining Social Imperialism: Use and Abuse of an Idea," *Social History* 1 (1976), pp. 265–90; Eley, "Social Imperialism in Germany," in Joachim Radkau and Imanuel Geiss (eds.), *Imperialismus im 20. Jahrhundert: Gedenkschrift Für George W.F. Hallgarten* (Munich: Beck, 1976).

14   Frederick Cooper and Ann Laura Stoler, *Tensions of Empire: Colonial Cultures in a Bourgeois World* (Berkeley: University of California Press, 1997), p. 4.

15   Marcel van der Linden, *Workers of the World: Essays Toward a Global Labor History* (Leiden: Brill, 2008); Michael Denning, "Wageless Life," *New Left Review* 66 (December 2010), pp. 79–97.

16   Peter Linebaugh and Marcus Rediker, *The Many-Headed Hydra: The Hidden History of the Revolutionary Atlantic* (Verso Books, 2002).

17   For the term "red Atlantic," see David Armitage, "The Red Atlantic," review of *The Many-Headed Hydra: Sailors, Slaves, and the Atlantic Working Class in the Eighteenth Century* by Peter Linebaugh and Marcus Rediker (London, 1990), *Reviews in American History* 29:4 (2001), pp. 479–86. Sidney Mintz offered some of the classic formulations of black Atlantic modernity. See David Scott, "Modernity That Predated the Modern: Sidney Mintz's Caribbean," *History Workshop Journal* 58:1 (January 1, 2004), pp. 191–210. More recently, see Stephan Palmié, *Wizards and Scientists: Explorations in Afro-Cuban Modernity and Tradition* (Durham: Duke University Press, 2002). The best-known work, although less relevant in this particular context, is Paul Gilroy, *The Black Atlantic: Modernity and Double Consciousness* (Cambridge: Harvard University Press, 1993).

18   See especially Uday Singh Mehta, *Liberalism and Empire: A Study in Nineteenth-Century British Liberal Thought* (Chicago: University of Chicago Press, 1999) and Jennifer Pitts, "Empire and Legal Universalisms in the Eighteenth Century," *The American Historical Review* 117 (2012), pp. 92–121. More broadly, see Domenico Losurdo, *Liberalism: A Counter-History*, trans. Gregory Elliott (London: Verso Books, 2011). For excellent analyses of the German case, see Matthew P. Fitzpatrick, *Liberal Imperialism in*

Germany: Expansionism and Nationalism, 1848–1884 (New York: Berghahn Books, 2008) and Jens-Uwe Guettel, *German Expansionism, Imperial Liberalism and the United States, 1776–1945* (Cambridge: Cambridge University Press, 2012).

19 Michel Foucault, *History of Madness*, trans. Jonathan Murphy and Jean Khalfa (1961; New York: Routledge, 2006) and Linebaugh and Rediker, *The Many-Headed Hydra*.

20 Gerhard von Scharnhorst, "Entwicklung der allgemeinen Ursachen des Glücks der Franzosen in dem Revolutionskriege und insbesondere in dem Feldzug von 1794," *Neues militairisches Journal* 8 (1797), pp. 1–154, pp. 16–17, 23, 28, 48.

21 Karl August Freiherr von Hardenberg, "Über die Reorganisation des Preußischen Staats" (September 12, 1807) (Rigaer Denkschrift). German History in Documents and Images (Washington, DC: German Historical Institute), http://germanhistorydocs.ghi-dc.org/.

22 General Rapp, *Danziger Zeitung*, July 1813, cited in Grosse Generalstab (ed.), *Das Preussische Heer der Befreiungskriege*, 3 vols (Berlin: E.S. Mittler, 1912), 2:315n1.

23 "Verordnung über den Landsturm vom 21. April 1813," in Maximilian Blumenthal (ed.), *Der preussische Landsturm von 1813: Auf archivalischen Grundlagen* (Berlin: R. Schröder, 1900), pp. 163–78.

24 Carl von Clausewitz, *On War* (1832; Princeton: Princeton University Press, 1976), p. 479.

25 The literature on this topic is vast. For a good overview, see Hans Ulrich Wehler, *Vom Feudalismus des alten Reiches bis zur defensiven Modernisierung der Reformära, 1700–1815*, vol. 1 of *Deutsche Gesellschaftsgeschichte*, 5 vols (Munich: C.H. Beck, 1987). Especially important for this work has been the work of Hartmut Harnisch and Jan Peters. See Hartmut Harnisch, *Kapitalistische Agrarreform und industrielle Revolution: Agrarhistorische Untersuchungen über das ostelbische Preussen zwischen Spätfeudalismus und bürgerlich-demokratischer Revolution von 1848/49, unter besonderer Berücksichtigung der Provinz Brandenburg* (Weimar: Böhlau, 1984); Jan Peters (ed.), *Konflikt und Kontrolle in Gutherrschaftsgesellschaften: über Resistenz- und Herrschaftsverhalten in ländlichen Sozialgebilden der Frühen Neuzeit* (Göttingen: Vandenhoeck & Ruprecht, 1995). See also Reinhart Koselleck, *Preussen Zwischen Reform und Revolution* (Stuttgart: Klett, 1975); Hanna Schissler, *Preussische Agrargesellschaft im Wandel* (Göttingen: Vandenhoeck und Ruprecht, 1978).

26 See especially John K. Thornton, "'I Am the Subject of the King of Congo': African Political Ideology and the Haitian Revolution," *Journal of World History* 4 (1993), pp. 181–214.

27 Georg Wilhelm Friedrich Hegel, *Phenomenology of Spirit*, trans. Arnold V. Miller (1807; Oxford: Clarendon Press, 1977); Orlando Patterson, *Slavery and Social Death: A Comparative Study* (Cambridge: Harvard University Press, 1982).

28 Joan Dayan, *Haiti, History, and the Gods* (Berkeley: University of California Press, 1995), pp. 36–9.

29 Susan Buck-Morss, "Hegel and Haiti," *Critical Inquiry* 26 (2000), pp. 821–65. Buck-Morss builds on the work of Pierre-Franklin Tavares, including "Hegel et Haiti ou le Silence de Hegel sur Saint-Domingue," *Chemins Critiques* (1992), pp. 113–31. Also important in the discussion is Nick Nesbitt, "Troping Toussaint, Reading Revolution," *Research in African Literatures* 35:2 (July 1, 2004), pp. 18–33, and Nesbitt, "The Idea of 1804," *Yale French Studies*, no. 107 (2005), pp. 6–38. See also Susan Buck-Morss, *Hegel, Haiti, and Universal History* (Pittsburgh: University of Pittsburgh Press, 2009).

30 I develop this point further in "Раса против революции в Центральной и Восточной Европе: от Гегеля до Вебера, от крестьянских восстаний до 'полонизации'" [Race against Revolution in Central and Eastern Europe: From Hegel to Weber, from Rural Insurgency to "Polonization."] *Ab Imperio* (2014), pp. 23–57.

31 The use of the terminology of emancipation and abolition occurs regularly in the works of Karl Marx and Friedrich Engels. See, for example, *Manifest der Kommunistischen Partei* (1848), Karl Marx and Friedrich Engels, *Werke*, 37 vols (Berlin: Dietz, 1956), 4:459–93.

32 Karl Marx, "The Secret of Primitive Accumulation," ch. 26 in *Capital*, vol. 1, trans. Ben Fowkes (1867; New York: Penguin Classics, 1976), pp. 873–76.

33 This seemingly paradoxical outcome could be compared to the process described by Perry Anderson in which the same processes of economic development in early modern Europe led to the end of serfdom in Western Europe and the rise of serfdom in Eastern Europe. Perry Anderson, *Lineages of the Absolutist State* (London: New Left Review Books, 1974).

34 The argument presented in this paragraph is developed in Andrew Zimmerman, introduction to *The Civil War in the United States*, by Karl Marx and Friedrich Engels (New York: International Publishers, 2016). See also Andrew Zimmerman, "From the Rhine to the Mississippi: Property, Democracy, and Socialism in the American Civil War," *Journal of the Civil War Era* 5 (2015), pp. 3–37.

35 W.E.B. Du Bois, *Black Reconstruction: An Essay Toward a History of the Part Which Black Folk Played in the Attempt to Reconstruct Democracy in America, 1860–1880* (1935; New York: Free Press, 1998). See also David R. Roediger, *Seizing Freedom: Slave Emancipation and Liberty for All* (Brooklyn: Verso, 2014).

36 What follows is based on my *Alabama in Africa: Booker T. Washington, the German Empire, and the Globalization of the New South* (Princeton: Princeton University Press, 2010).

37 Booker T. Washington, *Vom Sklaven Empor: Eine Selbstbiographie*, trans. Estelle Du Bois-Reymond (Berlin, 1902), p. vi.

38 On the conception of Togo as a *Musterkolonie*, see Dennis Laumann, "A Historiography of German Togoland, or the Rise and Fall of a 'Model Colony,'" *History in Africa* 30 (2003), pp. 195–211.

39 A.G. Hopkins, *An Economic History of West Africa* (New York: Columbia University Press, 1973), p. 126.

40   Andre Gunder Frank, "The Development of Underdevelopment," *Monthly Review* 18 (1966), pp. 17–31. There are many important critiques of dependency theory, but no persuasive refutations of its basic thesis of combined and uneven development rather than liberal modernization theory as an explanation of global inequality.

41   On colonial temporality, see especially Johannes Fabian, *Time and the Other: How Anthropology Makes Its Object* (New York: Columbia University Press, 1983).

42   George Steinmetz, *The Devil's Handwriting: Precoloniality and the German Colonial State in Qingdao, Samoa, and Southwest Africa* (Chicago: University of Chicago Press, 2007).

43   For an excellent analysis, see Kevin B. Anderson, *Marx at the Margins: On Nationalism, Ethnicity, and Non-Western Societies* (Chicago: University of Chicago Press, 2010).

44   Marx and Engels, *The Civil War in the United States*.

45   Marx, *Capital*, vol. 1, p. 873.

46   Rosa Luxemburg, *The Accumulation of Capital*, trans. Agnes Schwarzschild (1913; London: Routledge: 1951). David Harvey's concept of "accumulation by dispossession" is an important recent application of Luxemburg's work. See David Harvey, *A Brief History of Neoliberalism* (New York: Oxford University Press, 2007).

47   Against this view, see Guettel, "The Myth of the Pro-Colonialist SPD."

48   Karl Kautsky, *Sozialismus und Kolonialpolitik: Eine Auseinandersetzung* (Berlin: Vorwärts, 1907), pp. 18–20.

49   N. Gordon Levin, *Woodrow Wilson and World Politics; America's Response to War and Revolution* (New York: Oxford University Press, 1968); Arno J. Mayer, *Wilson vs. Lenin: Political Origins of the New Diplomacy, 1917–1918* (New York: H. Fertig, 1969).

50   Marilyn Lake and Henry Reynolds, *Drawing the Global Colour Line: White Men's Countries and the International Challenge of Racial Equality* (Cambridge: Cambridge University Press, 2008). This stands in tension with the picture of Wilsonianism offered in Erez Manela, *The Wilsonian Moment: Self-Determination and the International Origins of Anticolonial Nationalism* (New York: Oxford University Press, 2007).

51   On continuities between Kautsky and Lenin, see Lars T. Lih, *Lenin Rediscovered: What Is to Be Done? In Context* (Chicago: Haymarket Books, 2008).

52   Frederick Lugard, *The Dual Mandate in British Tropical Africa* (Edinburgh: W. Blackwood and Sons, 1922).

53   See, for example, Reichskolonialministerium, *Deutsche und französische Eingeborenenbehandlung* (Berlin: Dietrich Reimer, 1919).

54   Lugard was also exemplary in his admiration for German colonialism. See his *Rise of Our East African Empire*, 2 vols (Edinburgh: W. Blackwood and Sons, 1893), 1:402–03. The most important supporter of German colonial methods, perhaps, was E.D. Morel, who continued to defend German

colonialism even after the First World War. William Roger Louis, "Great Britain and German Expansion in Africa, 1884–1919," in Prosser Gifford and William Roger Louis, with Alison Smith (eds.), *Britain and Germany in Africa: Imperial Rivalry and Colonial Rule* (New Haven: Yale University Press, 1967), pp. 3–46, p. 35.

55 Carl Schmitt, *The Concept of the Political*, trans. George Schwab (1932; Chicago: University of Chicago Press, 2007), p. 79.

56 Carl Schmitt, *Die Rheinlande als Objekt internationaler Politik* (Cologne: Rheinische Zentrumspartei, 1925).

7

The Racial Economy of *Weltpolitik*: Imperialist Expansion, Domestic Reform, and War in Pan-German Ideology, 1894–1918

Dennis Sweeney

In a speech at the congress of the Pan-German League in September 1919, Paul Bang called the combination of German military defeat and the revolution in 1918 an unprecedented "national catastrophe," which put Germany at the mercy of "foreign powers."[1] He fulminated against the Allied reparations commission and "international high finance" as threats to German economic and therefore political sovereignty; the spread of "Bolshevik incitement" throughout Germany and the "hideous class hatred" among workers igniting a "frenzy of self-annihilation" in the form of strikes; the expanding state-socialist control over the economy (*Zwangswirtschaft*) in the new German Republic, which meant the "destruction of free enterprise" and economic "enslavement and cafferization of Germans"; and above all "members of a foreign race" (i.e., Jews), who were behind all of these developments, turning Germans into economic "helots" and "slaves" in their own country. Indeed, Bang identified the underlying cause of military defeat and revolution in the interaction between economic activity and the entailments of "race": the steady erosion of the foundations of the "*völkisch* economy" by the increasing penetration of racially derived "oriental" economic practices, which engendered a series of crises captured under the rubrics of "the worker question, the big city question, the middle class (*Mittelstand*) question, the housing question, and the racial sexual problem," and undermined the strength of the German population and great power status. In order to facilitate the "rebirth" of Germany, Bang maintained, it was necessary to throw off foreign-Jewish controls over the German national economy, strip Jews in Germany of their citizenship, "restore a healthy, racially-oriented industrial development" by means of a program of "internal colonization," and re-embark on a path of imperial expansion, especially renewed colonization of "the East." In these ways, Bang gave expression to a central obsession with capitalism and social order and to a radical-nationalist imperial vision that emerged within the Pan-German movement during the Wilhelmine era and informed other *völkisch* and Nazi understandings of domestic and global order after the war.

Yet this obsession and its relation to imperialism have not been considered constitutive dimensions of radical nationalism in the recent historiography on the late nineteenth- and early twentieth-century German Right.[2] This is especially the case with studies of the Pan-German League, "spearhead" of radical nationalism or the New Right during the Wilhelmine era, center of the early postwar *völkisch* movement and precursor to the NSDAP.[3] If historians were once concerned to situate the histories of the Pan-German League and other nationalist pressure groups within the capitalist transformations and evolving class relations of the Wilhelmine era and to emphasize the centrality of imperialism to right-wing politics, studies of the Pan-German League or the German Right during the last thirty years or so have treated radical nationalism largely as a cultural-political phenomenon, separate from or hostile toward economic matters and located its origins only in relation to the domestic politics of the *Kaiserreich*.[4] From this perspective, the Pan-German pursuit of German ethno-national aggrandizement—namely, the "defense" and expansion of "Germandom" (*Deutschtum*)—is understood as a relatively static and self-originating phenomenon and can be explained without reference to wider transnational economic processes and social transformations as constitutive elements in its formation and its transformation over time.[5] Even recent studies that address Pan-German expansionist ideology interpret its economic dimensions as traditional or backward-looking schemes of "migrationist colonialism," instrumental and tactical efforts to form coalitions with other right-wing groups or interests, or "discourses" that were secondary to its main impulses—that is, as direct extensions of a core nineteenth-century nationalist orientation concerned only with population and territory and ill-prepared for the new order of multi-scalar, capitalist empires in the twentieth century.[6] But this exclusive focus on population and territory overlooks the multifaceted and comprehensive scope of Pan-German imperialist advocacy as well as its changes or displacements over time.

Rethinking radical-nationalist imperialism in the wake of the "imperial turn" in European history and renewed interest in the cultural-historical geographies of global capitalism, I argue that the Pan-Germans demanded not simply territory but also the creation of a globe-spanning, economically aggressive, and avowedly modern Greater Germany or German "world empire"—an imperialist goal that linked developments in the colonial "periphery" with politics "at home" in ways that fundamentally transformed radical nationalism during the prewar period.[7] The Pan-Germans pursued strategies of capitalist expansion, different from other "liberal" or export-oriented strategies of *Weltpolitik*, involving the promotion of competitive production and commerce, anchored in a German-dominated Central European economic zone but radiating outward into the global arena of "free trade." Their aims were to harness the de-territorializing and volatile spatial dynamics of global capitalism and to reterritorialize Germans within a nation-state empire that would rival competing "world empires." After 1900, these aims took on commitments to domestic economic and social reform, including radical-nationalist *Sozialpolitik* and schemes for "internal colonization" designed to prepare Germandom for its imperial mission abroad. In this context, ethno-cultural understandings of Germandom as a race evolved into bio-political definitions of Germandom as a population-race (*Volkskörper*) in need of cultivation and new "living space." During the First World War, this new form of what I will call racist biopower—a "technology of power" that constitutes and operates on human populations as discrete biological entities and insists that inferior populations must be subjugated or destroyed in order for superior populations to live and thrive—informed social policy debate, the demands of the annexationist movement, and the military occupation colonial policies in Eastern Europe.[8] In this essay, therefore, I argue that two interrelated components—capitalist expansion and racist biopower—came together to form the increasingly influential racial economy of Pan-German *Weltpolitik* and its commitment to war and ethnic cleansing.

1

The prevailing approach to radical nationalism overlooks the constitutive role of "modern" economic concerns, transnational capitalist processes, and geopolitical rivalry in the making and remaking of Pan-German conceptions of "the people" or Germandom in the late nineteenth and early twentieth centuries. The Pan-Germans certainly demanded new territory in order to retain emigrants leaving for other countries; and they took as their goal the completion of the German national state. But they always viewed the latter in terms of establishing Germany's "world power position" and pursing the "interests" of Germandom throughout Europe and overseas: that is, in forging a globe-spanning nation-state empire.[9] Moreover, the

Pan-Germans often understood the nation or *Volkstum* and the economy as separate phenomena and emphasized the primacy of the national above all other considerations, including economic considerations. In this context, they defined the German nation or people during the 1890s as an ethno-cultural unity, which evolved out of a shared descent, history, language, religion, legal tradition, culture (art, music, and customs), and territory;[10] and, drawing on the political-economic ideas of Friedrich List, they insisted that the economy must be a spatially bounded domain, congruous with the territorial nation. Their mission was in part an effort to ensure that trade, capital, and productive activities remained "German"—that is, in "German" ownership or at least redounded to the benefit of Germans.[11] But these categories were also inherently unstable and the initial ethno-cultural meaning of Germandom was transformed in the wider contexts of imperial rivalry, transnational capitalism, and colonial rule overseas during the late 1890s and early 1900s.

They were inherently unstable for several reasons. First, national characteristics and economic practices were intimately connected in Pan-German rhetoric: Germandom was understood to manifest itself in entrepreneurial and productive qualities and advantages that allowed Germans to excel in matters of work, trade, and accumulation, including "German diligence, German education, and German honesty"—a claim that rested on wider invocations of the superiority of "German quality work."[12] Second, radical nationalists insisted that Germans were an inherently colonizing and economically active people with a long history of colonization in Europe and outward "expansion ... across the globe." The very success of this activity, they acknowledged, set in motion the socio-spatial dynamics that threatened a homogeneous and territorially bounded Germandom and *Volkswirtschaft*: that is, it brought Germans into regular contact with non-Germans and sustained the cross-border movement of capital, commodities, and persons intrinsic to global capitalism and industrial growth.[13] Indeed, the Pan-German goal of transforming Germany into a global power rested on demands for state economic and military policies designed to promote German commerce and production, including the development of naval bases, coaling stations, global communications infrastructure (telegraph and cable), and especially colonies, which would provide territories for settlement, arable land for agricultural production, raw materials for industry, semi-luxury goods or "articles of mass consumption" for the home market, overseas markets for German goods, and nodal points for commodity exchange and capital penetration into other countries.[14]

In order to harness these movements and nationalize capital, the Pan-Germans pushed for the formation of a Greater Germany with a complex political and economic architecture that defined Germandom as a "ruling people." The first explicit plan for a Greater Germany was penned anonymously in 1895 by League chairman Ernst Hasse, who proposed an overlapping constitutional structure combining a "Greater German federation" with a "German customs union" that together would constitute a German-dominated Central Europe (*Mitteleuropa*). Drawing on a long-standing tradition of advocacy for the creation of a *Mitteleuropa*, which began with List and passed through Paul de Lagarde and Gustav Schmoller,[15] Hasse imagined the Greater German federation as an imperial polity, comprising "German" and "lower-German" peoples from the German Reich, the Netherlands, Belgium, Luxembourg, Switzerland, and Austria-Hungary; and governed by a presidium (the German Kaiser), an upper house made up of representatives from the individual states and chaired by a chancellor chosen by the Kaiser, and a lower house seating delegates from the Reichstag and the legislatures of the individual states. Citizenship (male) in the federation would be divided between residents and "full citizens."[16] The economic union would include these states of the German Federation as well as the non-German areas of the Baltic principalities, Poland, Ruthenia, Romania, and Serbia. Its officials would unify trade and tariff legislation, currency, weights and measures policy, inventor and patent law, post and telegraph systems, and trade and exchange law to create a single economic zone.[17] Hasse's plan, therefore, not only quantified populations by nationality and mapped the geography of ethno-national dispersion across Europe as a prelude to situating them in spatially segregated, German-dominated political and economic unions; it also made clear that the economic relationships within *Mitteleuropa* would establish Germans as a "ruling people over the lesser peoples," especially "Slavs" who would be dispersed and employed as "lower-level manual workers" in industrial concerns or on large agricultural estates, if they could not be Germanized or convinced to emigrate.[18]

During the wider debate over "world empires" inaugurated by Kaiser Wilhelm II's speech announcing Germany's status as a global power in January 1896, the Pan-Germans conceived of this German-dominated *Mitteleuropa* as the core region of an expansive and spatially variegated global empire that would promote German national capital and economic development abroad via "free trade."[19] Thus, despite the pedagogical benefits a "closed economic state" surrounded by "high Chinese walls" might have for Germans inclined toward cosmopolitanism, as Hasse put it in 1897, the League chairman and other Pan-Germans envisioned the creation of a "modern world empire" that acknowledged the reality of global integration—the "connections among all peoples," which had increased "a thousand fold" via the "development of communications infrastructure"—and the "global market."[20] The means to secure the well-being and growth of the German people in the "struggle for existence" in the twentieth century, according to Hasse, would therefore not be isolation from the world economy but rather in the pursuit of an aggressive *Weltpolitik* capable of carving out one of the "world economic zones," which were already forged by Britain and Russia and being pursued by France and the United States.[21] Such a zone would provide control over a large area of trade, investment, consumer markets, production, and raw

materials and thus render Germany economically independent, invulnerable
to the economic coercion of other world empires and capable of defending its
position in global markets. The focal point of this strategy would be efforts
to acquire new colonies outside of Europe, including the "protectorates"
or "cultivation territories" in Africa, Asia, and the South Pacific. In a way
analogous to *Mitteleuropa*, these colonies would require German "rule over
natural peoples and peoples of lower culture."[22]

It was precisely in this context of German economic expansion
overseas and colonial rule over "natural peoples," who were deemed
incommensurably different and unalterably inferior, that the Pan-Germans
began to pose the "race question" as a practical and urgent political
matter. This took place first during the late 1890s in relation to the settler
colony of German Southwest Africa where Pan-German demands for the
systematic "opening up of the land" to capitalist development focused
on the construction of infrastructure (railway, roads, etc.), support for
the Boers, an ethnically "related tribe" migrating from South Africa, and
schooling and recruitment of German women to travel to the colony and
marry German men. The overall aim was to establish a firm economic
foundation in the colony, anchored in the labor of the "colored natives,"
which would also "put an end to Hottentot uprisings."[23] By 1902, however,
the Pan-Germans began to complain of increasing numbers of "mixed
marriages," which threatened the "purity of blood" of the "German race,"
and "half-breeds," who transgressed the sexual and social boundaries
between colonizer and colonized and thus undermined the authority of
their colonial rulers. Max Robert Gerstenhauer, therefore, called for a new
"native policy" that would effect a "separation" of the "ruling race" from
the "native population" by banning marriage and "sexual traffic" between
German colonizers and colonized Africans and expelling all "half-breeds"
from leading positions within German economic, social, and political life.[24]
This call to institutionalize the "rule of colonial difference" intensified
during the German war against the Herrero and Nama peoples from 1904
to 1907,[25] and when they met at their annual congress in Worms in June
1905, the Pan-Germans proposed plans for the "future development of our
colonies" that envisioned initiatives to stimulate "economic production" in
the colony alongside more effective measures to isolate and manage the
"native" population. Formulating the latter measures, which included the
full dispossession of all colonial subjects and a ban on their right to carry
weapons, the deportation of "rebellious" subjects, and the introduction of
"reservations," townships, and a passport system to control their movements,
especially as laborers, entailed an effort to define, classify, and dispose of
various Southwest African peoples as racial groups or population-races
with specific qualities and responsibilities.[26]

This concern with securing labor for capitalist agriculture and industry in
the African colonies became an enduring dimension of the "race question,"
primarily because the "racial" distinctiveness of black Africans was defined

in relation to their suitability for recruitment as wage earners in a capitalist economy. The Pan-Germans addressed the race question as a "worker question" in the African colonies during the late 1890s, when they began to discuss the importance of "educating" black Africans "into labor." The war against the Herero and Nama focused this discussion on the various possible forms of labor coercion, and the latter received a formal airing at the Pan-German congress in Dresden in September 1906. Despite the general recognition of the differences between African "tribes," Eduard von Liebert favored the hut tax as the means for forcing colonized Africans to work for wages and attributed the reluctance to work as wage laborers or to produce commodities of good quality for the market to the natural "laziness" of the "Negro races" and their lack of "culture": that is, their lack of consumer needs or desires, which might serve as forms of labor market compulsion.[27] If Paul Samassa preferred corporal punishment (whippings) as the appropriate form of coercion, he too noted the alleged laziness of (male) "Negroes," who prefer "loafing about" to the wage labor stimulated by the prospect of acquiring "pretty objects." In addition to being able to force their many wives to work for them, Samassa explained, they preferred to engage in the wasteful exploitation of natural resources (*Raubbau*) rather than to forge an "ordered economy" (*geordnete Wirtschaft*) of capital accumulation and growth.[28] This fundamental difference was anchored, according to Samassa, in a foreign "brain structure" and its distinctive "physiological substrate," and manifested itself in the lack of cultural "achievements" to emerge from Africa and in the rudimentary economic practices of the "black race."[29] In these ways, the "race question" as a programmatic Pan-German concern first evolved out of discussions about capitalist labor imperatives in Southwest and East Africa.

2

This engagement with colonial subjects also became the starting point for bio-political conceptions of Germandom as a population-race, for Pan-German arguments about racial exclusivity in the colonies gave rise to conceptions of the distinctive "racial constitution" of Germans themselves. But a new schema of racist biopower directed at Germans developed in a process of translation, rather than simply transfer, from colonial "periphery" to imperial center over the prewar decade. It emerged fully only out of the intersection of colonialism overseas and class-political struggles over capitalism and imperialism primarily against the German Social Democratic Party (SPD) in the metropole, during which the Pan-Germans supplemented their imperialist advocacy with three new departures in the realm of domestic politics (*innere Politik*): a program of nationalist pedagogy designed to "cleanse" or renationalize politics; schemes for a racialized social policy and "internal colonization" designed to remake domestic socioeconomic order; and efforts to forge or participate in bourgeois-led class and party-political coalitions in defense of national capitalism and capable of neutralizing the SPD. In the course of this activity, the Pan-Germans embraced a new conception of Germandom as a population-race (*Volkskörper*) and came to conceive of domestic reform and expansion abroad as inseparable components of their wider imperialist mission to forge a Greater Germany.

Plans to renationalize politics were mooted in the wake of the dramatic SPD victories in the Reichstag elections of June 1903, when the Pan-Germans began to link socialist success to the consequences of rapid industrial transformation. The Pan-Germans responded to this threat to their imperial mission with their strongest criticism to date of the Kaiser's government which they blamed for the SPD advance and a new commitment to "prepare for the political rebirth of our people" at their congress in September 1903.[30] The first broad outlines of this effort came in late May 1904 from Julius Ziehen, who recommended the implementation of a program for "German national education" involving the introduction of a citizenship curriculum in schools, producing and disseminating a national "catechism" and orchestrating various other efforts to influence "public opinion" across a range of social sites from the family to the sphere of party politics. Such a program, Ziehen maintained, would help expel from Germany the "poison of all manner of harmful foreign" influences, especially foreign reading materials, trashy literature, and other "obscene goods" brought into the public sphere by cross-border commerce; restore "social peace" by eliminating "unpleasant" divisions that characterize "our current political life"; and silence the "enemy within" (Social Democracy).[31] During the next few years, the Pan-Germans grew increasingly concerned about the links between Social Democrats and foreigners, including contacts with black Africans and "treasonous" solidarities with "Slavic and Jewish nihilists and anarchists" in Russia, not least because modern industrial-economic imperatives were generating increasing movements of people within and across borders.[32] In this context, Karl Negenborn rolled out a plan for citizenship education at the League's congress in 1908. Mandatory for all schools above the elementary level, Negenborn's comprehensive and allegedly nonpolitical curriculum would instruct young people in the responsibilities associated with citizenship as a "profession": that is, familiarize them with "state tasks" and institutions, imbue in them an appreciation of "political relationships," and teach them to "know and love the fatherland."[33]

These plans were followed by a series of efforts to reverse the cultural hybridization of the city and to cleanse public life of the "foreign bodies" brought "into the life of our people," which were deemed responsible for the electoral gains and popularity of the SPD. These included calls for the creation of a uniform national "style" in 1907, encompassing everyday cultural expressions as diverse as architectural design and interior wall decoration;[34] a "*völkisch* press law" that would suppress the "international cultural spirit," the poisonous "importation from abroad," manifested in German newspapers and the work of "foreign" editors in 1909;[35] a ban on the use of foreign words in economic life—namely, the proliferation of foreign names for businesses, on-store signs and in-store windows—in 1912;[36] and numerous other measures, ranging from policies to reduce the number of foreign students at German universities to campaigns to remove foreign clothing and fashions, especially for women, from German stores.

In the wake of even more dramatic SPD victories in the Reichstag elections of January 1912, Heinrich Claß, who replaced Hasse as League chairman in 1908, took up these proposals for "cleansing" public and everyday life in his pseudonymously-authored reform plan entitled *If I Were the Kaiser*. Claß called for a program for national education, controls over the press and public culture (especially the theater), and even initiatives in the home, where a woman's duty was

> to keep her home holy and clean, free from all corrosive influences, and to maintain the sharpest boundary between it and everything that is impure: no book, no newspaper that could bring contagion can come into the home; no guest who is not unimpeachable will be tolerated, no outside company in which the spirit of moral cleanliness does not govern will be recognized.[37]

The chairman focused his ire on what he called the "Jewish-socialist" spirit of revolution, stoked by the pervasive "materialism," immorality, overindulgence, and "foreign" sensibilities fostered by the explosion of industrial growth and exemplified by the rootless ways of life in the big city, which poisoned culture and politics and fueled the Social Democratic movement.[38]

The second Pan-German departure in the realm of domestic politics centered on new schemes of racialized social policy and internal colonization, which were also conceived as responses to the deleterious consequences of unrestrained capitalism, especially in the form of Social Democracy. The outlines of this departure first emerged in debates over the colonial question at the League congress in Worms in June 1905, when Ludwig Kuhlenbeck delivered a programmatic speech on "the political consequences of race research" defining Germans and other populations as biologically discrete though "impure" population-races locked in a global struggle for existence and identifying the source of German racial impurity and "degeneration" in the modalities of a liberal or "one-sided capitalism."[39] The latter, according to Kuhlenbeck, contained an intrinsic drive for the acquisition of land, raw materials, and labor, bringing German settlers and traders into sexual contact with colonial subjects; created the commercial conditions under which a "Semitic type," so foreign to "Aryan ways," could flourish within Germany; stimulated demand for labor that drew unwanted "racial elements" (i.e., the Poles) to once "racially-pure parts of Germany" (Westphalia) or to the agricultural regions of Prussia, which were simultaneously depopulated by Germans migrating to the cities in search of higher paying jobs; and turned large cities into overcrowded, unhygienic sites for "negative breeding" among Germans—that is, increasing fertility among Germans of lesser racial value and declining fertility among Germans of greater racial value.[40]

Indeed, drawing on the ideas of Otto Ammon, Kuhlenbeck argued that negative breeding demonstrated that "the racial question is a class question and vice versa." For it meant that racially valuable and nationally minded middle-class Germans artificially limited their reproduction in order to maintain "a certain standard of living," while less "biogenetically privileged" members of the "proletariat" reproduced at much higher rates—a reference invoking workplace and social hierarchies grounded in racial difference linked to discussions of colonial labor.[41] Negative breeding was therefore racially and politically dangerous because higher rates of reproduction within the working class brought more recruits to the banner of international socialism. This was a sign, according to Hasse, of the increasing mental "degeneration" accompanying other manifestations of "physical degeneration" within the German population.[42]

The Pan-German response to these "threats" was not to oppose capitalism, with its positive contribution to the competitive "struggle for existence" and German prosperity, but rather to support forms of *Sozialpolitik* that would promote a class-based program for racial "selection" and thus protect the nation from Social Democracy. Kuhlenbeck pointed to possible programs (housing and social insurance) to support the *Mittelstand*, the "real reservoir of racial value," as part of a new reform movement or "national, racially-conscious socialism" in his 1905 speech,[43] but the first proposal for an explicit "Pan-German social policy" came from Arnim Tille in late 1905. Calling for the formulation of a modern "nationally-oriented human economy" that would replace the outmoded humanitarian and egalitarian concerns of Christian, liberal, and socialist reform policies, Tille imagined a scientifically based "societal biology" that privileged the nation over the individual and "the most fit" over the least fit, and combined biomedical intervention to suppress diseases with economic policies designed to create "job opportunities" and stimulate national economic growth.[44] Less than two years later, Hasse proposed a public health policy as a means to cultivate the collective physical and mental health of Germans by "protecting" the "Nordic racial components of the German people."[45] This was a scheme for "planned racial breeding" to ensure biologically healthy marriages among higher social strata—and bans on "marriages between Germans and Hereros or Hottentots" and "between mentally or physically sick or degenerate" Germans—and to provide medical care for the strong and healthy, while contemplating forced sterilization or "killing off everything of lesser value."[46] Concerned with the health of future generations, Hasse's plan also encompassed physical exercise regimes, workplace regulations, pronatal medical care, and public health improvements in urban areas.[47]

This wider vision of *Sozialpolitik* brought colonial native policy back to the metropole, where it evolved into a plan for the cultivation of the physical and mental health of the German *Volkskörper*. After 1905, the Pan-German obsession with emigration was supplemented by a newly pronounced emphasis on the dangers of immigration, prompting not only complaints about the presence of black Africans, Poles, and "eastern Jews" but also determined efforts to support the "return" of ethnic Germans from Russia to Germany, where they could replace "foreign" laborers in industry or agriculture.[48] In his treatise from 1907, Hasse proposed a domestic "race policy," involving immigration controls preventing "racially-foreign" people, including the Poles, Jews, Magyars, "half Mongolian Russians, and other similar peoples," from entering the country and measures to manage minority populations by restricting them to "special regions (reservations) with special rights." The threat posed by "colored natives" in Germany, Hasse suggested, could be dealt with by means of bans on "mixed marriages" and the separation of "racially-foreign" populations from Germans (e.g., in schools and in separate rail cars).[49] From 1908 to 1910, concern with immigrant labor accompanied growing fears of the "degeneration" the German population, defined and measured statistically by its overall birthrate, mortality rate, and morbidity rate. This double preoccupation prompted Armin Tille to call in 1911 for new measures—including laws banning racially unhealthy marriages and certificates attesting to the mental and physical health of couples planning to marry—to cultivate what was now explicitly called the German *Volkskörper*.[50]

During the final prewar years, the Pan-Germans folded their schemes for social policy into broader plans for "internal colonization." The latter was designed to cultivate the health of the *Volkskörper* by settling German farmers and agricultural laborers in underdeveloped regions of Germany, especially in the Prussian East, as a way of replacing "foreign" farmers and workers with Germans; rejuvenating the "farmers' estate" (*Bauernstand*), a nationally reliable, racially healthy social group compared to the socialist and racially "degenerate" urban proletariat; creating a "healthy" balance between industry and agriculture in order to reduce socioeconomic divisions and draw workers away from socialism; and ensuring a sufficient food supply in the event of war. This program would also eliminate the economic and social conditions that allegedly gave rise to what the Pan-Germans now regarded as a major racial threat: the influence of Jews. Indeed, in his 1912 treatise on domestic reform, Claß identified the causes of Social Democratic electoral success mainly in Germany's rapid and uncontrolled industrialization, which produced all of the "harmful consequences" addressed by internal colonization, on the one hand; and the influence of "racially-foreign" Jews, who as "bearers" of "materialism" thrived under conditions of unrestrained capitalism and introduced "subversion" into political life by turning Social Democracy and left liberalism into "tools of Jewry," on the other.[51] By mid-1914, therefore, Pan-German reform policy, as Liebert formulated it in his report to the July meeting of the League Managing Council, focused on three main issues: the "racial question" (i.e., the presence of or contact with foreigners), the "Jewish question," and the "question of the struggle against Social Democracy, which for the most part is under Jewish leadership."[52]

This increasingly urgent domestic reform mission, moreover, was hitched to renewed demands for aggressive "external" colonization and imperial expansion. The understanding of Germandom as a population-race with existential needs in a world of limited resources meant that neglect in the area of foreign policy would mean the decline and extinction of Germandom. The Pan-Germans, therefore, ramped up their public campaign on behalf of German imperial expansion, welcoming the possibility of war for the purpose imposing domestic unity and making a series of aggressive new demands: control over or annexation of Belgium and the Netherlands; the subordination of France to German economic and military interests and the seizure of some its territories in the east and north after the "evacuation" of their populations; colonial concessions in Africa (Morocco and *Mittelafrika*); land for colonial settlement to the south and east with guarantees from Austria-Hungary; and acquisition of new "settlement land" to the east from Russia followed by the "evacuation" of its populations.[53] Indeed, by the summer of 1914, expansion to the east was the priority.

The third major departure in Pan-German domestic politics after 1903 involved efforts to build a bourgeois class alliance and party-political coalition in defense of private property and national capitalism. These efforts began with the formation of the Imperial League against German Social Democracy, which coalesced in May 1904 from several different initiatives coming from the ranks of radical nationalists, heavy industrialists, and right-wing politicians during the fall and winter 1903–04.[54] Led by Liebert, the principal aim of the Imperial League was to forge a "closed phalanx of the national *Bürgertum*" against the revolutionary views and "terrorism" of the SPD, which threatened employer prerogative, private property, and Germany's "world mission" and quest for colonies.[55] The Imperial League brought Pan-Germans into closer contact with heavy industry as well as active participation in electoral politics from 1904 to 1907, when its leaders and activists campaigned on behalf of candidates from the "bourgeois parties," ranging from conservatives to left liberals, deploying all of the latest techniques of modern electioneering during the so-called Hottentot elections over the colonial budget in 1907.[56] The Pan-German League itself, moreover, sponsored direct electoral work for the first time during these elections, organizing its first "mass distribution" of campaign handbills, brochures, and voter handbooks, providing speakers for election meetings and encouraging local branches to mobilize voters and bring them to the polls in their districts.[57] These activities entailed new kinds of coordination with numerous other economic associations like the

German National Union of Commercial Employees, a lower-middle-class (*neuer Mittelstand*) occupational organization with connections to the League, and only three months after the elections, Liebert presided over the formation of a new umbrella organization for antisocialist workers, the League of Patriotic Workers' Associations.[58] Indeed, in the post-election analysis of the Pan-German leadership celebrating the victory of the "Bülow bloc" of conservatives and liberals of all stripes against the SPD and the Catholic Center Party, Alfred Geiger endorsed this first experiment in mass politics and urged the League to expand its social base of support by developing a "popular" or populist style of mobilization in order to appeal to the "masses of ordinary people," especially workers.[59]

The Pan-Germans lost their enthusiasm for electoral activity after the collapse of the Bülow bloc over the finance bill in 1909, but the massive SPD victories during the Reichstag elections of January 1912 generated a sense of economic and political crisis that placed radical-nationalist prescriptions for domestic reform and imperial expansion at the forefront of right-wing politics by 1914.[60] From 1909 to 1911, the Pan-Germans developed even closer ties to heavy industry by virtue of Alfred Hugenberg's appointment as Krupp director in 1909 and Emil Kirdorf's election to the League's executive committee in 1910. In 1912, moreover, the Pan-Germans sponsored two new independent initiatives with wider social resonances: the Army League, a nationalist pressure group lobbying for an expansion of the army, which was created in January 1912 by the Pan-German August Keim and attracted the support of large sections of big agriculture, long alienated by the Pan-German League's support for land redistribution and small farmers in the Prussian East; and the Society for the Promotion of Internal Colonization, a gathering point for middle-class land reformers and "internal colonizers," funded by Hugenberg and created by his associates Friedrich von Schwerin and Max Sering in April 1912. The latter organization risked provoking the mistrust of big agriculture, but Claß met with leaders of the Agrarian League to work out a *modus vivendi*, which included agreement over internal colonization measures, in the summer of 1913. At the same time, Claß's call for a coup d'état (*Staatsstreich*) in order to neutralize the SPD in 1912 was picked up by leaders of heavy industry, especially the Central Association of German Industrialists (CVDI) and in the fall of 1913, representatives from heavy industry, big agriculture, and the *Mittelstand* took up the theme of constitutional revision in their efforts to form a loose *Sammlung* (rallying) called the Cartel of Productive Estates.[61] This emerging bourgeois coalition, with its popular base of small farmers, artisans, small businessmen, and small property owners, provided the wider social support for Pan-German visions of national capitalism and plans for internal colonization in the metropole. It also became a fertile ground for the spread of Pan-German conceptions of race and race struggle and demands for imperial-colonial expansion beyond the borders of Germany, especially into Eastern Europe: the main ideological motivations of the "nationalist opposition" pressuring the government to risk war during the July crisis of 1914.[62]

3

When the long-desired war finally came in August 1914, the Pan-Germans immediately set about formulating their war aims, which were organized around the imperatives of economic-territorial expansion beyond the borders of Germany permanently to weaken "our enemies" and secure "our future" and domestic reform aimed at the "recuperation of our people, the guarantee of its physical and moral health for all times," in a memorandum intended for wide circulation—war aims that radicalized over the course of the long and bloody conflict.[63] The first imperative involved the acquisition of "land without people," territory to be seized from France in the west but especially from Russia in the east (the Baltic lands). In the latter case, some 220,000 square kilometers would be forcibly depopulated of their original inhabitants—estimated at seven million people—by means of "clearance" or "ethnic cleansing" (völkische Feldbereinigung) and resettled by Germans, including soldiers but also "return migrants" from Russia.[64] This radical demand, which the Pan-Germans knew would entail mass violence, was part of a wider plan for the political, ethnic-racial, and economic reorganization of Europe: that is, the creation of a Greater Germany as a multilayered imperial macropolity.

The political architecture of this empire centered on a German national state but included a vaguely defined "League of Germanic States" comprising Germans, Swedes, Danes, and Norwegians with common citizenship, forms of dictatorial rule in Belgium that would force French-speaking Belgians to serve as laborers in German industry, the political incorporation of Latvians, Estonians, and Lithuanians granted some form of civil status below the level of full citizenship, and restrictions placed on the movement of "coloured peoples," who would be confined to certain districts and port cities.[65] A racially differentiated and partitioned imperial macropolity, it included German colonies overseas and the additional colonies promised by victory in war (the Belgian Congo and the French Congo, Morocco, and Senegambia). In order to secure this polity, the Pan-Germans also called for the creation of a German-dominated economic zone or trading area (Mitteleuropa) encompassing the Netherlands, Switzerland, Scandinavia, Finland, Italy, Romania, and Bulgaria, as well as the colonies of the Netherlands, Italy, and Belgium—an economic architecture that would partition and nationalize industry, commerce, and trade but allow cross-border exchanges and facilitate the expansion of Greater Germany from its European continental base into the arena of global trade.[66]

These ideas became increasingly influential during the first three years of the war as the Pan-Germans installed themselves at the head of the annexationist movement and put pressure on the government to expand its war aims. They orchestrated the war aims petition, which included far-reaching demands for economic and territorial gains and settlement policies, of the six major economic interest organizations—the Agrarian League, German Farmers League, Westphalian Farmers Association, Reich-German *Mittelstand* League, CVDI, and even the export-oriented League of German Industrialists—sent to the government in the spring of 1915. They organized the meetings for and largely wrote the July 1915 Intellectuals' Declaration, signed by 1,347 professors, pastors, civil servants, politicians, and representatives from industry, agriculture, trade, and banking and demanding even more ambitious territorial and economic gains, including the extension of German economic influence to Turkey, the Near East, and the Persian Gulf, as well as social reforms designed to secure a healthy class of farmers. Claß and former Navy League Chairman Prince Otto zu Salm-Horstmar also led efforts from the summer of 1915 to the fall of 1916 to gather representatives of German and Austro-Hungarian industry and agriculture for a series of meetings to discuss the possibility of establishing closer economic ties between the two countries and of creating a Central European customs union (*Mitteleuropa*). Moreover, the Pan-Germans began to establish lines of communication with leading government and military officials; entered into several government ministries and semipublic organizations responsible for war policy (e.g., the Baltic Council and League for the Liberation of Ukraine); and played an active role in the occupation administrations, most notably in *Ober Ost*, the military authority in the occupied Baltic lands, beginning in 1915.

The second and related dimension of this imperialist vision—the "recuperation of our people"—centered on an urgent program of internal colonization and "racial cultivation," which would address the problems attendant upon capitalist industrialization and prepared Germans for a "war of annihilation" between races or "race war." In the memorandum, Claß pointed to threats to the "racial constitution" of Germandom and the possible remedies, ranging from population and immigration controls to economic reorganization which were included in prewar Pan-German schemes of *Sozialpolitik* and internal colonization.[67] In October 1915, Deputy League Chairman Leopold von Vietinghoff-Scheel developed and extended this program of domestic reform to include a much larger and coordinated effort, based on the "fundamentals of biology," to cultivate the German *Volkskörper*. Since the latter was not an "image, a metaphor," but rather a living dynamic organism, "an actual body of the nation" resting on the "foundation of a blood community," as Vietinghoff argued, its deliberate cultivation required biomedical interventions regulating procreation and economic and social reforms facilitating the process of racial "selection"—in short, a new kind of state capable of organizing the "internal development" of the *Volkskörper* according to a "total plan."[68]

Like their demands for annexation, these Pan-German schemes for the management of the "life" of the German *Volkskörper* seemed to be gaining traction in wider nationalist circles and even influencing government policy. Indeed, state intervention into the sphere of biological reproduction had become the subject of intense national debate and policymaking on matters related to childbirth but also to venereal disease, contraception, and abortion, and the parties of the Reichstag even formed a Select Committee on Population Policy in May 1916. Moreover, the Pan-German version of racist biopower informed the Military High Command's memorandum on racial policy, internal colonization, and imperial expansion, entitled "German Population and Defense Strength" and submitted to the government in September 1917. But by this point, the Pan-Germans and the radical-nationalist annexationist camp had begun to lose much of their momentum and influence.[69]

For the government's reliance on the SPD and the socialist labor movement for its ability to wage war and the growing strength of the majority parties in the Reichstag brought multiple setbacks to the Pan-German cause over the course of 1917, not least the July "Peace Resolution" passed by the SPD, Center Party, and Progressive Party—setbacks which became the stuff of renewed radical-nationalist mobilization. The Pan-Germans responded to the Peace Resolution by entering the ranks and leadership of the Fatherland Party, a large right-wing propaganda organization, with support from heavy industry, agriculture, the *Mittelstand*, and nationalist workers' organizations, formed in September 1917 and designed to mobilize public opinion behind the annexationist camp.[70] They also ramped up their publicity apparatus in support of more and more extreme plans for imperial expansion. The most revealing plan in this regard came from Felix Hänsch, who wrote a book entitled *On the Threshold of the Greater Empire*, which mapped the coordinates of a multiscalar, globe-spanning empire, designed to secure the requisite economic foundation and "living space" (*Lebensraum*) for the German *Volkskörper* by means of territorial acquisition and ethnic cleansing or population "exchanges," especially in Eastern Europe and Central Africa; a German-dominated "central and southeastern European Economic Bloc" from Western Europe to the Persian Gulf; and the sprawling infrastructure necessary for a world empire (coaling and naval stations, cable and telegraph, transportation networks, and colonial dependencies) that would allow German economic independence and the ability to participate as an equal in global "free trade."[71]

After the Treaty of Brest-Litovsk in March 1918, when the way seemed open for realizing many of the aims of the annexationist movement, the Pan-Germans indulged in even more concrete and comprehensive "dreams" for remaking "the East" in particular. In the most detailed expression of this kind, Vietinghoff proposed the creation of "White Russia" in addition to Ukraine and other states in Eastern Europe as separate "satellite" states within a German "sphere of influence," extending from the Baltic Sea to the Black Sea and based on a German-controlled waterway. In relation to Ukraine, he mused about the possibility of forming a German-Ukrainian company that would finance the rail, road, and canal systems in the new Eastern European state with German capital in order to control its economy and block its transportation links with Russia. Most striking, Vietinghoff suggested that these satellite states of Eastern Europe would only be provisional political structures in this region for other European peoples, who would over time give way to the economically creative and "colonizing will" of German settlers expanding out from a series of seams, ramparts, and rings of settlement established along the waterway networks controlled by Germany; and that ethnic Germans in Russia, who were uprooted by the war, could migrate to "gathering points" (*Sammelplätze*) in Southern Bessarabia, the Kherson province, and the Crimea, establish their own "self-administration," and serve as future outposts of an ever-expanding Germandom.[72] Not surprisingly, in the summer of 1918, the Pan-German leadership was preoccupied with the introduction of a more expansive *Kolonialpolitik* in regions even beyond the Black Sea: namely Transcaucasia, which they now hoped would be turned into a "protectorate" of Greater Germany.[73]

The growing strength of the forces of democracy, revealed in the government's vague promise of postwar democratic reform in its "Easter Offer" of April 1917, the formation of the antiwar Independent Social Democratic Party, and the mass strikes in the munitions industry of the same month, also became the stimulus for more comprehensive Pan-German schemes for domestic reform. In response to what Claß referred to as the "international powers of revolution and money" (i.e., Social Democrats and Jews), the Pan-Germans developed more detailed plans for the reorientation of the state, constitution, legal system, juridical definitions of German citizenship, immigration and border control policy, and social and economic programs around the imperatives of internal colonization and "racial cultivation."[74] Moreover, race scientists and theorists within the *völkisch* movement began to identify a broader array of sites for bioracial intervention, which now included excess luxury, the proliferation of "trashy" fiction and cheap movies, women's employment, and the "nervous tempo of industrial production" itself, and the physician Fritz Lenz even produced a catechism for "racial hygiene" that addressed all of these issues.[75] Not surprisingly, this preoccupation with national-racial "decomposition" within the German people (*Volkstum*) prompted Konstantin von Gebsattel to push for the Pan-German leadership to take up the banner of antisemitism statutorily and openly and Claß to define Jews as "the most dangerous enemy" of Germany before a meeting of the Managing Council of the League in July 1917.[76] If the risk of losing members as well as momentum in their efforts to build a broad-based annexationist movement still held League leaders back from taking this step, defeat and revolution in 1918 would eliminate all remaining hesitation to embrace antisemitism openly.

****

The German military defeat and November Revolution in 1918 also put an end to radical-nationalist imperialist fantasies, but they did so only temporarily. In the immediate aftermath of war and revolution, the Pan-Germans and *völkisch* nationalists brought war into the domestic arena, embracing new forms of mass mobilization and counterrevolutionary organization in efforts to extirpate the "internal enemies" deemed responsible for the collapse of the authoritarian *Kaiserreich* and the economic crisis—"Bolsheviks" (i.e., Social Democrats and communists) and Jews—and to cultivate the health and purity of the German *Volkskörper*. But as the outlines of the postwar international order began to emerge, radical nationalists demanded new efforts to renationalize or reracialize the domestic "German economy," the return of territories lost in the postwar settlement, including overseas colonies, and renewed imperial expansion to the east on the European continent in order to attain world power status. In formulating these demands for a new postwar German Empire, the Pan-Germans rejected the "outmoded" tenets of nineteenth-century "classical political economy" or liberal capitalism in favor of new, twentieth-century modes of "spatial-economic thought" that conceived of large regional economic zones as the only basis for expansive world empires organized around the imperatives of race struggle.[77]

This postwar ideological orientation contained many new elements, but it also drew on long-standing Pan-German visions of an economic aggressive and racially partitioned world empire—visions that reveal the centrality of capitalism to the emergence and evolution of radical nationalism, especially its embrace of bioracism. The latter emerged out of a process of tension and contradiction between the pursuit of capitalist expansion, on the one hand, and demands for the aggrandizement of Germandom, on the other. The Pan-Germans' demands for economic expansion and industrial growth—a central imperative of German national strength—could only help to sustain the very movements of commodities, capital, and people and the proliferation of social interests that challenged their naturalized construction of an ethnically and culturally uniform Germandom—a challenge that gave rise to Pan-German explanations of cultural difference, social inequality, and political opposition to their imperial designs, first in the colonies and then in the metropole, as the products of biologically derived hierarchies or foreign ("un-German") contamination. In this new context of racial-biological explanation, the spatial dynamics of global capitalism came to represent an existential threat to the health of the German *Volkskörper*. Conversely, the goal of a racially pure German *Volkskörper* demanded an empire with fortified partitions and boundaries, immune to the diverse cultural influences and "racial" elements of other peoples—a disruption of the spatial openness and volatile logic of processes of capitalist accumulation. It was this dialectic between capitalism and bioracial formation that propelled the Pan-Germans—in their response to Marxist socialism—increasingly to insist on the qualities of German *Eigenart* and to demand with ever-greater urgency that the government police the borders, unity, and purity of the German "race" or *Volkskörper* by 1914. During the war, open military confrontation and total mobilization turned their bio-political project into an armed "race struggle" and *Daseinskampf*.

From this perspective, therefore, the distinctive violence of radical nationalism, especially its commitment to war, might best be understood not in self-contained attempts to form an ethnically or racially homogeneous nation-state, but rather in efforts to integrate these two unstable logics— capitalist and bioracial—into a dynamic and expansionist nation-state empire. The creation of Greater Germany, based in a German-dominated *Mitteleuropa*, required economic dispossession beyond the borders of metropolitan Germany, especially within key industrial and agricultural regions in Northern France, Belgium, Eastern Europe, and Africa. It also required commercial relationships and financial instruments that would subordinate the productive, extractive, and financial activities— and laborers—in other European and extra-European states to German economic priorities. Similarly, the internal biological imperative of the German *Volkskörper* required sustained bio-political efforts to ensure its "propagation" (*Fortpflanzung*) or continued "unfolding" (*Entfaltung*), which ultimately meant the management, expulsion, or destruction of other population-races. Indeed, for these reasons, the Pan-Germans insisted that state borders could never be permanent because the "borders of peoples are constantly subject to changes"[78] and that war was a sacred duty in the service of a higher cause. It was, according to Franz Sonntag, the principal means by which to secure the expanding economic foundations of Germandom, to revise state-territorial boundaries in accordance with the ongoing biological expansion of the German race; and to cultivate the internal qualities of the German *Volkskörper* by eliminating all that was politically and racially foreign or "rotten, brittle, life threatening." From this perspective, modern warfare was not "the monstrous agent of destruction acting in a blind rage, but rather the careful innovator and preserver, the great doctor and gardener, who guides humanity on its path to higher development."[79]

Notes

1   "Die Grundbedingungen unseres wirthchaftlichen Wiederaufbaus,"
     Deutschlands Erneuerung [*DE*] 11 (1919), pp. 755–70.

2   For recent work, see Johannes Leicht, *Heinrich Claß 1868–1953. Die
     politische Biographie eines Alldeutschen* (Paderborn: Schöningh, 2012);
     Stefan Frech, *Wegbereiter Hitlers? Theodor Reismann-Grone. Ein völkischer
     Nationalist* (Paderborn: Schöningh, 2005); Rainer Hering, *Konstruierte
     Nation. Der Alldeutsche Verband 1890 bis 1939* (Hamburg: Christians, 2003).

3   The term comes originally from Fritz Fischer, *Krieg der Illusionen. Die deutsche Politik von 1911 bis 1914* (Düsseldorff: Droste, 1969), p. 349.

4   The most important study is Geoff Eley, *Reshaping the German Right: Radical Nationalism and Political Change after Bismarck* (New Haven: Yale University Press, 1980). But see the still indispensable Fischer, *Krieg der Illusionen*; Fritz Fischer, *Griff nach der Weltmacht. Die Kriegszielpolitik des kaiserlichen Deutschland 1914/18* (Düsseldorff: Droste, 1961); Dirk Stegmann, *Die Erben Bismarcks. Parteien und Verbände in der Spätphase des Wilhelminischen Deutschlands* (Cologne: Kiepenheuer & Witsch, 1970).

5   This general trend was set by Roger Chickering, *We Men Who Feel Most German: A Cultural Study of the Pan-German League, 1886–1914* (Boston: George Allen & Unwin, 1984).

6   Woodruff D. Smith, *The Ideological Origins of Nazi Imperialism* (New York: Oxford University Press, 1986), esp. pp. 91–4, 105; and Peter Walkenhorst, *Nation—Volk—Rasse. Radikaler Nationalismus im Deutschen Kaiserreich 1890–1914* (Göttingen: Vandenhoeck & Ruprecht, 2007), pp. 170, 179, 235.

7   See, above all, David Harvey, *Spaces of Global Capital Capitalism: Toward a Theory of Uneven Geographical Development* (London: Verso, 2006); Manu Goswami, *Producing India: From Colonial Economy to National Space* (Chicago: The University of Chicago Press, 2004).

8   I derive the term "racist biopower" from the analysis in Michel Foucault, *"Society Must Be Defended": Lectures at the Collége de France 1975–1976* (New York: Picador, 2003), pp. 239–60.

9   *Allgemeiner Deutscher Verband* (April 25, 1891), p. 26, in Bundesarchiv Berlin [BAB], R 8048/1.

10 Ernst Hasse, "Das deutsche Volkstum," *Alldeutsche Blätter [AB]*, no. 5 (January 29, 1899), pp. 37–8.

11 "Deutscher Handel und deutsches Kapital," *AB*, no. 37 (September 2, 1894), pp. 151–2.

12 "Deutschlands Weltstellung und der Weiterbau am deutschen Nationalstaat," *AB*, no. 2 (January 7, 1894), p. 5.

13 Hasse, "Das deutsche Volkstum," p. 38.

14 "Das Deutsche Reich im Weltverkehr," *AB*, no. 36 (September 6, 1896), p. 162; Ernst Hasse, "Handel und Seemacht," *AB*, no. 50 (December 12, 1897), pp. 261–2.

15 Jörg Brechtefeld, *Mitteleuropa and German Politics: 1848 to the Present* (New York: St. Martin's Press, 1996).

16 *Großdeutschland und Mitteleuropa um das Jahr 1950* (Berlin: Druck und Verlag von Thormann & Goetsch, 1895), pp. 42, 44–6.

17 Ibid., p. 47.

18 Ibid., pp. 8, 48.

19 See "Deutschlands Weltstellung," p. 5.

20 Ernst Hasse, *Deutsche Weltpolitik* (Munich: JF Lehmann, 1897), pp. 14, 2.

21 Ibid., p. 6.

22   Ibid., p. 14.

23   "Stellungnahme des Allgemeinen Deutschen Verbandes zu den in Deutsch-Südwest-Afrika herrschenen Wirren," *AB*, no. 23 (June 3, 1894), p. 94.

24   Max Robert Gerstenhauer, "Ansetzung deutscher Familien in Südwestafrika," *Deutsche Kolonial Zeitung*, no. 50 (December 11, 1902), p. 505.

25   Partha Chatterjee, *The Nation and Its Fragments: Colonial and Postcolonial Histories* (Princeton: Princeton University Press, 1993), p. 12.

26   *AB*, no. 23 (June 4, 1904), pp. 192–5; Joachim Graf von Pfeil, *Deutsch-Südwest-Afrika. Jetzt und Später* (Munich: JF Lehmann, 1905), pp. 5–6, 12–13.

27   Eduard von Liebert, *Die deutschen Kolonien und ihre Zukunft* (Berlin: Bossische Buchhandlung, 1906).

28   Paul Samassa, *Die Besiedlung Deutsch-Ostafrikas* (Leipzig: Deutsche Zukunft, 1909), pp. 129–37.

29   Ibid.

30   *Sitzung des Geschäftsführenden Ausschusses [SGA]* (September 11, 1903), pp. 2–3 in BAB, R 8048/40. The quote is from Heinrich Claß, *Die Bilanz des des neuen Kurses* (Berlin: Selbstverlag des ADV, 1903), p. 41.

31   *AB*, no. 23 (June 4, 1904), p. 195; Julius Ziehen, *Über Volkserziehung im nationalem Sinn* (Munich: JF Lehlmann, 1904), pp. 19, 23.

32   See Claß' speech at the Dresden congress in "*Alldeutscher Verbandstag*. Dresden, 2. September 1906," in BAB, R 8048/56.

33   "Die Notwendigkeit staatsbürgerlicher Erziehung," *AB*, no. 38 (September 18, 1908), pp. 317–20.

34   Hasse, *Die Zukunft des deutschen Volkstums* (Munich: JF Lehmann, 1907), p. 167.

35   Stauff, "Ein völkisches Pressegesetz," *AB*, no. 39 (September 25, 1909), pp. 350–1.

36   "Entschliessung," in BAB, R 8048/86, p. 12.

37   Daniel Fryman [Heinrich Claß], *Wenn ich der Kaiser wär—Politische Wahrheiten und Notwendigkeiten* (Leipzig: Dieterich'schen Verlagsbuchhandlung, 1912), p. 121.

38   Ibid., pp. 20, 22, 30, 36.

39   "Die politischen Ergebnisse der Rassenforschung," *AB*, no. 25 (June 24, 1905), pp. 215–16.

40   Ludwig Kuhlenbeck, *Rasse und Volkstum* (Munich: JF Lehmann, 1905), pp. 16–23.

41   Ibid., p. 28.

42   Hasse, *Die Zukunft*, pp. 71–2.

43   Kuhlenbeck, *Rasse und Volkstum*, pp. 18, 24.

44   "Alldeutsche Sozialpolitik," *AB*, no. 50 (December 16, 1905), pp. 428–9.

45   Hasse, *Die Zukunft*, p. 50.

46 Ibid., pp. 74, 73, 83, 89.

47 Ibid., pp. 72–3, 105.

48 *SGA* in Berlin (October 22, 1905), pp. 7–10, in BAB, R 8048/50; *SGA* (June 16, 1906), pp. 4–5, in BAB, R 8048/55.

49 Hasse, *Die Zukunft*, p. 61.

50 "Aus den Gauen und Ortsgruppen," *AB*, no. 18 (May 5, 1912), pp. 157–8.

51 *Wenn Ich der Kaiser wär*, pp. 30, 32, 36–7.

52 *SGA* (July 4, 1914), pp. 19–20, in Breslau, BAB, R 8048/95.

53 Ibid., pp. 149–56, 168–70.

54 Klaus Saul, *Staat, Industrie, Arbeiterbewegung im Kaiserreich. Zur Innen- und Aussenpolitik des wilheminischen Deutschland 1903–1914* (Düsseldorf: Bertelsmann Universitätsverlag, 1974).

55 Andreas Grießmer, *Massenverbände und Massenparteien im wilhelminischen Reich. Zum Wandel der Wahlkultur 1903–1912* (Düsseldorf: Droste, 2000), p. 74.

56 Ibid.

57 "Flugschriften-Literatur für die Wahlen," *AB*, no. 2 (January 12, 1907), pp. 12–13.

58 Klaus Mattheier, *Die Gelben. Nationale Arbeiter zwischen Wirtschaftsfrieden und Streik* (Düsseldorf: Pädagogischer Verlag Schwann, 1973), pp. 90–1.

59 "Auschuß- und Vorstands-Sitzung des Alldeutschen Verbandes zu Berlin am 9. Und 10. Februar," *AB*, no. 7 (February 16, 1907), p. 51.

60 See especially Eley, *Reshaping*, pp. 321–30.

61 Ibid., pp. 316–21; Stegmann, *Die Erben*, pp. 360–400; Fischer, *Krieg der Illusionen*, pp. 388–90.

62 Fischer, *Krieg der Illusionen*, pp. 640–59.

63 Heinrich Claß, *Denkschrift betreffend die national-, wirtschafts- und sozialpolitischen Ziele des deutschen Volkes im gegenwärtigen Kriege* (October 20, 1915), pp. 8–9, in BAB, R 8048/633.

64 Ibid., pp. 30, 31, 43, 45.

65 Ibid., pp. 23–6, 35, 63–4, 65.

66 Ibid., p. 62.

67 Claß, *Denkschrift*, pp. 13–19.

68 "Grundlinien künftiger innerer Arbeit," *Der Panther* 10 (1915), pp. 40, 42, in BAB, R 8048/536.

69 *Denkschrift der Obersten Heeresleitung über die deutsche Volks- und Wehrkraft*, in *Bundesarchiv Koblenz*, BArch Koblenz, N 1022/14, pp. 87–187.

70 Heinz Hagenlücke, *Deutsche Vaterlandspartei. Die nationale Rechte am Ende des Kaiserreiches* (Düsseldorff: Droste Verlag, 1997).

71 Hänsch, *An der Schwelle des grösseren Reiches. Deutsche Kriegsziele in politisch-geographischer Bergründung* (Munich: JF Lehmann, 1917), pp. 10, 180, 183–97.

72 Vietinghoff to Manteuffel, May 24, 1918, pp. 48–72, in BAB, R 8048/642.

73 *SGA*, June 29/30, 1918 in Berlin, BAB, R 8048/119, 12–27, especially 13 and 14.

74 See his opening speech at the Pan-German *Verbandstag* in Kassel, *AB*, no. 42 (October 13, 1917), pp. 414–15.

75 See Felix Kuh, "Neue Aufgaben der deutschen Arbeit," *DE*, 6 (1917), pp. 524–36; Lenz, "Merkworte zur Rassenhygiene," *DE*, no. 3 (June 1917), pp. 272–3.

76 *SGA*, July 7/8, 1917 in Berlin, BAB R 8048/114, p. 10.

77 For the outlines of this critique, see Bang, "Das 'Erfurter Programm' der deutschen Industriellen," *Deutsche Zeitung*, no. 366 (August 20, 1924) in BAB, R 8048/249, p. 131.

78 Hasse, *Deutsche Grenzpolitik* (Munich, 1906), p. 5.

79 Franz Sonntag, "Wir Alldeutschen und der Weltkrieg," *Der Panther* 10 (1915), p. 14 in BAB, R 8048/536.

8

The Prussian Commerce Ministry, the *Deutscher Werkbund*, and Germany's Global Commercial Ambitions

John V. Maciuika

The Prussian Commerce Ministry as a 'micro-culture' of Wilhelminist reform

A growing body of literature on Wilhelmine reform movements and middle-class activism has been dismantling characterizations of Germany's Second Empire as a reservoir of structural defects that contributed to the disastrous First World War and Hitler's subsequent rise.[1] This chapter builds on recent studies of Wilhelmine reform in individual cities and regions by tracking reform impulses in a place where they have seldom been identified: within the Prusso-German bureaucracy. Across the two-thirds of German territory comprising Prussia, the Prussian Ministry of Commerce and Industry (*Königlich Preussisches Ministerium für Handel und Gewerbe*) sowed the seeds of a far-reaching reform program stemming from decidedly middle-class "Wilhelminist" sensibilities.[2] Wilhelminism, as originally set forth by the historian Hartmut Pogge von Strandmann, consisted of a certain prewar reformist attitude. According to von Strandmann, the Wilhelminist outlook was future-oriented, yet respectful of the nineteenth century's traditions and achievements. It was statist, yet supportive of the Second Empire's burgeoning capitalism. Further, Wilhelminism was forward-looking with respect to innovations in industry and technology, yet maintained awareness of the "social problem." Finally, Wilhelminism was sympathetic to reforms of the state for purposes of national efficiency, yet skeptical of the ability of either Conservative or Social Democratic platforms to actually achieve reform.[3]

This chapter focuses on the overlooked Wilhelminist reform program of Theodor Möller, a cosmopolitan Westphalian industrialist-turned-politician who served as Prussian Commerce Minister between 1901 and 1905. To be sure, the label "Wilhelminist" has been used by historians retroactively, and not by individuals like Möller in the early years of the twentieth century. Nevertheless, Möller advanced what should be recognized as Wilhelminist policies. He did so with the help of a loyal cadre of *hoch-bürgerlich* undersecretaries and senior civil servants, among them Heinrich Jakob Neuhaus, Hermann von Seefeld, Fritz Dönhoff, and Hermann Muthesius.[4] Together these officials managed to avoid Kaiser Wilhelm II's active opposition to progressivism in the fine arts of painting and sculpture, for—importantly—official opposition did not extend from these "high" arts down to the applied arts and finished goods industries, which were the Commerce Ministry's purview.[5] Removed from the censorious attention directed by the Kaiser at the Foreign Office and Minister of Culture in their planning of the German exhibition at the St. Louis World's Fair of 1904, for example, Möller developed reforms in a ministerial "micro-culture" that owed much to the minister's own background and initiative.

At the heart of Möller's policies were far-reaching reforms in technical education and applied arts education. These had significant implications for artists and finished goods producers, both of whom were aided by an upswing in the German economy in the mid-1890s that stimulated greater interest in the applied arts and emerging field of design. Even as they favored modern industries, Möller's reforms sought to align industrial producers on a local basis with pedagogical changes being effected at the Commerce Ministry's extensive network of applied arts schools. The thirty schools administered by the ministry stretched from Aachen in the west to Königsberg in the east, from Flensburg in the north to Breslau in the south. In ways that would affect Prussia's and Germany's finished goods industries, economic policies, and emergent modern design culture well past Möller's retirement from the Commerce Ministry in 1905, the ministry's reforms connected industries, commercial enterprises, and a self-proclaimed "new movement" (*neue Bewegung*) of artists, craftsmen, and architects, many of whom were hired by Möller to modernize Commerce Ministry applied arts schools.[6]

Significantly for the history of German architecture, applied arts, and industrial design, Möller's policies also paved the way to the foundation of the Deutscher Werkbund in October 1907. Specifically, Möller founded the State Trades Board (*Landesgewerbeamt*) in 1905 as a subagency (*Nebenamt*) within the Commerce Ministry. In doing so, he and such leading members of the State Trades Board as the architect and privy councilor Hermann

Muthesius introduced the organizational principles and aesthetic philosophy that would later be embedded in the Werkbund. The Werkbund—private, national, and *hochbürgerlich*-proud—was the pre–First World War era's leading Wilhelminist association devoted to German design as an agent of economic expansion and cultural reform. As Prussia's pioneering State Trades Board did before it, the Deutscher Werkbund would bring together industrialists, craftsmen, entrepreneurs, artists, architects, and government officials. While the State Trades Board met regularly to coordinate these diverse parties and interests within Prussia, the Werkbund operated at the national level as a private organization (albeit with some government members, notably the architect Muthesius, as public-private connecting figures). Both the Board and the Werkbund embarked on explicit missions to improve German products, boost international export competitiveness, and educate German producers and consumers alike about quality and taste. As early as 1901, and soon after his appointment as minister, Möller would write to a family member: "without further development of exports we cannot feed the 800,000 people who are added to our population every year. From this standpoint...trade agreements are a question of national survival."[7] Möller further believed that Germany's political power was a function of its economic well-being, while left-wing newspapers such as *Vorwärts (Forward)* feared that with Möller's appointment as Minister of Commerce and Industry, the ministry might as well be renamed "Ministry of the German Industrialists' Association."[8]

Between 1907 and 1914, the Werkbund aggressively carried forward the policies initiated by Möller's Commerce Ministry and its State Trades Board. As it grew in membership and influence, the Werkbund moved the needle significantly when it came to the "modernization" of German finished goods production through what its leadership called "artistic intervention."[9] Heavy industry, of course, would always retain preeminence in the prewar German economic and political landscape. Yet by 1914 the Werkbund, which self-identified as a "cartel for quality," grew to include such powerhouse German firms as Krupp, Mannesmann, AEG, Daimler, Benz, and Bosch. By the time of its first national exhibition in Cologne in summer 1914, and as will be detailed below, the Werkbund had expanded its connections with government to include the German Foreign Office, the Chancellor's Office, the Colonial Office, and the Interior Ministry.

Beginning in 1903, within the Commerce Ministry's ranks and, later, in the leadership of the Deutscher Werkbund, the work of one innovator clearly stands out: that of Hermann Muthesius (1861–1927). Born in the small Thuringian village of Gross-Neuhausen, Muthesius rose above firm roots in the trades *Mittelstand* to become a multilingual, cosmopolitan government architect (*Regierungsbaumeister*) and Commerce Ministry privy councilor (*Geheimes Regierungsrat*). He entered service in the Prusso-German bureaucracy in the early 1890s, after several years assisting the Berlin architecture firm of Ende and Böckmann in the design of government buildings in Japan. Perhaps more than any other single Commerce Ministry reformer, Muthesius employed what one of his Werkbund colleagues, Fritz Hellwag, later termed the architect's "concentric talents" in writing, policy making, the applied arts, and architectural design to advance the interests of the bourgeois class (*Bürgertum*) both within and outside government circles.[10] To Ernst Jäckh, the Werkbund's managing director beginning in 1912, Muthesius represented the most decisive personality in the organization, for "he alone had the accurate conception of politics ... as a synthesis of all human relations, ranging from physical matters to the metaphysics of psychology, from 'material' to 'form.'"[11]

Within the Commerce Ministry's micro-culture of reform, Muthesius took the lead in crafting Minister Möller's sweeping applied arts decrees, such as the Instructional Workshops Decree of 1904.[12] He was also the guiding hand in the reform of Prussia's applied arts schools for service to a modern economy, using his years of travel and government reporting in England to cherry-pick leading techniques of applied arts and technical education from such schools as William Richard Lethaby's Central School of Arts and Crafts and Charles Robert Ashbee's Guild and School of Handicraft. By the time Möller assigned Muthesius to head the applied arts department at the newly created State Trades Board, the architect was well prepared to organize the Board's first meetings in the sumptuous assembly hall of Berlin's Anhalter Bahnhof.

At the first Board meetings in 1905, Muthesius and other members of the leadership promoted synergies among the industrialists, crafts producers, school directors, entrepreneurs, and artists who had been summoned to participate. All the while during his work for the Commerce Ministry and State Trades Board, Muthesius continued operating a home-based architectural practice, where he and a team of junior architects (among them Martin Wagner, future director of urban planning for Berlin) designed explicitly reform-minded *bürgerliche Landhäuser* (suburban bourgeois country houses) for such Commerce Ministry colleagues as Heinrich Neuhaus, Hermann von Seefeld, and Gustav von Velsen. Muthesius's architectural designs and writings on architecture and cultural reform were all of a piece with his campaign to embed the Wilhelminist program developed within the Prussian Commerce Ministry in the Deutscher Werkbund.

The transformations at Möller's Commerce Ministry began taking place during the period after Muthesius returned, in 1903, from nearly seven years as a government reporter stationed at the German Embassy in London. Four years later, Muthesius would catalyze the founding of the national Werkbund association in October 1907. Looking back at the four years between 1903 and 1907, we can detect a significant divergence in disciplinary historiographies. On the one hand, Muthesius is well enough known in art and architectural history circles as an architect, theorist, prolific author, and "Father of the Werkbund," even if his work within the government remains greatly underemphasized. On the other hand, and for a wide variety of reasons that spans generations, scholarship specific to German history has overlooked the ways in which Möller and his Commerce Ministry subordinates incubated the aesthetic principles and organizational philosophy of the Deutscher Werkbund from inside the Prussian state apparatus. This omission on the part of both fields appears all the more remarkable when it is recalled that among historians of art, architecture, and design, the Deutscher Werkbund is the most oft-cited precedent for Walter Gropius's Weimar-era Bauhaus school, along with the permutations of *Sachlichkeit* (and *Neue Sachlichkeit*) propagated there. In short, the government policies that produced applied arts reforms beginning in 1903, and a new State Trades Board beginning in 1905, make Möller's Commerce Ministry a leading contributor to the development of twentieth-century methods of German industrial and architectural design. Möller's micro-culture of reform introduced practices oriented to sober, objective design (*Sachlichkeit*) and purposeful functionality (*Zweckmässigkeit*) that were promoted nationally by the Werkbund and later developed even more famously at the Bauhaus, Germany's foremost propagator of twentieth-century avant-garde design.[13]

The Commerce Ministry and the evolving Prusso-German administration

Of course, Möller's successes arose out of a particular set of Wilhelmine historical circumstances. The most important of these, this chapter argues, were the conflictive, evolving institutional landscape of nineteenth-century German government administration; policy opportunities conferred by perceived economic and political necessities that are examined below; and synergies arising from Germans working on problems widely perceived to be in separate spheres, but which in fact turned out to share much common ground. Thus, in the adaptive, improvisational manner that was common under conditions of "the Empire and Prussia in a battle for supremacy," to borrow a phrase from the title of Hans Goldschmidt's impressive but underappreciated study of Wilhelmine governance, *Das Reich und Preussen im Kampf um die Führung* of 1931, Möller found opportunities to propagate reforms in a Prussian ministry that had originally never been meant to survive in the Second Reich administrative environment at all—at least not according to the Second Reich's chief architect, Chancellor Otto von Bismarck.[14]

From 1880 to 1890, for the ten years that Bismarck included service at the helm of the Prussian Commerce Ministry in his wide-ranging portfolio, the Chancellor drew upon the process known as *Personalunion*, or consolidation of powers in a single post, as a means to expand imperial authority at the expense of a particularist Prussian hegemony. Thus in 1871, Bismarck's successful conversion of the Prussian Foreign Ministry

(*Ministerium für Auswärtigen Angelegenheiten*) into an Imperial Foreign Office (*Auswärtiges Amt*) became "the model example for the elevation of Prussian ministries into the Reich with the simultaneous preservation of the member state's interests."[15]

The techniques of *Personalunion* also came into play with the Prussian Ministry of Commerce. Within a month of Kaiser Wilhelm I's appointment of Bismarck as Prussia's Commerce Minister in September 1880, Bismarck informed the Kaiser that in a united Germany "there can exist no specifically Prussian commerce, just as there can be none specific to Saxony, Bavaria, or Württemberg."[16] The kingdom of Bavaria had, in fact, gone so far as to dissolve its own Commerce Ministry in 1871, anticipating the absorption of its state commerce ministry into a *Reichsministerium*, while the grand duchy of Baden dissolved its Commerce Ministry in 1881.[17]

Amid a continuing flurry of imperial reorganization efforts of such economic affairs as banking, commerce, taxation, and customs, Bismarck obtained approval for the establishment of a new Division of Economic Affairs (*Abteilung für wirtschaftliche Angelegenheiten*) within the Imperial Interior Ministry in October 1880. In November of that year, he oversaw the additional founding of a Peoples' Economic Advisory Council, or *Volkswirtschaftsrat*. As the historian Friedrich Facius explains, all of these measures "bespoke Bismarck's conviction to become master (*Herr*) of the prevailing tumult of economic problems" to which the "question of departmental organization was most intimately linked."[18]

While Bismarck's establishment of new imperial departments was one thing, his efforts to absorb the Prussian Commerce Ministry into an imperial structure were quite another. Despite the Chancellor's insistence that "the Prussian Commerce Ministry is in the long run a political impossibility, just as is one from Mecklenburg or Saxony," Prussian legislators stubbornly blocked Bismarck's bid to replace the Prussian Commerce Ministry with imperial departmental equivalents.[19] As late as 1889, Bismarck would maintain that "an independent Prussian Minister of Commerce will never exist again."[20] But his greatest wish as Prussian Commerce Minister— to absorb the Prussian ministry into a branch of the Imperial Interior Ministry—was repeatedly thwarted by Prussian legislators reluctant to surrender economic policy functions to the Reich.[21] Moreover, the very agencies and subdepartments originally created by Bismarck to replace the Prussian ministry quickly found themselves overwhelmed, over the course of the 1880s, by the demands of administering Bismarck's sweeping new social policies. For example, Bismarck's newly created Imperial Interior Ministry's Division of Economic Affairs had to oversee statistical data-gathering on poverty, accidents, and the demographics of emerging professions; a vast system for workers' insurance; and even measures for "defense against social democracy" (*Sachgebiet Abwehr der Sozialdemokratie*). Yet as it did so, the new division was effectively blocked from becoming the *Kaiserreich*'s center of policy making in the realm of commerce.[22]

The nature and consequences of Theodor Möller's reforms

Against this institutional background, the figure of Theodor Möller offers an interesting historiographical conundrum. It goes virtually without saying that Möller is an unknown in art historical circles. Or, rather, art and architectural historians have naturally focused more on individual "artist" architects like Muthesius, rather than on the ministers like Möller who hired them to help carry out intra-governmental institutional change.[23] Yet Theodor Möller is certainly known in the field of German history, although the bulk of historians' attention has concentrated on his failures. In particular, historians have analyzed Möller's central role in the "Hibernia Affair"—a botched state takeover of the private Hibernia Coal Company in 1905. Far less has been written about his successes. Partly for this reason, this chapter argues that Minister Möller should be regarded, in fact, as an unsung hero for implementing reforms that would come to be championed by architectural and design historians when they spotted the fruits of these reforms in the progressive Deutscher Werkbund design association. To put it in German historiographical terms, Möller's Prussian Commerce Ministry and its micro-culture of progressive reform policies represent exactly one of the "unexplored spaces" of reform specified in the book *Wilhelminism and Its Legacies*. The editors of this 2003 essay collection write in their Introduction: "One of the pressing needs of Wilhelmine historiography is to deconstruct the long-established dichotomous framework of 'modernizing economy' and 'backward political culture' in order to open up the interesting and underexplored spaces in between."[24] Möller's micro-culture of reform, taking place in a Commerce Ministry that narrowly avoided absorption into the imperial administrative structure by Chancellor Bismarck, in fact represents a vital element of forward-thinking political culture that helped guide the modernization of one sector of the *Kaiserreich*'s growing commercial economy.

Both the failures and the reforms of Theodor Möller need to be reconsidered in this light. German historians chiefly remember Möller for two reasons. First, Theodor Möller made a name for himself as a National Liberal Party strategist and Reichstag member in the 1890s. He showed particular talent in steering his party toward the revived policy of *Sammlungspolitik*, or "politics of rallying together," by which disparate groups and constituencies were unified, for practical purposes, via compromise. His success in this arena and in negotiating German international trade agreements prompted Kaiser Wilhelm II to name Möller Prussian Commerce Minister in 1901.[25]

By 1905, however, the so-called Hibernia Affair would all but destroy Möller's reputation. A flurry of scholarly articles and other historical literature emphasizes the Hibernia Affair as a failed attempt at state monopoly capitalism. This was, in other words, an attempt by the Prussian state to engineer the hostile state takeover of Germany's second-largest producer of coal, the Hibernia Coal Company, through the secret purchase of a majority of the company's stock. Although this plan was almost certainly directed by various top members of the state administration, Commerce Minister Möller was the state's point man. He worked clandestinely with the Dresdner Bank for the purchase of stock shares on behalf of the state's military and railway authorities. For their part, military and railway officials felt that unprecedented levels of vertical and horizontal integration among German companies were endangering both the military and railway system's access to uninterrupted supplies of coal. Acquiring majority control of Prussia's second-largest coal producer would remove the threat to the military and railways from growing cartels which, through their great concentrations of companies, could put the state at risk should there be a spike in price or other crisis that would cut off the state's access to vital energy supplies.

When industrialists and bankers like Hugo Stinnes, August Thyssen, and Carl Bleichröder got wind of the state's stock-purchasing scheme shortly before the state achieved the requisite 51 percent majority ownership of the company's stock, they reacted swiftly by blocking all further stock purchases. Newspapers like Maximilian Harden's *The Future* (*Die Zukunft*) quickly exposed the state's subterfuge. Möller, who had originally emerged from the ranks of industrialists only to become the state's major agent in this perceived betrayal of his former compatriots in Rhineland industry, paid the price with his forced resignation. The Hibernia Affair was a political and public relations setback for the administration, and to this day Möller is remembered most for this notoriously failed attempt to consolidate the state's position in the face of the advancing forces of German industrial capitalism.[26]

However, Möller's tarnished reputation takes on a far brighter hue if we turn from this German historiography to examine his ministry's efforts in the context of German architectural and design history. In particular, Möller began his tenure at the Commerce Ministry with a kind of master-stroke of "Wilhelminist" hiring: He appointed two prominent designers, the artist Peter Behrens and the longtime government architect Hermann Muthesius, to help modernize Prussia's crafts and design fields. Following two full days of interviews with Theodor Möller in 1902, Peter Behrens commented favorably to his friend, the writer Richard Dehmel, that he had left the Commerce Minister's office at Number 2 Leipziger Platz with the impression that the ministry was engaged in an exciting, "drastic reorganization."[27]

It was no small feat for Möller to win Behrens as the new director of Prussia's flagship applied arts school in Düsseldorf. Behrens, already Wilhelmine Germany's best-known artist and designer, would catapult to even greater prominence in 1907 as chief designer of factory and administration buildings, office furniture, industrial lighting, advertising

posters and brochures, domestic appliances, and letterhead for Emil
Rathenau's AEG, Germany's "general electric" company (*Allgemeine
Elektrizitäts-Gesellschaft*). Assisting Behrens in this work was a group of
young apprentices (and future twentieth-century "star-architects") that
included Walter Gropius, Ludwig Mies (Ludwig Mies van der Rohe after
1914), and the visiting Swiss architect Charles-Édouard Jeanneret, later
"Le Corbusier" (after 1920).[28] These young architects would, in time, rise
to prominence in the formation of what would come to be known as the
twentieth-century's "International Style" of architecture, propagated by Le
Corbusier in Paris and by Gropius and Mies at the Bauhaus school.

It was precisely under Möller's tutelage, then, that Commerce Ministry
employees like privy councilor Muthesius and school director Behrens
were given free rein to bring together progressive design thinking,
economic development policy, and educational reform in the applied
arts for the improvement of German production quality and export
competitiveness. Further, it is no exaggeration to note that the Prussian
Ministry of Commerce, originally marked by Bismarck for evisceration and
absorption into the larger imperial ministerial structure some fifteen years
earlier, evolved instead into Germany's most progressive state promoter
of what would soon come to be known as avant-garde design. Without
a doubt, there existed numerous centers of innovation in the arts and
design in Wilhelmine Germany.[29] But the implications of Kaiser Wilhelm
II's appointment of a Westphalian industrialist plucked from the ranks
of successful National Liberal Party leaders in the Reichstag—that is,
from the realm of "praxis" rather than from the *Beamtenkultur* of civil
service insiders—are considerable. This is not to deny the significance of
the "Hibernia Affair" as a Prussian state misadventure, or as a blunder in
which Prussian industrialists handed the state a black eye. But it should
significantly mitigate historians' long-accepted conclusion that Möller
himself was a liability who contributed little during his tenure at the
Commerce Ministry between 1901 and 1905.

Möller's legacy does not end with his applied arts reforms, founding of
the State Trades Board, and incubation of the private Werkbund association
between 1905 and 1907. Rather, it includes the close imbrication of the
Werkbund's design and commercial activities in the Imperial German
government's increasingly expansionist commercial policies in the years
prior to the First World War, especially after 1911. To fully appreciate this,
it is necessary to examine realignments among leaders in the Wilhelmine
design community, and their increasingly close relationships to counterparts
in the commercial and political establishments, between 1911 and 1914.
These relationships and realignments reveal key features of Wilhelmine
modernity and underscore the need to analyze Wilhelmine modernity on
its own terms—that is, without viewing the Wilhelmine era's political and
architectural cultures in the rear-view mirror of Weimar-era modernist
developments.

The 1914 Deutscher Werkbund exhibition in Cologne and German government policy

When scholars of Weimar-era architecture and design look at Wilhelmine precedents, they tend to highlight the Deutscher Werkbund's heated debates over "types" or "typification" (*Typisierung*) in design at the organization's one and only pre–First World War national exhibition in Cologne. And for good reason: the Deutscher Werkbund Congress and exhibition in the summer of 1914 produced a showdown of fundamental importance to the subsequent history of twentieth-century German architecture and design. The weekend conference of this summer-long exhibition, held on July 3–4 in a Behrens-designed congress hall on the grounds of the First Werkbund Exhibition in Cologne, featured keynote speakers familiar to all present: Hermann Muthesius gave the conference's opening address, and, as was also customary, Friedrich Naumann closed the conference with a rousing speech on the final night.[30]

There is a long-standing consensus among historians of architecture, art, and design about what took place. At the conclusion of Muthesius's speech on July 3 entitled "The Future Work of the Werkbund" ("Die Werkbundarbeit der Zukunft"), the artist Henry van de Velde rose to read a statement prepared the night before opposing virtually every recommendation Muthesius's speech had just made. The ensuing storm of controversy dominated the remainder of the conference: speakers rose to attack or defend the apparent heart of Muthesius's speech—his advocacy of "types" in design and industry—while others supported van de Velde's impassioned defense of artists' individual creative freedom. When it finally came time for Friedrich Naumann's closing address, entitled "The Werkbund and the World Economy" ("Werkbund und Weltwirtschaft"), the charismatic politician did his best to rally his audience around a common goal by assuring them that the Werkbund, despite its differences, was destined to raise the status of German exports and cultural production to unprecedented heights. Increased exports were a national necessity, Naumann reminded his audience, for Germany's great good fortune—its ever-growing population—required a steady expansion of exports to sustain the health and wealth of the nation. Naumann did not refer to the fact that Theodor Möller had been making exactly these arguments in his justification of new applied arts policies as far back as 1901.

As soon as the conference closed, Werkbund members who had been in attendance began writing articles and letters in a contentious, drawn-out effort not only to determine what, exactly, had just transpired, but also to try to influence subsequent developments. It was clear to all that Henry van de Velde had countered Muthesius's presentation of ten "guiding principles" (*Leitsätze*) justifying "types" (*Typisierung*) in design with ten "counter-principles" (*Gegenleitsätze*) defending artistic individuality against the encroachment of industrial, political, and economic imperatives. Ten days before delivering his lecture, Muthesius had circulated his principles among the fourteen speakers scheduled to address the conference. Where Muthesius's keynote address traced the development of types as an historical process, his ten theses distilled the speech into a set of principles that the Werkbund—in concert with industry and the state, and virtually by decree—would use to set new standards for exports and for industry.

Muthesius appears intentionally to have kept his theses general, sweeping, and maddeningly unspecific with regard to execution or to the practical implications for artists, industry, retailers, and the state. He avoided using the word "standardization" (*Standardisierung*), although his coinage of the term *Typisierung* ("making of types") left room for listeners to infer this; he also never outlined the exact structures of authority that would be needed to put such a comprehensive scheme into place. Muthesius's first priority, it seemed, was to steer the organization toward acceptance of the new direction, and one thing appeared certain: if the Werkbund followed the new course, the nature of its activities would be altered forever, enlarged to an extent that the Werkbund would henceforth work closely with industry and the state to establish readily identifiable, artist-designed "types" for seemingly every scale of product manufactured by Werkbund industries.[31] If Muthesius had his way, typical, "tasteful" products of high-quality would be made available in unprecedented quantities for coordinated, worldwide distribution as German national exports in an expanding *Weltwirtschaft*, or global economy. Or, as he put it in his theses: "Starting from the conviction that it is a matter of life and death for Germany constantly to ennoble its production, the Deutscher Werkbund, as an association of artists, industrialists, and merchants, must concentrate its attention upon creating the preconditions for the export of its industrial arts." And in another thesis: "Germany's advances in applied art and architecture must be brought to the attention of foreign countries through effective propaganda" (Theses 6 and 7).[32]

The foundations for unprecedented involvement by the state in promoting Werkbund affairs had already been affirmed publicly in 1912, at the fifth annual congress of the Werkbund in Vienna—the first to be held on foreign soil. Werkbund President Peter Bruckmann of Heilbronn repeatedly emphasized to the Werkbund membership—and to newly invited representatives of the Prussian Commerce Ministry, the Imperial Foreign Office, and the Ministry of the Interior, together with their counterparts in the Hapsburg Imperial administration—that the Werkbund must "in the next few years be recognized and respected by the imperial and state authorities as the official representative of the German applied arts."[33]

As it had in the Prussian Commerce Ministry's school reforms in the first decade of the twentieth century, architecture and architects would lead the way in coordinating the applied arts and ensuring Germany's continued development toward a contemporary "harmonious culture" in the second decade (Thesis 1). And though the Werkbund would never reach a scale of operation to rival the influence of German heavy industry, it is worth noting that between 1907 and 1914, corporate membership in the Werkbund's "cartel for quality" would grow from 143 to more than 300 companies, including the aforementioned Bosch, Bayer, BASF, Daimler, Benz, Krupp, and Mannesmann companies. These firms joined AEG, an early Werkbund giant, in representing Germany's increasingly influential mechanical, chemical, transport, armaments, and electrical industries.[34]

What the Werkbund membership would gradually come to know in the weeks between the Congress of July 3–4 and the outbreak of the First World War in early August is that Muthesius and Naumann—with Werkbund members like Gustav Stresemann and Ernst Jäckh, the Werkbund managing director, in key supporting roles—represented forces at work in German politics and in the Werkbund that far exceeded the ability of individual artists or small, private institutions like Karl Ernst Osthaus's German Museum for Art in Commerce and Industry (*Deutsches Museum für Kunst in Handel und Gewerbe*) to mount effective, meaningful resistance. Muthesius and Naumann, as two of the Werkbund's most influential founders and leaders, had also come more than ever to represent two even more formidable factions joined in alliance in the radically charged political environment that was Wilhelmine Germany between 1911 and 1914. Muthesius had long represented the interests of the Prussian Commerce Ministry, which now became joined in a constellation of ministerial and governmental actors that reflected the unique political circumstances of these increasingly tension-filled, jingoistic years. Chancellor Bethmann-Hollweg and three powerful ministries—Minister Clemens von Delbrück's Imperial Interior Ministry, Reinhold Sydow's Prussian Commerce Ministry, and Arthur Kiderlen-Wächter and Gottlieb von Jagow's Imperial Foreign Office—gradually aligned themselves with increasingly risky, aggressive bids to expand German foreign trade and territorial influence. They lent greater support to commerce, exports, and the finished goods industries, in spite of the continued political dominance of coal, iron, and steel producers in concert with agrarian Conservatives. In the nomenclature of the powerful but fractious industrial interest groups, the Chancellor and these three ministries grew more receptive to light industry's Association of Industrialists (*Bund der Industriellen*, or BDI) and the Hansa League for Commerce, Trade, and Industry (*Hansabund für Handel, Gewerbe, und Industrie*), relative to their traditional backing of heavy industry's Central Association of German Industrialists (*Centralverband Deutscher Industrieller*, or CDI).[35]

Naumann, for his part, was no creature of the ministerial bureacracy, but the left-leaning progressive mouthpiece of an expansionist program for a German-led trade zone in Central Europe and the Balkans—a region he popularized as "Mitteleuropa" in his best-selling eponymous book of 1915. But Naumann was anything but alone in promoting plans that reflected Germany's bid to rise into the ranks of such global powers as Britain, France,

Russia, and the United States. Werkbund managing director Ernst Jäckh, a longtime Naumann disciple, emerged as the forceful advocate of an alliance, spearheaded by German banking interests, that aimed to stretch "from Berlin to Baghdad" via the Austro-Hungarian Empire, the Balkans, and the Ottoman Empire. Naumann, Jäckh, and Gustav Stresemann—a National Liberal Reichstag member and the galvanizing head of the Association of Saxon Industrialists (the BDI's single largest corporate member)—were all aggressive promoters of imperialism at a time in Germany when, as the historian Klaus Wernecke has noted, "the word imperialism had no negative associations for its proponents."[36]

In domestic policy, Naumann was a hopeful advocate of ever-elusive representative democracy as a safeguard against socialist revolution and, simultaneously, as a weapon against heavy industrialists and feudal landowning Junkers allied in their stubborn maintenance of tariff rates favorable to Germany's purveyors of "iron and rye." While Muthesius and Naumann had never been able to agree on a proper *Sozialpolitik* for the treatment of Germany's workers, trade expansionism and imperialism provided a common ground for the Commerce Ministry privy councilor and Württemberg's leading progressive politician.

To men like Muthesius, Naumann, and Jäckh, then, the Werkbund operated at the intersection of art's claims to represent a civilizing German *Kultur* and industry's claims to political influence commensurate with its growing preeminence in German economic life. And while Theodor von Möller (the *von* was conferred upon his retirement in 1905) had long left the scene, his successor at the Commerce Ministry, Clemens von Delbrück, had defended Hermann Muthesius in the Prussian Chamber of Deputies (*Abgeordnetenhaus*) following the architect's bare-fisted denunciation of entrenched, "traditional" applied arts producers in his inaugural for the ministry-supported Berlin College of Commerce (*Handelshochschule*) in early 1907.[37] A few years later, Delbrück would bring his Commerce Ministry experience to bear on his leadership as Imperial Minister of the Interior, working closely alongside Chancellor Bethmann-Hollweg.

Like other organizations top-heavy with a membership drawn primarily from the Wilhelmine *Bürgertum*, the Werkbund embodied what Geoff Eley has discussed as a growing Wilhelmine bourgeois push for "equality of status" (*Gleichberechtigung*) in a political system singularly ill-prepared to brook compromise, or to embrace new and increasingly powerful bourgeois and working-class interests.[38] Yet given the imperial Wilhelmine political system's unwillingness to broaden the franchise or alter the fundamental structure of government, leading Werkbund figures such as Naumann and Muthesius adjusted their views in ways that remained loyal, in the end, to the conservative power structures they served. Their advocacy of "types" in 1914, occurring as it did in the context of larger political efforts to accelerate trade, concentrate production, and increase Germany's colonial and global influence, can hardly be considered apart from the political programs that began working their way through ministries as diverse as the Imperial Interior Ministry, the Foreign Office, the Colonial Office, the Prussian Commerce Ministry, and the Reich Chancellor's Office between 1912 and 1914—years that the historian Thomas Nipperdey has described as a time of "stable crisis."[39]

Perhaps the defining event for these years was the Reichstag election of January 1912, which yielded results that shook the German Empire to its foundations: the Social Democratic Party captured an unprecedented 34.8 percent of the vote. With its 110 delegates, the party formed the Reichstag's largest bloc, a feat all the more considerable in view of the party's illegality between 1878 and 1890.[40]

The resulting intensification and radicalization of German politics affected virtually every party, interest group, and political association. Changes in the organization of the Werkbund fit into this matrix of larger shifts, in which government ministries and interest groups struggled to make progress on constructive domestic and foreign policies amid antisocialist agitation that ranged from mild to hysterical. For the next two years, Chancellor Bethmann-Hollweg swung between two equally problematic poles in domestic policy. Appeasement of the socialists' loud calls for a just social policy (*Sozialpolitik*) was impossible, since this was anathema to Prussia's controlling Junker and heavy industrial interests, to say nothing of the Kaiser. On the political Right, heavy industry's CDI maintained repeated hardline calls for the dissolution of the Reichstag, the banning of public demonstrations, and resurrection of Bismarck's antisocialist laws. Heavy industry and agrarian leaders alike attacked Bethmann-Hollweg and Delbrück for refusing to disband the Reichstag and crush the socialists. The Chancellor and Interior Minister Delbrück, for their part, would disappoint moderates and especially the Left as well, paying only lip service to the idea of greater recognition and support for workers in 1912 before backing off entirely from the development of a social policy by early 1914.[41]

If the government of Bethmann-Hollweg was not experiencing complete paralysis in these areas of domestic policy, then it certainly had very little maneuvering room. For groups that represented commercial, trade, and finished-goods manufacturing interests, however, the dilemmas being faced by Bethmann-Hollweg and Delbrück actually opened an unprecedented— if by no means assured—window of opportunity. The BDI, for one thing, emerged as a natural partner to Werkbund interests. It had formed initially in 1895 to unite small and middle-sized finished goods industries, which typically did not belong to cartels, in an effort to break the overwhelming influence and domination of well-organized, cartellized heavy industry.[42]

For another, the BDI enjoyed gradually increasing ties to the Hansa League for Commerce, Trade, and Industry, a second, even younger interest group dominated by light manufacturing industries. The Hansa League had formed in 1909 during battles over the reform of imperial finances and represented a further important step in the organization of Wilhelmine commercial, banking, and white-collar employee (*Privatangestellten*) interests. Active members and leaders of these groups like Emil Rathenau, Gustav Stresemann, and Friedrich Naumann railed against the government's unfavorable treatment of finished goods industries as compared to its sustained support for tariff agreements favorable to the old alliance (*Sammlung*) of heavy industry and agriculture.[43] In fact, the BDI and its closest political ally, the National Liberals of the "broad middle" of Basserman and Stresemann, had been agitating for years to gain fair representation for commercial, banking, and light manufacturing interests in the Imperial Interior Ministry's Economic Commission for Industry (*Wirtschaftliche Ausschuss beim Reichsamt des Innern*).[44] Complaining about the stubborn and ongoing refusals of Conservatives to accept inheritance taxes and to roll back finished goods tax hikes that were damaging to German commerce and consumers, Naumann had protested, "Liberals pay the most taxes, but get little say [in government]. Social Democrats provide the most soldiers of all the parties and get even less."[45]

Bethmann-Hollweg and Delbrück did not expand light industry representation on the Economic Commission, just as they refused either to ban the socialist party outright or appease it with a meaningful social policy. They did, however, step up calls for imperialist expansion and initiatives promoting Germany's commercial success. A "gunboat diplomacy" dimension of this policy shift fell short, as the brinksmanship of Chancellor Bethmann-Hollweg and Foreign Minister Alfred von Kiderlen-Wächter during the Morocco Crisis of 1911 raised the ire of the French and British and failed to produce the hoped-for wave of nationalist fervor that would carry Conservatives to victory in the elections of 1912. Kiderlen-Wächter, a close friend of Ernst Jäckh from their days in Constantinople, worked closely with Bethmann-Hollweg on foreign policy until his unexpected death on December 30, 1912.[46]

A second dimension of this policy, a bid for expanding Germany's trade territories in order to compete effectively with such global powers as Britain and the United States, seemed to offer greater prospects. For example, the Foreign Office responded well to calls from the BDI and Stresemann, its most influential member, to mobilize Germany's worldwide network of diplomatic consulates as energetic facilitators of German commerce and foreign trade. German diplomatic outposts in Rio de Janeiro, Beirut, Calcutta, Genoa, and other cities received official notice of the Werkbund and its bid to improve the quality of German products and support German culture through the cooperation of artists, manufacturers, and merchants. The Chancellor's Office also requested that consulates furnish it with addresses of all German businesses and professionals operating in foreign territory who could serve as appropriate conduits for Werkbund propaganda, which the Chancellor's Office wished to have businesses disseminate as widely as possible in these countries.[47] Where Möller's State Trades Board organized on a state level in Prussia beginning in 1905, and the Werkbund organized on a national level as of 1907, the government now pursued synergies among artist-designers, German producers, and international distributors of high-quality German products beginning in 1912.

In a related effort, the Chancellor and Foreign Office arranged free passage on a luxury steamer from South America to Germany for Major Joâo Simplicio de Carvalho, Brazil's incoming Minister of Transport and one-time War Ministry attaché, so that he could tour the planned Werkbund Exhibition of 1914. He was to be shown German industry's finest examples of locomotives, passenger train cars, automobiles, and planes, and was to be treated as an honored minister of state throughout his visit. As the Chancellor noted in a letter to the German consul in Brazil, the Krupp Company, a Werkbund corporate member, would also take Major Carvalho on a tour of the legendary Krupp steel works in Essen.[48] Here family patriarch Gustav Krupp von Bohlen und Halbach would usher the Brazilian dignitary through explanations of the Krupp steel-production process, followed by a visit to sales displays of Germany's finest steel-plated armor, naval guns, artillery field pieces, and railway wheels and rails.[49] Between the Werkbund Exhibition and the Krupp tour, Foreign Office officials expressed confidence that Major de Carvalho's "far-reaching influence would soon be of benefit to German commerce, German industry, and shipping."[50]

As the Foreign Office was given to understand through documentation submitted by Ernst Jäckh and Carl Rehorst, the Werkbund Exhibition Planning Committee was working to assure that official foreign visitors would encounter the best selection of German industrial products in Cologne as well. For strategic reasons, the planning committee had chosen to abandon the Werkbund's traditional emphasis on the "*quality of the exhibitor*" and instead decided to focus attention on the "quality of the *exhibited products*" (emphasis original). "This broadening of the exhibition's base," explained Rehorst's and Jäckh's annotated report to the Standing Committee for German Industrial Exhibitions, "will especially help to realize the goal of the exhibition in its national-economic dimension, far better than if one were to limit oneself only to people and firms that are in the Werkbund and have already been won over to its ideas."[51] In other words, the Cologne Exhibition committee was opening its doors to all German industries and products deemed to be of sufficient quality. This move cast the Werkbund as a kind of umbrella organization whose principles stood to become those of the invited, non-Werkbund German industries as well. The Foreign Office further used the Werkbund Exhibition for training and education of its diplomatic and consular staff that attended both the exhibition and supplementary Werkbund lectures on various national efforts to promote quality in Germany's export industries.[52]

None of the Foreign Office's measures, of course, proceeded in a vacuum. Interior Minister Delbrück, for example, assured Foreign Minister Gottlieb von Jagow that the Werkbund Exhibition had his full support.[53] The Imperial Colonial Office (*Reichs-Kolonialamt*), too, signed on to display Germany's colonial products in its own Werkbund Exhibition pavilion. Colonial Office officials laid particular emphasis on exhibiting examples of Germany's colonial architecture, which they felt were in dire need of improvement given the sophisticated colonial buildings of the rival British Empire.[54]

The Prussian Commerce Ministry, too, participated by arranging for its applied arts schools to exhibit in Cologne.[55] Beyond the Werkbund Exhibition, the Commerce Ministry stepped up its involvement in domestic economic organization between 1910 and 1914 as well. Commerce Minister Reinhold Sydow, appointed in July 1909 following Clemens Delbrück's accession to Imperial Minister of the Interior, enlarged the influence of the Commerce Ministry to a far greater degree than either Delbrück or Möller before him.[56] For example, the Commerce Ministry asserted its authority over aspects of the electric power industry and the coal industry after 1910. A ministerial decree of July 1912 ordered state-led, public-private associations to assume control of the generation and distribution of electric power in the name of serving the public and preventing "private exploitation."[57] Likewise, Commerce Minister Sydow re-energized ministerial efforts begun under Möller to purchase a controlling interest in the Hibernia Coal Company. The Commerce Minister was not interested in an outright state takeover of the coal industry; rather, and as the historian Hans-Heinrich Borchard has shown, Sydow "wanted to enlarge the state's financial possessions only to an extent that would allow the state to exercise influence over price, production, and supply."[58]

The ministry's actions with respect to the electrical and coal industries suggest that what may have been planned for the Werkbund—had not the outbreak of war one month after Muthesius's speech to the Werkbund Congress of 1914 superseded all other plans—was a way to convert it, as well, into a form of state-led, public-private association. In this guise, the Werkbund could oversee design and production quality in an array of finished goods industries that would be subjected to increasing discipline and concentration, much as von Sydow's ministry was doing with the electrical and coal industries. The ten theses distributed by Muthesius at the Werkbund Congress in July 1914, in fact, represent a road map for exactly such state-guided action, making it no surprise that the Werkbund's artistic community would erupt in opposition to state control.

Light-industry interest groups, too, mobilized to urge greater government recognition of their importance to the German economy. Naumann and Stresemann strengthened ties between the BDI and Hansa League to the point where the two associations formed a special "industry council" (Industrierat) for non-cartellized German export industries in late 1912. Hartmann Oswald Freiherr von Richthofen, a banker and National Liberal who assumed the post of business manager for the Hansa League in May 1912, proclaimed to a Hansa League audience in Dresden on November 17, 1912, that a new "mercantile imperialism," a "healthy—not chauvinistic—imperialism," was henceforth to serve as the inspiration for Hansa League activities.[59]

Here, and as the historian Dirk Stegmann has noted, von Richthofen was following a course set by BDI spokesman Stresemann just one week earlier. In a speech at the second "Hansa Week" in Berlin on November 11, where Naumann and Professor Hans Delbrück, a "socialist of the lectern" and editor of the *Prussian Yearbooks* (*Preussische Jahrbücher*) had also spoken, Stresemann asserted: "The success of a people's global economic policies (*Weltwirtschaft*) is dependent on the global politics (*Weltpolitik*) of that people. The times have changed... and if the world outside is being divided up [among established colonial powers], then Germany must also participate."[60]

Such remarks went hand in hand with the Hansa League's domestic policy efforts. As commentator Emil Lederer observed in 1912: the Hansa League sought for the first time ever, and "in a consequential manner," to bring the "small tradespeople and small merchants into a state of economic and political solidarity with the entire urban upper-middle class (*städtischen Bürgertum*)."[61] This was congruent with Stresemann's own campaign to encourage group identity among private industrial and commercial white-collar employees, known as *Privatbeamten*. Stresemann specifically targeted the *Privatbeamten* so as to stimulate a middle-class political awareness disinclined to support trade unions.[62]

In concert with official policies and with measures being taken by interest groups and associations, Friedrich Naumann and especially Ernst Jäckh stepped up measures to sketch a prewar road map for German imperialism. Friedrich Naumann's *Die Hilfe* (*Assistance*) generally "took a strongly imperialist line," while Jäckh, a regular contributor, launched a series of additional publishing projects to spell out the terms for a bold, expansive, German-led alliance.[63] The foundation of the German-Austro-Hungarian Economic Association in September 1913, only a year after the Werkbund's Congress in Vienna, lent fuel to Jäckh's vision of a gigantic trading bloc dominated politically and economically by Germany.[64] Such programs for customs unions and various degrees of unification of East Central Europe under German hegemony were certainly part of a long tradition of discussions among pan-Germanists and colonialists like Albert Ritter, Heinrich Class, Paul Rohrbach, and others; it seems significant in this context that Jäckh, as the Werkbund managing director, propagandist, and close liaison to the Foreign Office, pushed so strongly for such a program at a time when the Foreign Office and other ministries were acting especially favorably toward the Werkbund as an official representative of German export ideals and cultural values.[65]

Jäckh optimistically wrote in 1913: "Helgoland and the fleet can protect Germany and hold England at bay. Baghdad and the Railway can threaten England at its sorest spots—at the Indian and Egyptian borders. This is what England has to fear."[66] He was certainly not alone among German banking and commercial forces in advocating a "Berlin to Baghdad line"—a rail line and axis of trade projected to stretch well beyond Germany, Austria-

Hungary, through the Balkans and Turkey, and ultimately to the Persian Gulf.[67] Cultivating Germany's alliance with the Ottoman Empire had been one of Jäckh's and Kiderlen-Wächter's specialties, and although skeptics regarded the Ottoman Empire derisively as the "sick man of Europe," Ottoman territory represented to many Germans the Wilhelmine Empire's last and best hope of coming to dominate a portion of the globe that had not yet been claimed by any other colonial power. Jäckh would continue efforts to draw the Ottomans and Germans closer together as head of the German-Turkish Union, which, with funding from Werkbund firm owner Robert Bosch, would hold a competition for a "House of Friendship" to symbolize the coming together of the two empires.[68]

In the plans of Jäckh, Naumann, and Stresemann, as well as Pan-Germanists like Paul Liman and Heinrich Class, Germany would be able to purchase badly needed raw material supplies from new markets in the Balkans, Turkey, and beyond. In exchange, these allies and trade partners would receive products from Germany's burgeoning, Werkbund-influenced finished goods industries. Commercial, banking, and industrial interests in the BDI, Hansa Bund, and Association for Trade Agreement Negotiations generally backed these types of measures, while Jäckh's patriotic and boosterist propaganda publications detailed ambitions for challenging England's "Pax Britannica" with an alternative "Pax Germanica." To promote this cause, Jäckh produced such publications as *Germany in the Near East Following the Balkan War* of 1913, *Greater Germany* of 1914, *The Rising Crescent: On the Path to German and Turkish Union* of 1915, and *Werkbund and Mitteleuropa* of 1916.[69] Jäckh's program was notably more expansive than Naumann's calls for a Pan-German and East Central European *Mitteleuropa*, although Naumann's book of the same name, published in 1915, espoused similar economic ambitions.[70] Jäckh's prewar publications are, in fact, perhaps the furthest projection of a Pan-German global economic and political power scenario that squared with the evolving policies of government and the lobbying efforts of Germany's largest industrial associations between 1911 and 1914. They are also of a piece with Muthesius's July 1914 lecture, "The Future Work of the Werkbund," and with Naumann's address a few days later, "The Werkbund and the World Economy."

The outbreak of the First World War and Germany's general mobilization in early August eclipsed the Werkbund's increasingly fractious internal struggles and effectively ended the First Werkbund Exhibition in Cologne. The proximity of the exhibition and the city to the Western Front assured that within days, visitors to the Werkbund's exhibition halls would be replaced with initial waves of wounded German soldiers.[71] Jäckh, Naumann, and Muthesius would continue a variety of Werkbund propaganda efforts in service of the German war effort, including the blatantly anti-French "Werkbund Fashion Show" in the Prussian Chamber of Deputies in 1915, the "House of German-Turkish Friendship" architectural competition in

1916, and various additional publications.[72] However, the painful events and privations of a devastating, four-year mechanized war gradually made it apparent that the expansive plans of the Werkbund, the government, and light-industry associations would suffer the same disastrous fate as the government's military campaign. The Werkbund would survive as an organization, but never again in the particular Wilhelmine configuration it had achieved as part of a nexus involving government ministries, industrial and commercial interests, and leading Werkbund architects, craftsmen, and artist-designers. The interaction of these various forces had done the most to shape the Cologne Werkbund Exhibition of 1914; it was these forces that young architects and Werkbund members like Walter Gropius would seek to escape after completing army service as a sergeant in a Hussar Reserve Regiment in 1918. Bruised by his battles with Muthesius during an active but futile effort (with Henry van de Velde and Karl Ernst Osthaus) to topple Muthesius from the Werkbund Exhibition organizing committee in 1914, Gropius would move on to found his very local, yet also very cosmopolitan and internationally influential "State Bauhaus in Weimar" (*Staatliches Bauhaus in Weimar*, where the design and manufacture of "types" would soon become a Bauhaus watchword) in the spring of 1919. Gropius, Bruno Taut, and other young Werkbund artists felt lingering bitterness toward the much-older Muthesius, whom they viewed as the domineering agent of increased state involvement in the Werkbund in 1914. As a result, Bruno Taut and Gustav Adolph Platz severely downplayed any debts that the theories and practices of Weimar-era architects clearly owed to the foundational writings of the former Werkbund vice president.[73]

Conclusion: Re-evaluating Wilhelmine institutions and reform milieus

The complexity of political, economic, and cultural forces in Germany between 1900 and 1914, as seen through the evolution of ministries like the Prussian Commerce Ministry and organizations like the Deutscher Werkbund, demonstrates the need for specificity in any discussion of a Wilhelmine reform milieu, whether inside or outside government. The micro-culture developed by Theodor Möller at the Prussian Ministry of Commerce was a key element in bringing innovators like Muthesius and Behrens to promote new configurations in applied arts education, finished goods production, and commercial design and distribution. It would certainly be too much to credit Möller with the formation of the Deutscher Werkbund, but it is fair to say that his leadership allowed Muthesius and the ministry's State Trades Board to pioneer the assembly of craftsmen, artists, school directors, entrepreneurs, industrialists, and government officials in 1905 that provided the blueprint for the Werkbund beginning in 1907. Similarly,

Möller was not responsible for the radical transformation of the Werkbund after 1912 into the willing servant and agent in the state's bid to expand German commercial distribution and participation in global markets. But as an industrialist operating within the tradition of a strong, top-down Prussian bureaucratic system, he did set in motion the kinds of new relations among industrialists, applied arts designers, and government ministries that would find their own peculiarly Wilhelmine—and Wilhelminist—manifestations on the eve of the First World War.

What might all of this have to tell us about the nature of Wilhelmine modernity? Our study suggests, at the very least, some ways of rethinking the concept of Wilhelmine modernity itself. For one thing, it seems insufficient merely to bracket government administration as if it existed separately from, or had only limited connection to, the social, economic, and cultural developments that the Commerce Ministry aimed to affect. Greater attention also needs to be paid to the multiplicity of professions pursued by Wilhelmine personalities such as those discussed here, so that state "bureaucrats" and bourgeois professionals working outside the government might at times be recognized as one and the same. Möller, for example, flourished as an industrialist, became a respected Reichstag member, and then led the Ministry of Commerce and Industry. Muthesius is perhaps a more dramatic example: Here was the son of a Thuringian master mason who rose from the *Mittelstand*; became valedictorian of his Berlin architecture class; published more than a dozen books on the theory, practice, and history of architecture; further served as a diplomatic attaché in London for seven years while reporting to the Prussian government on all manner of British domestic industrial and educational affairs; and, finally, founded a Werkbund association that he gladly placed at the disposal of his government superiors even as he helped mold it into the most progressive architecture and design association of the pre–First World War era.[74]

The list of accomplishments across several fields by single individuals underscores the need to recognize how interwoven the seemingly disparate fields of Wilhelmine professional activity were. Kevin Repp's valuable book on reformers and critics in the Wilhelmine context employs the term "anti-politics" as a way to understand the seemingly endless proliferation of reform activities outside of traditional government institutions. The implications of our analysis in this chapter, however, call for pushing Kevin Repp's argument one step further. This chapter's findings open up the possibility that the character of Wilhelmine modernity was such as to allow seemingly disparate fields of activity to relate and affect one another in ways that future, more specialized generations might overlook, particularly in light of the ways in which historical knowledge came to be categorized and revised to fit trenchant historical debates about cataclysmic events post-dating the Wilhelmine Empire. How else are we to understand the emergence of separate historiographies in German history and German architectural history which, in focusing on the same period of years, come up with entirely separate accounts of the significance of people and events (e.g., Theodor Möller, the founding of the Deutscher Werkbund, and the Werkbund Exhibition of 1914)? More than just the plethora of reform movements that practiced an "anti-politics" of reform outside of government, Möller and Muthesius demonstrate that a micro-culture of Wilhelminist ministerial reform produced far-reaching political, economic, and cultural effects. It is precisely the overlapping disciplines and interpenetrating nature of institutions during the prewar era that call upon us to recognize the richness of Wilhelmine German modernity, even as the *Kaiserreich* faced ongoing, and eventually calamitous, contradictions and crises.

Notes

1   Celia Applegate, *A Nation of Provincials: The German Idea of Heimat* (Berkeley: University of California Press, 1990); Alon Confino, *The Nation as Local Metaphor: Württemberg, Imperial Germany, and National Memory, 1871–1918* (Chapel Hill: University of North Carolina Press, 1997); Jennifer L. Jenkins, *Provincial Modernity: Local Culture and Liberal Politics in Fin-de-Siècle Hamburg* (Ithaca, NY: Cornell University Press, 2003); Kevin Repp, *Reformers, Critics, and the Paths of German Modernity: Anti-Politics and of the Search for Alternatives, 1890–1914* (Cambridge: Harvard University Press, 2000). The author would like to thank the editors, anonymous reviewers, and the constructively critical reader Denise Costanzo for their helpful suggestions in the preparation of this chapter.

2   The present chapter owes much to a book of essays dedicated to Hartmut Pogge von Strandmann and his ideas where the editors write in their Introduction: "One of the pressing needs of Wilhelmine historiography is to deconstruct the long-established dichotomous framework of 'modernizing economy' and 'backward political culture' in order to open up the interesting and underexplored spaces in between." Geoff Eley and James Retallack, "Introduction," in Geoff Eley and James Retallack (eds.), *Wilhelminism and Its Legacies: German Modernities, Imperialism, and the Meanings of Reform, 1890–1930, Essays for Hartmut Pogge von Strandmann* (New York: Berghahn, 2003), p. 6.

3   Ibid., pp. 8–9.

4   An early analysis of Möller's policies can be found in John V. Maciuika, *Before the Bauhaus: Architecture, Politics, and the German State, 1890–1920* (Cambridge: Cambridge University Press, 2005), especially ch. 4, "The Convergence of State and Private Reform Impulses in the Deutscher Werkbund," pp. 137–70, which, for all its details, does not bring the Wilhelminism of von Strandmann, or the idea of a Prussian ministerial reform "micro-culture" into the discussion.

5   On the fine arts, see Peter Paret, *The Berlin Secession: Modernism and Its Enemies in Imperial Germany* (Cambridge: Harvard University Press, 1980) and Maria Makela, *The Munich Secession: Art and Artists in Turn-of-the-Century Munich* (Princeton, NJ: Princeton University Press, 1990).

6   Hans-Joachim Hubrich points out that many anti-royal academy, progressive
     trends around the turn of the twentieth century, including the Applied Arts
     Movement (*Kunstgewerbebewegung*), the *Jugendstil*, and promoters of a new
     Sachlichkeit or objectivity, were commonly grouped under the umbrella term
     neue Bewegung, or "new movement," and were not necessarily perceived at
     the time as being in tension or conflict with one another. See Hans-Joachim
     Hubrich, *Hermann Muthesius: Die Schriften zu Architektur, Kunstgewerbe,
     Industrie in der "Neuen Bewegung"* (Berlin: Gebr. Mann Verlag, 1981), p. 9.

7   Letter from Theodor Möller to his daughter, Irmgard Möller, May 5, 1901,
     as quoted in Heidrun Walther, *Theodor Adolf von Möller, 1840–1925:
     Lebensbild eines westfälischen Industriellen* (Neustadt an der Aisch: Verlag
     Degener & Co., 1958), pp. 67–8. Unless otherwise noted, all translations are
     by the author.

8   Ibid., p. 152, quotation from p. 62.

9   On the Deutscher Werkbund, see Joan Campbell, *The German Werkbund: The
     Politics of Reform in the Applied Arts* (Princeton, NJ: Princeton University
     Press, 1978); Kurt Junghanns, *Der Deutsche Werkbund: Sein erstes Jahrzehnt*
     (Berlin: Henschelverlag, 1982); Frederic J. Schwartz, *The Werkbund: Design
     Theory and Mass Culture before the First World War* (New Haven, CT: Yale
     University Press, 1996); see also Frederic J. Schwartz's "Afterword" to the
     reissued *Jahrbuch des Deutschen Werkbundes 1913: Die Kunst in Industrie
     und Handel* (Berlin: Gebr. Mann Verlag, 2000), pp. 18–32; and Matthew
     Jeffries, *Politics and Culture in Wilhelmine Germany: The Case of Industrial
     Architecture* (Oxford: Berg Publishers, 1995). The Werkbund's later history
     and influence are usefully examined by Paul Betts in *The Authority of
     Everyday Objects: A Cultural History of West German Industrial Design*
     (Berkeley: University of California Press, 2004). For a view of the formation
     of the Werkbund that builds on the earlier literature but offers a significantly
     different account of its formation based on documents from the Prussian state
     archives, see Maciuika, *Before the Bauhaus*, especially ch. 4.

10   Fritz Hellwag took the occasion of Muthesius's fiftieth birthday to praise the
     architect's "concentric talents, which developed early" in "Kunstgewerbliche
     Rundschau," *Kgbl*, N.F. (1911), p. 138.

11   Ernst Jäckh, *Der goldene Pflug: Lebensgeschichte eines Weltbürgers* (Stuttgart:
     Klett Verlag, 1957), p. 196.

12   See John V. Maciuika, "'Sachlicher, wirtschaftlicher, zweckmässiger': 100
     Jahre 'Lehrwerkstätten-Erlass' vom Preussischen Ministerium für Handel und
     Gewerbe" ["More Objective, Economical, and Purposeful": The Centennial of
     the Prussian Ministry of Commerce and Industry's "Instructional Workshops
     Decree"], *Scholion* 4 (2006), pp. 120–31.

13   For a recent account, see Barry Bergdoll and Leah Dickerman (eds.), *Bauhaus
     1919–1933: Workshops for Modernity* (New York: Museum of Modern Art,
     2009). For a reading of pedagogies and policies linking the Bauhaus to the
     Wilhelmine era, see John V. Maciuika, "The Politics of Art and Architecture at
     the Bauhaus, 1919–1933," in Peter E. Gordon and John C. McCormick (eds.),
     Weimar Thought: A Contested Legacy (Princeton, NJ: Princeton University
     Press, 2013), pp. 291–315.

14 Hans Goldschmidt, *Das Reich und Preussen im Kampf um die Führung* (Berlin: Carl Heymanns Verlag, 1931).

15 Ibid., pp. 12–13. Also Hans-Ulrich Wehler, *Deutsche Gesellschaftsgeschichte. Band 3: Von der "Deutschen Doppelrevolution" bis zum Beginn des Ersten Weltkrieges, 1849–1914* (Munich: C.H. Beck, 1995), p. 816.

16 Kaiser Wilhelm I appointed Otto von Bismarck to become Prussian Minister of Commerce and Industry on September 13, 1880. Reichskanzler Fürst von Bismarck, Immediatbericht an Kaiser Wilhelm I, 12. Oktober 1880, as reprinted in Goldschmidt, *Das Reich und Preussen*, pp. 282–4, quotation from p. 283.

17 Hans-Heinrich Borchard discusses Bismarck's role as Prussian Commerce Minister in *50 Jahre Preussisches Ministerium für Handel und Gewerbe, 1879–1929* (Berlin: Reichsverlag H. Kalkoff, 1929), p. 31. For the broader ministerial context, see Friedrich Facius, *Wirtschaft und Staat: Die Entwicklung der staatlichen Wirtschaftsverwaltung in Deutschland vom 17. Jahrhundert bis 1945*, Schriften des Bundesarchivs 6 (Boppard am Rhein: Harald Boldt Verlag, 1959), especially pp. 63–4.

18 Friedrich Facius notes that October 1880 marked the first use of the term "economy" (*Wirtschaft*) in official imperial decrees. He sees the introduction of this term, which was not entirely new at the time, as part of Bismarck's effort to redirect the Prussian government's control over "commerce and trade" (*Handel und Gewerbe*) toward an imperially administered "economy" (*Wirtschaft*) through the new branch of the Interior Ministry, the Department of Economic Affairs (*Abteilung für wirtschaftliche Angelegenheiten*). See Facius, *Wirtschaft und Staat*, pp. 65–77, and especially p. 70, note 138.

19 Bismarck quoted in Borchard, *50 Jahre*, p. 31.

20 Quotation from Hans Rothfels, "Zur Geschichte der Bismarckschen Innenpolitik," *Archiv für Politik und Geschichte* 7 (1927), p. 307.

21 Goldschmidt, *Das Reich und Preussen*, especially "Mangelnde Verwaltungsbefugnisse des Reichs und preussischer Ressortpartikularismus," pp. 15–16. Bismarck's first apparent official mention of the desire to create an Imperial Ministry of Commerce came in 1874; see the discussion of Bismarck as Prussian Commerce Minister in Borchard, *50 Jahre*.

22 Facius, *Wirtschaft und Staat*, pp. 70–1.

23 While the fields of art and architectural history credit Hermann Muthesius as being the "Father" of the Deutscher Werkbund, their practitioners have left largely unexamined the degree to which this design association was in fact incubated within the Prussian administration. It has most often been argued that the Werkbund arose as a natural extension of the work of reform-minded individuals like the crafts entrepreneur Karl Schmidt, the pastor-turned-politician Friedrich Naumann, the architect and civil servant Muthesius, and other leading figures advocating reforms in Germany's applied arts.

24 Eley and Retallack, "Introduction" to *Wilhelminism and Its Legacies*, p. 6.

25 Möller, in fact, became Theodor *von* Möller in 1905, as was the custom when one was declared *Amtsmüde*, relieved of one's ministerial post, and "failed upwards" to become a titled aristocrat and effectively neutralized member

of the Prussian House of Lords (*Herrenhaus*). See Heidrun Walther, *Theodor Adolf von Möller, 1840–1925: Lebensbild eines westfälischen Industriellen* (Neustadt an der Aisch: Verlag Degener & Co., 1958); also Borchard, *50 Jahre*, pp. 52–5; 149–50; Stefan Hartmann, "Theodor Adolf von Möller," in Historische Kommission bei der Bayerischen Akademie der Wissenschaften (ed.), *Neue Deutsche Biographie* 18 (Berlin: Duncker & Humblot, 1994), pp. 634–5. On the revival of *Sammlungspolitik*, see Geoff Eley, *Reshaping the German Right: Radical Nationalism and Political Change after Bismarck* (New Haven, CT: Yale University Press, 1980), p. 349.

26   On the Hibernia Affair, see the accounts in Charles Medalen, "State Monopoly Capitalism in Germany: The Hibernia Affair," *Past and Present* 78 (February 1978), pp. 82–112; also the correspondence between Maximilian Harden and Walther Rathenau in Hans Dieter Hellige (ed.), *Walther Rathenau—Maximilian Harden: Briefwechsel, 1897–1920* (Munich: Gotthold Müller Verlag, 1983), pp. 375–81; Gerald D. Feldman, *Hugo Stinnes: Biographie eines Industriellen, 1870–1924* (Munich: C.H. Beck), pp. 92–9; Hans Fürstenberg, *Carl Fürstenberg: Die Lebensgeschichte eines deutschen Bankiers, 1870–1914* (Berlin: Ullstein,1931), pp. 400–15; Walther, *Theodor Adolf von Möller*, pp. 86–100.

27   Letter from Peter Behrens to Richard Dehmel, November 27, 1902, as quoted in Gisela Moeller, *Peter Behrens in Düsseldorf: Die Jahre von 1903 bis 1907* (Weinheim: VCH Verlag, 1991), p. 22.

28   Behrens is rightly remembered today in architectural histories as the western world's first corporate image designer. On Behrens, see Peter Thomas Föhl and Claus Pese (eds.), *Peter Behrens: Vom Jugendstil zum Industriedesign. Katalog zur Ausstellung in der Kunsthalle Erfurt* (Weimar: Klassik Stiftung Weimar, 2013); Stanford Anderson, *Peter Behrens and a New Architecture for the Twentieth Century* (Cambridge: MIT Press, 2000); Gisela Moeller, *Peter Behrens in Düsseldorf: Die Jahre von 1903 bis 1907* (Weinheim: VCH Verlagsgesellschaft, 1991); and Tilmann Buddensieg, *Industriekultur: Peter Behrens und die AEG 1907–1914* (Berlin: Mann Verlag, 1979).

29   For a survey of other centers of Wilhelmine design innovation, see Maciuika, "Design Reform in Germany's Central and Southern States, 1890-1914" in *Before the Bauhaus*, pp. 25–68.

30   Hermann Muthesius, *Die Werkbundarbeit der Zukunft und Aussprache darüber* (Jena: Eugen Diederichs, 1914); and Friedrich Naumann, "Werkbund und Weltwirtschaft" in Naumann, *Werke*, 6, pp. 331–50.

31   There is no evidence in the archives of the "Norms for German Industry" (*Deutsche Industrie-Normen*, or DIN) that Muthesius collaborated directly with various branches of industry or with the Association of German Engineers (*Verein deutscher Ingenieure*) in the development of his theses. Among the items at the DIN Archive that are helpful for understanding the gradual development of standards, types, and norms for German industry, see "Begründung des Ausschusses für wirtschaftliche Fertigung," Versammlung im Reichswirtschaftsamt, 23. February 1918, in *Mitteilungen des Ausschusses für wirtschaftliche Fertigung* 1 (1918), pp. 1–5; Karl Strecker (ed.), *Verhandlungen des Ausschusses für Einheiten und Formelgrössen in den Jahren 1907 bis 1914*

(Berlin: Julius Springer Verlag, 1914); W. Hellmich, "Der Normenausschuss der Deutschen Industrie," *Mitteilungen der Normenausschuss der Deutschen Industrie* 1 (January 1918), pp. 1–2; J. Wallot (ed.), *Verhandlungen des Ausschusses für Einheiten und Formelgrossen in den Jahren 1907 bis 1927* (Berlin: Verlag Julius Springer, 1928).

32 This was essentially the point of Muthesius's first of ten theses distributed to his Werkbund colleagues. For the original text and a translation of all ten theses, see Appendix B in Maciuika, *Before the Bauhaus*; see also the concise and insightful synopsis of the "Werkbund debate" by Stanford Anderson, "Deutscher Werkbund—the 1914 debate: Hermann Muthesius versus Henry van de Velde," in Ben Farmer and Hentie Louw (eds.), *Companion to Contemporary Architectural Thought* (London/New York: Routledge, 1993), pp. 462–7.

33 Deutscher Werkbund, *Die Wiener 5. Jahresversammlung des Deutschen Werkbundes vom 6. Bis 9. Juni 1912* (Berlin: Geschäftsstelle des Werkbundes, 1912), pp. 7, 10–11.

34 Matthew Jeffries, *Politics and Culture in Wilhelmine Germany*, p. 202.

35 The CDI represented heavy industry, led by coal, iron, and steel, which exerted particular influence through its control of prices and supplies of raw materials. The BDI contained industries in which textiles, foods production, light machinery and instrument-making, and wood and paper industries predominated. Since 1906, the two organizations had engaged in an extended on-again, off-again effort to function in a joint Partnership of Interests, or *Interessengemeinschaft*, but such cooperation could not be achieved until the government's formation of an official War Commission (*Kriegsausschuss*) in 1915. The Hansa League represented more of a broad mix of *Mittelstand* trades workers and commercial and white-collar employees. It is worth noting, however, that industrialists like AEG owner Emil Rathenau spoke at the organization's founding in 1909. See Hans-Peter Ullman, *Der Bund der Industriellen: Organisation, Einfluß und Politik klein- und mittelbetrieblicher Industrieller im Deutschen Kaiserreich 1895–1914* (Göttingen: Vandenhoeck & Ruprecht, 1976), pp. 34–48, 184–92, 214–15; Dirk Stegmann, *Die Erben Bismarcks, Parteien und Verbände in der Spätphase Wilhelminischen Deutschlands: Sammlungspolitik 1897–1918* (Köln: Kiepenheuer & Witsch, 1970), pp. 176–8, 242–4.

36 Klaus Wernecke, *Der Wille zur Weltgeltung: Außenpolitik und Öffentlichkeit im Kaiserreich am Vorabend des Ersten Weltkrieges* (Dusseldorf: Droste, 1970), p. 294.

37 When this matter arose for debate in the Prussian Chamber of Deputies, Delbrück defended Muthesius as an "expert colleague" and an "indispensable public servant." Referring indirectly to the conservative Association for the Economic Interests of the Crafts, which had called for Muthesius's dismissal, he added that "the applied arts cannot be elevated by philistines." Minister Delbrück to Fachverband für die wirtschaftlichen Interessen des Kunstgewerbes, May 15, 1907, reprinted in "Der Fall Muthesius: Ein Vortrag mit Akten und Briefen," *Hohe Warte* 3 (1907), p. 238. See also *Verhandlungen des Preussischen Hauses der Abgeordneten*, 23. Sitzung am February 3, 1908, p. 1527, as cited in Hubrich, p. 277.

38 Eley, *Reshaping the German Right*, p. 349.

39 Thomas Nipperdey, *Deutsche Geschichte, 1866–1918, Zweiter Band: Machtstaat vor der Demokratie* (Munich: C.H. Beck, 1992), pp. 748–57.

40 Nipperdey, *Deutsche Geschichte*, pp. 745–8; Carl Schorske, *German Social Democracy, 1905–1917: The Development of the Great Schism* (Cambridge: Harvard University Press, 1955), pp. 224–35; Margaret Lavinia Anderson, *Practicing Democracy: Elections and Political Culture in Imperial Germany* (Princeton, NJ: Princeton University Press, 2000).

41 Stegmann, *Die Erben Bismarcks*, pp. 246, 269–73, 415–20.

42 Ullman, *Der Bund der Industriellen*, pp. 27–33, and Stegmann, *Die Erben Bismarcks*, p. 33.

43 Ullmann, *Der Bund der Industriellen*, pp. 214–16, and Stegmann, *Die Erben Bismarcks*, pp. 178–81.

44 Stegmann, *Die Erben Bismarcks*, pp. 136–8, 218–21. Chancellor Bülow resisted BDI attempts to enlarge its presence from the dismal proportion of five out of thirty-five members of the *Wirtschaftsausschuss*. Increases in 1909 and 1910 in the total number of members making up the commission also neglected to accord the BDI a significantly larger proportion of representatives.

45 Naumann, "Von wem werden wir regiert?" *Die Neue Rundschau* 20:2 (1909), p. 636, as quoted in Stegmann, *Die Erben Bismarcks*, p. 180.

46 Jäckh first met Kiderlen-Wächter in Constantinople on August 6, 1908, see Kiderlen-Wächter to his wife, Hedwig Kypke, August 7, 1908, in Ernst Jäckh (ed.), *Kiderlen-Wächter, der Staatsmann und Mensch: Briefwechsel und Nachlass* (Stuttgart: Deutsche Verlags-Anstalt, 1924). Kiderlen-Wächter died of a heart attack at age forty after serving as foreign minister for two and a half years. See also Stegmann, *Die Erben Bismarcks*, pp. 244–5, and V.R. Berghahn, *Germany and the Approach to War in 1914* (London: MacMillan, 1993), pp. 105–15.

47 Bundesarchiv/Federal Archives-Berlin, BArch R901/18350, replies from German Consulates in Genoa, Jassy, Beirut, Singapore, Calcutta, and Batavia to Chancellor Bethmann-Hollweg, April 10, 1913; April 8, 1913; April 16, 1913; December 24, 1913; January 24, 1914; and February 7, 1914, respectively; German Consulates in Beirut, Kristiania to Deutscher Werkbund Geschäftsstelle, April 16, 1913; April 29, 1913, pp. 53–142. The correspondence and attached lists of German firms active on foreign soil are interspersed in this file with Werkbund documentation and a site plan by Rehorst of the Cologne Exhibition grounds. For a discussion of Krupp and other industrialists at the Werkbund Exhibition, see Jeffries, *Politics and Culture in Wilhelmine Germany*, pp. 218–19.

48 Correspondence between Imperial Foreign Office and Freiherr von Stein, German Consul of Porto Alegre; between Chancellor Bethmann-Hollweg (Im Auftrag gez. Johannes) and Freiherr von Stein; and between Bromberg & Cie.-Hamburg and Foreign Office, numerous letters all related to Carvalho's arrangements and dated between May 4, 1914, and June 30, 1914, Bundesarchiv/Federal Archives-Berlin, BArch R901/18350, pp. 147–151b.

49   Where the Werkbund would enter into a hopeful new phase by welcoming foreign dignitaries to an exhibition for the first time in 1914, the Krupp "Cannon King" (*Kanonenkönig*) was adding to a long list of foreign customers: Krupp sold armor, artillery, shells, and other materials to fifty-two foreign governments before the First World War and sold 24,000 artillery pieces to the German military as well. As William Manchester notes, in Essen alone Krupp's "eighty smoke-shrouded factories ... used more gas than the city surrounding them, more electricity than all Berlin, and constituted a huge city within a city, with its own police force, fire department, and traffic laws ... [and] Essen was only the apex of an iceberg" of Krupp factories and foreign holdings. Because the Krupp industrial empire was a family-owned business, Krupp represented, in effect, a one-man arms race, a fact that Manchester renders effectively throughout his exhaustive study, *The Arms of Krupp: 1587–1968* (Boston: Little, Brown and Co., 1968), here pp. 263–4, quotation from p. 253.

50   Freiherr von Stein, German Consul in Porto Alegre to Chancellor Bethmann-Hollweg, April 8, 1914, Bundesarchiv/Federal Archives-Berlin, BArch R901/18350, p. 148b.

51   "Auszug aus dem Protokoll der Plenar-Vorstandssitzung der Ständige Ausstellungskommission für die Deutsche Industrie am 29 April 1913 ... in Verbindung mit mündlichen Ausführungen des Geschäftsfuhrers Herrn Dr. Jäckh," in Bundesarchiv/Federal Archives-Berlin, BArch R901/18350, pp. 59–64, quotation p. 63.

52   Clipping from *Kölnische Volkszeitung* (n.d.), in BArch, R 3101/616, p. 35.

53   Staatssekretär des Innern (Delbrück) an Gottlieb von Jagow, Staatssekretär des Auswärtigen Amtes, February 27, 1913, in BArch, R 901/18350, 7a–8b.

54   Chancellor Bethmann-Hollweg to the general consulates in Singapore, Batavia, Calcutta, and the imperial consulates in Bombay and Columbo, August 14, 1913 (gez. Goetsch, im Auftrag), pp. 94–94b; also "Das Kolonialhaus auf der Deutschen Werkbundausstellung in Coeln 1914," Sonderabdruck aus dem *Deutschen Kolonialblatt* no. 14 (July 15, 1913), clipping in BArch R901/18350, p. 93. This file makes numerous mentions of drawings of buildings submitted from German colonial outposts, and while none were extant in this file, it does suggest an interesting avenue for further research on the design of German colonial architecture. For a nonarchitectural discussion of Wilhelmine Germany's colonial aspirations, see Woodruff D. Smith, "Colonialism and Colonial Empire," in Roger Chickering (ed.), *Imperial Germany: A Historiographical Companion* (Westport, CT: Greenwood Press, 1996), pp. 430–53.

55   See Deutscher Werkbund, *Deutsche Werkbund Ausstellung Cöln 1914: Offizieller Katalog* (Köln: Verlag von Rudolf Mosse, 1914), pp. 37–42.

56   Sydow was to be the longest-serving Commerce Minister after Bismarck. He trained as a lawyer and served both as a judge and as a director of the telegraph section of the Imperial post. Borchard, *50 Jahre*, pp. 64–6.

57   Ibid., p. 70. A fine topic for further research would be to trace the specific effects that this ministry-initiated oversight had on a firm like Emil Rathenau's AEG company.

58   Like Möller before him, Sydow faced considerable opposition from several quarters. But unlike Möller, Sydow emerged victorious in the takeover battle, in war circumstances, of course, achieving full recognition of the state's takeover in February 1917. Borchard, *50 Jahre*, p. 67.

59   Stegmann, *Die Erben Bismarcks*, pp. 344–51, quotation from p. 347.

60   Ibid., p. 347.

61   Emil Lederer, *Die wirtschafltichen Organisationen und die Reichstagswahlen* (Tübingen: 1912), p. 51, as quoted in Stegmann, p. 344.

62   Stresemann obtained results when he put direct pressure on Interior Minister Delbrück to back the BDI in the context of what Stresemann called Germany's *Weltpolitik* (global politics). In 1910, Delbrück's ministry dropped its previous opposition to Stresemann's call for insurance for private employees of large businesses. Stresemann had assured Delbrück that unless the government sanctioned new insurance programs for private employees, the Interior Minister would find "1.8 million private business employees in the state of Saxony alone voting socialist" in the next election. Delbrück's ministry introduced a bill for private insurance—to the surprise and consternation of Commerce Minister Sydow—but this did not stop the Social Democratic Party from winning its largest victory to date the elections of 1912. See Ullmann, *Der Bund der Industriellen*, pp. 215–20.

63   Quotation from Fritz Fischer, *War of Illusions: German Politics from 1911 to 1914*, trans. Marian Jackson (Dusseldorf: Droste, 1975), p. 236. See also Campbell, *The German Werkbund*, pp. 93–8.

64   Fischer, *War of Illusions*, p. 237.

65   See Wernecke, *Die Wille zur Weltgeltung*, pp. 288–310.

66   Ernst Jäckh, *Deutschland im Orient nach dem Balkankrieg* (Strassburg: Verlag Singer, 1913) as quoted in Wernecke, *Die Wille zur Weltgeltung*, p. 292.

67   See Fischer's discussion of "Groups and Associations aiming at Berlin-Baghdad as the 'New German Objective' " in *War of Illusions*, pp. 446–58. The historian Karl Erich Born calls the Berlin-Baghdad railway project, which was first conceived by the Ottoman Sultan Abdul Hamid II in 1887, "the most spectacular enterprise undertaken abroad by German banks." See Born, *International Banking in the 19th and 20th Centuries*, trans. Volker R. Berghahn (Warwickshire: Berg Publishers, 1983), pp. 138–46.

68   For a discussion of this competition, to which Jäckh invited twelve Werkbund architects including Peter Behrens, Bruno Taut, and Paul Bonatz, see Wolfgang Pehnt, *Expressionist Architecture*, pp. 71–2. For Jäckh's discussion of the project in several places in connection with the larger goals of the Werkbund and German foreign policy, see *Werkbund und Mitteleuropa* (Weimar: Gustav Kiepenhauer, 1916), pp. 16–18; *Der goldene Pflug*, pp. 202, 322–34; and especially Deutscher Werkbund and Deutsch-Türkischen Vereinigung (eds.), *Das Haus der Freundschaft in Konstantinopel, ein Wettbewerb für deutscher Architekten* (Munich: F. Bruckmann, 1918).

69   Jäckh, *Deutschland im Orient nach dem Balkankrieg*; Ernst Jäckh and Paul Rohrbach, *Das Grössere Deutschland*, as described by Paul Rohrbach in "Zum Weltvolk hindurch!" in *Preußische Jahrbücher* 4 (1914) as cited

in Fischer, *War of Illusions*, pp. 448–9, 449, note 20; Ernst Jäckh, *Der aufsteigende Halbmond: Auf dem Weg zum Deutsch-Türkischen Bündnis* (Stuttgart: Deutsche Verlags-Anstalt, 1915); Jäckh, *Werkbund und Mitteleuropa*.

70   Naumann's *Mitteleuropa* was to become the politician's best-selling, most-translated, and most-discussed publication. Friedrich Naumann, *Mitteleuropa*, in Naumann, *Werke*, 4, pp. 485–835.

71   "Die Deutsche Werkbundausstellung Köln," *Mitteilungen des Deutschen Werkbundes* (1915), pp. 1–2.

72   The Werkbund Fashion show is discussed in "Der Ausschuß für Mode-Industrie des Deutschen Werkbundes," *Mitteilungen des Deutschen Werkbundes* (1915), pp. 6–8; Ola Alsen, "Erste Modeschau des Werkbundes, Unter dem Protektorat der Kronprinzessin," *Elegante Welt* 1915 (Nr. 9), pp. 5–10; see also Adelheid Rasche, "Peter Jessen, der Berliner Verein Moden-Museum und der Verband der deutschen Mode-Industrie, 1916 bis 1925," *Waffen- und Kostümkunde* 37 (1995), pp. 65–92. Muthesius's most nakedly jingoistic articles from the war-era are *Der Deutsche nach dem Kriege*, in the pamphlet series "Weltkultur und Weltpolitik: Deutsche und österreichische Schriftenfolge," eds. Ernst Jäckh-Berlin und Institut für Kulturforschung-Wien (Munich: F. Bruckmann, 1915; 2nd ed. 1916); and *Die Zukunft der deutschen Form*, in the series "Der Deutsche Krieg: Politische Flugschriften," no. 50, ed. Ernst Jäckh (Stuttgart, Berlin: Deutsche Verlags-Anstalt, 1916).

73   Both the architect Bruno Taut and the art historian Gustav Adolph Platz omitted Muthesius entirely from their account of modern German architecture's rise. See Bruno Taut, *Die Neue Baukunst in Europa und Amerika* (Stuttgart: Julius Hoffmann Verlag, 1929); Gustav Adolph Platz, *Die Baukunst der Neuesten Zeit* (Berlin: Propylaen-Verlag, 1927). Platz's comprehensive, 600-page survey and catalog even omits Muthesius from its exhaustive register of major and minor architects active in Germany between 1895 and 1927, the year of Muthesius's death.

74   A fourteen-page bibliography of Muthesius's article and book publications can be found in Hubrich, *Hermann Muthesius*, pp. 317–31.

9

Prevention, Welfare, and Citizenship: The War on Tuberculosis and Infant Mortality in Germany, 1900–30

Larry Frohman

If one wanted to characterize the young century from the standpoint of hygiene, it would simply have to be named the century of prophylaxis. The most noble task of the modern doctor is to prevent disease.[1]

There are many ways to approach the history of the welfare state, and one's understanding of the subject depends to a large degree on the path one takes and the questions that are asked along the way. This essay will take as its point of entry the social programs established to prosecute the war on tuberculosis and infant mortality in Germany from the turn of the last century through the 1920s, specifically the work of the tuberculosis and infant welfare centers (*Tuberkulose-* and *Säuglingsfürsorgestellen*). Preventive social hygiene, or medical relief, programs to combat tuberculosis and infant mortality are central to the history of modern Germany not only because of their role in the epidemiological transition. These programs also have a much broader relevance because the refiguring of the rights and duties of citizenship raised

This is a substantially abridged version of an article that originally appeared under the same title in *Central European History* 39:3 (September 2006), pp. 431–81.

a set of questions concerning the relation between preventive social hygiene, individual freedom and well-being, and modernity that are paradigmatic for understanding the modern welfare state.

After 1900, the need to secure the health of the nation, and through this its economic and military power, made the problems of tuberculosis and infant mortality—and the social question more generally—into a matter of overriding national importance. When coupled with the growing authority of the social and biomedical sciences, this imperative of "national self-preservation" provided a compelling rationale for the vast expansion of public programs to rationalize the hygienic habits of the individual. It was in relation to this perceived national interest in individual health that the social problems of infant and tuberculosis mortality, as well as something akin to a social "right to health" for the sick and endangered segment of the population, could be constructed and the social programs to secure this right justified. In turn, this transformation of the health and hygiene of the private individual into a matter of public, political concern set in motion a fundamental reconsideration of the distinction between the public and the private. This transformation made preventive social hygiene (as well as other productive and reproductive practices) into the site of a new kind of social politics, and tuberculosis and infant welfare provide an ideal means of studying the micropractices through which the public/private distinction, and thus the social substance of citizenship, was refigured.[2]

The development of these preventive social hygiene programs was made possible by the emergence of a new emphasis in social knowledge, a social perspective on poverty, which was based on the idea that dependency, disease, and delinquency were more the product of the social conditions of the lower classes than their cause. The acceptance of this idea gave birth to a new, distinctly progressive approach to the social problem known as "social relief" or "social welfare" (soziale Fürsorge) which was qualitatively different from mid-century poor relief and charity with their individualist, voluntarist, and highly moralizing understanding of pauperism.[3] These new programs became an essential element of a larger preventive project, whose roots lay in the social hygiene tradition, but whose parameters were defined by sanitary reform and bacteriology. The root of the problem was that the bacteriological revolution was an incomplete one. Although Robert Koch, Louis Pasteur, and others succeeded in identifying specific pathogenic microorganisms as the cause of the most important contagious diseases, they were much less successful—at least in the short run and especially for tuberculosis—in developing a clinical cure. The failure of Koch's tuberculin therapy meant that, for the foreseeable future, the only way of combating this endemic, chronic disease would be to keep people from getting sick in the first place, and the absence of a proven medical treatment reinforced the idea that preventing disease was more economical and effective than attempting to cure the sick. On the other hand, the bacteriological understanding of the cause of disease and the means of its transmission did make it possible to formulate rules of hygienic comportment that would protect self and others. This insight shifted the center of gravity of preventive public health from the sanitary reform of the physical environment to the individual, whose hygienic consciousness—that is, the knowledge of the causes of disease and the desire to act in a responsible manner on the basis of this knowledge— was increasingly seen as the key to breaking the cycle of contagion and infection.

The social perspective on poverty also entailed the recognition of new forms of interdependence, solidarity, and citizenship. Since any individual could become a source of contagion, the fortunes of this individual could not be a matter of indifference to the community, which found itself potentially obligated—in ways which were unimaginable for classical liberalism—to take both positive steps to promote the health of the individual and measures to compel the individual to act in certain ways (or to refrain therefrom). In the words of one popular anti-tuberculosis tract, even though the poorer classes may be disproportionately victimized by *Volkskrankheiten* such as tuberculosis, "since rich and poor must live together, and since the fortunes of all social strata are woven together ever more closely by both the development of new means of transportation and by economic relations, it is, therefore, a duty of the community to enter into a war on tuberculosis to protect its underprivileged members and thereby to protect itself."[4]

This progressive idea of social citizenship was intrinsically ambiguous.[5] The social dimension of individual need could be invoked with equal legitimacy to subordinate the rights of the individual to those of the nation or race (i.e., future generations) or to support the demand for more extensive social services to compensate for those concrete disadvantages suffered by specific individuals as a result of their particular position within this interdependent social whole. Perhaps the most important question raised by these preventive social hygiene programs is to what extent were the potential benefits of these programs predicated on the social disciplining and the medicalization of these target populations—understood here as the use of coercive measures to rationalize the lifeworld of the working classes in accordance with the norms of middle-class culture and the modern social and medical sciences.

Many of the most influential readings of the German welfare state have suggested that, emancipatory aims and pedagogical strategies notwithstanding, the preventive social programs developed during this period ultimately subordinated the rights of the individual to those of the *Volk* and race and were, therefore, essentially repressive and potentially totalitarian.[6] One of the great strengths of the social discipline paradigm has been its ability to capture the logical connections between the constitution of need, surveillance of the needy and endangered, measures to discipline and otherwise influence the behavior of this population, and the constitution of their subjectivity. Without underestimating the importance of this literature, it is important to point out that these studies have often been too quick to take the explication of this logic for a description of the reality of assistance practice and to conclude that the logic of social discipline precludes a priori the possibility that social intervention could have enhanced in any genuine way the rights and welfare of the needy population. However, much of this literature has been informed by what could be called a teleological perspective that finds the seeds of National Socialist social policy—with its extreme coercive and deadly tendencies— already being sowed in the *Kaiserreich*. Accordingly, the social discipline paradigm has made it difficult to ascertain whether there might have been genuinely liberal or emancipatory dimensions in the progressive conception of social citizenship that guided at least elements of the preventive social welfare practices underway in the imperial and Weimar periods. In the empire and the Weimar Republic, the architects of preventive social welfare primarily came from the social-hygiene, rather than the eugenic, tradition, and they saw these programs as a means of promoting the development of the individual and, by enhancing the welfare of disadvantaged individuals, increasing the strength of the nation. The challenge is to simultaneously think both discipline and emancipation without succumbing to the temptation to reduce the one to the other.

In the following pages, I will argue that the working classes valued these preventive medical relief programs much more than has generally been noted and that their attitude toward these programs has important consequences for the way the history of the welfare state should be written. If the working classes were more receptive than allowed by the social discipline paradigm, and if the new hygienic ideas and practices promoted by these programs did not have to be forced upon an unwilling audience, then there is less need to insist upon their essentially disciplinary character, more space to examine how these new hygienic practices were justified and negotiated, and more need to analyze both the concrete ways in which they impacted the health and well-being of the needy and what these programs tell us about the nature of social governance and social citizenship rights at the birth of the welfare state. In what follows, I will argue that the combination of hygienic education and conditional incentives, rather than coercion, was the cornerstone of the preventive social hygiene programs relating to tuberculosis and infant mortality. Not only did the tuberculosis and infant welfare centers have little capacity to coerce their target populations. They had, I suggest, little need to do so because a substantial proportion of working-class women felt that the hygienic knowledge and medical consultations provided by the centers helped them meet some of the pressing problems that they faced in their everyday existence.

Before turning to the empirical study, however, it is necessary to say a few words about how this shift in perspective on social welfare programs relates to the problematic of modernity and "the social." Many of the contributions to a recent roundtable in the *American Historical Review* use global and postcolonial history to show that the imagination of modernity has drawn its energy from the diverse ways in which Europe has distanced itself from its extra-European Others, as well as from its own medieval past.[7] Of particular value in the present context are the contributions by Dipesh Chakrabarty and Lynn M. Thomas.[8] Chakrabarty and Thomas both emphasize the need to understand the rootedness of diverse modernist projects in the contexts of their own times, the normative value of these projects, the existential investment of historical actors in them, and the need to accept the modernity and utopian content of such local, "native" visions of reform. Building on these arguments and venturing a generalization, I suggest that the modernity of German social welfare grew out of both an overwhelming sense of the loss of origins, authority, and tradition and an awareness of the irreversibility of such loss. Without absolutes on which to rely, it became imperative to engage in reflexive thinking, to artificially reconstruct man's relations with nature and society, and to develop systematic bodies of knowledge to guide this process and give legitimacy and authority—even if only provisionally so—to the anticipated ends. Although few of the social reformers and social workers described below lived in the disenchanted world conjured up by Nietzsche and Weber, they were moderns nevertheless. The social reform project described here was all about creating new, more modern subjects, and these reformers were confident that their labors would yield a better world. Science was their anchor in the unnerving sea of modernity, regardless of both the particularity of this knowledge and the forms of power that it generated. Science, and the new science of social hygiene in particular, defined their understanding of the un- or not-yet-modernity of the world of the laboring classes; it enabled them to imagine the difference between what was and what might be; and it inspired them to bridge this gap. The concept of modernity thus enables us to understand the inner logic of this social reform project, the permanence and pervasiveness of such projects in times of far-reaching social change, and the urgency that it held for its practitioners.

Patrick Joyce has criticized what he has called the untheorized ontologization of the social and, more recently, the cultural, a move that has transformed these into foundational categories that are then used to "explain" action and meaning.[9] The notions of intrusiveness or coercion against which I argue can be seen as one particular form of class-based social causality, and in the following I try to avoid such problems by establishing a looser, more contingent, but hopefully more compelling connection between discourse, practice, and power. By attending to the intersection between science-based social-welfare efforts and the active negotiation of those efforts by their intended working-class recipients, we see the formation of an explicitly local social modernity, one in which the evolving meanings of the social, the subject, and the citizen were formed as much by the interests and investments of the recipients of social welfare as by the progressive reformers who were mobilizing its scientific and pedagogical tools.

1

Beginning around the turn of the century, welfare centers to combat tuberculosis and infant mortality evolved rapidly as the practical embodiment of the logic of prevention. The rationale for such centers seems to have been quickly accepted as self-evident, and the support of public officials, social reformers, and the working classes themselves led to the rapid spread of these centers before and during the First World War. The first tuberculosis welfare center was opened in Halle in 1899. By 1905, there were forty-two such centers, and the number grew to 321 in 1910, 1,145 in 1915, and over 3,000 by 1926.[10] The first infant welfare centers were established in Berlin and Munich in 1905, and their numbers grew at an equally rapid pace during the early war years before exploding between 1917 and 1922.[11] As a result, by the early 1920s, it was possible to speak of something approaching a seamless network of such centers covering the entire country, or at least its urban areas.

The early welfare centers were established by both voluntary associations and municipal governments. Their tasks were broad in scope, though these diverse activities were unified by a common focus on prevention.[12] They were staffed by a physician who worked on either a voluntary or paid basis and by one or more social workers or "sisters." Some of these women were graduates of the first social work (or social women's) schools, while others came to the job through their work as visitors for the local orphans council or poor board. Their training, modest as it was, made these social workers into agents of modernity. They were advocates of scientific hygiene, rationalized housekeeping, and the maternalist resolution of social conflict, and their authority over their clientele was increasingly legitimated in scientific terms.

The strategies that one adopted for combating a *Volkskrankheit* naturally depended on one's understanding of the source of infection and the means by which it was spread. On this point, there was universal agreement: "The center from which all infection spreads is the tubercular person, who through his expectorations hurls tuberculosis bacteria into the environment."[13] If infectious expectorations were the means by which this epidemic *Volkskrankheit* perpetuated itself, then the logical first step in breaking its grip was to survey the general population, seek out the quite literally hundreds of thousands of sources of contagion, and destroy them by treating each case in the appropriate manner. This was the mission of the welfare centers, whose guiding principle was:

> to track down and attack (*Erfassen*) [the sources and victims of infection]. Before anything is done, all cases under consideration must be surveyed and classified according to the nature of the proposed measures, which extend from the simplest enlightenment all the way

to sanatorium treatment...It is only through the centers that the war on tuberculosis is approached from the epidemiological perspective of combating epidemic disease rather than that of curative treatment or the restoration of the labor power. Consequently, observation and diagnosis are not restricted to curative measures for the afflicted individual, but also embrace his entire surrounding environment. [The centers] weave a net in conjunction with all of the other offices charged with hygienic observation of the population, and their primary goal is the systematic and timely discovery of all sources of contagion and their neutralization.[14]

The family was the alpha and omega of prevention because tuberculosis was most often spread by living or working together for a sustained period of time in an enclosed space with someone who already had the disease, and it was thus within the physical and social space of the family that the sick had to be isolated.[15] Since sanatoria were not an effective means of combating epidemic disease and since compulsory institutionalization was politically unacceptable, isolating the sick here meant less their physical removal than what might be called outdoor isolation or the "sanitization (*Assanierung*) of the tubercular family in its own home." This involved educating both the sick and the healthy on nature of infection and the basic rules of hygiene required to protect themselves and others from the disease so that the sick would no longer pose a danger to the population within which they lived.[16]

One of the key innovations of the early social state were the practical outreach strategies for seeking out their potential clientele and encouraging them to visit the centers, rather than deterring such visits, and the immediate goal of both the tuberculosis and infant welfare centers was to persuade their respective clienteles to visit the centers so that potential medical problems could be caught early and treated while the prognosis was still good. Once there, physicians and social workers would have—at least temporarily—a captive audience. However, a one-time visit would only have minimal impact on the health of the individual, and the rationalization of preventive care depended on finding a way to maintain regular contact between the welfare centers and their target population over the entire period when the latter were sick or endangered.

The most important incentive that the tuberculosis welfare centers could offer were medical examinations and, for those who met the criteria, the recommendation to the responsible agency of a sanatorium treatment. They also provided material assistance to facilitate the isolation of the sick individual within the family. This was accompanied by constant enlightenment, advice, and admonishment concerning the principles of domestic hygiene and practical suggestions on how to translate this theoretical knowledge into everyday habits to keep their environment clean and germ-free.

The maternal advice and infant welfare centers also provided free medical examinations, which gave working-class women the opportunity to consult a physician or nurse concerning the many minor, and sometimes not-so-minor, medical problems pertaining to their own pregnancies and the health of their infants (and later their young children). The other popular strategy adopted by many maternal advice and infant welfare centers in the decade before the war was to pay small premiums to the needy mothers. The promotion of breastfeeding was the axis around which all infant welfare programs pivoted, and it was hoped that these programs would encourage women to nurse their children—and reward them for doing so. But the centers had to have a way of making sure that these women were holding up their end of the bargain, and these premium programs obligated mothers to bring their infants to the centers for regular examinations and to agree to unannounced house visits so that social workers could verify that they were in fact nursing their children.

The threat to withhold these benefits undoubtedly gave social workers a degree of leverage over their clientele. However, since most of the women who participated in these programs had already nursed earlier children, it appears that these incentives often reinforced decisions that had already been made on other grounds. On the other hand, it is difficult to see these premiums as an effective means of disciplining working-class women because they only amounted to around 5–7 percent of the potential earnings of these women and were thus not large enough to offset the economic pressures on unmarried mothers and other poorer women whose children were most at risk.[17] While some mothers either chose not to participate in these programs or stopped bringing their children to the centers once they were no longer eligible for premiums, a substantial number of women regularly brought their children in for much longer periods; neither of these patterns is consistent with the claim that the effectiveness of these premiums depended on their disciplinary power. And while some physicians argued that those women who took the money and ran, so to speak, demonstrated that many women were not susceptible to the enlightenment and advice offered by the centers, others argued that, even though these women may have initially been enticed into the centers by purely financial considerations, the consultations and house visits could not have been without effect on their attitudes and habits.[18] Moreover, the literature on the youth welfare system has repeatedly emphasized how the resistance of working-class youth and families to reform schooling steadily ate away at the legitimacy of the Weimar welfare system.[19] However, there are few signs of such open, principled resistance to tuberculosis and infant welfare programs, and this may well reflect the fact that these programs were not as intrusive, coercive, or unwelcome as correctional education programs (or tuberculosis sanatoria) were often perceived to be.[20]

The real issue, though, is not so much whether the physicians and social workers who worked in the tuberculosis and infant welfare centers tried to get something out of their clientele, but rather the terms of exchange between the two. The basic purpose of these programs was to encourage needy women to behave in certain ways, and it would have been self-defeating for these programs to have made their terms of eligibility so harsh as to discourage their potential clientele from taking advantage of the assistance they offered.

In his excellent study of the war on tuberculosis in France, David Barnes wrote that "once the key notions of hygienic urgency and social danger were accepted, the progression from assistance to surveillance to confinement was just a small logical step."[21] And if Barnes had been writing about Germany, this strong version of the social discipline paradigm would have concluded by reflecting on the exclusionary and potentially genocidal consequences of this logic. However, although these outreach programs represented an important expansion of the institutional capacity of the nascent social state to identify and monitor needy and endangered populations, it is not clear whether these administrative knowledges were directly and logically translated into disciplinary control over these people, whether social reformers aspired to such control, or whether they in fact needed to rely on coercion and discipline to achieve their goals. In fact, it is precisely the assumptions that underlie this inferential chain that need to be examined.

2

The start of the systematic war on infant mortality in Germany has traditionally been dated to 1904–05. In the former year, Empress Auguste Victoria declared in a letter to the League of Patriotic Women (*Vaterländischer Frauenverein*) that the welfare of infants and children constituted a matter of urgent "patriotic" concern that should become the focus of united action by both philanthropic circles and state agencies. Her involvement led to the rapid mobilization of interested conservative notables, high-ranking bureaucrats, and the state medical establishment. The first major initiative of this officious infant protection movement was the founding of the Kaiserin-Auguste-Victoria-Haus (KAVH), which was to become the focal point of official efforts to combat infant mortality.

Although these representatives of the official infant protection movement undoubtedly had a conservative agenda, the success of their programs depended to a large degree on their ability to enlighten and persuade their clientele. The movement could not have grown so quickly, however, if it did not enjoy broad local support among a wide variety of social and political groups. Although the infant protection movement was by no means ignorant of social factors, the social problem of infant need was constructed primarily via the representation of working-class women as ignorant of the basic tenets of modern infant feeding and care.

"The enemies," wrote Arthur Schlossmann, the founder of the influential Association for Infant Welfare in Düsseldorf (*Verein für Säuglingspflege im Regierungsbezirk Düsseldorf*, founded 1907) and one of the leading figures in the infant protection movement, are "ignorance and indifference."[22] Social reformers and social workers viewed the war on infant mortality and tuberculosis as part of an effort to rationalize hygienic habits and elevate the culture of the working classes. In the parlance of the time, it was a *Kulturkampf*, or cultural struggle, and these reformers expected that elevating the culture of the working classes—in the form of more extensive knowledge of the principles of scientific infant care—would increase the personal responsibility of these women and in the long run render welfare largely superfluous. This was the essence of the Progressive social contract and the Progressive strategy for solving the social problem, especially its influential maternalist variant.[23]

The precondition, though, for educating these women was to establish the authority of the medical profession and convince working-class women to defer to the knowledge of doctors and social workers, rather than place their faith in old wives' tales. It was a commonplace within the infant protection movement that the greatest challenge to the authority of physicians and social workers, and the greatest obstacle to educating the working classes, were older, experienced mothers (and grandmothers), whose authority, and often their fatalistic attitudes toward child-raising as well, was based on their own experiences with pregnancy, childbirth, infant care—and infant mortality.

The most important determinant of infant mortality was whether children were nursed or bottle-fed. Breastfeeding appeared to provide so much leverage over the problem of infant mortality because it promised to render artificial feeding—with all of its attendant dangers—superfluous for the vast majority of women who were believed to be capable of nursing their children. However, at the heart of this campaign to promote breastfeeding there was an irresolvable conflict between those who saw expanded breastfeeding as a measure that could be adopted in anticipation of those social reforms that were regarded as the only definitive solution to the social question and those conservatives who regarded declining breastfeeding rates as a sign of the immorality of the age and as a problem that could best be addressed through religious renewal, rather than social reform. The value of breastfeeding could easily be integrated into the ideology of motherhood and the act of nursing taken as a sign of the moral worth of the mother herself. In the words of one Dr. Herzog, the director of the Mainz Association for Maternal and Infant Welfare, "those mothers who can nurse their children, but who do not do so, commit a sacrilege against their children! ... Breastfeeding is the most sublime maternal obligation. To be nursed is the most basic of all human rights!"[24] In its most distilled form, this rhetoric culminated in the assertion that "there is no such thing as a social question for children who are nursed by their mothers" (*Das Brustkind kennt keine soziale Frage*).[25]

This last statement, however, came from Heinrich Finkelstein, the director of the Berlin Children's Asylum and an important advocate of social hygiene programs, and the support of people such as Finkelstein for hygienic education and breastfeeding undoubtedly reflects both skepticism that working-class living conditions could be substantially improved in the short term and a confidence that higher rates of breastfeeding could bring immediate results even in the absence of such change.[26] The openness of the working classes to hygienic enlightenment was the product of a number of factors, not the least of which was the growing willingness of the Social Democrats to support pragmatic social reforms at the municipal level. However, underlying this entire process was the medicalization of the working classes.[27]

The success of the preventive project depended on the informed collaboration of working-class women, and communication between physicians and working-class mothers depended on a combination of scientific authority, personal tact, personal engagement, and the ability to offer these women something that they valued. As one doctor explained, when women came to the welfare center, the goal of the physician was to influence them to adopt more rational habits by "helping to instruct the inexperienced, convince the unwilling, encourage the discouraged, disperse prejudices, counter false advice, and clear away obstacles ... The medical arts collaborate with civic patriotism in this great task."[28]

Since the infant protection movement could not rely on the printed word to get its ideas across, the infant welfare centers were in part so valued because they gave doctors and social workers the opportunity to communicate directly with working-class women while giving these women a rare opportunity to consult with a physician. They also relied increasingly on visual media. Virtually every aspect of the new, scientifically approved methods for the care and feeding of infants and toddlers was illustrated in the *Atlas der Hygiene des Kindes* edited by Leo Langstein, who became director of the KAVH in 1911, and Fritz Rott, the director of the institution's information department.[29] The individual plates eschewed all but the most basic textual commentary and illustrated these new methods through the side-by-side contrast of proper and improper methods and simple genre-like pictures depicting how a conscientious and informed working-class woman would act when faced with a specific problem concerning her child. What was perhaps most fascinating about the *Atlas* was its use of charts and pictures (Figure 9.1) to establish readily comprehensible norms concerning the relationship between feeding and infant health and development, that is, how much an infant should eat at a specific age, how much of what kinds of foods should be fed to children at what age, the weight and height to be expected of a normal child at different ages, and even the color and texture of healthy and unhealthy baby poop, which were indicators of the quality and appropriateness of their food and the proper functioning of the digestive system. Some of these were meant

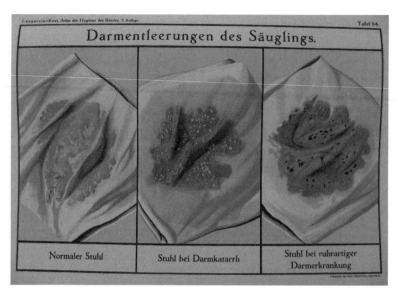

FIGURE 9.1 *Sample page from Langstein's* Atlas der Hygiene des Kindes *that establishes readily comprehensible norms concerning the relationship between feeding and infant health and development.*[30]

as models for mothers to follow, but others simply represented medical norms that could not be imposed upon either infants or their mothers. But what they did achieve was to give women a baseline so that they could see if their child was in any respect not developing properly and—and this is what was most important to physicians—take timely preventive action based on this knowledge.

How successful were these programs? Critics have argued in a curiously schizophrenic manner that these infant welfare programs were simultaneously intrusive and ineffective because their success depended on imposing upon working-class women values and habits, which, if not exactly foreign to these classes, could not be easily or consistently adopted by women who lacked the time, the money, and sometimes the infrastructure (i.e., running water) to put them into practice.[31] Though not unreasonable, these arguments are—in their stronger versions—overstated.

On the one hand, the reasoning itself is partly flawed. Though the elimination of sickness and infant mortality as class phenomena may very well have depended on fundamental change in the social conditions of the working classes, the earnings and the living conditions of the vast majority of the working classes were not so constrained that there was no margin for doing things in a different way. The primary goal of these preventive social programs was to shake working-class women out of their oft-lamented indifference by cultivating a hygienic consciousness that could translate into countless everyday measures—from cleaning a pacifier to washing one's hands to storing milk in a different place. While it is impossible to quantify the cumulative impact of these Enlightenment programs, it seems wrong at some basic level to dismiss them a priori as misguided, misogynist, and ideologized attempts to impose middle-class notions of respectability on women who had neither the proper culture nor the material preconditions needed to put them into practice.

A second way of assessing the disciplinary dimension of these programs is to look at how women voted with their feet. In other words, how many of these women patronized the welfare centers, and did they do so in ways that reflect a positive attitude toward these programs and that might have resulted in substantial benefits to themselves and their infants?[32] Though there is no nationwide data on the coverage rates of the infant welfare centers in the prewar years or statistics showing how long what percentage of women from various social classes brought their infants to the centers for consultations, or their reasons for doing so, the data that is available (primarily for the larger cities that were the leaders in the infant welfare cause) attests to vibrant activity on the part of the welfare centers and a strong interest in these services on the part of the working-class women who were their target audiences.

Though it would be risky to describe any of these cities as typical, the trend is clear. These coverage rates would have been impossible to achieve without the active cooperation of working-class women, and the wartime and postwar maternity allowance programs provided a huge boost to the infant welfare movement, with two-thirds or more of the newborns coming under the supervision of the welfare centers in many cities by the mid-1920s.[33] Whatever the obstacles involved in visiting these centers, whatever the possible indignities entailed by house visits, and whatever the difficulties involved in applying the advice they received, it seems clear that a substantial proportion of working-class women felt that the trade-off was worth it and that the centers contributed in some way or another to their welfare and that of their children.

The influence of eugenics on German public health policy has been widely documented and viewed as one of the main lines of continuity from the Wilhelmine to the Nazi periods. Eugenic thought challenged the infant protection movement most directly through its insistence that infant mortality was a valuable mechanism of natural selection that helped maintain the quality of the race. The infant welfare movement did not reject the underlying belief that different individuals' superiority or inferiority was natural—since this was common currency of welfare community at that time—as much as it argued that concerns about the counterselective and dysgenic effects of infant welfare programs were largely misplaced. While German child savers claimed that even children who were born weak and debilitated could develop into strong, healthy, and productive individuals if carefully nourished and cared for, what weighed more in their dialogue with eugenics and racial hygiene was their insistence that infant mortality could simply not have the positive selective influence often attributed to it because such a large proportion of infant mortality was due to general, social conditions, not natural differences in human fitness. From this perspective, infant welfare programs were legitimate and necessary means of counteracting the negative influence of social conditions. For welfare practitioners—as opposed to the intellectuals gathered in the various racial hygiene societies—there was little need to provide an immediate answer to the question of whether at some indefinite point in the future infant mortality rates might sink to such a level that their efforts would begin to have some dysgenic effects.

Although eugenics achieved new influence in public health and welfare communities during the war, the development of infant welfare programs during the Weimar years was not dominated by a single and social hygienic and eugenic discourses were intertwined in complex ways. The leading figures in the field—Langstein, Rott, Schlossmann—all continued to argue for the expansion of preventive social hygiene programs in order to counteract the impact of social conditions on infant welfare and maximize the health, fitness, and productivity of the population. In practice, such programs were indistinguishable from the positive programs to promote the birthrate and welfare of racially valuable families proposed by eugenicists. By and large, though, the infant welfare movement did not engage with the question of what might eventually have to be done if the dysgenic effects of universal infant protection began to threaten the long-term fitness of the race; they had more immediate concerns, though Sigrid Stöckel has argued that their shared concern with human economy and the productivity of the population created a back door through which negative eugenics could, under certain circumstances, begin to influence infant welfare practice.[34] It was not inevitable, though, that it should do so, and it was the creeping crisis of the late 1920s and the massive attack on the Weimar welfare system during the Depression that altered the constellation of political forces that had made possible the development of universal preventive social hygiene programs since the turn of the century.

3

In the previous sections, we have described the logic of prevention that served as the organizing principle for the welfare centers and the strategies by which social workers and physicians worked to modernize and rationalize the hygienic practices of the working classes. This work was based on the presumption that these changes would, in fact, lead to a reduction in infant and tuberculosis mortality. Although these claims appear to be confirmed by the dramatic decline in mortality rates during the first third of the century, correlation is not the same as causality,[35] and the historical demographers who have studied this question have generally been quite skeptical of the contribution of social hygiene programs to this decline.

The terms of this debate were established by Thomas McKeown, who argued that the modern rise of population was due primarily to a decline in mortality from infectious disease, rather than increased fertility. McKeown attributed this decline to increased resistance to these diseases resulting from a rising standard of living and better nutrition, and he sought to buttress the explanatory power of this interpretation by showing that this decline could not be explained in terms of either sanitary reform or advances in medicine.[36]

In the present context, the most relevant critique of McKeown's work is the one put forward by Simon Szreter.[37] The element of Szreter's critique that is most relevant to the argument being made here is his claim that there were limits to what could be achieved through sanitary reform alone. While sanitary reform could reduce waterborne diseases such as cholera, he argued that sanitary reform could not affect those diseases that were attributable to the lack of hygiene *in the immediate living environment of the family* because it lacked the means to penetrate into the working-class household. Thus, Szreter suggests, the realization of any substantial reductions in mortality, especially infant mortality, beyond those already achieved by sanitary reform would have to depend on improvements in housing and the development of new hygienic attitudes and practices among the working classes.

However, the preceding pages have described the very process by which preventive social welfare penetrated into the working-class household and transformed its hygienic culture in ways that would have made it possible for the working classes to take advantage of the opportunities for improved hygiene created by sanitary reform, improvements in housing, and a rising standard of living.[38] The hygienic practices promoted by the infant and tuberculosis welfare centers (including both breastfeeding and the entire spectrum of other infant hygiene, care, and feeding practices) were basically good medicine; they succeeded in reaching a substantial proportion of their target populations; and it is, therefore, difficult to imagine that the modernization of so many individual household hygienic practices did not have a meaningful cumulative impact on mortality rates.

The failure to stem the decline in breastfeeding rates in the prewar years should not necessarily be taken to mean that these infant welfare programs had no impact at all on infant mortality. Although the promotion of breastfeeding may have the most popular measure for combating infant mortality, especially among conservatives, propaganda on behalf of breastfeeding was always embedded in a much broader campaign to enlighten working-class women about the principles of scientific infant feeding and care, including bottle-feeding and milk hygiene, and I would suggest that the indirect impact of these programs on elevating the hygienic consciousness of these women was as important as their direct impact on breastfeeding rates.

While sanitary reform and rising wages may have been the necessary precondition for better hygiene within the working-class household, they were not sufficient conditions, and they did not automatically lead to improved domestic cleanliness, more rational child-raising practices, or more conscientious efforts to stem the spread of tuberculosis. While better mothering was the key to taking advantage of whatever freedom of action there may have been under existing conditions, women first had to come to want to do things in new and better ways. Conversely, breastfeeding and the other hygienic practices promoted by the tuberculosis and infant welfare centers could have brought about real improvements within existing social conditions and thus offset, at least in part, the baneful effects of poverty without in any way prejudicing the cause of social reform. Herein lay the real appeal of the welfare centers: working-class women patronized them because they believed they could provide meaningful assistance in meeting the immediate, pressing problems which they faced in their everyday lives. However, improvements in hygienic practice required a certain margin of subsistence in regard to two scarce resources: time and money. At some level, this is a general condition of human progress, and this was the real issue lying behind the debate over women's work: what was the net impact of two incommensurable changes—increased resources and the better nutrition that they made possible, on the one hand, and, on the other, decreased time to devote to children and the home?

The error made by some contemporaries was to assume that, just because working-class women enjoyed some margin for improvement, the full exhaustion of this potential would enable them to push back the limits imposed by the social conditions in which they lived, negate the social dimensions of sickness and mortality, and thus abolish the social question through the sheer force of maternal skill and commitment.[39] The error of much of the modern social discipline literature has been its failure to appreciate the real improvements that were possible within these slowly easing constraints and to understand both the appeal of these centers to working-class women and the pivotal role of hygienic education in helping these women see why it was important to do things differently.

Hygienic enlightenment thus helped bring new values, habits, and expectations to the working classes, and it was the mechanism through which the potential of rising incomes and sanitary reform was translated into improved hygiene, better maternal and infant nourishment, more rational household management, and ultimately a more hygienic domestic environment. But if this is so, then how does this conclusion bear on the question of social discipline and the relation between social hygiene, citizenship, and welfare?

I would suggest that, although they may have harbored far-reaching plans for rationalizing the lives of the needy and elevating their cultural level, physicians and social workers had few, if any, means by which to directly compel their clientele to act, or refrain from acting, in specific ways. They could explain, preach, and plead, but the success of these programs ultimately depended on their ability to get their message across in terms the working classes could understand, to offer something that they wanted, and to do so on terms which these women found acceptable. Social workers might threaten to withhold some benefit or another from a recalcitrant working-class woman. But unless she were an unmarried mother whose child was a ward of the local guardianship court or youth authority, she could not be compelled to bring her child to the infant welfare center, and no external sanction could be imposed should she choose not to do so. The same held true for tuberculosis, though there was here a greater willingness—which was not put into practice until the rise of the Nazis—to consider more coercive measures.

We also need to be more attentive to the reception of this cultural project on the part of the laboring classes. Were these new hygienic ideas and practices any more foreign to the working classes than they had been to the middle classes several decades before, and did these newfangled ideas, in fact, have to be imposed upon the needy at all? Despite the moralistic view of working-class mothers held by many reformers, the advice they offered was good medicine, whose direct and indirect impact on infant mortality cannot easily be dismissed, and working-class women visited the tuberculosis and infant welfare centers because they recognized the value of the information, advice, and material assistance they received, even if it came wrapped in condescending language. And if the working classes were more receptive than has been implied by the stronger versions of the social discipline paradigm, and if these new hygienic ideas and practices did not have to be forced upon an unwilling audience, then there is less need to insist on the invasive and coercive character of these programs. Thus, unless we are willing to insist that all attempts to influence the behavior of others are nothing other than surface manifestations of a deeper, cunning logic of social discipline, then we need to take seriously the role of hygienic enlightenment and social learning and approach the history of the welfare state in new ways that are capable of better capturing the expanded social rights that flowed from the combination of enlightenment, conditional incentives, and social discipline embodied in these programs. In practice, relations between social workers and their clients were much more ambiguous than has generally been allowed. The encounter between the needy and the helping professionals of the nascent social state was a site of discipline, enlightenment, resistance, resentment, frustration, gratitude, manipulation, evasion, and uneasy collaboration. The needy may well have been entangled in the networks of knowledge, power, and surveillance through which they were constituted as objects of social intervention and paternalistic solicitude. But these programs also provided incentives whose benefits were tangible enough to entice the poor into the welfare centers and persuade them to open their doors, at least part way, to the social workers employed there.

Thus, I would conclude that there is a historical answer to the theoretical question raised above. Without denying their disciplinary potential, the tuberculosis and infant welfare programs that spread so rapidly between the turn of the century and the Great Depression did reflect a real concern for the welfare of afflicted and endangered individuals, and they were perceived as such by their clientele. Even though the social rights established by these programs may have been constructed in gendered terms around the domestic roles of women, they gave the Weimar welfare system a genuinely liberal, emancipatory dimension that has been systematically obscured by those who have written its history primarily in terms of the rise of social discipline or as the prehistory of Nazi eugenics. The Weimar welfare state may well have later become, in the eyes of some of its architects and critics, a dysfunctional machine for the production of social discipline.[40] But this should not lead us to forget that it also produced something else: welfare and greater social rights. It was only after the rise of the Nazis that the preventive project was refunctioned along racial lines and the rights of the individual definitively and systematically subordinated to those of the racial community.

Abbreviations

BAB   *Bundesarchiv Berlin—Reichsgesundheitsamt (R86)*
Muk   *Mutter und Kind*
SDV   *Schriften des Deutschen Vereins für Armenpflege und Wohltätigkeit*
UW   *Unser Weg*
ZfT   *Zeitschrift für Tuberkulose*

Notes

1   "Eine Musteranstalt für die Bekämpfung der Säuglingssterblichkeit," *Zeitschrift für ärztliche Fortbildung* 3 (1906), p. 1.

2   Michael Katz and Christoph Sachße, *The Mixed Economy of Social Welfare. Public/Private Relations in England, Germany and the United States, the 1870s to the 1930s* (Baden-Baden: Nomos, 1996).

3   I have developed these ideas at greater length in Larry Frohman, *Poor Relief and Welfare in Germany from the Reformation to World War I* (Cambridge: Cambridge University Press, 2008).

4   Adolf Thiele, *Die Schwindsucht: Ihre Ursachen und Bekämpfung gemeinverständlich dargestellt*, 3. verbesserte Aufl. (1915; Berlin, 1926), p. 53.

5   Most studies of Progressivism, or left liberalism, in Germany have been political histories, which have found it difficult to focus systematically on the social policy domain, and the Progressive persuasion in social policy—with all of its ambiguities and contradictions—has been charted much more effectively in studies of welfare and social work, especially child and youth welfare.

The important exception is Kevin Repp, *Reformers, Critics, and the Path of German Modernity. Anti-Politics and the Search for Alternatives, 1890–1914* (Cambridge: Harvard University Press, 2000).

6   Paradigm-setting examples include Detlev Peukert, *Grenzen der Sozialdisziplinierung. Aufstieg und Krise der deutschen Jugendfürsorge von 1878 bis 1932* (Cologne: Bund, 1986); and Paul Weindling, *Health, Race and German Politics between National Unification and Nazism, 1870–1945* (Cambridge: Cambridge University Press, 1989). Note that in this essay, "social discipline" refers to this German historiographical paradigm and not to the also familiar conception of discipline established by Michel Foucault, in which discipline speaks to the processes of subjectivation or the production of subjects and the incitement of those subjects to invest in disciplinary discourses. For that connotation, see especially his *Discipline and Punish: The Birth of the Prison*, trans. Alan Sheridan (New York: Vintage, 1995); *History of Sexuality, Vol. 1*, trans. Robert Hurley (New York: Vintage, 1990); "The Subject and Power," *Critical Inquiry* 8:4 (1982), pp. 777–95.

7   "Historians and the Question of 'Modernity,'" *American Historical Review* 116:3 (June 2011), pp. 631–751.

8   Dipesh Chakrabarty, "The Muddle of Modernity," *American Historical Review* 116:3 (June 2011), pp. 663–75, and Lynn M. Thomas, "Modernity's Failings, Political Claims, and Intermediate Concepts," ibid., pp. 727–40.

9   In particular, Patrick Joyce, "What Is the Social in Social History?" *Past and Present* 206 (February 2010), pp. 213–48, especially pp. 220–1.

10   Julius Emil Kayser-Petersen, "Die spätere Entwicklung des Tuberkulosefürsorgewesens in Deutschland im Rahmen der Tuberkulosebekämpfung," in Karl Heinz Blümel, (ed.), *Handbuch der Tuberkulose-Fürsorge*, 2 vols (Munich: Lehmann, 1926), vol. 1, pp. 25–39, citation 26 and K.W. Jötten, *Die Auskunfts- und Fürsorgestelle für Lungenkranke wie sie ist und wie sie sein soll*, 2. Aufl. (Berlin: Springer, 1926), pp. 11, 58ff. The most important studies of tuberculosis in Germany and the work of the welfare centers are Gerd Göckenjan, *Tuberkulose-Prävention und Spuckverhalten. Bedingungen, Ziele und Maßnahmen einer historischen Kampagne zur Einstellungs- und Verhaltensänderung* (=Veröffentlichungsreihe der Forschungsgruppe Gesundheitsrisiken und Präventionspolitik, Wissenschaftzentrum Berlin, 1989); Gerd Göckenjan, "Fighting Tuberculosis in Germany, 1890s–1920s," in Katz and Sachße, *The Mixed Economy of Social Welfare*, pp. 279–302; Flurin Condrau, *Lungenheilanstalt und Patientenschicksal. Sozialgeschichte der Tuberkulose in Deutschland und England im späten 19. und frühen 20. Jahrhundert* (Göttingen: Vandenhoeck & Ruprecht, 2000); Sylvelyn Hähner-Rombach, *Sozialgeschichte der Tuberkulose vom Kaiserreich bis zum Ende des Zweiten Weltkrieges unter besonderer Berücksichtigung Württembergs* (Stuttgart: Steiner, 2000); and Peter Reinicke, *Tuberkulosefürsorge: der Kampf gegen ein Geißel der Menschheit dargestellt am Beispiel Berlins 1895–1945* (Weinheim: Deutscher Studien, 1988).

11   On the German infant welfare programs, see Sigrid Stöckel, *Säuglingsfürsorge zwischen sozialer Hygiene und Eugenik. Das Beispiel*

Berlins im Kaiserreich und in der Weimarer Republik (Berlin: De Gruyter, 1996); Silke Fehlemann, "Armutsrisiko Mutterschaft: Mütter- und Säuglingsfürsorge im deutschen Reich, 1890–1924" (Ph.D. diss., University of Düsseldorf, 2004); Elmar Schabel, *Soziale Hygiene zwischen sozialer Reform und sozialer Biologie: Fritz Rott (1878–1959) und die Säuglingsfürsorge in Berlin* (Husum: Matthiesen, 1995); Karen Hagemann, *Frauenalltag und Männerpolitik* (Berlin: Dietz, 1990), 204–19; Weindling, *Health, Race and German Politics*; and Gustav Tugendreich, *Die Mutter- und Säuglingsfürsorge* (Stuttgart: Enke, 1910). German infant welfare programs can profitably be compared with similar programs in England and the United States. See Laura Marks, *Metropolitan Maternity. Maternal and Infant Welfare Services in Early Twentieth Century London* (Amsterdam: Rodopi, 1996); Jacqueline Wolf, *Don't Kill Your Baby. Public Health and the Decline of Breastfeeding in the Nineteenth and Twentieth Centuries* (Columbus: Ohio State University Press, 2001); and Deborah Dwork, *War Is Good for Babies and Other Young Children. A History of the Infant and Child Welfare Movement in England, 1898–1918* (London: Tavistock, 1987).

12   To get a sense of the scope of their work, see Ernst Stuertz, *Praktische Anleitung zur Organisation von Fürsorgestellen für Lungenkranke und deren Familien* (Berlin: Urban & Schwarzenberg, 1905); Arthur Kayserling, *Die Organisation der Auskunft- und Fürsorgestellen für Tuberkulöse nach den Grundsätzen der Seuchenbekämpfung* (Leipzig, 1906); Kayser-Petersen, "Die ersten Anfänge des Tuberkulosefürsorgewesens in Deutschland und im Auslande," in Blümel (ed.), *Handbuch der Tuberkulose-Fürsorge*, I: pp. 5–24; Ernst Becker, "Die Fürsorgestelle für Lungenkranke in Charlottenburg," *Zeitschrift für Tuberkulose* 8:5 (1906), pp. 391–403; and Reinicke, *Tuberkulosefürsorge*.

13   Kayserling, *Die Organisation der Auskunft- und Fürsorgestellen*, p. 7; in the same sense Johannes Nietner, *Die Tuberkulose als Volkskrankheit und ihre Verhütung* (Berlin: Zentralkom, 1911), p. 8.

14   Dr. Wendenburg, "Die westfälischen Tuberkulose-Fürsorgestellen," in *Tuberkulose ud Tuberkulosefürsorge* (=*Beiträge zur sozialen Fürsorge*, Heft 9 [1927]), pp. 67–83, note 67.

15   Stuertz, *Praktische Anleitung*, pp. 1–2; Ernst Pütter, *Die Berliner Auskunfts- und Fürsorgestellen für Lungenkranke, Alkoholkranke und Krebskranke im Jahre 1912* (Berlin: Hirschwald, 1913), p. 3; and the letter from the Deutsches Zentral-Komitee (June 23, 1914), Bundesarchiv (BArch) Berlin—Reichsgesundheitsamt R86 1170, Bl. 2836.

16   Kayserling, *Die Organisation der Auskunft- und Fürsorgestellen*, p. 8; and Martin Kirchner, "Wie muß die Tuberkulosebekämpfung beschaffen sein, wenn sie Erfolg verspreschen soll?" in *Tuberkulose-Ausstellung Berlin-Wilmersdorf*, pp. 10–18, especially p. 13.

17   Fritz Rott, *Umfang, Bedeutung und Ergebnisse der Unterstützungen an stillende Mütter* (=*Veröffentlichungen aus dem Gebiete der Medizinalverwaltung*, III. Band, 14. Heft, 1914).

18   Dr. Hirschfelder, "Bericht über das 3. Jahr der Mutterberatungsstelle in Crefeld," *Mutter und Kind* 5:1 (October 1912), pp. 10–12.

19 See Peukert, *Grenzen*; and Edward Ross Dickinson, *The Politics of German Child Welfare* (Cambridge: Harvard University Press, 1996).

20 Stuertz, *Praktische Anleitung*, p. 39. According to Jessica Robbins, open resistance to visiting tuberculosis nurses was also rare in the United States, something that she likewise attributes to their lack of coercive power over the families they visited. Robbins, "Class Struggles in the Tubercular World: Nurses, Patients, and Physicians, 1903–1915," *Bulletin of the History of Medicine* 71:3 (1997), pp. 412–34.

21 David Barnes, *The Making of a Social Disease. Tuberculosis in Nineteenth-Century France* (Berkeley: University of California Press, 1995), pp. 74–111, note 110.

22 Schlossmann, "Vorwärts?" *Mutter und Kind* 2:5 (May 1910), pp. 2–3.

23 Marie Baum, "Mutter- und Säuglingsschutz," *Blätter für Soziale Arbeit* 1:3 (March 15, 1909), pp. 15–16; and Baum, "Die zweite Konferenz des Vereins für Säuglingsfürsorge im Regierungsbezirk Düsseldorf," *Blätter für Soziale Arbeit* 1:5 (May 15, 1909), p. 28. It was the failure of this new social contract to hold that eventually turned the Progressive architects of the Weimar welfare system against their own creation in the late 1920s. See Young-sun Hong, *Welfare, Modernity, and the Weimar State, 1919–1933* (Princeton: Princeton University Press, 1998).

24 Dr. Herzog, "Was kann für die Hygiene des Säuglings in den Mutterberatungsstellen geschehen?" *Mutter und Kind* 4:9 (June 1912), pp. 4–6, note 5.

25 Heinrich Finkelstein in *Stenographischer Bericht über die Verhandlungen, Schriften des Deutschen Vereins für Armenpflege und Wohltätigkeit* 87 (1908), p. 40.

26 Arbeitersekretär Czieslik, "Ist die Fürsorge für Mutter und Kind in das Programm der Arbeiterschaft aufzunehmen?" *Zeitschrift für soziale Medizin* 4:2 (1909), pp. 210–24, and Stöckel, *Säuglingsfürsorge*, p. 194.

27 Alfons Labisch, "Doctors, Workers, and the Scientific Cosmology of the Industrial World: The Social Construction of 'Health' and the 'Homo Hygienicus,'" *Journal of Contemporary History* 20:4 (1985), pp. 599–615; Ute Frevert, "Akademische Medizin und soziale Unterschichten im 19. Jahrhundert. Professionsinteressen—Zivilisationsmission—Sozialpolitik," *Jahrbuch des Instituts für Geschichte der Medizin der Robert Bosch Stiftung* 4 (1985), pp. 41–59.

28 Adolf Deutsch, "Die Beratungsstellen des Frankfurter Verbands für Säuglingsfürsorge," *Unser Weg* 2:8 (April 1911), pp. vi–vii.

29 The book was first published in 1918 and reissued in a third edition in 1926/27 under the title *Atlas der Hygiene des Kindes und des Kleinkindes*.

30 Langstein and Rott (eds.), *Atlas der Hygiene des Kindes* (Berlin: Preuß, 1926), plate 84.

31 Ute Frevert, "'Fürsorgliche Belagerung': Hygienebewegung und Arbeiterfrauen im 19. und frühen 20. Jahrhundert," *Geschichte und Gesellschaft* 11 (1985), pp. 420–46; Ute Frevert, "The Civilizing Tendency of Hygiene. Working-Class Women under Medical Control in Imperial Germany," in John Fout

(ed.), *German Women in the Nineteenth Century* (Teaneck, NJ: Holmes & Meier, 1984); pp. 320–44, and Frevert, "Akademische Medizin und soziale Unterschichten," in *Love and Toil. Motherhood in Outcast London, 1870–1918* (Oxford: Oxford University Press, 1993), Ellen Ross deconstructs the rhetoric of good mothering by tracing both the attractiveness of modern mothering and infant hygiene and the limitations placed upon the adoption of these practices by the material realities of working-class motherhood.

32 This is the position of Laura Marks in *Metropolitan Maternity*, p. 179. Wolf, *Don't Kill Your Baby*, pp. 114–15 and *passim*, also emphasizes the popularity of visiting nurses and infant welfare stations.

33 Although there is obviously room for exaggeration in these coverage rates, these figures do not seem out of line with data from American metropolises with comparable programs. For example, Wolf, *Don't Kill Your Baby*, p. 103, reports that in 1925 visiting nurses and infant welfare stations cared for 57 percent of the 58,000 infants born in that city.

34 Stöckel, *Säuglingsfürsorge*, pp. 97, 378ff.

35 See Stöckel's reflections on this point in *Säuglingsfürsorge*, pp. 359–65.

36 Thomas McKeown, *The Modern Rise of Population* (London: Arnold, 1976).

37 Simon Szreter, "The Importance of Social Interventionism in Britain's Mortality Decline c. 1850–1914: A Re-interpretation of the Role of Public Health," *Social History of Medicine* 1 (1988), pp. 1–37.

38 See Jörg Vögele, *Sozialgeschichte städtischer Gesundheitsverhältnisse während der Urbanisierung* (Berlin: Duncker & Humblot, 2001); Jörg Vögele, *Urban Mortality Change in England and Germany, 1870–1913* (Liverpool: Liverpool University Press, 1998); Jörg Vögele, "Urban Infant Mortality in Imperial Germany," *Social History of Medicine* 7:3 (1994), pp. 401–25; and John Brown, "Economics and Infant Mortality Decline in German Towns, 1889–1912: Household Behaviour and Public Intervention," in Sally Sheard and Helen Power (eds.), *Body and City. Histories of Urban Public Health* (Burlington, VT: Ashgate, 2001), pp. 166–93. For the failings of the welfare centers, see Jörg Vögele, Wolfgang Woelk, and Silke Fehlemann, "Decline of the Urban Penalty: Milk Supply and Infant Welfare Centers in Germany, 1890s to 1920s," in Sheard and Power, *Body and City*, pp. 194–213; and Wolfgang Woelk, "Von der Säuglingsfürsorge zur Wohlfahrtspflege: Gesundheitsfürsorge im rheinisch-westfälischen Industriegebiet am Beispiel des Vereins für Säuglingsfürsorge im Regierungsbezirk Düsseldorf," in Vögele and Woelk (eds.), *Stadt, Krankheit und Tod. Geschichte der städtischen Gesundheitsverhältnisse während der epidemiologischen Transition* (Berlin: Duncker & Humblot, 2000), pp. 339–59. By contrast, the connection between these programs and infant mortality rates seemed so obvious to the Chicago Commissioner of Public Health that he increased the number of infant welfare centers from four to twenty-five. See Wolf, *Don't Kill Your Baby*, p. 128.

39 Jane Lewis, *The Politics of Motherhood: Child and Maternal Welfare in England, 1900–1939* (London: Croom Helm, 1980), p. 65ff., effectively makes this point for England.

40 Hong, *Welfare, Modernity, and the Weimar State*, pp. 224–5.

10

Secularism, Subjectivity, and Reform: Shifting Variables

Tracie Matysik

In his 1905 classic *The Protestant Ethic and the "Spirit" of Capitalism*, Max Weber mentioned almost as an aside that the Calvinist-Puritan protagonists of his study had no "ethical programs of reform." They were concerned solely with the "salvation of souls," and not with any kind of ethical culture.[1] Weber was referencing the German Society for Ethical Culture (henceforth DGEK, for *Deutsche Gesellschaft für ethische Kultur*), an ethics-reform group whose mission was to create a cultural space for secular-ethical life, to reflect on and mobilize around a secular orientation for individual values and actions in the world; and Weber was decidedly not a fan.[2] In *The Protestant Ethic*, Weber was tracing a subterranean historical process whereby the once-religious moral orientation and related activity of the Calvinists was gradually rationalized and made worldly. Weber's critique of the DGEK pertained to what he saw as the organization's naïve idea that ethics and ethical subjectivity were cultural phenomena that could be intentionally crafted and reformed. While ethical-culture reformers sought actively to propagate the secular, the "Protestant ethic" that became the "spirit of capitalism" bespoke the supposedly neutral social-historical process of secularization.

The goal of this essay is not so much to make sense of Weber's comment specifically but rather to address the context in which it arose. To do so involves thinking about three terrains of German cultural and intellectual life at the turn of the century, all of which came together in the DGEK and Weber's resistance to it: the status of secularism as a social movement, the problem of subjectivity as contemporaries articulated it, and the culture of reform. Each one of these terrains relates centrally to German cultural modernity, but in varied and often incompatible fashion, as I will discuss below. My central argument is that they are shifting variables in a modernity that must be thought of as multiple and incoherent, with interrelated parts that are moving in different directions and at different speeds. Their interaction at once lent vibrancy to the intersecting debates, even as it interrupted utopian or highly coordinated visions of reform.

Secular variations and subjectivity

Before turning to the DGEK and its conflicts, it is useful to visit each of the three domains in which it was operating, beginning with the secular and religious context it confronted. A narrative of secularization closely tied to Weber's thesis regarding the Protestant ethic and rationalization was once central to discussions of modernity.[3] In that narrative, a gradual decline in explicit religious belief had supposedly given way especially in Calvinist societies to a gradual rationalization of society, complementing general individualization (an emphasis on individual responsibility), industrialization, and the expansion of capital. Moreover, what had happened in Northern European and North American Protestant settings in Weber's account would supposedly unfold globally through the eventual geographic and cultural spread of modernization of the globe.

This narrative, however, has been definitively challenged in recent decades both globally and in Weber's own home.[4] Even as historians of diverse parts of the globe have observed the important persistence of varied religious practices and beliefs within the context of modernity,[5] so too have historians of Germany begun to talk about waves of secularization, desecularization, and "resacralization."[6] In the German case, the focus has been less on questions of belief or on how many individuals actually attended weekly church or synagogue services than on how religion came to form an integral part of modern political and social identities.[7] Having uncovered the ways in which Catholic, Protestant, and Jewish identities could all be fused to and mobilized by political and social interests, historians have made the provocative comparison to the age of Reformation and Counter-Reformation, some even talking about the late nineteenth century as a "new confessional age," epitomized by its own "wars of religion," or "culture wars," in which tolerance of difference had little place.[8]

If the history of secularization has been called into question, so too has the meaning of the "secular" itself. With histories of religion focusing less on professions of belief and more on the interaction between religious affiliations and sociopolitical interests, it has become unsatisfying to think of secularism as the mere removal of religion and faith from public life. Rather, it is clear that like the contours of modern religion, the contours of modern secularism had to be molded, its stance as "neutral" no longer tenable. Weber's narrative presented the secular as a "disenchanted" realm, but sociologists and historians have been more likely of late to focus on the concrete positive values propagated by secularists. Already in 1949, Karl Löwith had identified the secular as the disguised displacement of religious values, a claim echoing Carl Schmitt's 1922 premise that "all significant concepts of the modern theory of the state are secularized theological concepts."[9] In *Legitimacy of the Modern Age*, a tome too little acknowledged due to its literal and intellectual heft, Hans Blumenberg convincingly argued against Löwith and Schmitt, maintaining that secular modernity was neither replacement nor displacement of a religious epoch and must instead be taken as an era replete with values distinct to its technological capacity and intellectual curiosity.[10] Similarly, more recent theorists have rethought the category less as one defined by subtraction (the disappearance of religion) than, in the words of the editors of *Rethinking Secularism*, "as a presence. It is *something*"—although that something is remarkably difficult to pin down and varies from time to time, place to place.[11]

Theorists of late have zeroed in on a matter already identified by Blumenberg, namely the distinct type of subjectivity coinciding with formations of the secular. For Blumenberg, a new ethos of "self-assertion" facilitated the modern worldview, the basis for the pursuit of technological mastery over nature.[12] Charles Taylor offers a closely related argument in his *A Secular Age*. There Taylor presents the modern, secular world as one featuring the "buffered" self—a self that recognizes his or her individual belief system as one among many. These "buffered" selves are in contrast with what he calls "porous" selves, individuals so integrated into a particular belief system that they have no capacity for reflection on it.[13] Important for Taylor is the fact that buffered selves can reasonably come together and entertain their differences. The "secular" in this context thus does not so much refer to an absence of religious belief or practice as it does a particular formation of subjectivity that presupposes the possibility of autonomous (if contextually informed) choice and the ability to negotiate difference of belief and practice. The argument is crucial for Taylor's overall aim to defend the role of religion in the public and secular sphere.[14] It is also central to any understanding of the secular as a pluralist marketplace of ideas.

Others have cast a more critical eye on the supposedly rational and autonomous or buffered self of the secular—skeptical of its conceivability and critical of the social and ideological violence its myth helps to perpetuate. Authors such as Wendy Brown, Talal Asad, Saba Mahmood, and Michel de Certeau, among others, have sought to illuminate assumptions in realms such as scholarship, activism, medicine, and law about a certain kind of liberal, rational subject as the norm against which other types of subjectivities are measured. Attentive to a dichotomy similar to that which Taylor elaborates between the buffered and porous self, Brown writes of the culturally hegemonic logic behind the liberal conception of tolerance and the autonomous subject on which it is based. Such tolerance, she maintains, presupposes a subject who imagines himself or herself to be free to pick and choose belief and conviction, moral decision, and emotional attachment; that liberal tolerance also constructs an other who seems to have no such freedom, who is represented as "porous" in relation to a belief system, as Taylor might say. While the former is seen in the secular framework to "have" religious conviction or emotional investment as add-ons to a more primary rational self, the latter is represented as *being determined by* a religious conviction or emotional investment. The one is represented as reasonable and the other as a "fanatic."[15] In a study of Egyptian piety movements, Saba Mahmood has exposed a comparable logic. In her telling, western secular feminists are scandalized by the practices of female Egyptian pietists whose daily practices conform to and inscribe on their bodies what would seem to be a patriarchal system. From the rational, secular angle that privileges "agency" as the pursuit of a particular kind of autonomy, these women might look saturated by their religion. Through her own immersion in the piety circles, however, Mahmood exposes a complex world of emotion, rationality, education, and choice. Yet because the parts of that complex world are arranged and interlinked differently than that of the self-defined secular and rational, the choices and commitments and emotional structures of the pietists may be illegible to the "western feminist" researcher.[16] Whether in celebration or in critique, theorists of the secular thus seem to agree that its dominant discourse relies on this concept of a free subject, one who chooses for or against a religion, for or against a set of moral and emotional options; and its antithesis is a subject inseparable from its religiosity.

It is worthwhile dwelling for a moment on an important and related critique within religious studies that has emerged in recent decades. This critique began with an early argument by Talal Asad, who challenged the way in which religion had come to be represented as an autonomous domain of human existence. With his critique aimed explicitly at Clifford Geertz, Asad identified key moments in the history of Western European theorizing of religion, moments in seventeenth- and eighteenth-century thought when "religion" came to be identified: first, as having some sort of transhistorical "essence," distinct from other formations of power; and, second, as pertaining to a "distinctive mental state characteristic of all religions," one in which belief manifests itself as "a verbalizable inner condition."[17] For Asad, the discourse that arose in the seventeenth and eighteenth centuries, usually in the name of "religious tolerance" and usually at the hand of individuals of a Protestant background, corresponds to the "privatized idea of religion in modern society," in which religion becomes an optional category.[18] He identified as exemplary of these developments John Locke's definition of religion in his *Letter Concerning Toleration*, in which Locke understands "true religion" to be entirely separate from civil matters and to pertain solely to "the inward and full persuasion of the mind."[19] Not surprisingly, Asad's next book was devoted to the study of secularism; and much scholarship from other pens has followed him in seeing a connection between the Protestant influence on the evolution of "religion" as a universalized academic and theoretical category with a particular conception of an autonomous and rational subject at its core and the related presuppositions underpinning prevalent forms of secularism.[20] If, as theorists of secularism suggest, secular discourses presuppose a kind of buffered self whose beliefs can be seen as contained within the self and as chosen by that self, they do so in a line of continuity with a long-standing Protestant tradition that privileged the private conviction of the individual as the essence of religion and saw public activity and ritual as only secondary.[21]

Todd Weir's book *Secularism and Religion in Nineteenth-Century Germany* has shed new light on the contours of secularism in the specifically German context. Tracing the evolution of secularism from the 1840s into the twentieth century, Weir observes important distinctions along the way. First, he distinguishes organized secularism from explicit decline in belief, on the one hand, and broad sociological processes of a secularized state, on the other. Unlike the latter two developments, he claims, organized secularism explicitly advocated for its interest. Despite vast differences among variants of organized secularism, Weir suggests that their reform orientation and their advocacy of interest make them collectively a "fourth confession," especially in so far as their interests consisted often in acquiring recognition from the state similar to that the state granted to organized confessions. Taking up a suggestion from the political theorist and historian of secularism, Hermann Lübbe, Weir further observes that theories of secularization as broad and unintended sociological process—theories such as Weber's, for instance—sought to neutralize the radical and threatening dimensions of specific secular organizations and their reform projects.[22]

Weir's argument points to the reform element of this story. The ethics reformers were not just theoreticians writing independently about matters of belief; rather, they organized in explicitly reform-oriented associations. They mobilized also around matters of education, gender and sexuality, international relations, colonialism, science in public life, and, eventually, for and against the outbreak of war. In this diverse array of concerns, the secular ethics reformers nudged up against the entire spectrum of reform culture in the *Kaiserreich*.[23]

Accordingly, a word about reform culture more broadly is in order. The last two decades have seen a rise in studies about everything from social-welfare reform to land reform and *Lebensreform* of every variety. Much of this research is indebted to the critique of the *Sonderweg* thesis that David Blackbourn and Geoff Eley launched in their *Peculiarities of German History*.[24] In this work, they not only precociously challenged any normative model of modernity against which Germany should be measured—a move that would put their work later in good company with much postcolonial critique of modernity as presupposing a European norm—but they also drew attention to components of nineteenth- and early twentieth-century

German history previously underrepresented in the historiography. By removing the teleological lens that tied nineteenth-century developments to a necessary path toward National Socialism, they uncovered rather a much more dynamic "modern" industrial state, and they pointed to a more vibrant public culture of social and cultural reform. Their point was not to unhinge any connection between nineteenth-century Germany and its Nazi inheritor but rather to suggest that National Socialism did not need a turn away from liberalism or "modernity" to take root. The challenge to historians was thus to understand in a new light what that vibrant public culture in the Wilhelmine era looked like. In a complementary argument, Detlev Peukert's thesis in his field-defining essay "The Genesis of the 'Final Solution' from the Spirit of Science" suggested a narrative in which the explicitly progressive social-science and social-reform projects of the *Kaiserreich* continued into the National Socialist era, shifting their bureaucratic practices fairly easily to fit a dramatically altered ideological focus.[25] While historians have hotly contested Peukert's now inverted teleology, in which liberalism and progressive social science paved the way for Nazism's deadly aims, his provocation further supported a generation of scholarship on reform in both the Wilhelmine and Weimar eras.[26]

If a virtual consensus now exists about the vitality of the culture of reform in the *Kaiserreich*, disagreement thus remains about the meaning of that vitality. Several years ago, Matthew Jeffries briefly surveyed the field and lamented that no synthesis exists.[27] And yet, what much literature of late has told us is that the vitality of the reform culture resided in its very resistance to synthesis and its inability to foster totalizing projects. Dennis Sweeney, for instance, suggests that we focus on the sources of conflict in the reform movement. He has expressed concern that an overall modernity paradigm—whether Foucauldean, Weberian, Peukertian, or other—that emphasizes an increasingly disciplinary, rationalized, and scientized society obscures the variations in ideological commitments and tactics that the wide range of reform projects presented. He further notes that such a paradigm of modernity simultaneously tends to emphasize an increasingly powerful and autonomous state. It thus misses the diverse relations that different elements of civil society held with the state, the different lobbying efforts they made to the state, and the different ways they took on functions of the state. Drawing upon a vast array of historiography on social reform, he concludes rather that what defined the reform culture was the way that competing reform groups vied with one another to define the social, and with it the state and modernity.[28] Here I want to take up Sweeney's suggestion that we focus on the sites of contestation and to add the matter of secularism and subject-formation to his triplet of categories that were being contested.

In what follows, I will treat a set of discussions evolving out of the DGEK that reveal how considerations of reform, secularism, and the subject of reform intersected. Participants debated what it meant for secularism to be a concrete social movement: was it to be an explicit alternative to religion? Must it offer a comprehensive and unified *Weltanschauung*? Or could it work in a more open fashion? Did modern secularism mean religious tolerance or antireligion? And what was the relationship of secularism to rationalism, to materialism, and to scientific practice and belief? Moreover, these discussions were relatively unique in that they explicitly addressed the makeup of the subject upon whom reform depended. My approach is greatly informed by Weir's observation about the difference between those who represented the secular as a neutral category—in both intellectual and sociological terms—and those who adopted an explicit stance of advocacy for a particular secular social program. But here I zero in on the attention to the matter of secular subjectivity. By attending to the intellectual arguments made within the secular movement—the different intellectual positions taken by its participants—we see not only how problems about subject-formation were central to the articulation of the meaning of both secularism and reform but also how different assumptions about subject-formation contributed to evolving fault lines within the movement. Like Taylor, Asad, and other recent theorists of the secular, ethics reformers shared the assumption that the formation of the modern subject was a matter central to their topic. However, as we will see below, there was hardly any consensus in the DGEK and related secularist organizations about a rational or buffered or private self as the quintessential secular subject. Moreover, it was disagreement about the nature of both the secular and the makeup of its subject that made it difficult for ethics reform to cohere as a reform movement. Coherence existed, but primarily in terms of the perpetuation of discord and discussion.

Pluralism and the limits of tolerance

The DGEK first formed in October 1892. The immediate prompt to organize was a Prussian legislative initiative pertaining to the confessional nature of public schools, a move that the founders of the DGEK saw as counter to their secularist hopes for Prussia and Germany.[29] The idea of "Ethical Culture" itself derived from the movement founded a few years earlier by the German-Jewish-American Felix Adler, who had visited Berlin in the spring of that year.[30] Where Adler's movement had begun as a secular-Jewish alternative to traditional religion, however, the DGEK emphasized pluralism and conversation. They consequently set out to provide a forum in which individuals, "independent of all religious and political persuasions," could participate in the discussion—avoiding doctrine at all costs.[31] The only limitation on participants would be the commitment to a vaguely humanist definition of "ethical culture" as "a condition in which justice and truth, humanity, and mutual respect reign."[32] The practices or methods of the society built directly upon the idea that ethics was a category to be interrogated. In the introduction to a periodical that they founded entitled *Ethische Kultur*, Gizycki explained the idea of the journal as follows:

> *Ethische Kultur* assumes readers who have the ability truly to love humanity and to strive for knowledge of the truth—who want to effect all of the changes in social life that are necessary for the well-being of all, who love sincerity and, far from all darkness of infallibility, are willing to hear the opinions of others and to change their own or to give up their own as soon as they recognize sufficient bases to do so. We would want the person with these characteristics as our reader and co-worker, no matter whether he is conservative, liberal, socialist, believing or unbelieving, learned or not learned.[33]

While a variety of different perspectives were represented among the founders of the DGEK, the overall project of tolerance and exchange of viewpoints could be said to be one informed by the idea of the buffered secular self. There was perhaps no better theoretical statement to this effect than the seminal *Gemeinschaft und Gesellschaft*, written by Ferdinand Tönnies.[34] The author was not only a founding figure in German sociology but also an intellectual spokesperson for the DGEK in its initial years. In the book he had argued that with the shift from a social organization that privileged group identity and tradition to one that emphasized individual autonomy and rationality went a parallel shift from a traditional morality that would be defined by self-sacrifice and group consideration to a "modern" ethic that demanded self-interestedness and future-oriented calculation. If in *Gemeinschaft* a moral code was said to be already in place, the challenge for the individual in *Gesellschaft* was that he or she had to make individual decisions about moral valuations. In one strain of the argument, Tönnies suggested that a shift to modern *Gesellschaft* forces religious belief to give way to scientific and rational inquiry.[35]

This strain of Tönnies' argument was not so different from what Weber would suggest three decades later with his notion of "disenchantment" in the modern age.[36] Alongside this relatively straightforward depiction of secularization as disenchantment or loss of religion, however, Tönnies also offered another narrative, one in which the homogeneity of belief in *Gemeinschaft* gives way to a contest for public opinion (*öffentliche Meinung*) in *Gesellschaft*.[37] In this second narrative, Tönnies presented public opinion as the moral voice of society. Public opinion stands, according to Tönnies, above the state, ready to judge the rightness or wrongness of the state's actions. Intrinsically, it is a site of contestation, but a site of contestation that always seeks homogeneity or monopoly. In a rare break from a staunchly scientist tone, Tönnies stated that modern public opinion in the current era could act as a vital force in society when it involves personal interaction and demands participation from individuals. But, when dominated by the mass media—as he felt public opinion then was—it becomes depersonalized, looming as just one more alienating force over against the lone individual of *Gesellschaft*.[38] As Tönnies maintained in public writings, the purpose of the DGEK was to promote a rigorous science of ethics that would infuse public opinion with considered reflection and provide for individuals insight into the wide array of available moral frameworks. Most urgently, while he accepted the condition of modern *Gesellschaft*, he feared an unchecked growth of an ethic of capitalist self-interest. The alternative, he maintained, would be a rigorous and rational science of ethics that would enable individuals to make choices about their own moral orientation.[39]

Whatever Tönnies' explicit prescription for modern life, the ingredient he thought essential was clear: the autonomous subject who consumed public opinion and in principle had the rational capacity to weigh options about belief privately. To be sure, he agonized about the mechanism by which public opinion intersected with subjective interiority, emotion, and rational contemplation. The result in *Gemeinschaft und Gesellschaft* was a fusion of ideas from Spinoza, Schopenhauer, and Darwin, among others, that amounted to a fascinating conception of a biologically and socially determined entity that nonetheless had evolved to be self-determining. The particular formula was unique, but it resonated with the pressing problem confronting ethics reformers of the time: the overwhelming sense of individuals as materially determined, a position fostered by the general popularization of science and materialist philosophies after 1848, together with the need to understand those individuals as capable of making moral decisions upon which cultural and social reform depended.[40]

Not surprisingly, many defenders of established confessions spoke out against the DGEK and its appeal to secularism as pluralism and tolerance. Chief among the critics was Adolf Stöcker, the Protestant preacher and vocal antisemite, who denounced the DGEK as a product of the "Jewish press."[41] More surprising, however, were the criticisms launched from within seemingly secular circles. Illuminating on this front is the criticism that came from the pen of Eugen Heinrich Schmitt, who was envisioning a rebirth of "religion" in a very modern, materialist guise. Based in Budapest, Schmitt had founded the League for the Religion of Spirit (*Bund der Religion des Geistes*), a project inspired by Hegel, Feuerbach, and other leading figures of German materialist thought. According to Schmitt's vision, a new "religion" or *Weltanschauung* (worldview)—and he moved regularly between the two terms—would be based on the fundamental divinity of humanity. Two things worried Schmitt most about the DGEK. First, he was concerned that the DGEK was misrepresenting the public, when in fact most people were committed to one *Weltanschauung* or another. Second, and perhaps more important for Schmitt, he worried about the DGEK's "misconception of the independence of moral consciousness from *Weltanschauung*, the illusion that the human essence can be split in two pieces."[42] Here he was referring to the DGEK's idea that individuals could hold one belief while bracketing it in pursuit of public dialogue. Schmitt's concern was with "the harmony of the whole person with himself."[43] The idea of private belief and public openness, for Schmitt, defied the primary purpose that religion or *Weltanschauung* was supposed to fulfill, namely the facilitation of that harmony between self and world.

This challenge from Schmitt helps to frame an even more hostile conflict between the DGEK and Ernst Haeckel, the outspoken Darwinist in Germany and a leading voice for science in the German public sphere. One might expect a certain cooperation between the secular DGEK and the secular Haeckel. Like the founders of the DGEK, Haeckel was eager to found a new ethics, one that would be based on modern scientific rather than received religious principles. As with Schmitt, however, a fit was not to be found. Unlike Schmitt, who was based in Budapest, the Jena-based Haeckel was able to attend the founding meeting of the DGEK. There he advocated for explicit adoption of a fully natural-scientific *Weltanschauung* as the basis of ethics to the complete foreclosure of religious residues.[44] In so far as he privileged science as the basis for ethics, his position would seem to be close to that articulated by Tönnies, who had in fact cited Haeckel on the matter in his *Gemeinschaft und Gesellschaft* and who wrote often of the need to pursue ethics with modern scientific methods.[45] But there was a slight shift from Tönnies to Haeckel that made all the difference. For Haeckel, a natural-scientific *Weltanschauung* did not promote ecumenicism or neutrality of religious belief; rather, a natural-scientific *Weltanschauung* must *replace* religion altogether. Not only did Haeckel advocate science as the sole legitimate intellectual and ethical orientation for modern life; as a replacement for religion, a scientific *Weltanschauung* was to assume an all-consuming role in the mind and comportment of its practitioners. As he explained in a publication defending his stance shortly after the founding meeting, "I consider it impossible to resolve the ethical problem without also addressing the religious problem; because they are intimately connected. Both have their roots in that inner sanctuary of the thinking person which he calls his *Weltanschauung*."[46] In other words, much like Schmitt, Haeckel objected to the premise of a split subject, one that held internal beliefs privately while entertaining multiple perspectives publicly.

Even more starkly than Schmitt, though, Haeckel objected to the stance of tolerance that the DGEK took. He publicly denounced the project as "so general that anyone could support it."[47] In Haeckel's view, the DGEK failed to recognize the ideological war that was underway, the waging of which required full commitment of its participants. While he was long vocal on this topic, he expressed himself most thoroughly in his *Riddle of the Universe* (*Welträtsel*) a few years later. There he not only spoke of the absolute conflict between religion and the sciences but he also took aim directly at Catholicism, whose history he described as "an unscrupulous web of lies and deceit." Endorsing the *Kulturkampf* as necessary to ward off the cultural "danger" posed by Germany's Catholic population, Haeckel heralded his own monistic philosophy as the natural-scientific heir to German

Protestantism and the only intellectual framework suitable to lead Germany into the twentieth century. While there was no room in his *Weltanschauung* for established religions in general, Catholicism in particular, he maintained, threatened to undermine science as the guiding light of ethics and it thus had to be battled to the bitter end. There was accordingly no room for tolerance or pluralism in Haeckel's view. Like Tönnies, he understood humans as fundamentally determined creatures; and only a *Weltanschauung* that fully and exclusively embraced science could provide insight into the fundamentally harmonious condition of humans in nature. Conceptions of a divisible moral self—of "free will"—could only be inherited relics of a Christian viewpoint that must be confronted vigorously.[48]

It is important to observe that all of these positions—the pluralist/tolerance model of Tönnies and the DGEK, the humanist-materialist "religion" of Schmitt, and the scientistic anti-religious *Weltanschauung* of Haeckel—fall in some fashion on the side of secularism. Moreover, they all derived from some form of secularized Protestantism (*Kulturprotestantismus*, as it has been dubbed).[49] Yet the divisions are easy to identify. Using recent theoretical terms, we may say that Tönnies and the DGEK were working with the model of the buffered self that Taylor describes. Behind their project of public conversation lay an explicit presupposition of a secular and autonomous subject who could detach his or her self and internal beliefs from external, public concerns—this despite the fact that its spokespersons tended to embrace materialist or monist philosophies and with them various forms of determinism. Conversely, both Schmitt and Haeckel presuppose some form of porous subject—the kind of subject recent theorists claim secularism attributes to religious life, subjects for whom there is no clear divide between external social life and private belief or thought. For Schmitt and Haeckel, these subjects will be fully infused with the cultural framework in which they exist, be that a scientific or religious framework. Despite being a standoff between different varieties of secularism, it looks very much like those that Brown sees in secular confrontations with religious societies or subjects, when the secular-buffered subject meets the supposedly porous or infused subject and the limits of secular and rational tolerance thereby come into relief.

There were, to be sure, other points of discord—both actual and potential—between the DGEK and their critics. Most relevant, perhaps, was the cosmopolitan self-conception of the DGEK founders, on the one hand, and elements of cultural chauvinism on the part of its critics, on the other. While founders of the DGEK made an effort to envision something like a universal humanity, their critics all envisioned more of a local and global competition among relatively well-defined groups. So Stöcker feared the Jewish influence within German circles and Haeckel took aim especially at Catholic influences, both in the name of a German nationalism, while Schmitt disparaged Chinese cultural development and warned of a similar "decline" for Europe on the whole.[50]

On this front, it is tempting to think that the DGEK's project of multiple perspectives and tolerance really was about a cultural openness, and that may well have been partially the case—though such a statement needs to be qualified a bit. At least in their early years, for instance, DGEK founders had relatively little to say about European colonialism, for instance—this despite their regular emphasis on universal humanity and individual moral autonomy. Nonetheless, real political differences certainly did play a role in early discussions. In each case, the limits of tolerance for the DGEK seemed to be reached where national and racial chauvinism coincided with conceptions of porous selves.

In subsequent years, however, that neat and tidy delineation seemed to break down. A new round of controversy took place in 1903–05 that illustrates a shifting of positions. The controversy broke out when the spiritual turn of Friedrich Wilhelm Foerster, a founding leader of the movement, emerged. Importantly, the basis of Foerster's turn was not so much a new conviction regarding a transcendent god as a concern about the status of the individual in the modern world. While self-identifying now in a loosely Christian fashion, his concerns remained in a real sense this-worldly and secular. In a series of articles, he explained his concern that the modern individual is adrift, left to rely on reason alone in moral and spiritual matters. In contrast to this modern form of atomism, Foerster maintained, individuals need the influence of moral tradition and community—the "consensus of the wise"—in the development of moral orientation. Most revealing, he insisted that the individual perceive this tradition or "consensus of the wise" as a type of "inner experience" or "intuition"—a kind of social internalization that the individual perceives as a priori wisdom.[51]

Foerster was lambasted for this turn, both at organizational meetings and in the pages of *Ethische Kultur*. Making it clear that Foerster no longer had any place in the DGEK, Franz Staudinger—another founding member of the organization—spelled out the problem. Insisting that the DGEK remained committed to pluralism in belief—in keeping with the principles Foerster himself had drawn up more than a decade earlier—Staudinger instead framed the matter in terms of reason and emotion. Emotion, he acknowledged, is an important component in the motivation for moral action. Yet without reason as its guide, he warned, things like emotion and inner conviction can be mobilized for morally dubious purposes as easily as for commendable ones. Remembering shamefully his own chauvinist-nationalist enthusiasm in his youth at the Prussian victory over France, Staudinger insisted that it bore all the traits that Foerster associated with inner experience and intuition. Accordingly, he concluded, only reason should be trusted as the arbiter of moral matters, with emotion held to a subservient role.[52]

In this standoff, in which Foerster ultimately withdrew from the activities of the DGEK for the time being, it would seem at first glance as if we find yet another straightforward illustration of the distinction between buffered and porous selves, with Staudinger now speaking for the buffered self and castigating Foerster for his conception of a porous self. Staudinger adhered to the idea of a subject capable of removing itself from its surroundings in order to reflect on them, while Foerster was newly committed to the way that inherited cultural tradition decisively shapes and infuses the thinking and feeling subject. But upon closer inspection, it seems the alignments had actually shifted a bit. As a final shot in his engagement with Staudinger, Foerster made a plea that the DGEK stick to its original pluralist roots.[53] In terms of the marketplace-of-ideas model of secularism, Foerster— the spokesperson for the porous self—remained its defender. While he personally endorsed a kind of religion of social tradition, he continued to understand the DGEK fundamentally as a site for the reasonable exchange of perspectives.[54] Moreover, in so far as Staudinger spoke for the DGEK at this moment and excluded Foerster from its ranks, the organization had shifted from one of neutral pluralism to one of explicit antireligion. In terms of buffered and porous selves, nothing lined up in the way recent theorists of secularism might lead us to expect. To be sure, one finds at the outset the buffered self and the politics of tolerance facing off against porous selves and singular worldviews. However, Stöcker aside, these standoffs were taking place all *within* the generally secular camp. By 1905, the lines had shifted such that the buffered self no longer even coincided with the politics of tolerance, whereas the porous self became tolerance's companion.

To understand these intellectual shifts, it is helpful to reflect on institutional transformation and the context of reform. Much had happened in the years between 1892 and 1905. While anti-Catholicism had long been a staple element in some of the secular or free-thinker circles, its vehemence grew after *Sammlungspolitik*, a form of coalition-building that brought the Catholic Center Party into the government and sought to reintegrate the once marginalized Catholic populace into the German nation.[55] At the same time, discussions about confessional practices in public schools surfaced anew, eliciting further organizational activity and realignment.[56] Out of the campaigns arose a branch organization of the DGEK known as the German League for Moral Education (*Deutsche Liga für Moralunterricht*), an organization that was at times more strident in its explicit hostility to religion than was the DGEK itself.[57] The resulting mood in the DGEK proved on all fronts less accommodating of religious difference and more inclined to antireligion on the whole. Rudolf Penzig in particular, who had assumed a leadership role in the DGEK and the editorship of *Ethische Kultur*, pushed the DGEK in this direction in order to present a stronger public stance against collaboration between church and state.[58] Not coincidentally, it was Penzig himself who had first called out Foerster and his new religiosity at an annual meeting in 1903.[59] Ultimately this institutional slide toward antireligion would culminate in the forming of the Weimar Cartel, an umbrella organization for diverse free-thinker groups. While it would not form until 1909, the trend toward collaboration between associations and with it the slide by the DGEK toward antireligion was well underway by 1903–05.

Reflections on secularism and reform

I want to conclude by reflecting on what this story tells us about the nature of secularism, reform, and German modernity. Most important, when we look at the free-thinker milieu in Germany, we see *varieties* of competing secularisms and related conceptions of the secular subject. There is no easy alignment of conceptions of rational autonomous subjects with secularism as real or staged neutrality and the politics of tolerance. While such an alignment did exist in the early days of the DGEK, the organization not only quickly revealed the limits of its own tolerance—not against religion, interestingly, but against antireligious stances; it also yielded not long thereafter to a decidedly not neutral stance of antireligion itself. Moreover, the autonomous-rational subject of 1892's secularism lost the capacity for tolerance and entertainment of difference by 1905.

Perhaps the slippage of the DGEK from pluralism and into antireligion is indicative of something peculiar about the nature of secularism as an explicit reform project, bringing us back to Weber's critique and Weir's analysis. One of the points that recent critics of secularism return to repeatedly is the idea that secularism presents itself as neutral while in fact carrying with it all sorts of cultural baggage—presuppositions about the nature of the self, of social interaction, of bodily comportment, and of scholarly and legal categories. Indeed, Weber presented his own *Protestant Ethic* as an objective social-scientific study, even though the reader today will detect in it not only a strong dose of anti-Catholicism but also an implicit critique of domestic Liberal politics in Germany.[60]

The tension between staged neutrality and partisan critique is even more pronounced in the explicit reform project of the DGEK. Indeed, perhaps Weber was so annoyed by the DGEK precisely because the effort to tie neutral secularism to reform—an inherently *oriented* type of social organization—couldn't help but reveal the lie of neutrality itself. In this sense, the DGEK illustrates especially visibly the ruse of neutrality that secularism upholds; at the same time, it reveals a much more complicated picture in which the pretenses to neutrality, tolerance, and rational autonomy cannot even maintain themselves as aligned pretenses.

In terms of reform, the story of secularism reminds us that reform was always a project of contestation, a staking of claims even when reform presented itself as politically or culturally neutral. In the case of the DGEK, these claims revealed themselves through conflict and the limits of toleration, namely through what had to be excluded. At the outset, the organization had to exclude Haeckel; soon it would be Foerster. There were also uncomfortable alliances in the formation of the Weimar Cartel that could not survive the onset of the First World War, as pacifist and internationalist factions—now including Foerster again—were suddenly incompatible with the more nationalist factions. And in all of these episodes, competing conceptions of the secular subject came to the fore. If those competing conceptions of the subject changed from conflict to conflict, they give us insight into the very different building blocks reformers were using in their efforts to reshape society—and the difficulty the reformers thus had in coalescing around a sustained and singular vision of reform. My point is not that secular ethics reform was thus doomed to failure due to its internal conflicts. Indeed, quite the opposite was the case. Its conflicts seemed to feed the dynamism of the movement, keeping it vital right up to 1933. My assertion here is, rather, that these competing views of secular subjectivity—and the inability to settle on one model—not only illustrate the malleability of secularism as a social and intellectual phenomenon but perhaps also point to a crucial dimension of reform culture more broadly. What is unique in the DGEK is solely that it explicitly thematized the conflicts around its most basic starting points— especially the makeup of the moral subject—making the fault lines and their galvanizing potential more visible than other reform movements might do.

Notes

1   Max Weber, *The Protestant Ethic and the "Spirit" of Capitalism, and Other Writings*, ed. and trans. Peter Baehr and Gordon C. Wells (New York: Penguin, 2002), p. 35.

2   H.H. Gerth and C. Wright Mills, "Introduction," in Gerth and Mills (eds.), *From Max Weber: Essays in Sociology* (New York: Oxford University Press, 1946), p. 11.

3   A classic statement was Peter Berger, *The Sacred Canopy: Elements of a Sociological Theory of Religion* (Garden City, NY: Doubleday, 1967); a complementary intellectual history is Owen Chadwick, *The Secularization of the European Mind* (Cambridge: Cambridge University Press, 1975). In the German context, a symptomatic example of the writing of religion out of the narrative is Hans-Ulrich Wehler, *Das deutsche Kaiserreich 1871–1918*, 4th edn (Göttingen: Vandenhoeck & Ruprecht, 1980).

4   A turning point in the literature was Peter Berger (ed.), *The Desecularization of the World: Resurgent Religion and World Politics* (Washington, DC: W.B. Eerdman, 1999). More recent works include Michael Warner, Jonathan Van Antwerpen, and Craig Calhoun (eds.), *Varieties of Secularism in a Secular Age* (Cambridge: Harvard University Press, 2013); Rajeev Bhargava (ed.), *Secularism and Its Critics* (New York: Oxford University Press, 2005); Hent de Vries and Lawrence Sullivan (eds.), *Political Theologies: Public Religions in a Post-Secular World* (New York: Fordham University Press, 2006).

5   A poignant statement is Dipesh Chakrabarty, *Provincializing Europe: Postcolonial Thought and Historical Difference* (Princeton: Princeton University Press, 2000).

6   Thomas Nipperdey's *Religion im Umbruch. Deutschland 1870–1918* (Munich: C.H. Beck, 1988) is commonly cited as the turning point in modern

German historiography. See also Hartmut Lehmann, "Von der Erforschung der Säkularisierung zur Erforschung von Prozessen der Dechristianisierung und der Rechristianisierung im neuzeitlichen Europa," in Hartmut Lehmann (ed.), *Säkularisierung, Dechristianisierung, Rechristianisierung im neuzeitlichen Europa* (Göttingen: Vandenhoeck & Ruprecht, 1997), pp. 9–16, and Helmut Walser Smith and Chris Clark, "The Fate of Nathan," in Helmut Walser Smith (ed.), *Protestants, Catholics, and Jews in Germany, 1800–1914* (Oxford: Berg, 2001); Anton Rauscher (ed.), *Probleme des Konfessionalismus in Deutschland seit 1800* (Paderborn: Schöningh, 1984). Very important for the view that the nineteenth century was not one of secularization, but rather of a translation of religion into new forms of expression, has been Lucian Hölscher (ed.), *Datenatlas zur religiösen Geographie im protestantischen Deutschland von der Mitte des 19. Jahrhunderts bis zum Zweiten Weltkrieg*, 4 vols (Berlin: W. de Gruyter, 2001).

7   On Catholicism, see David Blackbourn, *Marpingen: Apparitions of the Virgin Mary in Nineteenth-Century Germany* (New York: Knopf, 1994); Jonathan Sperber, *Popular Catholicism in Nineteenth-Century Germany* (Princeton: Princeton University Press, 1984); Margaret Lavinia Anderson, "The Limits of Secularization: On the Problem of the Catholic Revival in Nineteenth-Century Germany," *The Historical Journal* 38:3 (1995), pp. 647–70. On Protestantism, see Dagmar Herzog, *Intimacy and Exclusion: Religious Politics in Pre-Revolutionary Baden* (Princeton: Princeton University Press, 1996); Gangolf Hübinger, *Kulturprotestantismus und Politik: zum Verhältnis von Liberalismus und Protestantismus im wilhelminischen Deutschland* (Tübingen: J.C.B. Mohr, 1994); Michael Gross, *The War against Catholicism: Liberalism and the Anti-Catholic Imagination in Nineteenth-Century Germany* (Ann Arbor: University of Michigan Press, 2005). A very brief but interesting account of the interaction of different confessions in an age of growing democracy can be found in Margaret Lavinia Anderson, "Afterword: Living Apart and Together in Germany," in Smith and Clark (eds.), *Protestants, Catholics and Jews in Germany*, pp. 317–31.

8   Olaf Blaschke, "Das 19. Jahrhundert: Ein Zweites Konfessionelles Zeitalter?" *Geschichte und Gesellschaft* 26 (2000), pp. 38–75; Lisa Swartout, "Culture Wars: Protestant, Catholic, and Jewish Students at German Universities, 1890–1914," in Michael Geyer and Hartmut Lehman (eds.), *Religion und Nation, Nation und Religion: Beiträge zu einer unbewältigten Geschichte* (Göttingen: Wallstein, 2004), pp. 157–75.

9   Karl Löwith, *Meaning in History: The Theological Implications of the Philosophy of History* (Chicago: University of Chicago Press, 1949); Carl Schmitt, *Political Theology: Four Chapters on the Concept of Sovereignty*, trans. George Schwab (Chicago: University of Chicago Press, 2005), p. 36.

10   Hans Blumenberg, *Legitimacy of the Modern Age*, trans. Robert Wallace (Cambridge: The MIT Press, 1983). For a more sustained treatment of Blumenberg, Löwith, and Schmitt, see Tracie Matysik, "Blumenberg's Multiple Modernities: A Spinozist Supplement to *Legitimacy of the Modern Age*, *Germanic Review*," *Germanic Review* 90:1 (2015), pp. 21–41.

11   Craig J. Calhoun, Mark Juergensmeyer, and Jonathan Van Antwerpen, "Introduction," in Calhoun, Juergensmeyer, and Van Antwerpen (eds.), *Rethinking Secularism* (New York: Oxford University Press, 2011), p. 5.

12 Blumenberg, *Legitimacy*, p. 138.

13 Charles Taylor, *A Secular Age* (Cambridge: Belknap Press, 2007), pp. 37–42.

14 Hent de Vries speaks of the post-secular, in at least one of its meanings, in complementary terms, in which a self-understood "secular" state recognizes the ongoing necessary presence of one or more religious communities in its realm. See Hent de Vries, "Introduction," in de Vries and Sullivan, *Political Theologies*, p. 3. See also the discussion between Jürgen Habermas and Taylor in Eduardo Mendieta, Jonathan Van Antwerpen, and Craig Calhoun (eds.), *The Power of Religion in the Public Sphere* (New York: Columbia University Press, 2011), pp. 15–69.

15 Wendy Brown, "Subjects of Tolerance: Why We Are Civilized and They Are the Barbarians," in de Vries and Sullivan (ed.), *Political Theologies*, pp. 298–317. See also Wendy Brown, *Regulating Aversion: Tolerance in the Age of Identity and Empire* (Princeton: Princeton University Press, 2006).

16 Saba Mahmood, *Politics of Piety: The Islamic Revival and the Feminist Subject* (Princeton: Princeton University Press, 2012), pp. xii, 1–39.

17 Talal Asad, *Genealogies of Religion: Discipline and Reasons of Power in Christianity and Islam* (Baltimore: The Johns Hopkins University Press, 1993), pp. 28–9, 48.

18 Ibid., 48–9.

19 John Locke, *Two Treatises of Government and a Letter Concerning Toleration* (New Haven: Yale University Press, 2003), p. 219.

20 Talal Asad, *Formations of the Secular: Christianity, Islam, Modernity* (Stanford: Stanford University Press, 2003).

21 The literature is vast, but good examples in addition to Asad include Russell McCutcheon, *Manufacturing Religion: The Discourse on Sui Generis Religion and the Politics of Nostalgia* (New York: Oxford University Press, 1997); Derek Peterson and Darren Walhof (eds.), *The Invention of Religion: Rethinking Belief in Politics and History* (New Brunswick, NJ: Rutgers University Press, 2002). A subtle example of history writing that illustrates the struggle between "religious" and "secular" viewpoints and their presuppositions about subject-formation is Michel de Certeau, *Possession at Loudun*, trans. Michael Smith (Chicago: University of Chicago Press, 2000).

22 Todd Weir, *Secularism and Religion in Nineteenth-Century Germany: The Rise of the Fourth Confession* (New York: Cambridge University Press, 2014), pp. 1, 12–14. See also Todd Weir, "Germany and the New Global History of Secularism: Questioning the Postcolonial Genealogy," *Germanic Review* 90:1 (2015), pp. 6–20.

23 I discuss the ethics-reform movements in more detail in Tracie Matysik, *Reforming the Moral Subject: Ethics and Sexuality in Central Europe, 1890–1930* (Ithaca: Cornell University Press, 2008).

24 David Blackbourn and Geoff Eley, *The Peculiarities of German History: Bourgeois Society and Politics in Nineteenth-Century Germany* (New York: Oxford University Press, 1984).

25 Detlev Peukert, "The Genesis of the 'Final Solution' from the Spirit of Science," in Thomas Childers and Jane Caplan (eds.), *Re-evaluating the Third Reich*

(New York: Holmes and Meier, 1993). More elaborated and subtle versions of the narrative are to be found in *Grenzen der Sozialdisziplinierung: Aufstieg und Krise der Jugendfürsorge von 1878 bis 1932* (Cologne: Bund, 1986).

26 See Young-sun Hong's essay in this volume for a thorough discussion as well as Edward Ross Dickinson, "Biopolitics, Fascism, Democracy: Reflections on Our Discourse Concerning Modernity," *Central European History* 37:1 (2004), pp. 1–48; and Kevin Repp, *Reformers, Critics, and the Paths of German Modernity: Anti-Politics and the Search for Alternatives, 1890–1914* (Cambridge: Harvard University Press, 2000).

27 Matthew Jefferies, *Imperial Culture in Germany, 1871–1918* (New York: Palgrave, 2003), p. 192.

28 Dennis Sweeney, "Reconsidering the Modernity Paradigm: Reform Movements, the Social and the State in Wilhelmine Germany," *Social History* 31:4 (2006), pp. 405–34.

29 Marjorie Lamberti, *State, Society, and the Elementary School in Imperial Germany* (New York: Oxford University Press, 1989), pp. 155–63; Marjorie Lamberti, *Jewish Activism in Imperial Germany* (New Haven: Yale University Press, 1978), pp. 126–7. For an argument against the bill on the grounds that it privileged students from "recognized religions," and thus persecuted children of nonconfessional or "dissident" orientation, see "Wir Dissidenten und der neue Volksschulgesetzes-Entwurf," *Freireligiöses Familien-Blatt* 1:3 (1892), pp. 17–18.

30 Howard B. Radest, *Felix Adler: An Ethical Culture* (New York: P. Lang, 1998), p. 10. See also James F. Hornback, "The Philosophic Sources and Sanctions of the Founders of Ethical Culture" (Ph.D. diss., Columbia University, 1983).

31 Georg von Gizycki, "Introduction," *Ethische Kultur* 1:1 (1893), p. 1.

32 Note 1 of the "Satzungen der Deutschen Gesellschaft für ethische Kultur," printed in Friedrich Wilhelm Foerster (ed.), *Einführung in die Grundgedanken der ethischen Bewegung. Zur Ausbreitung des Wirkens der Deutschen Gesellschaft für ethische Kultur* (Berlin: Deutsche Ges. für ethische Kultur, 1896), p. 3. See also Gizycki, "Introduction," p. 1; Friedrich Jodl, "Was heißt 'ethische Kultur'?" *Ethische Kultur* 1:1 (1893), p. 2.

33 Gizycki, "Introduction," p. 1.

34 See Ferdinand Tönnies, *Community and Civil Society*, trans. Jose Harris and Margaret Hollis (New York: Cambridge University Press, 2001), originally published as Ferdinand Tönnies, *Gemeinschaft und Gesellschaft. Abhandlung des Communismus und des Socialismus als empirischer Culturformen* (Leipzig: Fues, 1887).

35 Tönnies, *Community and Civil Society*, p. 182.

36 Max Weber, "Wissenschaft als Beruf," *Gesammelte Aufsätze zur Wissenschaftslehre* (Tübingen: J.C.B. Mohr, 1922), p. 536ff.; reprinted as "Science as a Vocation," in H.H. Gerth and C. Wright Mills (eds.), *From Max Weber: Essays in Sociology* (New York: Oxford University Press, 1946), p. 139ff.

37 For Tönnies's mature reflections on the problem of public opinion, see Ferdinand Tönnies, *Kritik der öffentlichen Meinung* (Berlin: J. Springer, 1922).

38 Tönnies, *Community and Civil Society*, p. 242. The parallels between Tönnies' view of public opinion and that of Jürgen Habermas are striking. See Jürgen Habermas, *The Structural Transformation of the Public Sphere: An Inquiry into the Category of Bourgeois Society*, trans. Thomas Burger and Frederick Lawrence (Cambridge, MA: The MIT Press, 1989).

39 Ferdinand Tönnies, *"Ethische Cultur" und ihre Geleite: 1) Nietzsche-Narren [in der "Zukunft" und in der "Gegenwart"]; and 2) Wölfe in Fuchspelzen* (Berlin: Ferd. Dümmlers Verlagsbuchhandlung, 1893); Ferdinand Tönnies, "Die ethische Bewegung," *Die Umschau* III (1899), pp. 842–5.

40 On the popularization of science, see Andreas Daum, *Wissenschaftspopularisierung im 19. Jahrhundert: Bürgerliche Kultur, naturwissenschaftliche Bildung und die deutsche Öffentlichkeit 1848–1914*, 2nd edn (Munich: Oldenbourg, 2002).

41 Adolf Stöcker, "Vereine und Kongresse," *Deutsche Evangelische Kirchenzeitung* 6:44 (1892), pp. 428–9.

42 Eugen Heinrich Schmitt, *Warum ist eine religiöse Bewegung Notwendigkeit? Ein Wort an die 'Gesellschaften für ethische Kultur* (Leipzig: Tanssen, 1892), p. 5.

43 Ibid., p. 7.

44 Georg von Gizycki (ed.), *Mitteilungen der Deutschen Gesellschaft für ethische Kultur* (Berlin: Ferd. Dümmler, 1892), pp. 20–1.

45 Tönnies, *Community and Civil Society*, pp. 105, 134.

46 Ernst Haeckel, "Ethik und Weltanschauung," *Die Zukunft* 1 (1892), p. 310.

47 Ibid., p. 310.

48 Ernst Haeckel, *Die Welträtsel: Gemeinverständliche Studien über monistische Philosophie* (Leipzig: Alfred Kröner, 1909), pp. 203, 208, 240.

49 A good discussion is Gangolf Hübinger, *Kulturprotestantismus und Politik: Zum Verhältnis von Liberalismus und Protestantismus im wilhelmischen Deutschland* (Tübingen: Mohr Siebeck, 1994).

50 Schmitt, *Warum ist eine religiöse Bewegung Notwendigkeit?* p. 4.

51 Foerster outlined the major theses of his argument in "Die Grenzen des bloßen Verstandes in Fragen der Lebens- und Menschenkenntnis," *Ethische Kultur* 13:1 (January 1905), pp. 3–4. He followed up his initial foray with comments in "Sprechsaal," *Ethische Kultur* 13:3 (1905), pp. 22–3; in "Sprechsaal," *Ethische Kultur* 13:6 (1905), p. 47; and "Erklärung," *Ethische Kultur* 13:12 (1905), pp. 93–4.

52 Staudinger elaborated the main points of his argument in Franz Staudinger, "Das Gemüt und die Wahrheit," *Ethische Kultur* 12:22 (1904), pp. 171–2; he followed up with further comments in "Sprechsaal," *Ethische Kultur* 13:2 (1905), pp. 15–16; and in "Sprechsaal," *Ethische Kultur* 13:4 (1905), pp. 30–1.

53 Foerster, "Erklärung," pp. 93–4.

54 Ibid.

55 Helmut Walser Smith, *German Nationalism and Religious Conflict: Culture, Ideology, Politics 1870–1914* (Princeton: Princeton University Press, 1995), pp. 117–27. On *Sammlungspolitik*, see Hans-Ulrich Wehler, *The German Empire, 1871–1918*, trans. Kim Traynor (Leamington Spa, UK: Berg, 1985), pp. 94–9. On organized forms of anti-Catholicism and the *Kulturkampf*, see Michael B. Gross, "Kulturkampf and Unification: German Liberalism and the War against the Jesuits," *Central European History* 30:4 (1997), pp. 545–66; and Gross, *The War against Catholicism*.

56 Lamberti, *State, Society, and the Elementary School*, pp. 161, 177–209.

57 On the brochures and publications, see, for example, *Konfessionelle oder Weltliche Schule? 3 Ansprachen in der Deutschen Gesellschaft f. ethische Kultur (Abt. Berlin) 14. Okt. 1904* (Berlin: Verlag für ethische Kultur, 1904). The branch founded the periodical *Weltliche Schule*, which ran from 1906 to 1920. Rudolf Penzig gave a first-hand account of the founding of the organization and the periodical in "Was haben wir getan?" *Deutsche Liga für weltliche Schule und Moralunterricht* 1:1 (1906), pp. 1–2.

58 Frank Simon-Ritz, *Die Organisation einer Weltanschauung: Die freigeistige Bewegung im wilhelminischen Deutschland* (Gütersloh: Chr. Kaiser/Gütersloh Verlagshaus, 1997), p. 132.

59 *Protokoll des siebenten ordentlichen Gesellschaftstages der Deutschen Gesellschaft für ethische Kultur 7* (Berlin: Siebenmark, 1903), pp. 7, 9. See also the discussion in Simon-Ritz, *Organisation einer Weltanschauung*, pp. 106–08.

60 A good discussion is Friedrich Wilhelm Graf, "The German Theological Sources and Protestant Church Politics," in Guenther Roth (ed.), *Weber's Protestant Ethic: Origins, Evidence, Contexts* (New York: Cambridge University Press, 1993), pp. 27–49.

11

War, Citizenship, and Rhetorics of Sexual Crisis: Reflections on States of Exception in Germany, 1914–20

Kathleen Canning

Introduction

The German defeat, revolution, and convening of a republic in 1918–20 mark a prolonged state of exception, in which the Kaiser's rule collapsed and competing sites of governmentality—revolutionary and republican—sprung up in its place.[1] The suspension of state power, its dissemination into the spheres of the public, and its reappropriation by that public in the winter of 1918–19 also signaled the end of another state of exception—the state of siege on the German home front, initiated in August 1914 and expanded into a military dictatorship by the summer of 1917.[2] This essay examines the social and political imaginary of citizenship that transformed the wartime state of exception into another—the provisional rule of the revolutionary councils that seized power in November 1918. The convening of new parties and new voters for democratic elections in early 1919 called upon citizens to imagine and institute new forms of political representation, thus replacing the emergency rule of institutions steeped in tradition—the Hohenzollern monarchy and the military—with new forms of governance built on republican citizenship.

If the mobilization of German civilians in defense of the *nation* and their apparent consent to the *Burgfrieden* and the Law of Siege constituted the opening acts in the wartime state of exception, their gradual withdrawal of this consent through everyday acts of disavowal and protest infused prewar visions and claims of citizenship with new demands for material goods, like bread, coal, and higher wages that intermingled with desires for new forms of political representation and participation and for peace without annexations.[3] Citizenship was increasingly imagined as the currency in which the state would recompense both civilians and soldiers for the burdens it had asked them to bear. If historians of the First World War are correct in viewing the mass mobilization of Germans in 1914 as successfully congealing a divided people into a nation for at least the war's first months, it is just as important to note the mutability of those identifications, which fueled new claims and expectations of nation and state as the war extracted ever more from both soldiers and civilians. If August 1914 saw "new social formations organized around a national identity," as Peter Fritzsche has argued, the capacity of the nation to contain those identifications broke down in the course of the war, fissured along the lines of class, gender, generation, and political affinity.[4] Citizenship took the form of mass demonstrations for bread, suffrage, and peace, articulating an excess of claims, identifications, and expectations that undermined the state's capacity to govern and attested to the readiness of citizens to act in its place.

The new rhetorics and identifications of citizenship drew everyday actors into the process of reimagining Germany—politically, culturally, and spatially. Germany had entered the war with citizenship—most notably the Prussian three-class suffrage—as one of the crucially unresolved dilemmas of Germany's modernity, one that bore directly upon the relations between the Wilhelmine state and the expanding civic publics, most notably that of working-class Social Democracy. With this dilemma only temporarily suspended by the "truce of the fortress," the significance of the suffrage question sharpened in the course of the war; in fact, suffrage reform was the foremost issue in the Kaiser's "Easter decree" of April 1917.[5] While the stakes of the long-term Social Democratic campaign against the Prussian three-class suffrage involved the citizenship rights of working-class men, in the course of the First World War, women came to occupy a more visible and controversial place in the discussions of *Staatsbürgertum* as one desired outcome of the war.

As such, citizenship became a vital part of the imagination of the future: from 1916 on, with no quick end in sight, planning for the war's aftermath became a crucial strategy, not only of military and state bureaucracies, but also of mobilized civilians, whose claims as citizens were still cognizant of prewar inequalities of class and gender but more explicitly embedded in their experiences of the wartime state of exception. Social reformers, intellectuals, and feminists active in the National Women's Service (*Nationaler Frauendienst*) pointed to the state's reliance upon the female "army" on the home front, highlighting its contribution to the war efforts as irreversible proof of women's readiness for the citizenship rights that radical, liberal, and socialist women's organizations had pursued since the turn of the century. At the same time, conservative military and medical authorities interpreted the calls for female suffrage as further evidence of a festering sexual crisis, the symptoms of which included the plummeting birthrate, rising rates of venereal disease, and rampant female promiscuity on the home front.[6] Fears and expectations that the conduct of total war both relied upon women and rendered them ungovernable—politically and sexually—became one of the ironies of the particular "modernities" of the First World War and an essential aspect of the contested futures of the war's aftermath.

Visions of citizenship and the state of exception on the home front

If the question of participatory political rights for women had preoccupied and divided the German women's movement from the mid-1890s on, radical and socialist feminists, organized into three different associations, waged a particularly vigorous campaign on the eve of the First World War for female suffrage.[7] While most German women's rights organizations suspended their campaigns upon the outbreak of war, some radical suffragists turned to pacifism and internationalism, situating their citizenship claims in an international context and firmly rejecting the necessity for war.[8] The home front became a virtual laboratory of citizenship, even as most feminist organizations subordinated their onetime suffrage claims to wartime service.[9] As suffrage claims became audible again in 1917–18, they drew readily upon the rhetorics of prewar suffrage campaigns regarding women's claims to equal political participation. As the intensifying war efforts transformed the daily lives of ever-widening circles of German women, the ranks of those envisioning and claiming capacity for citizenship swelled considerably beyond the groups of prewar suffrage advocates. Elisabeth Zillken, active in the circles of Catholic social reform, offered an outline of German women's new obligations as citizens (*Staatsbürgerpflichten*) in 1916, noting that the war was taking a bloody toll not only on working women but also on women whose main task was running the household in wartime. Suggesting that before the war women had not fully grasped the contexts and connections between their own "little households" and the broader arenas of state politics, Zillken took stock of women's readiness for citizenship: "If only we had understood in time, the importance of raising *Staatsbürgerinnen*, then much would have been easier, then we would now have better citizens."[10] Suggesting that the war had left no space in which citizenship remained irrelevant, Zillken emphasized that the "family is no longer a closed circle unto itself; rather hundreds of threads connect it to public life and draw its individual members out [into the public.]"[11] In

the pages of the monthly *Die Staatsbürgerin*, Dr. Ilse Reicke pointed to
the new realms of female expertise as incubators of citizenship: patriotic
and s*taatsbürgerliche* activities grew out of the knowledge and experience
women gained in contending with the effects of the war, the work of
"bandaging the wounded soldiers, caring for the crippled, comforting
the widows, helping the orphans, rebuilding the destroyed homes…"[12]
Dr. Marie Baum, a former factory inspector, suggested in a similar vein
that the field hospitals and lazaretts had become schools of both social
expertise and citizenship for female volunteers, noting the urgent need to
"politicize the life forces"—the people's health, nutrition, and education—
by training those who oversee them.[13] Not only had new spaces opened
on the home front for middle-class women to supervise the sphere of the
social, but the war also dissolved all divides between private households
and political economy, individuals and nation-state, prompting middle-
class women to reimagine the terms of their participation in both politics
and the social.

Female activists in the Social Democratic milieu issued claims for
citizenship rights in terms that acknowledged both women's contribution to
war efforts and their growing opposition to the war. Social Democratic Party
activist Luise Zietz, who would join the antiwar Independent Socialists when
the party split in 1917, emphasized that women who bore no responsibility
for the decision to declare war were nonetheless forced to carry its economic,
social, and political burdens. Although Zietz had supported female suffrage
before the war, her own participation in female relief work led her to
conclude that the war had delivered abundant evidence of women's capacity
for citizenship.[14] In her view the war had politicized women's relationships
to state, society, law, and administration, compelling them in the absence of
formal citizenship rights to seek redress for their hardships by taking to the
streets.

Unlike her middle-class compatriots, Zietz did not imagine a citizenship
cast in terms of morality or sentiment; rather class inequalities were in
the forefront of the citizenship she sought to enact. Addressing poor and
working-class women as future citizens, Zietz castigated the subtle and
disenfranchising hierarchies that underwrote wartime social welfare,
especially the practice of subjecting war wives and widows to tests of
their "need and worthiness" (*Bedürftigkeit* and *Würdigkeit*). State social
assistance was a social right, she claimed, not an act of benevolence or
charity, nor did it represent a "hand-out" from rich to poor.[15] Rather than
a barrier to citizenship rights or a marker of second-class citizenship, the
right of soldiers' families to claim and receive social benefits in wartime
was intrinsic to citizenship. Soldiers' wives, Zietz noted, should enjoy
rights that were firmly anchored in law (*gesetzlich garantiert*) and should
represent both a material and symbolic remuneration for the "ghastly
circumstances" war widows and wives endured, including their own
bodily vulnerabilities in wartime.[16] Furthermore, Zietz drew an intriguing

connection between the political and social rights women lacked on the home front and the precarious citizenship of working-class men, including soldiers at the front. One stark example thereof was the decision of local magistrates to strip soldiers of their voting rights when their pregnant wives applied for public assistance to pay the midwives' fees for delivery and postpartum care:

> We deprive our husbands of their right to vote if we seek expert help for our difficult hours [of childbearing]...We can scarcely bear to imagine our soldiers' response to hearing from their wives that they are losing their right to vote because of their very service in defense of the fatherland.[17]

Zietz underlined the citizenship claims of soldiers' wives by highlighting the fragility of their husbands' rights and noting how quickly working-class men, even soldiers in the trenches, could become dependents of the state in a time of emergency.[18] Recounting her own advocacy on behalf of those soldiers and their families, Zietz noted that the Interior Ministry subsequently resolved to cover midwifery services at no cost to soldiers' wives and to refrain from reclassifying soldiers' citizenship status in such cases. As this example reveals, class inflected wartime visions of citizenship but did not remain bound by the identification of class with "productive labor" or by the sharp distinctions between factory and family that underwrote Social Democratic Party and union politics before the war.

While the languages of *staatsbürgerliche Rechte/Staatsbürgertum* proliferated in the circles of both the bourgeois and social democratic women's movements, female workers and war widows constituted two additional social groups whose citizenship claims became increasingly vociferous after the winter of 1916.[19] The class-infused rhetorics of citizenship reverberated in the strikes of April 1917 and January 1918, in which hundreds of thousands of mobilized civilians called for an end to the militarized state of exception and the right to vote, along with an immediate armistice and the provision of food and coal.[20] Observers' accounts mention the overwhelming presence of women in these strikes, who appeared not only as supporters on the sidelines but often as strike leaders who demonstrated "the greatest courage and determination."[21] It is notable that the strike movements of 1917–18, in contrast to the protests over food and coal of 1915–16, raised demands for "fundamental reforms of the entire system."[22]

As women were drawn into much more direct subjection to and surveillance by the German state, especially after 1916, the potential for a sharpened consciousness of citizenship advanced. Flash points included the state's own escalating attempts to ascertain and assign female capacities for labor, childbearing, or national service within the new political economy of the home front. Female civilians could scarcely ignore the state's own desire to render women identifiable, accessible, and deployable, whether through appeals to the patriotism of female volunteers, the intensified scrutiny of the sexual behavior of soldiers' wives, or the contemplation of coercive measures like the forced "detention" (*Kasernierung*) of urgently needed female laborers for agricultural work.[23] New spaces of consciousness, negotiation, and subversion emerged as female civilians became more cognizant of their own indispensability to the militarized state. Despite the detrimental conditions of work in wartime factories, female workers seemed eager to learn new skills and earn higher wages, even while recognizing that their jobs were transitory. Yet the abandonment of protective measures at a time when the need for female labor was most acute opened other possibilities for distancing and critique, not least because the war on the home front began to reveal its own bodily perils, from unrestricted work hours to the handling of toxic powders and chemical ammunition components that sometimes singed or yellowed the skin and hair.[24]

The effects of censorship and of restrictions on women's right to assemble under military rule served as repeated reminders of the participatory political rights they lacked. These circumscriptions of civil rights inhibited more than potential political criticism of the war, but also stifled the sociability of survival on the home front—the exchanges of information that took place as women bargained on the black market or waited in line for bread, milk, or eggs, or as they traded news of troop movements or reports of the fallen. Strategies for managing the material and psychic challenges of everyday life were, in fact, on the agenda of many of the women's assemblies that the authorities banned, for example, seventeen meetings planned for March 1915 on "Women's Worries in Wartime" (*Frauensorgen in der Kriegszeit*) or several others that were to address "War and Profiteering in Food" (*Krieg und Lebensmittelwucher*) in May 1915.[25] That same summer, Luise Zietz drew this same connection between women's absent rights of political participation and their capacity to manage the dire circumstances of wartime when she asked,

> How much longer can women, who have demonstrated their political maturity, their capacity for citizenship to such a high degree, be deprived of the political rights that are increasingly indispensable in the face of the hardships they face?

If the privations of the home front constituted crucial lessons of citizenship during the war, activists like Zietz could anticipate their even greater impact at the war's end, when millions of German women would likely confront the impossibility of a longer-term reliance upon husbands as providers. The rights of citizenship, she noted, would be of even greater importance for war widows and single mothers, suggesting a crucial connection between political rights and the social and economic right to work and to state protection and welfare provision for working women, mothers, and children.[26]

Visions of citizenship as "feminization": Anticipating the aftermath of war

As the prosecution of war on the home front came to hinge ever more upon the mobilization and cooperation of German women, the scope of the state was trained more sharply on female civilians. As female workers acquired new skills and higher wages in sectors of industry that had been exclusively male, as they assumed men's union posts or donned their uniforms as streetcar drivers or mail carriers, they became more conscious of their own capacity to transgress previously held presumptions about women's natural inclinations and capacities in the realms of work, politics, households, and neighborhoods. Interestingly, this changing consciousness was seldom explicitly spoken or celebrated. Rather, it most often was expressed as a sober acknowledgment of new skills and capacities gained necessarily through the war's insatiable demand for women workers in crucial industrial sectors, especially armaments. While female reformers and activists recognized women's presence in the wartime workforce as part of the wartime state of exception, the perception of these changes as emancipatory is absent in their accounts.[27]

Interestingly, the trope of female emancipation emerges in the wartime writings of conservatives and nationalists, who interpreted feminization—of the population, the labor force, of mobilized publics on the home front—as fostering an inexorable emancipatory dismantling of gender ideologies and sexual hierarchies. Military and medical authorities, for example, assessed the dangers of a quantitative "feminization" of the German population, measuring male loss of life against the imminent certainty of a "female population surplus."[28] The preoccupation with feminization also focused on the alleged "excesses" of women's behavior in wartime, often linking the unbridled consumption and indulgence in luxury goods to young women's propensity for sexual promiscuity and marital infidelity.[29] Soldiers' wives, supported by state pensions, were the most frequent object of this concern with female governability.

Although citizenship did constitute a new language of politics during the war, the visions and claims it produced were changeable and often contradictory. From the official enactment of military rule, the suspension of civil and political rights among soldiers and civilians and the day-to-day crises in the provisioning of food, coal, and medicine, the wartime state of emergency lent citizenship a new resonance as a language of participation, one that helped shape the outlines of a republic that came into sharper view after the Kaiser's "Easter message" of 1917. While Social Democratic and radical pacifist activists spoke a language of rights, attaching their notions of citizenship to the end of the *Kaiserreich* and the inception of a democratic form of governance, the Protestant middle-class women's movement, which had opposed female suffrage before the war, embraced the idea of female citizens as *Staatstragende*, as future "carriers of the state" whose participation would be vital to the restoration of the nation in the aftermath of war.

At the same time, the more the state recognized and relied upon women's capacities on the home front, the greater was the apprehension of nationalists and conservatives about female *Staatsbürgertum*, whether in the guise of rights or duties.[30] For conservatives, women's citizenship loomed as a most drastic consequence of democratization, which after 1916 seemed an increasingly likely outcome of the war.[31] The state's dependence on female labor deepened with the passage of the "Hindenburg Law" (Auxiliary Service Law), fueling conservative fears that female intrusion into male industrial sectors would prove irreversible after the war. The Reichstag's Committee for Industry and Trade (*Ausschuss für Handel und Gewerbe*), for example, began to outline the process of demobilization in 1916, spurred perhaps in part, as Ute Planert argues, by the petition campaign of the League to Combat the Emancipation of Women that ultimately garnered over 300,000 signatures against female employment in "men's professions" (*Männerberufen*).[32]

Already in 1915 the highest level ministers and military commanders had begun to calculate the effects of mass mortality among men of reproductive age (*zeugungsfähige deutsche Männer*), prompting natalist appeals to women to help staunch the wartime loss of life. The nationalist right infused its rhetorics against feminization with a sense of foreboding about the future of the German family in the face of widespread "sexual demoralization," a term that entwined fears about plummeting rates of marriage and birth with worries about epidemics of venereal disease, infertility, and rampant female promiscuity.[33] By 1917–18, this search for remedial measures became increasingly desperate, as military doctors and district commanders, noting the declining rates of marriage and birth, sought to counter both population loss and "feminization of society" by tightening the scrutiny of soldiers' wives and sharpening the penalties for dissemination of information about birth control and abortion.[34]

Pronatalism was reinvigorated not only in the bureaucracies of military and state, but also in the tendency of the League and other right-wing activists to hold German women responsible for the "demographic compensation that the massive death of our people requires." They called for a "fundamental reckoning with the political associations of the women's movement" that favored the development of "free personalities" over the "duty to conceive and raise children."[35] Calling up the memory of the birth-strike debate of 1912 that had preoccupied and divided female Social Democrats on the eve of the war, right-wing activists of the League alleged that radical feminists and socialist critics of the war relied upon female informational networks to disseminate birth control information on the home front.[36] In 1916, the newly founded *Gesellschaft für Bevölkerungspolitik* (Association for Population Policy) convened a conference on the topic of population policy and the question of female labor, which explored the practicability of compulsory measures or sanctions to address the apparent indifference of German women to pronatalist propaganda.[37]

Other preoccupations of wartime population policy were the soaring rates of venereal disease that often originated in brothels at the front and was then passed from soldiers to their wives during home leaves, as well as worry about the availability and use of contraceptives on the part of both women and men. The relationship between venereal disease and birth control was obvious to medical authorities, who determined in 1918 that at least 800,000 soldiers were afflicted with venereal disease, of whom one-third were married men.[38] At the same time, authorities pointed to a declining marital fertility rate and to statistics indicating that many married women who had experienced infertility, miscarriages, or stillbirths had been infected with venereal disease. In one study conducted in Berlin in 1918, 304 of the 451 married women who had never been pregnant (67.3 percent) were infected with gonorrhea, while a similar percentage of 378 women who had only borne one child or had suffered miscarriages suffered from "infections of the reproductive organs" that were likely consequences of venereal disease.[39] While the "Committee on Population Policy" of the German Reichstag met in ten sessions in 1918 to address the urgent identification and treatment of venereal disease "among the troops and the entire population," it concluded at the same time that the "inhibition of conception" should now become an offense punishable by law.[40]

The virtual obsession with female reproductivity prompted energetic responses from feminists across the political spectrum. In the second volume of *Die sexuelle Krise*, Gretel Meisel-Hess commented sardonically on the "endless sea of words that poured out on the question of the population loss already in the second winter of the war," and on the scapegoating of the women's movement regarding the declining birthrate:

> Although the zealots have thrown themselves into imposing on our dejected people a national enthusiasm for bearing children, the sentiments and the social and economic prerequisites are entirely lacking at present. Never has the sexual drive, purely instinctually, diminished or constrained itself so fully, more than now when the fields of corpses stretch endlessly before us, when these sites of battle are fertilized with the cadavers of the most robust masculinity of our people. And we at home should think about making love, conceiving or birthing children under these conditions?[41]

In a different vein and in terms reminiscent of the birth-strike debate of the prewar years, Social Democratic activists also decried the "sentencing of women to compulsory child-bearing" as a likely outcome of the proposed criminalization of the dissemination and sale of contraceptives.[42] Yet now at the height of mobilization for female citizenship, during the winter and spring of 1918, the right to bodily integrity and reproductive self-determination acquired new meanings as crucial prerequisites for the exercise of political rights. Indeed, the state's interpellation of women's bodies as the source at which the recovery of lost "human material" must begin only served to heighten women's attention to the bodily transformations of wartime and to the significance of their bodies as potential sites of citizenship.[43] As the trenches swallowed ever larger numbers of soldiers, military planners nervously deliberated plans for the war's aftermath, casting the reinstatement of the shattered gender order as an urgent necessity.[44] The recognition that the "woman question" would be a "problem that may be impossible to solve" after the war, particularly if women gained suffrage rights, fueled the efforts of nationalist groups, such as the League to Combat the Emancipation of Women, to portray female suffrage and sexual self-determination as a force that "eats away at the marrow of our people in a much more insidious way than any other danger that currently threatens us."[45]

The declining birthrate, women's employment in "male industries," and the excesses of consumption and sexuality were indisputable focal points of anti-feminist mobilizations in wartime, when military planners resolutely anticipated a German victory. Nationalists and military authorities castigated female protesters on the home front, whether in bread lines or munitions factories, for violating the terms of the *Burgfrieden* (civil truce) of 1914. In the last years of the war, as the ideological ground for the stab-in-the-back legend was laid, pacifist feminists and socialists were increasingly maligned in terms that anticipated later charges of civilian betrayal of men at the front, even if gender has scarcely figured as a significant dimension of this legend's ideological potency.[46] Planert's study makes clear that even prior to "the new orientation" of 1917, which begrudgingly acknowledged that some form of democratization would almost certainly follow the war's end, antifeminists had come to regard female suffrage as a peril to a postwar gender settlement: "What kind of reward should the soldiers receive, if the female civilians at home are compensated with the right to vote?" asked one official of the *Antifeministische Liga* in early 1917.[47] A few months later, with the "new orientation" in full swing, the Bund's monthly journal aligned female suffrage with the dangers of a postwar democracy. The Bund warned that "thoroughgoing 'feminization' and 'democratization' would issue the death blow to our German heroes and to the German Reich."[48] Between these two assessments of the outcomes of suffrage reform a none-too-subtle shift occurs from the initial implication that the granting of female suffrage would impinge upon or nullify the rewards owed to returning soldiers, to the more drastic prediction that the conjoined processes of "feminization" and "democratization" could deliver a "death blow" both to the legacy of soldiers' heroism and to the Reich itself. Confronting the specter of feminization and democratization of citizenship rights in 1917, one inventive county administrator (*Oberregierungsrat*) from Oldenburg proposed a novel solution that was meant to circumvent the prospect of equal suffrage for *both* women *and* men of the lower classes. While the marital status and numbers of children had always been "a private matter of individual citizens" (*Privatsache der einzelnen Staatsbürger*), this official suggested that male heads of households (*Familienoberhäupte*) be accorded "a second vote, which they should submit on behalf of the rest of their (non-voting) family members," while fathers of four or more children should even be eligible to cast a third vote.

> This principle, which recognizes one form of female suffrage, must be upheld in the conduct of all public elections, in order to offer good faith recognition to heads of families, and especially to fathers of many children, for the contribution they have made to all of us (*die Gesamtheit*) by granting them greater participatory rights. This would mark the first step towards a new legal code that aims to strengthen the family as the most vital foundation of the state.[49]

This fantasy of a familial citizenship, which incorporated "one form of female suffrage" through the vote cast by husbands and fathers on behalf of their family members, also belongs to the imaginary of citizenship that took shape during the war. Against the backdrop of the surging and seemingly irreversible "surplus" of women, and the expanding public presence of women in protests on the home front, the individual participatory rights of women came to symbolize not only female dominance but also their unpredictability as a political force in the incipient democracy.

Citizenship under exceptional circumstances: Revolution

As the end of the war neared, the maneuvering toward tangible rather than envisioned citizenship intensified. Local governments deliberated the desirability of women's communal political rights, while radical suffragists, Social Democrats, and members of the Federation of German Women's Associations (BDF) put aside party and class differences in the interest of renewed efforts in favor of female suffrage. The fervor intensified as voter assemblies took place across Germany throughout the spring and summer of 1918; by fall, efforts to school future citizens were underway, with handbooks, courses, and assemblies offering *staatsbürgerliche Erziehung* (citizenship education) to women who would soon exercise "influence on the political and social reshaping of Germany."[50] Yet the last months before the revolution were replete with setbacks: In May 1918, a large majority in the Prussian *Abgeordnetenhaus* rejected equal suffrage in Prussia. On November 2, 1918, women's associations of different political persuasions sought an audience with the new chancellor, Prince Max von Baden, in order to present their demands for the realization of "political freedom and self-determination" for women, "who, also in Germany, have fought for political equality for decades."[51]

The arrival of citizenship coincided with the disaster of the German defeat and the bewilderment and exhilaration that followed the revolution and collapse of the *Kaiserreich*. While many contemporaries viewed the ascription of citizenship rights as an inevitable, even a just reward, granted to women and workers in return for and in recognition of their profound sacrifices for the war effort, others noted that the legal proclamation of citizenship rights was a necessary concession to the revolutionary movements, and thus represented a vital step toward ending the revolution and achieving social peace. Yet 1918–19 marks a turning point not least because the spaces for citizenship widened within every political milieu and party, and also because feminists were eager to experience citizenship, to prove themselves as citizens at a time when the state had to be rebuilt and the nation had come apart at the seams.[52]

Indeed some feminists disavowed all responsibility for the disastrous war and defeat, defining themselves as citizens who were unencumbered by the past and thus better able to envision a wholly new future than men.[53] Women were called to the "deathbed of the fatherland," noted Social Democrat Adele Schreiber in 1918, even though they bore no blame for the long and murderous war. Effecting a figurative departure from the nation in order to embrace the emergent republic, Schreiber evoked not only the male graves but also the grief of German women as the foundation of the "new Germany":

> The new Germany has emerged under conditions that differ from those we had anticipated: it is founded namely on the deaths of almost two million men. Two million graves of our strong men: what female suffering does this embody, what anguish on the part of mothers, soldiers' wives and their betrothed, their daughters and sisters! Germany is drained, impoverished, a plaything for the retribution and loathing of its opponents! And in these grim times women gain the right to vote![54]

The resolute refusal of Reichstag and military authorities to offer concessions on women's citizenship rights in the last months of the war, at the height of suffrage and antiwar campaigns, explains in part why the declaration of female suffrage seemed "to fall overnight from a storm cloud" and was described by many contemporaries as a shock.[55] Even the politically experienced Agnes von Harnack, who was thirty when the war began, served in the *Nationaler Frauendienst* during the war, and joined the DDP after the revolution, expressed incomprehension about the sudden inception of female suffrage:

> The end of the great war, which women endured silently, patiently, helping and healing throughout, has fundamentally and thoroughly transformed their position in public life. An event, which is impossible to write about today and the consequences of which remain unforeseen,

made women citizens with a dash of a pen, with a mere announcement in the daily paper ... [56]

Those conservative women who only reluctantly accepted the burden of citizenship for the good of the nation in 1918 were particularly distressed by its revolutionary inception. In a retrospective of 1921, Emma Föllmer remembered,

> The revolution dropped the right to vote in our laps. Many of us had not aspired to it, and some did not desire it at all. It was unexpected but swept us up like a torrent, from which came the captain's call: all men on board! [sic][57]

Even if many middle-class or nationalist women accepted the burden of citizenship, they expressed ambivalence about the sudden inception of rights, particularly under revolutionary circumstances. The right to vote, Harnack contended, must be viewed as "a gift, for we cannot call it an achievement" as only a minority of women had embraced this right before the war. "What was once merely a dream," Harnack noted—and not necessarily a "beautiful dream"—had now become a sober reality.[58]

The evident puzzlement and ambivalence among influential feminists to the proclamation of equal suffrage makes clear that no one, including female voters themselves, were quite sure of the consequences of the female vote for Germany's momentary crisis or political future. The pages of newspapers and political journals are replete with speculation on these very topics. Swirling through these sources is the palpable sense that the real work of defining citizenship and making it meaningful had only just begun in 1918: "The break with those who held power until now does not bring our task to an end," noted one contributor to the journal, *Die Frauenbewegung*: "Rather we are standing at the edge of something totally new which we must now create."[59] Female activists took note—some somberly, some with exhilaration—of the significance of the female demographic majority (*Frauenüberschuss*) in the voting booths. Marie von Bunsen's article, "Wir Wählerinnen," pointed to the responsibilities of female voters:

> The challenge we face is enormous. According to current estimates (we are) 55 percent of all voters; literally the fate of the National Assembly, of the German Reich, has been placed in the hands of women.[60]

Agnes von Harnack pointed to the "extraordinary responsibility ... the solemn duty" that now rested with the 40 million new voters, including 18.5 million men and 21.5 million women.

> Women represent a majority of three million and will, in fact, decide the outcomes of the elections ... And what it actually means to

decide the election becomes evident if we examine three of the major arenas that span both public and private life. Women will decide the future constitution of the German Reich; they will participate in future determinations of our foreign policy, our treaties and alliances with foreign peoples, and decisions regarding war and peace. In making this very clear, we call up once again that entire sea of blood and tears through which we have wandered these last four years. A decisive role in the future legislation will belong to women and they will finally be in a position to participate in deciding the issues of concern to them.[61]

Conjuring up the worst fears of the antifeminists, Agnes von Harnack suggested that the impact of the female vote crisscrossed the spheres of private and public and endowed women with a particular, formative agency not only in shaping the founding of the new republic, but also in determining the terms of war and peace against the backdrop of mourning, of "that entire sea of blood and tears," which appears as a particularly feminine trope of politics in the immediate aftermath of war.[62] The sum of these consequential duties, in Harnack's view, was a "thorough upheaval in the relationships of power between men and women" that would unleash in women the potential and even more, the obligation to saturate "a state founded by men with the influence of women."[63] In order to fulfill this call, Harnack argued that "the woman does not belong primarily in the home, but at every location where she can inform herself about questions of public life, party platforms, election formats and similar matters."[64] With this she offered a concise definition of participatory citizenship for women. Dr. Rosa Kempf underscored that the prospects for democratic self-governance hinged upon women's participation in the upcoming elections:

> The advancement of all of the people requires the participation of women in the self-governance of the people. For women should have the right to decide about the forms and structures in which they live and work and by which they want to be governed.[65]

The emphasis on *unterrichten* (instruction) and *selbst entscheiden* (deciding for themselves) echoed the widespread sense among female activists, both middle class and Social Democratic, that the masses of new female citizens urgently required schooling in order to practice participatory citizenship. It seemed self-evident to them that after all of these years of training for participatory citizenship, feminists were competent and capable of offering their own short course in citizenship to women with lesser political experience. As Social Democrat Adele Schreiber asserted in 1918,

> Millions of women, who had no knowledge of politics, are now in need of enlightenment. Until now the training of young women for citizenship has been utterly neglected. And at this point the training period that

remains for German women is terribly brief. "Learn to vote!" is the slogan of the day. But it is very difficult to learn to be a voter in such a short time, for that means becoming a conscious citizen with the capacity for independent judgment. And now begins the massive competition of all of the parties for the woman voter![66]

Yet at the same time even the Liberal Democratic Party (DDP) found it necessary to place the education and mobilization of the new female voters in the hands of men. Schreiber's private notes on her many speeches from this time period refer to one of the first election appeals of the DDP as calling upon *Deutsche Familienvater*! (German fathers!) with the following assurance:

> You will not need to change your standing in your domestic circle. Remain just the person you were and are now, but bring your wife and your daughter to the ballot box, even if it you are quite unaccustomed to parleying politics with them.[67]

Underlying the pragmatic question of 1918–19 about who would educate new women voters, or lead them to the polls, was the much more fundamental issue of whether participatory citizenship would fundamentally transform women and men or the relationships between them. These worries were articulated amid the disruptions of demobilization and the economic displacement of women, an issue over which the interests of women were sharply divided from those of men. If the dismissal of women workers from "men's jobs" had seemed self-evident during the war, once women actually *became citizens* a disjuncture suddenly appeared between their political and economic rights. Ironically, one of the tasks of new female citizens and their first elected representatives in the Reichstag was to prevent demobilization from "turning the political emancipation of women into a farce" by allowing their "economic servitude."[68] As Germany's first female factory inspector and later member of the Reichstag, Marie Baum (DDP) observed in 1919:

> If the examples from sectors of female industrial employment are any indication, we cannot fail to mention that hostility to women makes itself felt in every sector. I think that I may speak in the name of all German women in saying that we are in no sense unaware of the necessity of making jobs available to returning soldiers, as well as to the injured war veterans. In order to achieve this, we should look not only to working women, but also to those men who were not direct participants in the war. But this did not take place. Instead, universities closed their doors to women; teaching positions held by women were reassigned to men; women who had completed several years as apprentices in the rail system were told that there was no prospect for a job and to change their careers. If we immerse ourselves in their accounts, we encounter exceptional

hardships in individual cases and in some even complete economic collapse, along with incomparable emotional bitterness. For anyone who does not regard the term "Beruf" (calling) a hollow term can understand that it is unacceptable to rip people ruthlessly out of their professions (job).[69]

Baum's critique not only seeks to expose the hostility to women that became palpable during the demobilization process, but emphasizes as well the emotional and professional identifications of female workers and women professionals with their jobs. Her attention to the gendered constraints of the economic right to work might be read against the backdrop of women's new rights of equal political participation; both were inscribed in the Weimar Constitution.

Reordering gender:
Citizenship inscribed in law

The perception that the gender order had ruptured at the end of the war forms an important backdrop for the writing and enactment of citizenship in 1919–20. The task of fashioning a new state, new terms of governance, also compelled these newly mobilized and newly identified citizens to quickly set about the task of normalization, of overcoming this state of exception, not least through the process of writing citizenship into law (constitution) and mobilizing citizens to authorize the enactment of this constitution through voting. Indeed, the ability of citizenship to "interpret or even contain ... distress or discontent within the terms of its political language"[70] rested on its promise to *reorder* the relations between state and civil, military and civilian, men and women, and to envision a future after the catastrophe, in which the naming of new citizens became a crucial first step. A key site of this impulse to reorder, to put an end to the state of exception, took place in the National Assembly, which sought to transcend the ruptures of war and revolution, to pry citizenship from the social spaces that had made its declaration possible, and to restore it to the realm of the state. In months of deliberations, the Assembly ascribed new rights to explicitly gendered (embodied) citizens, and sought to anchor the legitimacy of the new state in a reinvigorated sexual division of labor in family and workplace.

Despite the reconciliatory impulses that underpinned the writing of citizenship in 1919—the compromises between capital and labor, republic and Reich/nation—some "states of exception" were less reparable than others. The postwar "female surplus," for example, meant not only that women constituted the majority of voters but also that for millions of women, especially war widows, the imagined return to their prewar status was unthinkable. The perceived female "excess"—a trope in which the quantitative excess of women signaled "emancipation" (women broken loose from social structures and mores), or a more diffuse sense of female ungovernability and unpredictability—stood in the way of overcoming Germany's particular postwar state of exception. The tense recognition that both femininities and masculinities had changed is palpable in the writing of citizenship into the Weimar Constitution.

Yet the naming of women as citizens—intended to modernize and reorder gender relations—set into motion processes that neither law nor realms of formal politics could ultimately contain. Not only did the meanings, claims, and self-identifications of citizenship exceed the strictures of the constitution, but competing notions of citizenship jockeyed to fill the unprecedented vacuum of political power created through defeat and revolution. Tensions emerged as well between different sites of republican citizenship—between the citizenship the National Assembly granted to women, for example, and the radical redefinition of citizenship that took shape within the workers' and soldiers' councils in 1918 and 1919 and that harnessed civil and political rights to a thoroughly reconceived politics of production.[71] While the citizen was to play "a direct, unmediated and active role in self-government," the rights of council citizenship were dependent upon and restricted by a citizen's location or relation to production. In restricting participatory rights in council governance to "workers of hand and head," the councils actually delimited the new republican rights of citizenship along the lines of class, which was necessarily a line of gender as well.[72]

Yet the newly declared participatory rights also authorized a new presence of women in public, transforming female figures, even those not explicitly positioned in politics, into objects of anxiety and unease. It is significant that none of the visions of citizenship bandied about in the National Assembly—whether radical, liberal, corporatist, or nationalist—made a pretense of universality. Rather, each approached the negotiations over citizenship as one site for the (re)articulation of norms and ideologies of gender that would realign the relations between the sexes and thereby resolve the postwar "gender crisis." The inscription of explicitly differentiated, embodied citizenship rights assigned women a particular place in the founding of republican democracy and the rejuvenation of the nation. The National Assembly's deliberations of reproductive rights, and the first sessions of the newly elected Reichstag, placed reproductive sexuality—under the guise of "population politics"—at the crux of both citizenship and republican governmentality. Cornelie Usborne's finding that female activists and "average women" in the later Republic appealed to legislators, even to the Chancellor, on matters of birth control and abortion makes clear that female citizens could both take the terms of citizenship seriously and yet form subjectivities that profoundly questioned and expanded its terms.[73] The postulates of citizenship, anchored in those early years, would continue to unsettle the Republic throughout the 1920s, neither fulfilled nor wholly expunged from its political culture. As a legal identity, fixed in time, place, and bodies, the edges and boundaries of citizenship were continually called into question, not only by the repeated crises of nation and state, but by the impossibility of a gender settlement in the process of ending war and founding the Republic.

Notes

1   This is an updated and revised version of an article published under the title "Sexual Crisis and the Writing of Citizenship: Reflections on States of Exception in Germany, 1914–1920," in Alf Lüdtke and Michael Wildt (eds.), *Ausnhamezustand und Sicherheitsregimes: Historische Perspektiven, Göttinger Gespräche zur Geschichtswissenschaft* (Göttingen: Wallstein, 2008), pp. 168–213.

2   A classic study of the wartime state of exception is still Gerald D. Feldman in his *Army, Industry and Labor in Germany 1914–1918* (Princeton: Princeton University Press, 1966). For more recent explorations of the transformation of the state during the war, see Jay Winter (ed.), *The Cambridge History of the First World War: Volume II: The State* (Cambridge: Cambridge University Press, 2014).

3   See, for example, Belinda Davis, *Home Fires Burning: Food, Politics and Everyday Life in World War I Berlin* (Chapel Hill: University of North Carolina Press, 2000); Maureen Healy, *Vienna and the Fall of the Habsburg Empire: Total War and Everyday Life in World War I* (Cambridge: Cambridge University Press, 2004); Tammy Proctor, *Civilians in a World at War 1914–1918* (New York: New York University Press, 2010); Adam R. Seipp, *The Ordeal of Peace: Demobilization and the Urban Experience in Britain and Germany, 1917–21* (Burlington, VT: Ashgate, 2009); Robert Weldon Whalen, *Bitter Wounds. German Victims of the Great War, 1914–1939* (Ithaca: Cornell University Press, 1984).

4   Peter Fritzsche, *Germans into Nazis* (Cambridge: Harvard University Press, 1998).

5   Feldman, *Army, Industry, and Labor*, pp. 336–7; Roger Chickering, *Imperial Germany and the Great War, 1914–1918* (Cambridge: Cambridge University Press, 1998), pp. 163–4; Seipp, *The Ordeal of Peace*, ch. 3.

6   On fears of sexual crisis, see Ute Planert, *Antifeminismus im Kaiserreich: Diskurs, soziale Formation und politische Mentalität* (Göttingen: Vandenhoeck & Ruprecht, 1998); *Kritische Studien zur Geschichtswissenschaft*, Bd. 124, especially Kapitel 5, "Geschlechterpolitik im ersten Weltkrieg." Also see Birthe Kundrus, "Geschlechterkriege. Der erste Weltkrieg und die Deutung der Geschlechterverhältnisse in der Weimarer Republik," in Karen Hagemann and Stefanie Schüler-Springorum (eds.), *Heimat-Front. Militär und Geschlechterverhältnisse im Zeitalter der Weltkriege* (Frankfurt: Campus, 2002), pp. 171–87.

7   Ute Gerhard, *Unerhört. Die Geschichte der deutschen Frauenbewegung* (Reinbek bei Hamburg: Rowohlt, 1990), pp. 288–92.

8   The "International Women's Congress" of pacifists and suffragists took place in 1915 in Den Haag, while socialist women held an international peace conference in Bern in the same year.

9   Ute Daniel, *Arbeiterfrauen in der Kriegsgesellschaft: Beruf, Familie und Politik im Ersten Weltkrieg* (Göttingen: Vandenhoeck & Ruprecht, 1989); Birthe Kundrus, *Kriegerfrauen. Familienpolitik und Geschlechterverhältnisse im Ersten und Zweiten Weltkrieg* (Hamburg: Christians, 1995).

10 Elisabeth Zillken, *Staatsbürger-Pflichten der Frau und Fraumenstimmrechtsbewegung*, hrsg. Vom Preussischen Landesverein für Frauenstimmrecht (Düsseldorf, 1916), p. 2.

11 Ibid.

12 Dr. Ilse Reicke, "Frauengedankem zum Kriege," *Die Staatsbürgerin* 6:2 (1917), pp. 25–6. This monthly was published by the *Deutscher Reichsverband für Frauenstimmrecht* under the editorship of Marie Stritt and, after 1918, of Adele Schreiber.

13 Universitätsbibliothek Heidelberg, Handschriftensammlung, Nachlass Marie Baum: H 2–27, "Sozialhygienische Bevölkerungspolitik," nach einem Vortrag gehalten am 29. Juni 1916, pp. 328–30.

14 Luise Zietz, "Die sozialdemokratischen Frauen und der Krieg," *Ergänzungshefte zur Neuen Zeit* 21 (1914–15), pp. 2–6.

15 Ibid., pp. 6–7.

16 Ibid.

17 Ibid., pp. 14–15.

18 Ibid., pp. 13–15. Zietz recounted her own activity on behalf of those soldiers and their families and the decision by the *Reichsamt des Innern* to provide midwife services at no cost to soldiers' wives and to refrain from reclassifying soldiers' citizenship status.

19 Whalen, *Bitter Wounds*, pp. 110–11.

20 Florence Hervé, *Geschichte der deutschen Frauenbewegung* (Cologne: PapyRossa, 1995); Willy Albrecht, Friedhelm Boll, Beatrix W. Bouvier, Rosemarie Leuschen-Seppel, and Michael Schneider, "Frauenfrage und deutsche Sozialdemokratie vom Ende des 19. Jahrhunderts bis zum Beginn der zwanziger Jahre," *Archiv für Sozialgeschichte* 19 (1979), pp. 459–510; and Rolf Helbig, Wilhelm Langbein, and Lothar Zymara, "Beiträge zur Lage des weiblichen Proletariats und dessen aktive Einbeziehung in den Kampf der deutschen Arbeiterklasse gegen Imperialismus, Militarismus und Krieg in der dritten Hauptperiode der Geschichte der deutschen Arbeiterbewegung" (Ph.D. diss., von Pädagogische Hochschule Clara Zetkin, Leipzig, Sektion Geschichte, 1973).

21 Hervé, *Geschichte der deutschen Frauenbewegung*, pp. 81–2. The presence of women in these strikes is documented by reports of the *Generalkommando* (formerly Deutsches Zentralarchiv Merseburg and now Geheimes Staatsarchiv Berlin), "Zusammenstellung der Monatsberichte des stellvertretenden Generalkommandos" (March 3, 1917–December 29, 1917), Rep. 77, Tit. 1059, no. 3, Bd. 1, as cited in Helbig et al., "Beiträge zur Lage des weiblichen

Proletariats," pp. 400–1. I have examined other records in the Geheimes Staatsarchiv regarding the trials and punishment of male and female strikers, but details about the strikes themselves prove elusive.

22 Albrecht et al., "Frauenfrauge und deutsche Sozialdemokratie," pp. 502–05; Anja Weberling, *Zwischen Räten und Parteien. Frauenbewegung in Deutschland 1918/19* (Pfaffenweiler: Centaurus Verlagsgesellschaft, 1994), pp. 14–15.

23 See Daniel, *Arbeiterfrauen in der Kriegsgesellschaft*; Kundrus, *Kriegerfrauen*; and Helbig et al., "Beiträge zur Lage des weiblichen Proletariats," pp. 123–8. For an illuminating comparison to Austria, see Healy, *Vienna and the Fall of the Habsburg Empire*, especially ch. 4, "Sisterhood and Citizenship: 'Austria's Women' in Wartime Vienna"; Lisa Todd, "'The Soldier's Wife Who Ran Away with the Russian,' Sexual Infidelities in World War I Germany," *Central European History* 44:2 (2011), pp. 257–78.

24 See, for example, Emmy Freundlich, *Die industrielle Arbeit der Frau im Krieg* (Vienna/Leipzig: Anzengruberverlag, 1918), pp. 51–4.

25 *Die Gleichheit*, 25:13, 78 and *Vorwärts* 9 (March 1915), as cited in Helbig, "Beiträge zur Lage des weiblichen Proletariats," pp. 313–14, 332–4.

26 Zietz, "Die sozialdemokratischen Frauen," pp. 36–8.

27 See, for example, Nachlass Adele Schreiber, Bundesarchiv Koblenz; Nachlass Marie Baum, Universität Heidelberg, Handschriftensammlung; as well as Henriette Fürth, *Die deutschen Frauen im Kriege* (Tübingen: Mohr, 1917); Elisabeth Altmann-Gottheiner, "Die volkswirtschaftliche Bedeutung der Frauenarbeit in und nach dem Krieg," *Recht und Wirtschaft* 5. Jg. (Berlin, 1916); Freundlich, *Die industrielle Arbeit*, among many similar texts.

28 Geheimes Staatsarchiv Berlin, Preußischer Kulturbesitz, Rep. 76 VIIIB, Nr. 2013, Zeitungsausschnitte. The relevant article here is from the *Volkswohl für Schlesien* (Breslau), February 5, 1918. The terms used to characterize female excessive consumption included "*Unwirtschaftlichkeit*," "*Wohlleben*," "*Vergnügungs- und Genußsucht*," among others.

29 *Die Gleichheit* printed reports of soldiers' wives from Nordhausen who were forced to defend themselves against the "unjustifiable reproaches on the part of the local authorities" (*ungerechtfertigte Anwürfe seitens der Ortsbehörden*) regarding transgressions of this nature. See *Gleichheit* 25:20 (June 25, 1915). This article is also cited in Helbig et al., "Beiträge zur Lage," pp. 320–1. Also see Oberst Max Bauer, *Der grosse Krieg in Feld und Heimat: Erinnerungen und Betrachtungen* (Tübingen: Osiander'sche Buchhandlung, 1922), pp. 153–7, which recounts the "sexual demoralization" caused by the behavior of women on the home front. On perceptions of the moral and sexual comportment of soldiers' wives, see Kundrus, *Kriegerfrauen*, ch. 10, "Sittenlose Kriegerfrauen," pp. 212–20. Also see Lisa M. Todd, "War Wives and Sexual Treason: State Surveillance of Public and Private Morals in Germany during the First World War" (Ph.D. diss., University of Toronto, 2005) and Todd, "The Soldier's Wife."

30 Planert, *Antifeminismus*, p. 184; Kundrus, "Geschlechterkriege."

31 Planert, *Antifeminismus*, pp. 180–1. Planert contends that only a small minority of men recognized women's entitlement to citizenship rights based on their wartime service.

32 Ibid., pp. 187–8.

33 Bauer, *Der große Krieg in Feld und Heimat*, pp. 155–7.

34 GStA, Pr. Kultusministerium, Rep. 76 VIIIB, Nr. 2013, Zeitungsausschnitte, 5, article from *Volkswohl für Schlesien*, February 5, 1918.

> Der Einfluß der Kriegszeit auf die Sterblichkeit war ein sehr ungünstiger. Nimmt man nun den gewaltigen Geburtenrückgang und die hohe Sterblichkeitsziffer, so dürften wir bei Kriegsbeendigung einige Millionen Menschen weniger zu verzeichnen haben. Eine große Rolle wird dann auch die Geschlechtsgliederung des Volkes spielen, zumal aller Voraussicht nach eine Verweiblichung der Gesellschaft Platz greifen wird. Es werden auf 1000 Männer etwa 1100 Frauen kommen.

35 Planert, *Antifeminismus*, pp. 205–06.

36 On the birth strike debate, see Anneliese Bergmann, "Frauen, Männer, Sexualität und Geburtenkontrolle: Zur Gebärstreikdebatte der SPD 1913," in Karin Hausen (ed.), *Frauen suchen ihre Geschichte* (Munich: Beck, 1983), pp. 81–108. Here also see Planert, *Antifeminismus*, pp. 206–08.

37 Planert, *Antifeminismus*, pp. 211–13.

38 GStA, Pr. Kultusministerium, Rep. 76 VIIIB, Nr. 2013, Nr. 2013, Zeitungsausschnitte, 5, article from *Volkswohl für Schlesien*, February 5, 1918.

39 GStA, Pr. Kultusministerium, Rep. 76 VIIIB, Nr. 2013, Zeitungsausschnitte, 37, article on "Bevölkerungspolitik und Geschlechtskrankheiten" von Prof. Dr. med. Tonton, Wiesbaden.

40 GStA, Pr. Kultusministerium, Rep. 76 VIIIB, Nr. 2013, Zeitungsausschnitte, 40–3, Report in *Berliner Börsenzeitung* (March 26, 1918) on "Bevölkerungspolitik im Reichstag" von Felix Marquart's report from *Hamburgische Zeitung* (March 27, 1918); and an article from *Freie Presse* (Straßburg im Elsaß) (April 18, 1918), "Die Verhinderung von Geburten."

41 Grete Meisel-Hess, *Das Wesen der Geschlechtlichkeit: Die Sexuelle Krise in Ihren Beziehungen zur sozialen Frage und zum Krieg, zu Moral, Rasse und Religion und insbesondere zur Monogamie* (Jena: Eugen Diederichs, 1917), p. 152.

42 GStA, Pr. Kultusministerium, Rep. 76 VIIIB, Nr. 2013, Zeitungsausschnitte, 43: "Die Verhinderung von Geburten," *Freie Presse* (Straßburg im Elsaß) (April 18, 1918). Here the author cites an article in *Die Gleichheit*.

43 On the significance of the bodily transformations of war for women, see Cornelie Usborne, "Body Biological to Body Politic: Women's Demands for Reproductive Self-Determination in the First World War and Early Weimar Germany," in Geoff Eley and Jan Palmowski (eds.), *Citizenship and Nationhood in Twentieth-Century Germany* (Stanford: Stanford University Press, 2007), pp. 129–45.

44   Planert, *Antifeminismus*, pp. 184–9.

45   Ibid., pp. 205–06. Here Planert cites propaganda of the Bund extensively.

46   See, for example, Boris Barth, *Dolchstoßlegenden und politische Desintegration. Das Trauma der deutschen Niederlage im ersten Weltkriege 1914–1933* (Düsseldorf: Droste, 2003), p. 386. See the remarks in the review by Patrick Krassnitzer on Barth's cursory analysis of the gendered dimensions of the stab-in-the-back legend: http://hsozkult.geschichte.hu-berlin.de/rezensionen/type=rezbuecher&id=3647&view=print.

47   As cited in Planert, *Antifeminismus*, pp. 205–06, 225. The cited passage in German is: "Was sollten etwa die Krieger für eine Belohnung erhalten, wenn die Heimkriegerinnen mit dem Wahlrecht belohnt werden?"

48   Cited in ibid., p. 229.

49   GStA, Pr. Kultusministerium, Rep. 76 VIIIB, Nr., Nr. Nr. 2013, Zeitungsausschnitte, 34, *Der Tag* (December 7, 1917), "Wahlrecht und Bevölkerungspolitik," vom Oberregierungsrat Düttmann, Oldenburg. The precise wording is: that male heads of household should be granted "eine zweite Stimme … die er gleichsam als Vertreter der übrigen Familienmitgleider abzugeben hätte."

50   Planert, *Antifeminismus*, pp. 226–7.

51   *Vossische Zeitung* 562 (November 2, 1918), Abendausgabe, p. 2. Also see Ute Gerhard, *Unerhört*, pp. 323–4.

52   See Julia Sneeringer, *Winning Women's Votes: Propaganda and Politics in Weimar Germany* (Chapel Hill: University of North Carolina Press, 2002), which examines the constructions of female citizenship by party political propaganda, and Heidemarie Lauterer, *Parlamentarierinnen in Deutschland 1918/19 –1949* (Königstein/Ts., 2002).

53   Schreiber, "Revolution und Frauenrecht," p. 9. Her formulation was: "Wir treten unbelastet in die Politik."

54   Adele Schreiber, *Revolution und Frauenrecht: Frauen lernt wählen!* (Berlin: Arbeitsgemeinschaft für staatsbürgerliche und wirtschaftliche Bildung, 1919), pp. 8–9.

55   Marie von Bunsen, "Wir Wählerinnen," *Vossische Zeitung* 624:286 (December 6, 1918), p. 2.

56   Dr. Agnes von Harnack, *Die Frauen und das Wahlrecht*, hrs. vom Ausschuß der Frauenverbände Deutschlands, o.J., p. 1. This brochure almost definitely appeared in late November or early December 1918.

57   Emma Föllmer, *Zwei Jahre politisches Frauenwahlrecht*, hrsg. Vom Vaterländischer Volksbund (Berlin, 1921), p. 3. "Das Frauenwahlrecht wurde uns mit der Revolution in den Schoß geworfen, von vielen nicht erhofft, von manchen so gar nicht erwünscht. Unerwartet, wie ein Sturzbach kam es jedenfalls für alle und wirkte wie der Ruf eines Kapitäns: Alle Mann an Bord!"

58   von Harnack, *Die Frauen und das Wahlrecht*, p. 2. The exact wording is: "Dieser Zustand, der vor wenigen Wochen noch ein Traum und nicht einmal ein schöner war, ist heute eine Realität …"

59 Elisabeth von Rotten, "Ansprache bei der Kundgebung zum Rechtsfrieden," *Die Frauenbewegung* 23 (1918), p. 19.

60 von Bunsen, "Wir Wählerinnen," p. 2.

61 von Harnack, *Die Frauen und das Wahlrecht*, pp. 2–3.

62 Ibid., pp. 2–3.

63 Ibid., pp. 4–5.

64 Ibid., p. 5.

65 Dr. Rosa Kempf, "Parlamentarismus und Frauenbewegung," *Die Staatsbürgerin* 6:10 (1918), pp. 122–3.

66 Schreiber, *Revolution und Frauenrecht*, pp. 10, 12.

67 Bundesarchiv Koblenz, Nachlaß Adele Schreiber, 1173/58, pp. 98–9.

68 Stadtarchiv München, Nachlaß Dirr, 300: "Die Tätigkeit der weiblichen Abgeordneten der Fraktion," von Dr. Rosa Kempf, pp. 4–5.

69 Nachlaß Marie Baum, Universitätsbibliothek Heidelberg, Handschriftensammlung, H 2–34: "Zur Frage der wirtschaftl Demobilmachung der Frauen," *Frauen-Rundschau der Düsseldorfer Nachrichten* 2. Bd., no. 23 (September 11, 1919).

70 Citations from Thomas Childers, "Political Sociology and the 'Linguistic Turn,'" *Central European History* 22:3/4 (September–December 1989), pp. 387–8. On the history of Weimar constitutional and legal theory, see Peter C. Caldwell, *Popular Sovereignty and the Crisis of German Constitutional Law* (Durham: Duke University Press, 1997).

71 On the *Räte* as sites of citizenship, see Peter Carl Caldwell, "The Citizen and the Republic in Germany," in Eley and Palmowski, *Citizenship and National Identity in Germany*, pp. 45–7; also see Benjamin Ziemann, "'Gedanken eines Reichsbannermannes auf Grund von Erlebnissen und Erfahrungen.' Politische Kultur, Flaggensymbolik und Kriegserinnerung in Schmalkalden 1926. Dokumentation," *Zeitschrift des Vereins für Thuringische Geschichte* 53 (1999), pp. 201–32; and Benjamin Ziemann, *Contested Commemorations: Republican War Veterans and Weimar Political Culture* (Cambridge: Cambridge University Press, 2013).

72 Caldwell, "The Citizen and the Republic," pp. 45–7.

73 Usborne, "Body Biological."

12

Anchoring the Nation in the Democratic Form: Weimar Symbolic Politics beyond the Failure Paradigm

Manuela Achilles

How to think Weimar[1]

It has long been held that Weimar democracy lacked the symbolic appeal necessary to bind collective sentiment and win popular support.[2] Recent revisionist histories, seeking to destabilize the teleologies that tend to mark this well-established literature, support Peter Fritzsche's assertion that Weimar was less a cumulative failure than a series of bold experiments.[3] The turn toward new approaches and perspectives, however, is uneven and incomplete even in studies that avoid conflating the fragility of the fledgling republic with the overall lack of democratic symbols and identifications. Detlev Peukert's pathbreaking analysis of the Republic in terms of a "crisis of classical modernity" is a case in point. While admonishing his readers not to ignore the Weimar experiment in democracy, Peukert adopts the conventional narrative when claiming that the first German republic had no founding ritual, and that this (alleged) absence in national history attests to a general lack of legitimacy.[4] Thomas Mergel, in his important re-evaluation of Weimar parliamentary culture, similarly attributes to the pro-republican left a certain tendency "toward a rationalistic understanding of politics, toward the underestimation of the emotional attachment to a flag."[5] This assertion of a fatal symbolic deficit is entirely in line with the earlier claim that the rationalistic optimism (Gotthard Jasper) of the republican forces led to a consequential underestimation of the integrative power of state symbols (Klaus Wippermann).[6]

What complicates the attempt to restore a degree of openness to the study of Weimar democratic culture is the fact that much of the postwar memoir literature confirms the negative historiographical verdict on the Republic's symbolic politics. Gustav Radbruch, a prominent legal expert and major representative of the moderate wing of the Weimar SPD, for instance, asserted after the fact that the Social Democrats made a mistake when they failed to accompany their republican engagement with the corresponding national music, but rather worked silently and with gritted teeth. Since then, Radbruch lamented, "we have learned that the world is not led by reason, but by trifles, or less informally said, that any politics requires symbols and fantasy."[7]

Recent reconsiderations of Weimar democratic culture, seeking to take a fresh look at the historical evidence, suggest that the tight fit between postwar memory and historiography is deceiving with regard to the facts. It is by now evident that Weimar republicans were not—as the standard historical narrative claims—deliberately antiritualistic.[8] On the contrary, republican officials in the federal and state administrations clearly recognized (and acted on) the political necessity to symbolically legitimate the emergent democracy. Arnold Brecht, one of Weimar's leading civil servants, expressed this when noting that German governments could not leave the creation and use of symbols to political parties and other groups which battled with one another under their separate symbols: "They needed official symbols for public appearance. They could not pursue their business without any form. They had to try, as far as this was possible, to emphasize what was integrative and unifying (*das Integrative, Zusammenfassende*)."[9]

As I have shown elsewhere, Weimar's symbolism of the democratic state and nation revolved around the Republic's foundational law and therefore might be termed a constitutional patriotism *avant la lettre*.[10] Radbruch's laudation on the occasion of the Republic's tenth anniversary in 1928 provides a good example of the narrative forms that democratic national symbolism took. Representing the government within the context of a carefully staged "celebration of the constitution" (*Verfassungfeier*) in the Berlin Reichstag, the law professor contextualized the republican achievements by recalling those who "have fought and bled for this constitution" and "remained faithful to their patriotic duty unto death."[11] "A constitution is like a shield that becomes all the more valuable to its bearer the more it shows the scratches and scars of past struggles," Radbruch proclaimed; "[it] is like a flag that emanates all the more honor and sacredness, the more it has been cut by swords and pierced by bullets." He concluded by proclaiming with an eye to the future that: "[t]he banner, the black-red-golden banner, will stand; the Weimar Constitution will stand; the German Republic will stand!"

Considering this and other evidence testifying to the republican concern with national representation, why is the negative verdict on the Republic's symbolic politics (and by extension on Weimar democracy more generally) so difficult to revise? For what reasons does the dominant historical discourse tend to return almost ceaselessly to the paradigm of (symbolic) lack and failure? The answer to this fundamental question of Weimar democratic culture lays not least in the post-1945 West German politics of history and memory. Seeking to dissociate the Federal Republic from a democracy that had given way to Nazi dictatorship, the emergent political and historiographical elites of West German democracy were eager to assert that Bonn was not Weimar. The *Weimar Komplex* (Sebastian Ullrich) of the Federal Republic congealed in the still widely held belief that the first German republic was marked (and marred) by a tragic paradox: that it was a republic without republicans, a democracy without democrats. Combining feelings of guilt for the atrocities committed under the Third Reich with anxieties about the viability of the second German democracy, this assertion of lack and failure supported the ideological stabilization of the Federal Republic. Weimar became a negative foil against which to define the positive achievements of its West German successor.[12]

Notably, the symbolic potency of the Weimar failure paradigm transcends the confines of German national history. As Rudy Koshar has observed in regard to the US political discourse,

> Weimar was and remains a metaphor of failure—and not just any old failure but rather the super-sized variety: the end of Weimar gave way in 1933 to Adolf Hitler. More than the symbol of an inability to master the complexities of modern democratic decision-making, Weimar, in this view, takes on the qualities of an existential disaster, the mother of all political failures, whose consequences go well beyond a lost election or bungled policy.[13]

How, then, can we "think" and "speak" of Weimar beyond the established teleological narratives of doom and failure? What, if anything, is the Republic's significance in a historiography that embraces the openness and contingencies of the first German democracy?

Building on the most productive insights of the past decades, it is sensible to ground the study of Weimar democratic culture in a critical reconsideration of Peukert's central terms, that is, "modernity" and "crisis." Rüdiger Graf has gone a long way in restoring to the contemporary meanings of "crisis," their optimistic and constructivist dimensions, thus challenging the term's pessimistic historiographical understandings and uses. In Weimar, Graf writes, "the crisis never appeared to be the precursor of doom, but its diagnosis was rather a call to action."[14] Understood as a moment of decision in which the future remained open, the diagnosis of crisis empowered historical actors to remake their world around new values and identities. This was true irrespective of whether the crisis was real or perceived.

The optimistic belief in the malleability of fundamental political, social, and economic conditions that Graf restores to the Weimar crisis discourse is essential to a full appreciation of the Republic's modernity. While the disintegration of traditional forms of self and community fueled an anxiety-driven desire for "order," the uncertainties of individual and collective identity that characterized the modern condition in the interwar years also provided an enlarged array of political actors with the opportunity to imagine and install new regimes or reform and solidify existing ones. Irrespective of whether the desired and projected orders were imagined as "old" or "new," the crucial indicator of their modernity is the fact that the state and nation—as designated by a particular set of symbols and practices—became qualities that could be created, shaped, staged, contested, and remade.

Once the general openness of the Weimar period is acknowledged and its history written from the start rather than its end, it is important to keep in mind that democracy was both a sectional interest and the constitutional frame within which the political contest over the representational forms and institutional structures of the state and nation took place. That the Republic faced disloyal opposition from the extreme political left and right, however, does not necessitate the conclusion that it suffered from a fatal symbolic deficit. In fact, the very intensity of the political struggle suggests that the democratic values the Republic represented and guaranteed were clearly understood especially also by those that rejected them. As the idea of experimentation is extended from the aesthetic to the political realm, the central question of Weimar democratic culture is thus no longer about lack or deficiency. Rather, the interest shifts to the integrative and disintegrative potentials of a relatively open and heterogeneous democracy based on a shared belief in the rule of law. As recent global developments have shown, the challenges of democratic integration in the face of fundamentalist opposition are as real and relevant today as they were a century ago in the aftermath of the First World War.

The remainder of this essay reconsiders the fundamental symbolic decisions and practices of the early Weimar Republic. The focus is on the symbolic politics of the national assembly as well as on the symbols of the state and nation commissioned by the Reich Art Custodian (*Reichskunstwart*), a government office situated at the intersection of art and politics. As will be shown, the need to legitimize the nascent democracy in the face of severe obstacles inspired a labor of democratic representation that transcended the confines of political camps, religious affiliation, social milieus, and perceived race. The particular strength of the republican symbolism—its integrative impulse—was also its greatest challenge: seeking to incorporate large sections of the conservative middle classes, Weimar democracy blurred the political margins of the nascent republic. There was no alternative, however.

Having lost their absolute majority in the federal election of 1920, Weimar republicans needed to turn enmity into loyal opposition and had to do so in the absence of diplomatic or economic success. It was a daunting task that would have stretched any democracy to its limits.

"Onwards over Graves": The symbolic politics of the Constituent Assembly

The revolutionary transition from *Kaiserreich* to republic was a complex process that created grave challenges as well as immense possibilities. Faced with the collapse of the old regime, the moderate left and bourgeois center formed a coalition under the leadership of Friedrich Ebert (SPD) who favored the constitutional path toward the reorganization of the war-torn state and society. The general election to the Weimar Constituent Assembly of January 19, 1919, produced a sweeping victory of the democratic forces, thus legitimizing ex post facto a moderate form of revolution while rejecting the reorganization of Germany along socialist lines.[15] As the historian Hagen Schulze has put it, "The voter had spoken and the result was: the German people wanted a black-red-gold revolution, not a red one."[16]

In the midst of a bitter confrontation with the radical left, the Provisional Government deemed it unsafe to convene the German National Assembly in Berlin. Frankfurt am Main, the seat of the 1848 parliament, was also dismissed because of its proximity to industrial and occupied territories. In the end, the choice fell on the provincial city of Weimar in the state of Thuringia. The city's Court Theatre, a focal point of German classical *Bildung* stretching back to the eighteenth century, was to serve as the major assembly hall. To secure the proceedings, several thousand troops under the command of General Maerker formed a ten-kilometer deep security cordon around the city.

Constituting itself in the aftermath of war and defeat, the National Assembly launched the republic in a decidedly low-key representative style. Friedrich Ebert epitomized the new symbolic sobriety when after his swearing in as President on February 11, 1919, he requested all further formalities to be dropped and simply went to his car.[17] Weimar schoolchildren and the town council waiting outside to salute him were disappointed. Friedrich Stampfer recalls in his memoirs that never before did the installation of a new head of state occur in such a simple form.[18] The *Berliner Tageblatt* explained, "Ebert is a calm and objective, almost prosaic man, who shuns all superficiality."[19] Yet although the President enjoyed considerable support among the liberal middle class, his representational matter-of-factness gave cause for concern. The *Berliner Tageblatt* urged Ebert to adopt a master of ceremonies, as well as a retinue and residence, "for we surely do not want the German Republic to break in an entirely petty bourgeois fashion with all the conventional forms of etiquette."

The allusion to "petty-bourgeois" habits and tastes points to the class bias in the public perception of Ebert's public performance as head of state. While the Social Democratic press saw in him the embodiment of the calm and self-reliant forces of socialism,[20] the reaction of the liberal press was ambivalent. Theodor Wolff of the *Berliner Tageblatt* praised Ebert's unassuming patriotism and common sense, but to him the socialist politician was neither a shining genius nor a high-ranking statesman. According to Wolff, the new President was the son of a labor movement that yielded diligent and critical spirits: "Ebert is good vintage from this soil which lays in the middle between the torrid and frigid zones."[21] The focus on the average, common, and even ordinary became problematic when Wolff envisaged the President after work behind a good bottle of wine. Noting that "his entire character is like his figure hearty and round," Wolff's invocation of homespun conviviality was only a short step away from right-wing derision. Wolff tried to forestall mockery by noting that monarchists on principle revered the most incompetent sovereign if the "dull coincidence of birth" had placed him in princely chambers. Nonetheless, his report reveals a desire for ceremony and splendor that the socialist media clearly rejected. The *Vorwärts* asserted already on the day of the assembly's opening that great pathos and grand gestures were incompatible with the working class.[22] From a socialist perspective, the republican sobriety signaled not so much a void or lack—for example, of political genius and appropriate etiquette or manners—but rather a radical break with the social inequalities and monarchic hubris of the *Kaiserreich*.

The moderate socialists' desire to symbolically mark the rupture between the old and new regime was overdetermined by the war experience and the enormous personal losses it had inflicted on the German people. Otto Meissner, the President's Chief of Staff, reports that Ebert rejected his suggestion to step up ceremonial display in his dealings with the diplomatic corps with the words: "Don't forget that we in Germany are living in a house of mourning!"[23] There can be no doubt that this grief and sorrow was deeply felt, as Ebert had lost two sons in the First World War. But also in a more general sense, republican ceremonial stood in the tension between the protocols of personal loss and the yearning for national renewal. In this situation, the Weimar coalition grounded the nascent Republic on the ethics of work, mourning, and self-restraint. It was no glorious start, but it was a start nonetheless. In the poignant words of the *Vorwärts*, the Republic was a new beginning that confirmed once more the right of all Germans to "plant hope over graves."[24]

It is important to distinguish the republican principle of hope, as expressed in the foundational narratives and practices of Weimar democracy, from the excessive expectations that historians have linked to the Republic's eventual collapse. Richard Bessel refers to the latter when asserting that "the Weimar Republic ultimately proved too weak and vulnerable to bear the burdens of unrealistic popular expectations and the demagogy which fed off them."[25] While this assessment captures the propaganda and sentiments especially of the extreme political left and right, republican politicians of the middle ground such as Ebert clearly understood the limitations imposed upon politics in a defeated and impoverished country; they never ceased to emphasize this fact. It was in spite of the postwar challenges that Weimar republicans embraced democracy as a most "precious possession."[26] After the national assembly adopted the republican charter on July 31, 1919, the liberal *and* Social Democratic press attributed to this day "the greatest historical significance."[27] Interior Minister David proclaimed proudly that "[t]he German Republic is from now on the most democratic democracy in the world."[28] Yet republicans also realized that their achievement was overshadowed by the popular outrage over the Treaty of Versailles. Chancellor Gustav Bauer, a moderate socialist like Ebert, articulated this when, in praising the Weimar Constitution, he declared, "Not even in this solemn hour, we can hope to veil the rift that runs through our people. The experiences of war and peace have driven us apart. We stand in party political antagonism." Bauer contrasted this reality of political polarization with the desire for national cohesion. In his view, Weimar democrats had the "duty and desire to once also speak of the other today. We are also compatriots, blood relatives, Germans."[29]

The constitutional symbolism of shared hegemony

The moderate forces dominating the National Assembly based the Republic on democratic foundations while pursuing a mixed strategy of continuity and change. The constitution, in its preamble, designated the German Federation (*Reich*) to be an entirely new structure, erected by the undivided German people on the bases of liberty, justice, peace, and social progress.[30] The first article then stipulated, "The German *Reich* is a republic. Supreme power emanates from the people." Article 17 prescribed the republican form of government for every German state. The constitutional principles of popular sovereignty and international reconciliation postulated a dramatic break with the monarchic and militarist doctrines of empire. At the same time, the constitution maintained the appellation *Reich* both in its title and throughout, thus retaining an important moment of historical continuity. The declared desire of the German people "to renew" rather than to merely "establish" its federation or *Reich* also excluded the idea of a radical break with the past. The same is true for the Constitution's Article 3, which determined the design of the national flag. Recuperating the "Greater German" democratic tradition of the 1848 revolution, the republican colors were black, red, and gold. Yet due to pressure from the reactionary right and the democratic center, the merchant marine kept the imperial black-white-red with the Republic's new national colors in the upper canton of the ensign next to the staff.

Historians usually consider the black-white-red flag a monarchic emblem or even the "emperor's flag" (Kaiserfahne).[31] This interpretation is correct in so far as it captures the flag's perception by the radical political left and right. Neither the origin nor the meanings of the imperial tricolor were that clear-cut, however—not even under the Kaiserreich. The Bismarckian state adopted black-white-red mercantile and war flags, as well as the standards of the Imperial House. The empire did not have a "national" flag until 1892, when black-white-red assumed that function. The expansion of civil society as a public arena of freely associating citizens, distinct from the monarchic state and beyond its arbitrary supervision, was crucial to this emergence of a national symbolism that was independent from the symbolic interventions of the dynastic state.[32] The First World War then greatly magnified the popular appeal of the black-white-red colors. Instrumental in this respect were tales of soldiers' patriotic sacrifice under the national flag and/or with the Deutschlandlied on their lips.[33]

Designating the sacrifices of the Volk-as-nation, the imperial flag was not incompatible with taking pride in democratic legacies and practices in the immediate aftermath of the First World War. When the defeated army returned to the German capital in early December 1918, black-white-red coexisted easily and playfully with both the red emblems of revolutionary change and the black-red-golden tricolor of the greater German democracy.[34] The constitutional flag compromise must be seen in relation to this plasticity of the national symbolism and within the broader context of international developments. Initially, the Weimar coalition favored the adoption of a black-red-gold national flag, leaving the hitherto black-white-red mercantile flag to regulation by federal law. The odds that this proposition would pass the Assembly's final vote diminished dramatically, however, when a large segment of the liberal democrats raised the old imperial flag against the perceived humiliation of the German nation by the Treaty of Versailles.[35] It was especially the so-called war guilt clause, naming Germany the sole culprit for the devastation, that tipped the constitutional flag debate toward a solution that included recognition of the black-red-white colors.

And yet, this move toward a dual solution was not intended to provide the political right with a potent symbol of antidemocratic resentment. The general impetus, rather, was to protect the moral integrity of the nation and their democratic representatives. Carl Petersen of the DDP articulated this when distinguishing the imperial flag's *national* symbolism from its abuses by a "deluded government."[36] It was no political sham when Petersen, speaking in the name of his party, sympathized with the black-red-golden legacy of 1848. But in his opinion, preserving the collective pride of the defeated German nation was more important. Over and again, the Senator from Hamburg summoned black-white-red as the symbol of Germany's economic strength and national revival. He then linked lowering the imperial flag with the Treaty of Versailles: "With all the cunning of the world's press," Petersen admonished the political left, "it will be proclaimed that we ourselves acknowledge that our old strength is broken. Nobody wants this. But this you must consider in this hour. One will also say: the fact that they have taken down the old flag proves their admission of guilt for the war."[37]

Speaking in support of a somewhat limited and confined tolerance for black-white-red, and against the motion of the independent socialists to adopt the red flag, Hermann Molkenbuhr of the MSPD distinguished the "pure trade flag" from the chauvinist and oppressive sides of empire: "On the oceans," he noted, "the black-white-red flag was not the representative of militarism and absolutism; on the ocean, the black-white-red flag covered the fruits of German economic industriousness and of the traffic that reconciles peoples." To preempt the political right from turning his argument to their advantage, the reformist socialist concluded:

> The militarist *Reich* has collapsed. It will remain buried, and if you intend to uphold it before the public with a black-white-red flag, this would be all that remained. But especially because you recognize the black-white-red flag as the symbol of the past, of the regime which has brought so much misery over Germany, because of this...the black-white-red flag must not be considered for the nation (*Reich*). In this respect, the only possibility is the old democratic colors, the colors of the Greater Germany, namely black-red-gold.[38]

The National Convention passed the flag compromise by a margin of 211 to 90 votes on July 3, 1919.[39] While admitting the black-white-red flag into the new democratic order, albeit in a diminished role, the Assembly abolished the imperial privileges of birth together with the symbols of status, honor, and achievement (Article 109) with the notable exception of orders and decorations conferred for merit or valor during the First World War (Article 175). German citizens were not permitted to accept titles or orders from a foreign government. Titles could be conferred only when descriptive of an office or calling. While academic degrees were not affected, titles of nobility were considered part of the family name and so could no longer be conferred. The Constitution held no provisions for a national anthem or national holidays.

Historians have long noted that the symbolic absences and compromises enshrined in the Weimar Constitution remained contested. It is equally true, however, that the National Assembly's decisions were deliberate and meaningful symbolic acts. The compromises over the Republic's name and flag were gestures of conciliation that aimed to integrate a vast majority of the German people into the Republic. The adoption of the imperial mercantile flag, moreover, was an act of political protest that sought to preserve republican national pride at least symbolically. Silences, too, at times spoke louder than words, at least in some quarters. The National Assembly's sober representational style related to a public that mourned the horrific losses of war and defeat. If there was hope (and there was), then it was hope over graves. The discontinuation of the imperial honorary practice, on the other hand, created an absence that signaled a radical break with the social and political inequalities of the old regime. While the constitutional symbolism of the state and nation was neither negligent nor empty, it was not comprehensive either. The new state still had to redesign everything from the federal service flags, seals, coins, and postage stamps to the architecture of railway stations, canals, post offices, and customhouses. The place where this work coalesced and congealed into form was the Office of the *Reichskunstwart*, to which we will now turn.

"Giving form" to the Reich:
State design between art and politics

Located at the intersection of art and politics, the *Reichskunstwart* was a newly established government agency that worked to transform the national symbols of sovereignty and authority (flags, coat of arms, border posts, etc.) as well as those of authentication and exchange (coins, bills, postage stamps). The office also helped orchestrate the state funerals for Walther Rathenau (1922), President Ebert (1925), and Foreign Minister Gustav Stresemann (1929), as well as the Presidential inauguration of Paul von Hindenburg (1925) and the annual celebrations of Constitution Day in Berlin.

Edwin Redslob, who directed the *Reichskunstwart* office from 1920 until Nazi Interior Minister Frick dissolved it in 1933, conceived of his task as a deliberate project of national "design" (*Formgebung*). The trained art historian documented and promoted the Republic's new symbolism with the help of richly illustrated brochures and articles. He monitored and fostered major developments in the realm of art, literature, music, and film, produced expert opinions on the taxation and export of German artworks, and also claimed influence on federal building projects.[40] Redslob's aim was to actively create or invent a German "tradition" that engaged the "fantasy of the people,"[41] while also refuting both imperial hubris and bureaucratic sterility.[42] In his view, "The symbols of authority of the federal government must not consist merely of phones and note pads in the office. There need to be other values, so that the sentiment of state can establish itself and fulfill the citizens also in their hearts."[43]

The *Reichskunstwart*'s concern with the creation of a modern national style can be traced back to the cultural agenda of the German Design and Industries Association (*Deutscher Werkbund*) of which he was an active member.[44] Founded in Munich on October 5, 1907, the Werkbund was a reform-oriented association of architects, applied artists, artisans, industrialists, and policymakers who shared an interest in establishing a partnership between product manufacturers and design professionals. The Werkbund's motto—*Vom Sofakissen zum Städtebau*—delineated a vast range of interests including the design of the imperial graphic arts (*Amtliche Graphik*).[45] Claiming the field of state design for its members, the Werkbund lobbied federal lawmakers across the political spectrum to support a motion that asked the government to consult qualified experts in all artistic matters such as the design of the republican bills and stamps, and to install an office at the Federal Ministry of the Interior that would guarantee the uniform administration of these tasks.[46] It was this interest-driven claim on national design that led to the establishment of the *Reichskunstwart* office in the winter of 1919. The Werkbund-inspired motion evidently passed without controversy. Parliament adopted it with *Heiterkeit* during the third reading of the Interior Ministry's budget on October 30, 1919.[47] Considering the heated debates over the national flag in the Constituent Assembly, the recorded amusement is rather ironic. National symbols in Weimar were hardly ever uncontroversial or a matter of cheerful unison.

After founding its artistic advisory bureau on December 15, 1919, the federal government left all further arrangements to Interior Minister Erich Koch (DDP). His favorite candidate for the *Reichskunstwart* position was Ernst Jäckh, a prolific advocate of Werkbund ideas and cofounder of the German Academy for Politics in 1920. Jäckh declined Koch's offer and instead suggested Dr. Edwin Redslob, the director of the Württemberg art collections in Stuttgart.[48] Born in Weimar on September 22, 1884, Redslob combined a deep appreciation of his hometown's humanist tradition with an ardent interest in *art nouveau* and Expressionism. He joined the German Werkbund in 1913, volunteered for the German army in 1914, and later sympathized with liberal democracy although it is unclear as to whether he ever joined that party.[49] All in all, Redslob's self-understanding as "mediator" and "intermediary" rendered him a remarkably suitable choice for the position as federal art custodian.[50]

Redslob started his work in the service of the Republic from the standpoint of radical innovation. Having accepted the *Reichskunstwart* position as of January 1920, he recalled his arrival in Berlin as a "time of first hopes."[51] His initial statements attest to this desire for a new departure. Comparing the events of the recent past to a "deforesting of the German forest," he asserted at the Leipzig Arts and Crafts Fair in August 1920 that it was time to "root up the old stumps and to plant new seeds" so as "to prepare … for a new cultivation." In his view, the future would be entirely different from the past and only one thing was certain: "there can be no thought of scraping along and muddling through any longer."[52]

The republican press generally supported Redslob's repudiation of a "faded yesterday."[53] Noting that the Republic lacked customary symbols, the journal of the republican school reform movement urged that "something fundamentally new must be created."[54] The *Vossische Zeitung* introduced Redslob as a "highly experienced expert" who possessed the "necessary mixture of skill and energy" to do away with the "still existing sanctified jog trot of the old regime."[55] The graphic art magazine *Das Plakat* wished for the *Reichskunstwart* to "sweep away with an iron broom the empty symbols of an expired past ... [and] take action so that the ... facilities of the federal railways and federal post office be designed in a sober and beautiful fashion."[56]

Redslob, indeed, shifted the state's representational center of gravity away from the monarchs and their families to the German *Volk* and nation. When Interior Minister Adolf Köster consulted him about the decoration of government offices, he recommended—in the best Werkbund tradition—the use of first-class reproductions of outstanding German artworks, contemporary poster art as well as photographs of cultural landmarks and industrial centers, all to be supplied by the federal printing office using the highest level of technical expertise.[57] Yet, although the *Reichskunstwart* cherished modern art and technology, he did not strive to radically erase all traces of the imperial past from public display. Rather, Redslob's declared aim was to foster the "pervasion of tradition with modernity."[58]

Redslob articulated this position in a draft letter to the Republican Youth Organization, Black-Red-Gold. The organization had complained that the German government did not follow the example of Czechoslovakia, which had destroyed the Austrian emblems of authority. Redslob rejected the underlying assumption that emblems of former German princes were signs of foreign domination. In his opinion, "It is the history of our own people that is at issue here, and it would amount to a falsification of history if all memories of the time that lies behind us were to suddenly disappear."[59] After admonishing the republican youth not to waste their energy on destructive action, the *Reichskunstwart* proposed in conclusion: "Let us rather consider how and where positive measures are to be taken, which always have a stronger effect than negative ones. ... You will find an ally in me wherever you do positive work."

In doing this "positive" work, the *Reichskunstwart* had to balance the forces of conservation and innovation with the symbolic decisions enshrined in the Weimar Constitution. To fill in the gap in the state's symbolic repertoire that resulted from the National Assembly's break with the honorary practice of the old regime, the *Reichskunstwart* commissioned commemorative emblems in memory of the Ruhr struggle and the tenth anniversary of the beginning of the First World War, as well as sports prizes to be awarded at athletic competitions on the Republic's Constitution Day. Foreign dignitaries received porcelain tea services in lieu of the customary medals. A special award for excellence in the realms of art and science was the "Eagle Shield of the German Reich" first awarded to Gerhart Hauptmann at the occasion of his sixtieth birthday in November 1922.

The *Reichskunstwart* was also instrumental in producing the federal coat of arms, which was the Republic's most important symbol of state authority. Displaying an eagle at its core, the emblem decorated official seals, documents, nameplates, and coins (often without the shield). As the motif had been associated with the monarchy, its republican adaptation was not uncontested. Seeking to break with imperial tradition, the architect Moritz Lehmann promoted a black-red-golden design featuring the letters "D R" for *Deutsche Republik*.[60] Although the proposal enjoyed some parliamentary support, the federal government dismissed the idea and instead asked Stephan Kekule von Stradonitz, a heraldry and law expert, to redesign the national eagle. The Prussian Office of Heraldry commissioned Professor Emil Döpler, the draftsman of the imperial coat of arms, to produce an alternative proposal. Döpler stripped the eagle of its monarchic attributes, including the crown, but otherwise maintained the original design. The federal government accepted this solution on September 1, 1919. President Ebert declared on November 11, 1919, that the German coat of arms display a one-headed eagle on a golden shield, with red beak, tongue, and claws. The government kept official prototypes defining the emblem's heraldic characteristics while referring questions of artistic detail to a particular design's purpose and function.[61]

Interestingly, the imperial eagle's symbolic de-coronation failed to stir a wave of right-wing indignation. The symbol's integrative "magic" apparently worked without dynastic attributes. Stradonitz understood this when asserting that the coat of arms could have been furnished with a people's crown or even aureole as such attributes were "trifles compared with the doubtlessly most fortunate choice of the heraldic image as such."[62] The public agreed but rejected Döpler's solution. Redslob found the design incompatible with a modern style of national representation and invited expressionist painter Karl Schmidt-Rottluff to draft a more suitable version for the federal seals and flags. Schmidt-Rottluff's sturdy wood engraving, however, drew much mockery especially from the conservative public. Redslob's next round of commissions was more successful. It produced official nameplates for the German consulates (by Tobias Schwab), railway services (by Otto Firle), finance ministry (by Rudolf Koch), and postal services (also Koch). Sigmund von Weech designed the republican state seals, which were adopted by presidential decree on March 30, 1922. This design also provided the pattern for the badges of the army and navy, as well as for coins, postage stamps, and murals. A particularly imposing variety was the four meter-high painting of an eagle adorning the entry hall of the new Stuttgart railway station.

Having commissioned this plurality of works, Redslob noted that the various republican eagles had one thing in common: they responded to a fundamental change in perception. "Our times see fundamentally differently," the *Reichskunstwart* wrote, "we need easily discernible clarity and simple forms. Above all," Redslob continued, "it is necessary to take into account the demands that lie in the nature of the object by virtue of its material, size and purpose."[63] Veteran heraldists such as Stradonitz shared the *Reichskunstwart*'s concern with function, practicality, and utility. Stradonitz stressed, however, that official designs needed to remain within the bounds of the official heraldic guidelines. This excluded "flying" or "sitting" eagles from federal use. Adhering to these guidelines was important because it helped distinguish the national eagle from "mere symbolizations," thus visualizing the dominion of state authority vis-à-vis society at large.

The republican appropriation of the eagle motif for the purpose of state representation was, overall, relatively successful. While the proliferation of designs at times caused confusion, resulting in the call for a "standard eagle," the motif as such remained beyond dispute. An article by F.H. Ehmcke for Redslob's *Amtliche Graphik* of 1925 explained the eagle's popularity by noting that "in it the painful and glorious past lives on." Ehmcke added that "in its sign the sublime state idea, for which our ancestors have lived and died, will be guided through the present toward a future that shall shine brighter for our descendants."[64] It appears that in the most integrative sense the federal eagle stood for the continuity of the Reich tradition rather than for a particular form of government or state. Allowing for a variety of modern and functional designs, yet circumscribed by history and heraldry, the eagle was perhaps the most "national" of all German state symbols under the Weimar Republic.

The creation of republican service flags posed different challenges since they had to accord with the compromise between two historical trajectories—anchored in the events of 1848 and 1871—that had joined course only recently under the Republic. In assisting the government in producing the official designs, Redslob limited his concern to the correct heraldic realization of the constitutional premises. Introduced by President Ebert on April 11, 1921, the conclusive "Flag Table of the Reich" differentiated the Republic's ten most important banners, five for each constitutional color combination (Figure 12.1). When the symbolic parity established by the chart did not quell the nagging flag dispute and the government asked its *Reichskunstwart* to propose a new solution,[65] he suggested adopting a national "unity flag" (*Einheitsflagge*). Combining the colors of both constitutional banners, Redslob's designs conjoined the competing colors with a version of the iron cross of the Teutonic Knights, a Crusader order. His favorite variation displayed a black cross pattée with a white border on a quartered red and golden ground (Figure 12.2).

FIGURE 12.1 *Flags of Weimar Germany (Flag Regulation of April 11, 1921).*

FIGURE 12.2 *Proposals for a German national unity flag, Reichskunstwart, 1926.*

Crisis as opportunity and openness as limit

The republican search for a national unity flag was increasingly hampered by a political climate that favored the decisive logic of "either-or" over compromise.[66] Yet, the obstinate attitude of the extremist left and right also provided the Republic with opportunity. It was, after all, the inability of the radical opposition to compromise and form a government that kept the forces of the republican middle ground in control of the federal state. Republican officials such as Redslob worked tirelessly to gradually win support in conservative circles not least by extending the Republic's symbolism. The vital question was one of political boundaries and symbolic limits. This emerged most clearly in the aftermath of the murder of Foreign Minister Walter Rathenau by anti-republican extremists on June 24, 1922. While the assassination is often seen as just one episode in a series of political murders that upset the early Weimar years, or as a precursor to the Holocaust, it was also a crisis of right-wing representation that provided the republican state and its supporters with the rare opportunity to turn public opinion against the subversive politics of the conservative right, and to advance and defend its own symbolism.[67]

As massive crowds turned out in defense of the Republic, the federal government orchestrated a carefully staged state funeral for the slain minister in Berlin. Republicans now also pushed more strongly for both the dissemination and protection of the national flag. City councils throughout the country voted to acquire the black-red-gold banner to fly at all public buildings.[68] Prussia instructed its entire administration to show the national flag together with the black-white state banner on official holidays. Flag manufacturers, being swamped with orders, found it impossible to satisfy the sudden increase in demand. A letter to the editor of the *Vossische Zeitung* detailed a citizen's desperate shopping odyssey in pursuit of a black-red-golden tricolor.[69] A female reader recommended self-help. Addressing herself to women who in her view were more practical than men, she advised to recycle the imperial flag by dying the white stripe yellow and reassembling the parts.[70]

As republican banners became both objects and manifestations of democratic desire, the old regime's emblems also appeared in a new light. The Social Democrat Otto Wels exclaimed on the day after Rathenau's assassination, "The symbols of the old monarchy must disappear!"[71] Wels admitted that many supporters of the Republic once followed the black-white-red flag from inner conviction. The murder of Rathenau by nationalist fanatics, however, delegitimized this practice. For republicans, Wels concluded, "the black-white-red flag has become the murder flag today!" The perhaps strongest expression of this desire to demarcate and defend the bounds of republican legitimacy was Chancellor Joseph Wirth's conclusion to his parliamentary speech in support of a law for the defense of the Republic.[72] After praising the slain government minister as a great statesman and friend, while urging the productive collaboration (*Mitarbeit*) of all, the Chancellor turned to the right and declared most dramatically: "There stands the enemy, who trickles his poison in the wounds of a people. There stands the enemy—and there is no doubt about it: this enemy stands on the right!"

Put on the defensive, the nationalist right avoided open confrontation and instead appropriated the republican language of fundamental constitutional rights. A comment by Oskar Hergt, the cofounder and chairman of the ultra-conservative DNVP, is exemplary of the nationalist rhetoric. Hergt declared: "Whoever attempts to overturn our state order by unconstitutional means places himself [sic] outside the legal order and therefore is not entitled to its protections. Those who, like the German National Peoples' Party, seek to attain their political aims solely along the constitutional path, however, can demand the same constitutional guarantees as all other citizens." It did not matter whether the anti-republican right truly believed in civil liberties for all. Hergt said it quite openly: granted that all German citizens were equal before the law, the constitution provided his party with the legal means to overthrow the republican state.

The democratic coalition was not blind to the fact that the nationalist embrace of the Weimar Constitution was purely strategic. The liberal democrats, for instance, cautioned that "[t]he allegedly 'peaceful and constitutional' fight against the Republic also leads to civil war."[73] Yet, the political right's appropriation of the constitutional argument was powerful because it undercut the inside/outside (friends/enemies) dichotomy the Weimar state needed to establish and maintain. The republican dilemma, therefore, was not about symbolic absence or passivity. Rather, the symbolism of shared hegemony on the basis of the rule of law opened the Republic to a conundrum all democracies face: how to integrate a plurality of opinions while protecting its core values against abuse and destruction.

To what extent should the republican state have censored languages and practices that openly contradicted republican visions and ideals? The short answer is that republicans, after having lost their absolute majority in 1920, were not in the position to exclude anybody or anything from the republican nation. They had to emphasize, as Arnold Brecht noted, the unifying and integrative tendencies of Weimar democracy. Seeking to draw large sections of the conservative middle class into the Republic, Weimar democrats opened the proverbial gates to declared political enemies who they also considered, as Chancellor Bauer said in his praise of the Weimar Constitution, "compatriots, blood relatives, Germans." In this situation, republican officials such as Redslob worked as patient and persistent proponents of a German national style that was "contemporary" as well as "traditional" and "broadly appealing."[74] Striving to engage the fantasy of the people yet rejecting militarist hubris and aesthetic excess, republican state design drew the symbolic contours of a pluralist mass democracy. It is in this perspective, too, that the Republic was the ultimate laboratory of German modernity.

Notes

1   Rudy Koshar, "How to Speak Weimar," *Montreal Review*, May 2014: http://www.themontrealreview.com/2009/How-to-Speak-Weimar.php [accessed June 30, 2014].

2   See, for example, Alois Friedel, "Die politische Symbolik in der Weimarer Republik" (Ph.D. diss., University of Marburg, 1956), p. 7; Hagen Schulze, *Weimar. Deutschland 1917–1933* (Berlin: Severin und Siedler, 1982), p. 424; Ian Kershaw (ed.), *Weimar: Why Did German Democracy Fail* (New York: Palgrave Macmillan, 1990).

3   Peter Fritzsche, "Did Weimar Fail?" *The Journal of Modern History* 68:3 (September 1996), pp. 629–56, here p. 647.

4   Detlev Peukert, *The Weimar Republic: The Crisis of Classical Modernity* (New York: Hill and Wang, 1993), pp. 5–6 and 35.

5   Thomas Mergel, *Parlamentarische Kultur in der Weimarer Republik* (Düsseldorf: Droste, 2002), p. 64.

6   Gotthard Jasper, *Der Schutz der Republik: Studien zur staatlichen Sicherung der Demokratie in der Weimarer Republik 1922–1933* (Tübingen: JCB Mohr, 1963); Klaus Wippermann, *Politische Propaganda und staatsbürgerliche*

Bildung: Die Reichszentrale für Heimatdienst in der Weimarer Republik (Cologne: Wissenschaft und Politik, 1976).

7   Gustav Radbruch, *Der innere Weg. Aufriß meines Lebens* (Stuttgart: KF Koehler, 1951), p. 177. See also Friedrich Stampfer, *Die vierzehn Jahre der ersten deutschen Republik* (Hamburg: Auerdruck, 1947), p. 304. Especially bitter is Albert Grzesinski, *Inside Germany* (New York: EP Dutton & Co., 1939), p. 139ff.

8   Bernd Buchner, *Um nationale und republikanische Identität: Die deutsche Sozialdemokratie und der Kampf um die politischen Symbole in der Weimarer Republik* (Bonn: Dietz, 2001); Nadine Rossol, *Performing the Nation in Interwar Germany: Sport, Spectacle, and Political Symbolism, 1926–1936* (Basingstoke: Palgrave Macmillan, 2010); Caroline Dorothée Lange, *Genies im Reichstag: Führerbilder des republikanischen Bürgertums in der Weimarer Republik* (Hanover: Wehrhahn, 2012); Michael Meyer, *Symbolarme Republik? Das politische Zeremoniell der Weimarer Republik in den Staatsbesuchen zwischen 1920 und 1933* (Frankfurt: Peter Lang, 2014); Benjamin Ziemann, *Contested Commemorations: Republican War Veterans and Weimar Political Culture* (Cambridge: Cambridge University Press, 2013). First attempts at synthesis are mostly in form of edited volumes: Bernd Buchner et al., *Weimar und die Republik: Geburtsstunde eines demokratischen Deutschlands* (Weimar: Weimarer Verlagsgesesllschaft, 2009); Christian Welzbacher (ed.), *Der Reichskunstwart. Kulturpolitik und Staatsinszenierung in der Weimarer Republik 1918–1933* (Weimar: Weimarer Verlagsgesellschaft, 2010); John Alexander Williams (ed.), *Weimar Culture Revisited* (Basingstoke: Palgrave Macmillan, 2011); Kathleen Canning, Kerstin Barndt, and Kristin McGuire (eds.), *Weimar Publics/Weimar Subjects: Rethinking the Political Culture of Germany in the 1920s* (New York: Berghahn, 2010).

9   Arnold Brecht, *The Political Education of Arnold Brecht: An Autobiography 1884–1970* (Princeton: Princeton University Press, 1970), p. 216; Arnold Brecht, *Aus nächster Nähe: Lebenserinnerungen 1884–1927* (Stuttgart: Deutsche Verlagsanstalt, 1966), p. 361.

10   Manuela Achilles, "With a Passion for Reason: Celebrating the Constitution in Weimar Germany," *Central European History* 43:4 (December 2010), pp. 666–89.

11   Speech as reported in Reichszentrale für Heimatdienst (ed.), *10 Jahre Weimarer Verfassung. Die Verfassungsreden bei den Verfassungsfeiern der Reichsregierung* (Berlin: Zentralverlag G.m.b.H., 1929), p. 111.

12   Sebastian Ullrich, *Der Weimar-Komplex. Das Scheitern der ersten deutschen Demokratie und die politische Kultur der frühen Bundesrepublik 1945–1959* (Göttingen: Wallstein, 2009).

13   Koshar, "How to Speak Weimar."

14   Rüdiger Graf, "Either-Or: The Narrative of 'Crisis' in Weimar Germany and in Historiography," *Central European History* 43, Special Issue on the "Culture of Politics: New Perspectives on the Weimar Republic" (2010), pp. 592–615, here p. 603. See also Moritz Föllmer and Rüdiger Graf (eds.), *Die "Krise" der Weimarer Republik: Zur Kritik eines Deutungsmusters* (Frankfurt: Campus, 2005).

15 Brecht, *Political Education*, pp. 142, 150.

16 Hagen Schulze, *Otto Braun oder Preussens demokratische Sendung* (Frankfurt: Ullstein, 1977), p. 240.

17 *Berliner Tageblatt*, February 12, 1919.

18 Stampfer, *Die vierzehn Jahre*, pp. 97–8.

19 *Berliner Tageblatt*, February 12, 1919.

20 *Vorwärts*, February 12, 1919.

21 *Berliner Tageblatt*, February 12, 1919.

22 *Vorwärts*, February 6, 1919.

23 Otto Meissner, *Staatssekretär unter Ebert—Hindenburg—Hitler: Der Schicksalsweg des deutschen Volkes von 1918–1945, wie ich ihn erlebte* (Hamburg: Hoffmann und Campe, 1950), p. 46.

24 *Vorwärts*, February 6, 1919.

25 Richard Bessel, *Germany after the First World War* (Oxford: Clarendon Press, 1993), p. 254f.

26 Brecht, *Political Education*, p. 215f.

27 *Vorwärts* 388, August 1, 1919; *Berliner Tageblatt* 352, August 1, 1919.

28 As reported in *Vorwärts* 388, August 1, 1919.

29 Ibid.

30 See Heinrich Oppenheimer, *The Constitution of the German Republic* (London: Stevens and Sons, 1923), pp. 219, 7–8.

31 Buchner, *Identität*, pp. 51, 47, 48. For a more differentiated approach, see Karl Rohe, *Das Reichsbanner Schwarz Rot Gold: Ein Beitrag zur Geschichte und Struktur der politischen Kampfverbände zur Zeit der Weimarer Republik* (Düsseldorf: Droste, 1966), p. 241f.

32 Kevin Repp, *Reformers, Critics, and the Paths of German Modernity: Anti-Politics and the Search for Alternatives, 1890–1914* (Cambridge: Harvard University Press, 2000), pp. 219–20, 222, 227, 242, 326.

33 Hans Hattenhauer, *Deutsche Nationalsymbole: Zeichen und Bedeutung* (Munich: Günter Olzog, 1984), p. 57.

34 Manuela Achilles, "Re-forming the Reich: Symbolics of the Republican Nation in Weimar Germany" (Ph.D. diss., University of Michigan, 2005), pp. 58–9 and ff.

35 *Das Kabinet Scheidemann, 13. February bis 20. Juni 1919, Akten der Reichskanzlei: Weimarer Republic* (Boppard am Rhein: H. Boldt, 1971), p. 315.

36 Ed. Heilfron (ed.), *Die Deutsche Nationalversammlung im Jahre 1919 in ihrer Arbeit für den Aufbau des neuen deutschen Volksstaaates* [DNV], vols 1–8, (Berlin: Norddeutsche Buchdruckerei und Verlagsanstalt, 1919–20); here vol. 5, p. 3007.

37 Ibid., p. 3009.

38 Ibid., p. 3017.

39 Ibid., pp. 3120, 3041.

40 See RKW to Maximilian Pfeiffer (May 17, 1920), Bundesarchiv–Lichterfelde [BArch], 32/1: p. 37.

41 RKW draft memo of June 1920, BArch, R 32/1: pp. 19, 31.

42 On Redslob's agenda, see Edwin Redslob, *Amtliche Graphik: Ein Beitrag zur Frage der unbewussten Kunsterziehung* (May 1921) [=*Plakat* no. 5], p. 1; Edwin Redslob, "Grundgedanken für die Arbeit des Reichskunstwartes," *Kunstchronik und Kunstmarkt 5* (October 28, 1921), pp. 75–8, BArch, R 32/1: p. 152ff.; Edwin Redslob, *Die Amtliche Graphik des Reiches und ihre Auswirkung auf Kunst und Handwerk* (Berlin: Phönix Illustrationsdruck und Verlag GmBH, 1925) [=*Gebrauchsgraphik* no. 2], pp. 7–9 and 58, BArch R 32/1: pp. 18–46 and 121; R 32/2: pp. 46–9, 56, 72–82, 89–107; R 32/28: pp. 45–7.

43 Redslob, *Gebrauchsgraphik*, p. 58.

44 On the search for a German national style under the Second Empire, see Matthew Jefferies, *Imperial Culture in Germany, 1871–1918* (New York: Palgrave Macmillan, 2003), pp. 90–2 and ff.; Wolfgang Hardtwig, "Nationale und kulturelle Identität im Kaiserreich und der umkämpfte Weg in die Moderne," in Helmut Berding (ed.), *Nationales Bewußtsein und kollektive Identität: Studien zur Entwicklung des kollektiven Bewußtseins in der Neuzeit 2* (Frankfurt: Suhrkamp, 1994), pp. 507–40. On the Werkbund: Joan Campbell, *The German Werkbund: The Politics of Reform in the Applied Arts* (Princeton: Princeton University Press, 1978); Peter W. Kallen, *Unter dem Banner der Sachlichkeit: Studien zum Verhältnis von Kunst und Industrie am Beginn des 20. Jahrhunderts* (Cologne: DME-Verlag, 1987); Frederic J. Schwartz, *The Werkbund: Design Theory and Mass Culture before the First World War* (New Haven: Yale University Press, 1996); John Maciuika, *Before the Bauhaus: Architecture, Politics, and the German State, 1890–1920* (Cambridge: Cambridge University Press, 2005).

45 See F.H. Ehmke's biting survey of the empire's coins, bills, and postage stamps, published by the Munich *Bund*: F.H. Ehmcke, *Amtliche Graphik*, Munich (October 1918).

46 For details regarding the Werkbund's role in the foundation of the *Reichskunstwart* office, see Ernst Jäckh, *Der Goldene Pflug: Lebensernte eines Weltbürgers* (Stuttgart: Deutsche Verlags-Anstalt, 1954), pp. 202–03. Interior Minister Koch acknowledged the Werkbund's involvement in a letter of December 5, 1919; BArch, R 32/1: 16.

47 Annegret Heffen, *Der Reichskunstwart. Kunstpolitik in den Jahren 1920–1933: zu den Bemühungen um eine offizielle Reichskunstpolitik in der Weimarer Republik* (Essen: Verlag Die Blaue Eule, 1986), p. 45, note 59.

48 Jäckh, *Der Goldene Pflug*, pp. 203, 9, 23f., 459.

49 See Heffen, *Der Reichskunstwart*, pp. 46–51; A letter of March 6, 1923, suggests that Redslob was voted into the DDP (*Parteiausschuss*) on March 3, 1926. BArch R 32/3: p. 208. Cf. Friedel, p. 51, note 3.

50 Christian Welzbacher, *Edwin Redslob: Biographie eines unverbesserlichen Idealisten* (Berlin: Matthes & Seitz, 2009), p. 12.

51 Edwin Redslob, *Von Weimar nach Europa: Erlebtes und Durchdachtes* (Berlin: Haude & Spenersche Verlagsbuchhandlung, undated), p. 165.

52 Edwin Redslob, *Die Werbekraft der Qualität. Vortrag auf der Leipziger Herbstmesse am 30. August 1920* (Berlin and Munich: Verlag Hermann Reckendorf, 1920), p. 4.

53 Ibid.

54 *Die Neue Erziehung* 1 12/13 (June 1919).

55 Max Osborn, "Der 'Reichskunstwart,' " *Vossische Zeitung* 22 (January 13, 1920).

56 *Das Plakat* 11:8 ("Formgebung im öffentlichen Verkehrsleben"), BArch, R 32/1: 45 (copy).

57 *Das Kabinett Wirth; Akten der Reichskanzlei*, pp. 533–4, note 5 (doc. 196).

58 Redslob, *Von Weimar nach Europa*, p. 58.

59 Heffen, *Der Reichskunstwart*, p. 124 and f.

60 Karlheinz Weissmann, *Die Zeichen des Reiches: Symbole der Deutschen* (Asendorf: MUT-Verlag, 1989), p. 104. The country's constitutional proper name was *Deutsches Reich*—also "D R."

61 Stradonitz in Redslob (ed.), *Die Amtliche Graphik des Reiches und ihre Auswirkung auf Kunst und Handwerk* = H.K. Frenzel (ed.), *Gebrauchsgraphik, Monatsschrift zur Förderung künstlerischer Reklame* 2:2, p. 33.

62 Ibid., pp. 34–7.

63 Edwin Redslob, "Die künstlerische Formgebung des Reichs" (Berlin, 1926), p. 6.

64 F.H. Ehmcke, "Amtliche Graphik als Recht und Pflicht," *Amtliche Graphik* (*Gebrauchsgraphik*), p. 5.

65 Redslob, "Die Künstlerische Formgebung," p. 6.

66 On the logic of either-or, see Graf, "Either-Or." The historian Hajo Holborn rejected Redslob's unity flag with the assertion that the issue could only be decided at the point of ultimate victory. In his opinion, it was necessary that one side succeeded in installing itself visibly and decisively at the very center of all political thinking and conduct. Hajo Holborn, "Review of Egmont Zechlin, *Schwarz-Rot-Gold und Schwarz-Weiß-Rot in Geschichte und Gegenwart* [Berlin 1926]," *Historische Zeitschrift* 141 (1930), pp. 130–4, here p. 133.

67 Manuela Achilles, "Nationalist Violence and Republican Identity in Weimar Germany," in David Midgley and Christian Emden (eds.), *German Literature, History and the Nation* (Oxford: Peter Lang, 2004), pp. 305–28; Manuela Achilles, "Reforming the Reich: Democratic Symbols and Rituals in the Weimar Republic," in *Weimar Publics/Weimar Subjects*, pp. 175–91.

68 *Vossische Zeitung* (June 29, 1922, evening edition).

69 H. Pollack, "Ich suche eine Fahne. Ein Kauf mit Hindernissen," *Vossische Zeitung* (August 10, 1922).

70 Margarete Caemmerer, "Die Fahnenfrage. Zu dem Artikel Slings 'Das Volk ohne Fahne,' " *Vossische Zeitung* (June 29, 1922).

71 Cited in Buchner, *Identität*, p. 93.

72 Speeches by Wirth and Hergt in *Gegen den politischen Mord! Reichstagssitzung vom 25. Juni 1922* (Schwerin IM, 1922).

73 Jasper, *Der Schutz der Republik*, p. 62.

74 Max Osborn, "Der 'Reichskunstwart,'" *Vossische Zeitung* (January 13, 1920). The German terms are "zeitgemäß" and "volkstümlich."

13

The *Werkbund* Exhibition "The New Age" of 1932

Jennifer L. Jenkins

In 1925, at a meeting of the German Werkbund in Bremen, the association's members hatched a plan to celebrate the group's twenty-fifth anniversary in 1932 with an exhibition. Initially proposed by the architect Richard Riemerschmid, the idea was approved by the general membership. The event's organization was turned over to Ernst Jäckh, the Werkbund's longtime business manager. Jäckh secured pledges from industry and government and planned an ambitious exhibition. Scheduled to be held in Cologne in 1932 and supported by the city's mayor, Konrad Adenauer, it was to be called "The New Age" (*Die neue Zeit*). With the decision to mount an international exhibit in Cologne, the Werkbund appeared to have come full circle, its plans for 1932 mirroring the moment of its celebrated show in Cologne in the summer of 1914. The prior event had announced the arrival of the association on an international stage. Its signature buildings—Bruno Taut's Glass Pavillion, the Factory and Office Building from Walter Gropius, and Henri van de Velde's Municipal Theater—showcased the group's stylistic diversity and the creative range of its members. Both aspects of its work were on full view in 1914. In fact, the plurality of positions on the relationship between art and industrial modernity had led to a fierce debate among the members following architect Hermann Muthesius's presentation on the virtues of standardization and his promotion of a partnership between modernist design and German commerce.[1]

If the keyword for the 1914 Cologne exhibition was plurality that of the 1932 exhibition was unity. "The New Age" was intended as an assertion of Germany's pre-eminence in modern architecture and design. It was to display the group's strong sense of internal unity as centered on the ethics and aesthetics of functionalism that underpinned *Neues Bauen*. However, many things about this exhibition were more illusory than real, the internal unity included. Histories of the Werkbund tell us that the exhibition never happened. Most lay the blame for this on the economic depression following "Black Tuesday," the stock market crash of October 1929, which drained the organization's funds as well as those of affiliated *Vereine* and municipal administrations, and made the staging of an expensive exhibition financially impossible. Others point to increasing strife within the organization, which weakened it internally, as well as the appearance of new enemies on the cultural scene. According to these accounts, as the coffers emptied and trade union support faded away, the Werkbund's championing of industrial functionalism was under siege from a newly resurgent design direction emphasizing the reactionary conceptions of *Handwerk* and *Heimat*.[2] In this narrative, a nationalist conception of culture triumphed over an internationalist view of civilization, and progressivism was defeated by reaction. The Weimar Republic died, and so too did the Weimar Werkbund.

Such accounts tell a familiar story of rise and fall, but one wonders if that is all that one can say? The exhibition, "The New Age," is at most a footnote in literature on the Werkbund. However, this phantasm, this-exhibition-that-never-happened, provides an interesting window onto both the late Weimar Werkbund and the categories that organize its historiography. This includes the vexed conceptual pairs functionalism/organicism, international/national (or *heimatlich*), and *Zivilization/Kultur*. These concepts are often paired up with the metacategories of modern/antimodern, which themselves are elided with the political designators of progressive and reactionary, creating a chain of associations that welds aesthetic debates to political ones. As a result, progressive design can be equated with industrial functionalism, both supposedly signifiers of a progressive, that is, social democratic politics. While the pairing of functionalism and Social Democracy largely held through the late 1920s, by the early 1930s primary sources tell us that such a one-to-one correspondence often did not exist. Design direction and political program no longer matched so neatly. In general, the more we look the more we find that much of the messy modernity of German architecture and design in the 1920s and 1930s, its contest for the future, did not fit such clearly designated categories. Much of its substance, including the work of female designers—more recently a topic of research—is thereby lost to view.[3]

A good deal of the confusion has been historiographically generated, stemming from a particular reading of the development of culture and politics in the years prior to 1933. Starting with influential texts, most notably Barbara Miller Lane's classic 1968 study *Architecture and Politics in Germany 1918–1945*, the histories of architecture and design were embedded into the political history of the Weimar Republic, making the one the signifier of the other. With this move the history of modernist design became a way of reading the development of German politics.[4] The origins of modernist architecture were located in the revolution of 1918 and the emergence of Germany's avant-garde. Weimar modernism was separated from its Wilhelminian predecessor, and progressive aesthetics was equated with progressive politics. With time such scripts became rigid, with studies placing architects and designers into strictly demarcated categories: left or right, socialist or nationalist, anti- or proto-fascist, progressive or reactionary.[5]

This research correctly highlighted the new, and intense, politicization of design during the Weimar Republic and drew attention to the controversies that arose after 1918 around large architectural projects, particularly those that aimed at social reform and drew on public funds. It usefully illuminated why the hostility surrounding the Bauhaus was not a side issue, and it showed how the form that housing took—with the flat roof, for example—generated resonant political symbols.[6] However, fusing of design with politics frequently elided the difficulties of such a linking. It often grappled unsuccessfully with the complexities of Germany's political histories *and* its histories of modernist culture. In dividing the modernists from the antimodernists/cultural pessimists, a line was drawn between Bruno Taut and Heinrich Tessenow—to use one example—which Taut's death in Turkey in 1938 as a political exile from Nazism and Tessenow's status as the teacher of Albert Speer confirmed all too neatly. Their shared work in the construction of Germany's first life-reform community, the garden city Hellerau in 1908, and the similarities in their work and ideas—their intense interest in creating new experiences of "lived space" and their shared belief that the built environment was indispensable in creating new forms of community—vanish from view.[7] Other uncomfortable stories, such as Mies van der Rohe's career in National Socialist Germany, the similarities between National Socialist design and its modernist West German successors, or the structural and ideological connections between progressive Weimar architecture and the most advanced forms of Nazi building—including the ways in which the nascent field of regional planning during the Republic was drawn directly into National Socialist plans for racial settlement—became either hard to see or impossible to explain.[8]

A way to bring these topics into view is to focus on the discourse of the designers and planners themselves—the architects and advocates of modernist development. Using what Frederick Cooper has called an "indigenous" rather than a normative concept of modernity, the complicated involvement of German modernist design not only with progressive social reform, but also with imperialist expansion and industrial egotism, comes into view.[9] The Werkbund occupies a central place in analyses of progressive design. But it is rarely, if ever, analyzed in its relationship to the state and seen as an imperial institution in itself, a particularly modern combination of industrial, political, and aesthetic forms of power.[10] For the politician Friedrich Naumann and his colleague Ernst Jäckh, as well as for cultural theorists such as Joseph August Lux and industrialists such as Walther

Rathenau, the domestic reform of national spaces and things was not separate from imperial visions and plans. In exploring these connections, few figures are better positioned for analysis than the organizer of the 1932 Werkbund exhibition, the publicist and professor Ernst Jäckh. Jäckh combined—in his actions, person, and history—the connections between modernist design and Germany's aspirations for *Weltpolitik* both before and after the First World War. Jäckh believed that the modernist aesthetic advocated by the Werkbund should be disseminated as an imperialist *Weltkultur*, a sign and symbol of Germany's industrial might. As this essay will show, the roots of the *neue Zeit* exhibition lay in Jäckh's ideas about German power in the world and in modernist art, design, and technology as expressions of that power.

1

The 1932 exhibition was one of the last acts of the Weimar Werkbund. The fact that we know so little about it makes the general point that we know much more about the association's beginning than its end. Its founding in 1907, and its endorsement of a stylistic break with nineteenth-century historicism in favor of an industrial aesthetic, is a more straightforward story than is the murky pattern of continuity and rupture which characterized the development of modern design from the late 1920s through the 1950s. The failure of the 1932 exhibition to occur has been traditionally seen as evidence of Weimar's progressive modernism collapsing under the accumulated onslaught of economic depression and right-wing political advance. Joan Campbell wrote, in one of the oldest of such accounts, that Jäckh's exhibition was an unabashed celebration of modernity—modern design, modern science, and modern technology—and an exemplar of Weimar's cultural and political progressivism. It supported the future-oriented ideals with which the association had always been identified. "Jäckh had in mind a novel type of exhibition that would survey all aspects of human thought and creativity," she wrote. "Its aim was to demonstrate the unity of the emerging modern world...and above all, to inculcate in every visitor the same faith in progress and enthusiasm for the future that inspired the efforts of the Werkbund itself."[11] According to Campbell, such an exhibition predictably crashed on the rocks of the early 1930s, its progressivism extinguished by the newly influential voices of cultural and political reaction. Jäckh's futuristic bloom could not survive in a *Blut-und-Boden* hothouse.

Such an account irons out not a few complexities. First, the Weimar Werkbund had already travelled a long way by 1932 from its prewar predecessor. The question of technology was in the ascendant in the organization, so eclipsing the association's prior discussions on the transformative power of art as to make them seem almost quaint. Mies van der Rohe, in a 1928 debate on the "New Age" exhibition, warned his colleagues that technology should be their focus and not art. "[T]he economic, technical and cultural life conditions have fundamentally changed," he wrote, "and technology and economy face completely new problems. It is of decisive importance that these issues are correctly perceived and find meaningful solutions."[12] Members concurred that technological change had introduced vital new areas for design, and their suggestions for how to harness this power were often neither enlightened nor tolerant. Ernst Jäckh fit squarely into this camp. He was also a more complex and distasteful figure than generally realized, and his ideas concerning Germany's leadership in modernist design, and its role in defining a new *Weltkultur*, were not necessarily progressive. Campbell saw Jäckh as a die-hard supporter of functionalism and *Neue Sachlichkeit*, but Jäckh himself spoke of going beyond *Sachlichkeit* to something with deeper spiritual reach and vision. "What does the idea of 'the new age' mean?" he wrote in the overall plan for the exhibition. "It shouldn't mean something novel or fashionable; it isn't just 'modernity' or only the 'new objectivity' (*Neue Sachlichkeit*)," he stated, but something grander and larger.[13] What did this mean?

In addition to being the organization's business manager, Jäckh had been its most consistent imperialistic advocate before 1919 and was one of its more power-obsessed members. He also holds the infamous honor of being the organization's last Weimar president, and during his short tenure (1932–33) he engineered the association's *Gleichschaltung* in the spring of 1933. In a meeting with Hitler and Alfred Rosenberg in April 1933, the three men discussed the terms under which the Werkbund would be folded into Rosenberg's *Kampfbund für deutsche Kultur*.[14] By this date, and with this action, it was clear that Jäckh's view of the intersection of art, technology, and German "spirit" lay closer to the ideas about modernist design, industry, and national power which motivated a radical wing of the National Socialist Party.[15] By contrast, the views of his opponents— uniformly defamed in older accounts as the handmaidens of reaction through their use of organic language—championed not an ideology of blood and race but older pedagogical and artistic processes, local forms of creativity, and a community-oriented sense of building, all of which had been previously seen as progressive.

A range of positions on how to combine art and technology existed inside the association in 1932. They moved across the political spectrum, and they confound a neat modern/antimodern split. The architects who spoke of organic design and development did not all agree with the National Socialist architect Paul Schultze Naumberg nor with Rosenberg's *Kampfbund für deutsche Kultur*. Werkbund member Hans Poelzig's articulation of the "avant garde position" of 1931, for example, was notable for its look backwards. In a speech to the Association of German Architects, Poelzig criticized functionalism for having become conformist and bound to industry. He expressed nostalgia for the ideas on radical creativity and social change made famous by Bruno Taut and his colleagues in the "Crystal Chain" correspondence of 1919.[16] Poelzig's speech showed that by the early 1930s a clear definition between older ideas of modern/antimodern, or *Kultur/ Zivilisation*, in discussions of design was in the process of breaking down. The fronts were no longer clearly defined; their boundaries had changed through years of intensive discussion and conflict, and dissention existed in each camp. Several key terms of Germany's design discourse—functionalism, *Sachlichkeit*, and organicism—now carried a range of meanings; in the late 1920s and early 1930s they would be fought over from both the left and the right in a fraught and bitter contest for the future of the association.

As the examples above show, discussions on the 1932 exhibition published in the Werkbund journal *Die Form* reveal a complex debate about cultural and political modernity that thwarts the categories traditionally used to read it. A close analysis of the debate around the *neue Zeit* exhibition shows the pieces of the familiar duo *Kultur/Zivilization* changing sides. Here the supporters of an "organic" art, such as Walter Rietzler, the editor of *Die Form*, expressed skepticism about the grandiosity of Jäckh's plan, while the advocates of industrial design—Jäckh's supporters—displayed a marked will to power. Jäckh's background is also germane. Seeing him as a benign supporter of progressivism is to believe his own self-promotion. Jäckh made a career of selling himself politically, and his myriad political connections were a constant in the many twists and turns of his career. From a left-liberal journalist in 1907, he became a rabid annexationist and Foreign Office contact in 1915, operating out of Berlin and Istanbul, before covering up that past by turning into a benign republican internationalist in 1920 on the way to cooperating with the National Socialists in the *Gleichschaltung* of the Werkbund in 1933. Insights from new literature on Wilhelmine imperialism can help unpack what he had in mind in 1932 when he spoke of his exhibition as a showcase for German *Weltkultur*. The idea that Germany would have a pioneering role in the modern design movement for Jäckh was never about internationalism and it had shockingly little to do with art. For him the Werkbund, *Weltkultur*, and the *neue Zeit* were concerned with technology, industry, Germanic culture, and state power.[17]

2

On April 1, 1912, Ernst Jäckh became the Werkbund's managing director. He had been the editor of the liberal Southern German *Neckar-Zeitung*, a supporter of the politician Friedrich Naumann, and the man responsible for introducing "American" styles of political campaigning into Naumann's successful election to the Reichstag in 1907. Due to his campaigning experience, Jäckh was hired in 1912 to take the Werkbund in a new direction.[18] Hermann Muthesius stressed to Jäckh, in persuading him to take the position, that "only you can complete the scaffolding that Wolf Dohrn and A[lfons] Paquet have prepared...we know of no one else, in whom we would place so much trust to save and protect the Werkbund."[19]

Jäckh's plans for strengthening the organization, both financially and in terms of membership, quickly materialized. The Werkbund grew in numbers, began the publication of a yearbook, and began establishing branches outside of Germany and Austria.[20] Yet the development of the organization in a traditional sense was not the reason that Jäckh was hired. Nor did he have any expertise in architecture and design, the Werkbund's central areas of activity. According to Naumann associate Theodor Heuss, "things like furniture construction...wallpaper patterns, city planning, graphic design, handweaving, and so on were either completely foreign or of no interest to him."[21] Jäckh was neither an architect nor a designer, and he was not particularly interested in art. What Muthesius meant with "saving" and "protecting" the Werkbund in 1912 went in the direction of business outreach, international connections, contracts, and trade. Jäckh had consistently sided with the business and industry-oriented side of the association; he was a strong supporter of Muthesius's imperialist interests and those of the Werkbund's longtime president, the Württemburg industrialist Peter Bruckmann.

Political connections were foremost in the appointment, and he had these in abundance. They included his friendship with Naumann—the man at the center of what Kevin Repp has called the "Wilhelminian reform milieu"—and his connections to journalists, politicians, writers, and administrators in state ministries: to Paul Rohrbach, Commissioner for Settlement in Southwest Africa from 1903 to 1906, a supporter of the modernization of Turkey and a publicist for the dismemberment of Russia, and to Hjalmar Schacht of the Dresdener Bank, later President of the Reichsbank and Economics Minister under Hitler. Hans Humann in the Reich Navy Office was another friend; he would provide Jäckh with a model for modernizing colonized places with his work in Qingdao. A conduit to Enver Pascha, Humann facilitated Jäckh's collaboration with the Young Turk leadership during the war.[22] All of these men were liberal imperialists, many were friends of Naumann's and supported his vision of expanding Germany's international trade as a motor for social reform projects at home. Jäckh himself was quite clear on this score. In his view Germany's rise in population, coupled with her industrial capacity, necessitated an economic program of industrial and trade expansion based on the import of raw materials and the export of high-quality manufactured goods. A rise in exports was to run hand in hand with industrial consolidation, urbanization, and political reform at home. As he wrote in 1913, support for Germany's growing population required in the first instance "the processing and refining of raw materials into finished manufactures and the export of these products into developed markets."[23]

Jäckh's primary political connections, however, and the ones that made him most attractive to Muthesius and Bruckmann, who led the Werkbund after 1916, were to the Foreign Office. Here friendship to the well-connected diplomat, and later Foreign Minister, Alfred von Kiderlen-Wächter provided the foundation. Jäckh's most powerful ties to industry, banking, and the Foreign Office ran through Kiderlen-Wächter, minister in Bucharest, interim ambassador in Istanbul, and Foreign Secretary between 1910 and 1912. Kiderlen had introduced Jäckh to the leaders of the Young Turk revolution of 1908, specifically the members of the "Committee for Union and Progress," and Jäckh furthered these connections in the years between 1908 and 1914. Most of Jäckh's ideas for Germany's cultural and industrial expansion targeted the Ottoman Empire as the most suitable arena.[24] "[T]he Orient of the Balkans and the Near East, the states in the Balkans as well as Turkey," he wrote, "remain as the most natural, the nearest, the almost neighborly area of development (Erschliessungsgebiet) for German labor, and the possibilities of this Orient increase yearly."[25] Jäckh's nickname was "Jäckh the Turk" (Türken Jäckh), and it was the promise of being able to continue his Ottoman projects, as well as the offer of a teaching position at the University of Berlin, in addition to his Werkbund duties that enticed him to take the position as its business manager. "We completely agree with the wish of the Foreign Secretary," wrote Muthesius (referring to Kiderlen), "that you will continue to pursue your oriental and foreign policy work in Berlin... which has been successful thus far in Heilbronn and Istanbul, in tandem with your leadership of the Werkbund."[26] Muthesius was referring—with Heilbrunn and Istanbul—to Jäckh's organization of a study trip to Württemburg in 1911 for Turkish politicians, including members of the Young Turk Committee of Union and Progress, who observed industrial plants, toured hospitals and schools, and heard lectures on German administration.[27]

Jäckh's relationships with the Young Turk leadership were known to the Foreign Office, as was his furthering of what, in 1914, became the Ottoman-German alliance. The historian Fritz Fischer described Jäckh was "the most important propagandist of Germany's eastern policy" during the First World War. He was a friend of Baron Max von Oppenheim, a notorious figure in Near Eastern politics in his own right and the founder of the "Information Service for the East," the office which prepared the ground for an Islamic uprising against the British Empire during the First World War. Fischer placed Jäckh in a group he called government liberals, those men grouped around Chancellor Bethmann Hollweg, his September Memorandum, and a wartime policy of expansion and annexation. A central aspect of the latter was the plan for Germany's extension east and south that went under the name of Mitteleuropa.[28] Fischer never mentioned that Jäckh was the administrative head of the Werkbund, but the Werkbund fits into this context. With the publicist Paul Rohrbach, Jäckh published a series of books and pamphlets during the war, including the series Der deutsche Krieg, which trumpeted Germany's imperialist war aims.[29] As part of this work, he championed the Werkbund's role in defining a Weltkultur as the cultural component of Germany's expansionist policies.

From its inception, the Werkbund had advocated the importance of bridging oppositional concepts: art and industry, matter and spirit. During the war Jäckh took this further, telling his colleagues that culture, politics, and economy were now interconnected aspects of the same expansionist program. In his vision, they merged into a new totality. He presented this view in a speech to the Werkbund Congress in 1915, and the title of the talk signaled its direction. Called "Werkbund and Mitteleuropa," it stated that the "Werkbund" was not only the name of a design organization. Rather, it was to designate the new Central European cultural order of an expanded German state. Jäckh began his lecture on the customary cultural ground, only to progress to a much more radical, future-oriented, political vision. "Art and politics," he stated, possessed "an inner unity."[30] So far, so familiar. Yet the next step was anything but business as usual. The unity between art and politics, he asserted, could be illustrated by analyzing the two terms of his title: "Werkbund" and "*Mitteleuropa*." His lecture outlined the following three points:

1. that the Werkbund has developed out of and towards the same laws of order/form as *Mitteleuropa*, both in will as in goal, moreover,
2. that this law of order is an organic principle, that achieves its artistic expression in the Werkbund and its political expression in Mitteleuropa, and finally
3. that this organic principle is essentially "German mind" (*der deutsche Sinn*) and "German ways" (*das deutsche Wesen*).[31]

According to one of the most perceptive historians of the Werkbund, Frederic Schwartz, its members "were trying to set up a world in which art and economy would speak the same language." He called this "experimenting in the open."[32] Jäckh took the experimenting one step further. He stated that art, economy, and politics, including foreign policy, were all aspects of the same national drive. *Weltpolitik* was incomplete without the founding of a *Weltkultur*, which was encapsulated in the modernist design furthered by his Werkbund colleagues. Moreover, both Werkbund and *Weltkultur* would work together to create a coming new order. This, he wrote, would be organized as an association, a "Werkbund," binding together "a particular community of peoples (*einer gewissen Völkergemeinschaft*)."[33] With this speech, Jäckh moved beyond Naumann's conception of *Mitteleuropa*—which he claimed was too narrowly focused on economic policy and was too constrained geographically, being limited to Germany and Austria-Hungary—and set out a more expansive vision. The larger *Mitteleuropa*, he told his audience—pointing to the alliances between Germany, Austria-Hungary, and the Ottoman Empire—was not fantasy but reality, a set of facts on the ground. "Today *Mitteleuropa* is no longer a utopia," he wrote, "as a four-fold political alliance it is already an actual fact."[34] The new branches of the Werkbund that he helped to found after 1912, with locations in Sweden, Belgium, Holland, Switzerland, and Hungary, also mapped this emerging new space.

Thus the Werkbund defined the culture for which *Mitteleuropa* was the state. A new *Weltkultur* would result from the fusion of Germany's modernist design with the dynamism of German industry, both of which would operate on the territory of German-dominated Middle Europe.[35] However, following the war and Germany's defeat Jäckh's open chauvinism had become a liability. He professionally remade himself with breathless speed, submerging his annexationist identity and emerging in 1920 in the guise of a liberal internationalist and the founder of the German Academy for Politics (*Hochschule für Politik*) in Berlin. What did "modernity" mean to a man such as this? How many meanings did it have?

3

Jäckh unveiled his plan for "The New Age" at the Werkbund Congress in Breslau in 1929.[36] Some of the aspects were familiar. As was fitting for the twenty-fifth anniversary of the association, the exhibition would highlight all sides of the issue of "quality work." Similar to the Werkbund's latest exhibitions—the *Weissenhof Siedlung* of 1927 and the Breslau exhibition in 1929—architecture would hold pride of place.[37] Industrial organizations were particularly strong supporters of the exhibition.[38] Cologne was to receive a number of new buildings, including social housing, a number of public buildings and hygienic installations ("a central market hall, slaughterhouses and livestock areas, schools and clinics"), and a completely new university.[39] Jäckh was adamant that these buildings were to be "social" constructions and not just "for show." He had a contemptuous view of *Schaubauten* and *Schauarchitektur*. The new housing was to be a permanent addition to the cityscape, intended "to relieve the housing shortage." "It means mobilizing the thinking around this exhibition in order to provide lasting social and economic accomplishments," he claimed, "in order to solve actual and necessary building issues through the systematic cooperation of local, national and international forces and values."[40] This was business as usual. Other aspects of the exhibition, however, were more surprising, its scale and reach above all, as well as its stance on technology. Jäckh wanted the exhibition not just to be new. He wanted it to be revolutionary. It was not only to break with past practice. Rather, it was to offer what he claimed to be a completely new set of perspectives on modern life. Rather than displaying objects, interiors, or buildings, the exhibition aimed to show a fundamental change in identity and perception. It targeted the particular *forms of seeing and feeling* that Jäckh claimed characterized the coming time. These were to be made concrete and palpable. This was a distinctly futuristic step.

Jäckh defined the exhibition's concept using a diagram with seven intersecting circles. As he stated, the exhibition would cover the following topics:

the necessity and possibility of a new view of the world (*Weltsicht*); the new image of the universe; new directions in physics; philosophy in the age of technology; the transformation of human relations; the transformation of biological thinking; the body-soul problem and changes in modern medicine; radical change in the fine arts; the search for a new understanding of being, and the fourth dimension as the mark of a new worldview.[41]

Here one sees that the focus was no longer, as the Werkbund's focus had been, on remaking objects, buildings, and spaces. Here attention was put on the design of humans and human identity, their philosophy, relations, and body–soul issues as viewed through the lenses of biology, technology, and modern science. Modernity, he said, was a style and was, thus, empty. The "New Age" was a change of life-form that would create a "new man." Jäckh's accompanying diagram with its seven circles was as amorphous as was the description. It reached from circle one, "the conception of the world" (*Weltbild*), to circle seven, "ordering of the world," with stops at "the moulding of man," "building and living," and "the shape of the state." Via the concepts surrounding the circles, Jäckh mapped the movement from the particular to the universal. Amorphousness was not particular to the 1929 plan. It never became more concrete. The more one reads the more amorphous it becomes. One is not surprised that not a few Werkbund members wondered how such a concept could be concretely exhibited.

The answer was technology. As became clear, the goal of the exhibition was to show an ideal of the new man, formed in the image of technology and extolling a vision of German industrial power. Jäckh claimed that technology held the various pieces of the exhibition concept together, and he conceived of technology in a particular way. It was not encapsulated in objects or represented through particular styles. Rather, technology was the essence of the "New Age" and was the defining element in the coming period of world history. Technology was a force that enveloped and transformed objects, landscapes, relations, bodies. He spoke of "cinema eyes" and "radio ears" as examples of the coming transformations in perception and experience that the exhibition would display. Germany represented a high form of this stage of cultural development, which operated, according to Jäckh, according to universal principles. It would triumph throughout the world, transforming individuals and societies in its own image. This was not a matter of human choice. In fact, individual choice and human agency were noticeably absent in Jäckh's descriptions. While Jäckh had always had this tick—he had spoken in these terms for some time—what is interesting was the amount of consensus that his ideas generated in the period after 1929. Newspapers from the right to the left commented favorably on the exhibition plans.[42]

But not all in the Werkbund agreed. Walter Rietzler, editor of *Die Form* between 1927 and 1932, pointed to the "conflicts and fights" over the exhibition that were roiling the organization. Rietzler was in many ways Jaeckh's opposite number. Trained as a musicologist, he had directed the city art gallery in Stettin and was one of the Werkbund's founding members. As Campbell pointed out, "his sympathies generally lay with the creative element in the Werkbund rather than with its 'politicians'," and he had disagreed with Jäckh on the question of *Weltkultur* since the war. In 1916, when Jäckh published *Werkbund and Mitteleuropa*, Rietzler published a counter piece. His book *Die Kulturarbeit des Deutschen Werkbundes* emphasized art and creativity as the core of the Werkbund's mission rather than the intersection between cultural policy and state power. Rietzler felt that an exhibition which claimed to define a "new age" before that age had begun, and which was taken up with the idea of a coming period of world history, at a time when the Weimar Republic was under considerable strain, was far too grandiose.[43] Moreover, its urge toward spectacle showed distinct contempt for the practical and pedagogical work of the Weimar Werkbund. Rietzler was not an antimodernist. He recognized the importance of technology, and he supported *Neues Bauen*. As he wrote, "from the first mention of the idea it was clear that technology would have to be a large part of the exhibition." Technology, wrote Rietzler, "is, after all, that power through which the new era manifests itself most clearly." Yet it mattered greatly how one presented and displayed technology, as an object subject to human control or as an impersonal world historical force. For Jäckh it was the latter; his new man was not a private individual but a collective subject created by world historical forces. This seemed to be popular, as other members worried that the exhibition would potentially not take technology seriously enough. One wrote on the danger of presenting only a superficial experience—an aestheticization—of technology through the exhibition. "One danger easily arises via this perspective," he wrote, "essentially that one makes—from modern forms which come out of life and out of technology—an aesthetic affair only, a type of decoration. How one can confront this danger can't be ascertained…"[44]

Paul Betts has written perceptively on the changes in German design culture as the 1920s merged into the 1930s. "[M]odern design experienced surprising success after 1929," he writes, "yet its victory came at a certain price. For the triumph of modern design went hand in hand with the disappearance of its former reform idealism. The once powerful political pathos of functionalism had given way to a severe *Neue Sachlichkeit* divorced from any real social vision."[45] That this change was in the air was undeniable. In 1930, Mies van der Rohe championed a view of modernity as an aesthetic principle emptied of social and political content. "The new age (*die neue Zeit*) is a fact," he wrote, "it exists completely independently of whether we say 'yes' or 'no' to it."[46] Likewise, the exhibition "Eternal Forms" (*Ewige Formen*), held in Munich in 1931, attempted to confer an ahistorical timelessness onto functionalist objects, narrating the history of modernist design as a history of technological change that now excised the social visions that had previously accompanied the Werkbund's championing of functionalism. Older understandings of modern/antimodern were in the process of changing places.

Jäckh went further. He didn't only empty modernist design of social vision; he began filling it with a new one. "Werkbund" went from being a designation for an architectural style or a social program to becoming a claim (*Weltkultur*) about how German industry, technology, and business—German capitalism—would shape the rest of the world. As he wrote in the exhibition concept, the coming time, the "New Age," was one of great changes:

> The five continents of the five divisions of the earth will melt together to form one interconnected continent of a unique global unity... on which no area or space is unknown... we live in a transformed and different space: we live in a space that is simultaneously larger and smaller than that of all of world history preceding us; we truly live "in year one," or in the first decade of a new conception of space, and a new measurement of time... it is now a question of understanding all of the consequences, to seize and "realize" the new reality in all of its aspects.[47]

He may have been a globalist before his time, but describing him as a simple progressive, a defender of the "modern" unproblematically understood, was quite far off the mark. His messages to Alfred Rosenberg, that perhaps the "New Age" exhibition could be used to advertise National Socialist ideas, are testament to this fact.

Notes

1   On the Werkbund and its exhibition in 1914, see Frederic J. Schwartz, *The Werkbund: Design Theory and Mass Culture before the First World War* (New Haven: Yale University Press, 1996); John Maciuika, *Before the Bauhaus: Architecture, Politics and the German State, 1890–1920* (Cambridge: Cambridge University Press, 2005).

2   As Paul Betts noted, after 1929 the Werkbund's support from the political left, namely from trade unions and socialist organizations, which was "once solid... had evaporated." Betts, *The Authority of Everyday Objects: A Cultural History of West German Industrial Design* (Berkeley: University of California Press, 2004), p. 26. The Werkbund had 3,000 members in 1929; the numbers fell thereafter. See Joan Campbell, *The German Werkbund: The Politics of Reform in the Applied Arts* (Princeton: Princeton University Press, 1978), p. 296, and ch. 8 for the decline in membership.

3   Despina Stratigakos, *A Woman's Berlin: Building the Modern City* (Minneapolis: University of Minnesota Press, 2008) and the classic study of Maud Lavin, *Cut with the Kitchen Knife: The Weimar Photomontages of Hannah Höch* (New Haven: Yale University Press, 1993).

4   Barbara Miller Lane, *Architecture and Politics in Germany, 1918–1945* (Cambridge: Harvard University Press, 1968); Peter Gay, *Weimar Culture: The Outsider as Insider* (New York: Harper & Row, 1968); Francesco Dal Co, *Figures of Architecture and Thought: German Architecture Culture* (New York: Rizzoli, 1990). Eric Weitz, *Weimar Germany: Promise and Tragedy* (Princeton: Princeton University Press, 2007), repeats several of these assumptions.

5   Peter Fritzsche takes up the problems of outdated categories of right and left in analyzing Weimar culture and politics, proposing an analysis of the period as a series of "experiments with modernity." See Fritzsche, "Did Weimar Fail?" *The Journal of Modern History* 68:3 (September 1996), pp. 629–56. Edward Ross Dickinson's argument for analyzing Weimar and Nazi eugenics also turns on breaking down older assumptions about the "progressive" and the "reactionary" in order to better understand the messy modernity of the 1920s and the transition into the 1930s as the state came under National Socialist control. Dickinson, "Biopolitics, Fascism, Democracy: Some Reflections on Our Discourse about 'Modernity,'" *Central European History* 37:1 (2004), pp. 1–48.

6   John Willett, *Art and Politics in the Weimar Period: The New Sobriety, 1917–1933* (New York: Pantheon, 1978), remains a fine resource on this topic.

7   The best study for understanding this shared terrain is Kathleen James-Chakraborty, *German Architecture for a Mass Audience* (London: Routledge, 2000).

8   On the connections between National Socialist design and its postwar West German counterparts, see Betts, *Authority of Everyday Objects*. Culture and politics did not cleanly divide into modern and unmodern expressions. Modernist design fueled fascist cultural imaginings and progressive architects, such as Taut, were not immune from nostalgia about organic forms of community. Taut creatively mobilized romantic conceptions of such in his public housing projects. On fascism and modernism, see Ruth Ben-Ghiat, *Fascist Modernities: Italy 1922–1945* (Berkeley: University of California Press, 2001); Roger Griffin, *Modernism and Fascism: The Sense of a Beginning under Mussolini and Hitler* (Houndmills, Basingstoke: Palgrave Macmillan, 2007). An important new analysis of Weimar's political and stylistic diversity can be found in James-Chakraborty, *German Architecture for a Mass Audience* and in her edited volume, *Bauhaus Culture: From Weimar to the Cold War* (Minneapolis: University of Minnesota Press, 2006), as well as in John A. Williams (ed.), *Weimar Culture Revisited* (New York: Palgrave Macmillan, 2011) and in Kathleen Canning, Kerstin Barndt, and Kristin McGuire (eds.), *Weimar Publics/Weimar Subjects: Rethinking the Political Culture of Germany in the 1920s* (New York: Berghahn, 2010).

9   Frederick Cooper, *Colonialism in Question: Theory, Knowledge, History* (Berkeley: University of California Press, 2005). See also Dipesh Chakrabarty's distinction between normative discourses of modernity and those of lived experience, which he called History I and History II, in *Provincializing Europe: Postcolonial Thought and Historical Difference* (Princeton: Princeton University Press, 2010).

10 The exception would be Maciuika's fine study *Before the Bauhaus*.

11 Campbell, *German Werkbund*, pp. 202–3.

12 Werkbund Archiv Berlin (hereafter WBA Berlin) ADK 3-396/28: Mies van der Rohe, "Zum Thema: Ausstellungen," *Die Form* 4 (1928), p. 121.

13 WBA Berlin ADK 3-401/29: Ernst Jäckh, "Idee und Realisierung der internationalen Werkbund-Ausstellung 'Die Neue Zeit' Köln 1932," *Die Form*, Heft 15 (1929), p. 406.

14 Jäckh was the Werkbund's executive secretary from 1912 to 1922, its second vice-president in 1930, and its president in 1932. Throughout his life he was proud of his connections to powerful politicians. It was thus in character that he was proud to have organized the meeting on April 1, 1933, with Hitler and Rosenberg to discuss the *Gleichschaltung* of the Werkbund via its takeover by the *Kampfbund für deutsche Kultur*. On June 10, 1933, the organization's members voted to surrender control to the other organization. Jäckh was proud of his role in the decision. His memoir claimed that with this action, he preserved a "relative autonomy" for the organization, but this was false. Jäckh, *Der goldene Pflug: Lebensernte eines Weltbürgers* (Stuttgart: Deutsche Verlags-Anstalt, 1954), p. 195. See also Campbell, *German Werkbund*, p. 295, and Betts, *Authority of Everyday Objects*, p. 27.

15 A group around Josef Goebbels in the early to mid 1930s championed German modernist art, in particular Expressionist painting, as exemplifying Germanic racial strength. Ernst Piper, *Nationalsozialistische Kunstpolitik: Ernst Barlach und die "entartete Kunst": eine Dokumentation* (Frankfurt: Suhrkamp, 1987).

16 Poelzig "summarized the avant-garde position in 1931. Addressing the *Bund deutscher Architekten* (BDA) he criticized the advocates of *Neue Sachlichkeit* for unthinkingly equating art with technology. Instead, Poelzig called for an artist's architecture that would go beyond rationalistic functionalism to reflect the spirit of the age as interpreted by the creative personality." Campbell, *German Werkbund*, p. 216.

17 Campbell wrote that some members of the Werkbund worried that Jäckh's "main appeal would... be to German nationalists, neoconservative officials, and doctrinaire intellectuals, rather than to the international community of artists." *German Werkbund*, p. 205. They were not wrong.

18 As Theodor Heuss put it, "Jäckh bringt den Werkbund in Schwung," in *Erinnerungen 1905–1933* (Tübingen: R. Wunderlich, 1963), pp. 114–15. On Jäckh's "American" tactics, see pp. 59–64 of this volume.

19 Letter from Muthesius reprinted in Ernst Jäckh's memoir, *Der goldene Pflug*, p. 196.

20 For figures on new sources of funding and membership after 1912, see WBA Berlin D 52: Ernst Jäckh, "5. Jahresbericht des Deutschen Werkbundes 1912/13," p. 97.

21 Heuss, *Erinnerungen*, p. 115. This made him "ganz unbefangen in den langsam beginnenden Richtungsstreiten," according to Heuss, and all the more influential in shifting the organization's emphasis toward imperialism and industrial expansion.

22 Kevin Repp, *Reformers, Critics and the Paths of German Modernity: Anti-Politics and the Search for Alternatives, 1890–1914* (Cambridge, MA: Harvard University Press, 2000). On Rohrbach, see George Steinmetz, *The Devil's Handwriting: Precoloniality and the German Colonial State in Qingdao, Samoa and Southwest Africa* (Chicago: University of Chicago Press, 2007); Fritz Fischer, *Germany's Aims in the First World War* (London: Chatto and Windus, 1967), pp. 9–10, 124–5. In his memoir, Jäckh speaks at length of his friendship with Schacht and Rohrbach, with whom he made a trip to Turkey in 1909. He described Rohrbach's articles on the Baghdad railway and his work for the *Deutsches Baghdadkomitee für Humanitätszwecke* and described Schacht as "Archivar in der Dresdener Bank, Mitglied des Jungliberalen Vereins und hatte Interesse an Orient." See Jäckh, *goldene Pflug*, p. 151.

23 Ernst Jäckh, "Deutsche Wirtschaftspolitik—von Helgoland bis Baghdad," in *Deutschland im Orient nach dem Balkankrieg* (Munich: M. Mörike, 1913), p. 13.

24 See Ernst Jäckh, *Der aufsteigende Halbmond: Auf dem Weg zum deutsch-türkischen Bündnis*, 6th edn (Stuttgart: Deutsche Verlags Anstalt, 1916); the essays were published in *Deutschland im Orient nach dem Balkankrieg* and correspondence reprinted in *Der goldene Pflug*.

25 Jäckh, "Deutsche Wirtschaftspolitik," p. 12.

26 Jäckh, *goldene Pflug*, p. 93. Letter from Muthesius to Jäckh reprinted in *goldene Pflug*, p. 196. For information on Jäckh's membership in Orientalist associations, see Jürgen Kloosterhuis, *"Friedliche Imperialisten" Deutsche Auslandsvereine und auswärtige Kulturpolitik, 1906–1918*, vol. 2 (Frankfurt: Lang, 1994).

27 The "Committee for the Turkish Study Trip" had a distinguished membership including Field Marshall General Colmar von der Goltz, Dr. J. Riesser, the president of the export association the *Hansabund*, the chairman of the Central Association of German Industrialists, Max Roetger, and others. On the Turkish side, twelve ministers, three governors, six professors, thirteen businessmen, thirteen officers, six politicians, and four journalists attended. Jäckh wrote about the event for Naumann's journal *Die Hilfe*. See *goldene Pflug*, p. 211 and Kloosterhuis, "Friedliche Imperialisten," vol. 2, p. 581.

28 Fischer, *Germany's Aims*, pp. 122–31, 101–3.

29 Unlike Rohrbach, Jäckh supported an adamantly pro-Turkish policy during the war. Rohrbach, by contrast, broke with German-Turkish policy over the issue of the Armenian Genocide. See Paul Rohrbach, *Armenien: Beiträge zur armenischen Landes- und Volkskunde* (Stuttgart: Engelhorn, 1919).

30 WBA Berlin: Ernst Jäckh, *Werkbund und Mitteleuropa: Vortag auf der Jahresversammlung des Deutschen Werkbundes in Bamberg* (Weimar: Kiepenhauer, 1916), p. 5.

31 Jäckh, *Werkbund und Mitteleuropa*, pp. 5–6. The German reads,

>   dass der Werkbund aus dem gleichen Formgesetz und zu dem gleichen Formgesetz geworden ist, wie Mitteleuropa—im Willen wie im Ziel; ferner 2. dass dieses Formgesetz das organische Prinzip ist, dass im Werkbund

seinen künstlerischen Ausdruck und im Mitteleuropa seinen politischen
Ausdruck gefunden hat; und schliesslich 3. dass dieses organische Prinzip
im Grund der deutsche Sinn, das deutsche Wesen ist.

32 Schwartz, *Werkbund*, p. 8.

33 Jäckh, *Werkbund und Mitteleuropa*, p. 6.

34 Ibid., p. 6.

35 Ibid.

36 Jäckh, "Idee und Realisierung," pp. 401–21.

37 As Jaeckh wrote, "Qualitaet … als ein ebenso technisches, wie aesthetisches,
    wirtschaftliches und soziales, kulturelles wie nationales Problem." Ibid., p. 402.

38 The Verband Rheinischer Industrieller, which represented 830 firms, supported
    the exhibition. In an Ausstellungs- und Messeamt communication of January
    18, 1929, it was stated that "es stellt die überwiegende Zustimmung der
    Wirtschaft zu dem Plan der Ausstellung 'Die Neue Zeit' fest." See ibid., p. 402.

39 Ibid., p. 405.

40 Ibid.

41 Jäckh, *goldene Pflug*, p. 204. Theodor Heuss also supported the idea of the
    exhibition:

    > "Die neue Zeit"—das ist nicht bloß Radio, Flugzeug, Elektrifizierung jedes
    > Kuhstalles, Tonfilm, Waschmaschine, Flachdach, Kohlenverflüssigung,
    > Sport, Dieselmotor, Jazz, Offsetdruck. Es ist auch dies, aber es ist zugleich
    > mehr … Die Aufgabe ist international gesehen, oder wenn man so will,
    > universal, sie ist im weitesten Sinne "politisch", indem sie nicht bloß einen
    > Querschnitt durch das Greifbare und durch das Gekonnte geben will,
    > sondern das Werdende ertasten, erspüren und zeigen will … dass die grosse
    > Einheit eines Rhythmus, an die sie glaubt, in staatlichen und nationalen
    > Individualitäten ihren mannigfaltigen Ausdruck findet, daß die Spielarten
    > und Sonderungen einem Höheren und Verbindlichen eingeordnet bleiben.

    Heuss as quoted in *goldene Pflug*, pp. 205–6.

42 WBA Berlin ADK 3-400/29a: Dr. Karl With, "1932. Das Echo des Werkbund-
    Programms für die internationale Ausstellung 'Die Neue Zeit,' " *Die Form*,
    Heft 22 (1929), pp. 612–15.

43 WBA Berlin ADK 3-3999/29: W. Rietzler, "1932" *Die Form*, Heft 1 (1929),
    pp. 1–3.

44 WBA Berlin ADK 3-923/29: Lotz, "1932" *Die Form* (1929), p. 441.

45 Betts, *Authority of Everyday Objects*, p. 30.

46 Ludwig Mies van der Rohe, "Die Neue Zeit," *Die Form* (1930), p. 406,
    reprinted in Kristiana Hartmann (ed.), *Trotzdem modern. Die wichtigsten
    Texte zur Architektur in Deutschland 1919–1933* (Braunschweig/Wiesbaden:
    Vieweg, 1994), p. 230.

47 Jäckh quoted in Schwartz, *Werkbund*, p. 43.

14

Women on the Verge of a Nervous Breakthrough: Emancipation, Sexuality, and Female Political Subjectivity

Marti M. Lybeck

Schoolteacher Anna Philipps, one of the historical subjects of this essay, began the 1920s by asking herself and then her colleagues and friends whether she might be a homosexual. Ten years later, she was asking the National Socialist Party to protect her from the homosexual cabal she thought was puppet master to the corrupt Weimar state. Philipps felt called to narrate and document this transformation, elaborating on her changing interpretations of herself as a gendered and sexual self as well as her relationship to the state and her (albeit vague) notions of a better modern Germany.[1] Because she was a person with little public standing or clout in her own time or since, Philipps's book presents an opportunity for examining the process by which ordinary people might engage in the modern struggle to control their own futures. As women, the writers considered in this essay had to confront the dynamic of political modernity that empowered commoner men through their authority in the household. They were part of the "first wave" of women seeking to emancipate themselves from legal frameworks, social norms, and elite intellectual discourses that denied women the capacity and right to self-determination. Their writings challenge fraternal modernity by asserting their rights to support themselves, to make their own decisions, and to assert a political voice. A characteristic of modernity is the struggle of those excluded from its expansive promises to claim inclusion and to be taken seriously as subjects. In taking them seriously, I trace how that process of claiming happened for the ordinary individual.

Philipps's wild swing from curious exploration to repressive moral politics was extreme and idiosyncratic, yet it was part of a larger pattern seen among the overlapping groups of women seeking independence and careers and members of the women's movement between 1880 and the 1930s. Why did women who called into question the patriarchal norms of their society, forging unconventional lives that rejected family roles, nevertheless align themselves with aggressive nationalist authoritarianism?

The question concerning the combination of female assertion and conservatism is not new, but the important dimension of sexual subjectivity has only recently become an analytical factor. Many scholars have examined the politics of the organized women's movement and the phenomenon of conservative women activists. The literature on the former has focused primarily on organizations and prominent spokeswomen. Here an original triumphal narrative of female empowerment has been complicated by analysis of whether moderate feminism contributed to acceptance of Nazism.[2] Frieda von Bülow and Käte Schirmacher are two prominent examples of the latter trend, emancipated women who combined outspoken feminism with extreme aggressive nationalism.[3] The strongest interpretive thread has emphasized the politics of social motherhood, which the German women's movement shared broadly with other European, Latin American, and North American feminisms.[4] As scholars have shown, legitimating political activism through the concept of motherhood did not determine whether the resulting politics were socialist, radical, liberal, or conservative, nor was motherhood ideology limited to actual mothers or women who idealized existing models of bourgeois motherhood.[5] Analysis of the leaders of explicitly conservative organizations has emphasized opportunist and power-seeking motives, seeing them as exemplars of a strategy that allowed combining personal activism and impeccable respectability.[6]

The writers of the sources used in this essay, with the possible exception of Ella Mensch, were neither conservative leaders nor central figures in the organized women's movement. Their political claims do not fit easily into conservative orthodoxy and they did not emphasize motherhood in their attempts to reconcile proudly "emancipated" lives with political ideologies. They came to my attention through the role that discourses of homosexuality played in their lives and publications. In their texts, the issue of sexuality comes to the fore in ways that "motherhood" or "morality" arguments sometimes efface.

Women's and sexual emancipation efforts and effects proceeded apace in the period bracketing the First World War. In addition to the campaigns of the organized women's and homosexual emancipation movements, the New Woman became a legible figure. She promised, and threatened, a female subject position of autonomy from male and family tutelage.

Emancipation is used here not as a simple abolition of legal restrictions—the familiar triumphal narrative of fighting repression—but rather as a complex subjective negotiation of the individual's place in his or her social world. Emancipation narratives and the media-circulated figure of the New Woman opened imaginative spaces and suggested fictive personae that were not completely realizable. Yet even partial emancipation was the first step toward full modern subjectivity that proceeded to the work of subject formation. For these historical subjects, it was aligned with the assertion of an autonomous subject position. Questions of autonomy played an important role in Enlightenment thought on the relationships between self, state, and society. It increasingly pointed toward the concept of a subject authorized to make considered decisions. Not all people could be autonomous; much theorization was and is required to create the category of citizens with sufficient autonomy of judgment to be considered worthy of political participation. Yet, autonomy often appears as an isolated and abstracted achievement of modernity, marked in votes or jobs. In using the term empirically to analyze women's writing, the more contingent and fraught elements of seeking autonomy become apparent. As conditions of modernity eroded the embedded categories of relational power in the family, the social hierarchy, the church, and the patriarchal state, individuals who wanted to have social and political standing, respect, and influence struggled to fashion themselves to fit existing cultural categories of autonomy. These complicated aspirations to autonomy, in part, motivated real choices to live outside existing family roles, to pursue education and careers, to reimagine one's relationship to structures of authority, and to formulate political positions that otherwise seem inexplicably strange.

On a small scale, this essay explores a different model of writing political history, one that operates on an intimate level. Political histories have tended to focus on actions, organizations, and ideas, perhaps considering individual lives in biographies of major figures. Biographies typically follow set scripts that seek cohesion and progression. Instead I propose to analyze individual lives to investigate how political considerations figured into the conflicted subject formation of individual women. Theirs were intimate conflicts with friends and colleagues, involving specific aspects of sexuality. The decisive nexus that motivated political affiliation was the relationship between authority and desire. Approaching politics through this nexus on the individual level promises to reveal much about the political dimension of women's emancipation that has previously eluded examination. Beyond that, it may reveal deeper dynamics of political affiliation itself, not as a choice of ideology, self-interest, or style, but as rooted in individual experience, aspiration, fear, and desire.

The three life stories examined in this essay, Ella Mensch (1859–1935), Anna Philipps (b. 1881), and Selli Engler (1899–1982), follow three generations of women engaged in gender change. Ella Mensch was among the first generation to attend university in the 1880s; for her, the move meant a bold appropriation of new space. She advocated for feminist causes and women teachers, and worked on her own as an editor and journalist.[7] Her polemical writing in the first decade of the twentieth century critiques the direction taken by other feminists, asserting praise for the nationalist conservatism of Bismarck and opposition to any form of personal or sexual emancipation. Anna Philipps followed her father's footsteps into a teaching career that led to higher education and civil service status. Under Weimar conditions, this rather ordinary schoolteacher began to see herself as both a desiring subject and a civil servant deserving of public respect and professional reputation. These claims were previously considered masculine privileges. Selli Engler was even more of an outsider than Philipps. She seems not to have had any higher education, yet she aspired to be a writer. She found her readers, market, and followers among the new public of homosexual women that coalesced in Berlin in the second half of the 1920s. For a short time, Engler promoted herself as a leader within the homosexual rights movement, exerting her influence through personal example, exhortation, and didactic fiction.

The three figures share some contradictory characteristics that make them especially fruitful choices for examining the unexpected paths of German political modernity. They were "ordinary" women from provincial middle-class origins seeking emancipation, but their life stories reveal protagonists who might easily be dismissed as cranks and oddballs. Their texts' irritation and resentment, often escalating into outrage, suggest an intense process of subject-formation taking place as they articulated their peevish arguments in manifestos and exposés. At times, each could easily be taken as representative of *Mittelstand* proto-Nazi sentiments. Mensch identified herself as a conservative nationalist throughout her writing career. Philipps and Engler did not start out with strong political alignments, but in the 1930s, both apparently appealed to Hitler and the Nazi Party. I read their essays and stories as reflecting a process of mastering the contradictions encountered in the imagined intersections between gendered emancipation, sexuality, and state authority. These figures were not isolated, but neither were they typical of activists in women's movements. Their status as in-between figures, constantly negotiating between new possibilities and received concepts of the individual, the state, and desire, makes them useful as subjects of political analysis.

The precarious space of their new subject positions might partially explain their conservative alliances. Conservative conceptions offered symbols of stability and security that could anchor identities breaking away from the security of family networks and nineteenth-century gender roles. The lives of all three unfolded in emerging and tenuous social configurations of the new same-sex environments. Considering the unaccustomed burden of supporting themselves financially further reinforces the conclusion that a fantasy of intimate connection with and backing of a strong and dynamic nation or party likely did offer comfort. Many scholars have demonstrated the appeal of conservative mobilization for women; to some degree those arguments also apply in these cases. But, often, those turns to the conservative also entailed rejection of feminism. This essay is not focused on the nationalist conservatism of women like Paula Müller-Otfried of the Protestant women's group. Rather, I investigate how lived and avowed emancipation combined in self-fashioning with ideological alignments otherwise clearly antifeminist. If we assimilate these voices too quickly to the comforts of conservatism in general, we lose an opportunity to analyze with more subtlety the interrelationships between what we might call progressive feminist claims, feminine desire, and individual assumptions about politics and the state in a time of rapid social and political change.

In these and other women's texts of the era, sexuality in all its many aspects was a very central concern on social, institutional, and individual levels.[8] With a few notable exceptions, claiming sexual autonomy was one of the most problematic aspects of women's moves toward self-emancipation.[9] These three cases, in dealing with issues of homosexuality, bring that individual struggle to define sexuality explicitly into the already complicated confrontation of emancipation and politics. My claim is that including the sexual resonances of emancipation is crucial for understanding the broader issues outlined above. The story of German homosexual emancipation has largely been told within the binary of state and subject, where the subject seeks to throw off state repression.[10] Despite the more flexible conceptions of power and the productive function of the apparatus of the state in its extended manifestations enabled by Foucault's analysis in *The History of Sexuality* and elsewhere, an analysis of desire versus state makes the embrace of the state in the gender emancipation process hard to grasp except as false consciousness. Close reading of the texts suggests another alternative: that women sought conservative authority and moral standards as a key element in legitimating feminine desire. I analyze this as a two-step process in which emancipation invokes threatening sexual questions. In response, individual subjects ally themselves with structures and ideologies available from the past in order to create conceptual space for those desires compatible with their ideas about authority and the autonomous subject. In other words, gender emancipation did not facilitate longing for sexual freedom. Each writer framed aspirations to emancipation with the discipline of sexual behavior. In this process, sexual desire became a metaphor for desire understood more generally. Rejection of unregulated sexuality became key to asserting and legitimating desire in other realms, including claiming space in the public sphere. An active role in policing other emancipating women's sexuality allied the individual ideologically with the mission of national renewal, suggesting alliances with others proclaiming that mission.

Ella Mensch—first-generation university student

Ella Mensch received one of the first doctorates in literature awarded to a German woman in Zurich in 1886. Early women university students like Mensch were obliged to study abroad because German universities did not admit women to degree programs until 1908. Women students encountered significant barriers to academic achievement; probably no more than one hundred doctoral degrees were awarded to German women prior to 1908.[11] Prospective students needed family consent and financial support. Yet, former students' memoirs reflect their experience of intense emotions as they broke social barriers, felt the thrill of intellectual stimulation, and lived in small close groups away from family oversight. Many formed networks of influential women lasting into the 1920s.

Like the protagonist of her student novel *On Outpost Watch: Novel of My Student Days in Zurich*, Mensch grew up as the daughter of an influential teacher in a rural area near Stettin.[12] The 1903 novel depicted the situation of pioneering women students in Zurich twenty years earlier. Shortly after its publication, Mensch's ideas about gender and politics appeared in a very different work, *Bildstürmer der Frauenbewegung* (*Iconoclasts of the Women's Movement*).[13] This strange, yet insightful text was part of the series *Großstadtdokumente*, a collection of independent volumes on crime, prostitution, and entertainment in Berlin, Vienna, and Hamburg. Despite the volume authors' academic credentials, the books' popularity relied on titillation, informing respectable readers about the shocking realities of the urban underworld in a suitably authoritative and scientific tone.[14] Mensch's book fit the paradigm because she exposed and denounced an "erotic epidemic" within the women's movement after the turn of the century.

Mensch's publications, including the periodical *Frauen-Rundschau*, made her a visible figure in the print public sphere in Germany in the 1900s. As an activist, she advocated expanding posts for women teachers and joined the fight against prostitution and pornography. After the turn of the century, she wrote with political authority as a conservative feminist. An undated photograph shows her in a collar and tie as a typical New Woman of the late nineteenth century.[15]

The conservative political consciousness of the novel's protagonist, Fanny Stantien, could be based in memory or perhaps constitute a rewriting of her student experience as she later wished she had lived it. Either way, the character made the forces that shaped conservative feminism explicit: "She had not forgotten the opinion of those in her circle of relatives and friends about women's education—that it was at best an inspired whim to be tolerated. For these circles she was always the 'emancipated one.' And the group that considered itself as the privileged representatives of progress in Zurich had long counted her among the 'reactionaries.' "[16] The vision of a woman in Fanny's position was always doubled—she saw herself and her emancipatory moves through the eyes of her scandalized home environment, but was also aware of how out of step she appeared to university progressives and radicals. Fanny struggled to explain her transgressions against the assumptions of each reference group.

Fanny's encounters with the Social Democratic male student Stümke gave her the opportunity to argue directly for conservative feminism. In response to Stümke's claims that "women cannot expect anything from a state that is a military power," Fanny drew on the history and heroes of German nationalism: "We want to win our portion and place in the solid construction that the work of a Lessing, a Fichte, and a Bismarck has created." In her vision of the future, conservative feminists would carry out the next step in the chain of nation-building achievements. Anti-feminist conservatives, she argued, would "recognize soon enough that they must be revitalized with ideas from the women's camp." As Mensch has Fanny express it, feminism would be meaningless unless it could develop in "a state that has conservative means of power at its disposal."[17] Mensch's argument balances radical social change with conservative allegiance to the stability and protection offered by the state of the nationalist imagination.

Crucially, Mensch's conservatism understood sexual morality alongside the national state as the essential bedrock of an orderly society. In the early days of women's pursuit of education, "much depended on the conduct and appearance of the individual. Awkwardness and tactlessness could make things difficult for those who followed." The novel's title refers to its dominant theme of moral watchfulness: "Fanny Stantien had brought this feeling—that one stood 'on the outpost watch' and had to avoid all extravagance—along with her and didn't have to acquire it through unpleasant experience as many others did."[18]

Fanny's purpose in the novel is to impose social and sexual discipline on those, like her friend Linda, who were in danger of "unpleasant experience." Linda confided in Fanny that she was tempted to enter into a modern free love relationship. Fanny pointed out the dangers that sexual activity posed for women's achievements, reputation, and emotional well-being. Predictably, Fanny's position was confirmed later in the novel by the caddish betrayal Linda suffered at her lover's hands.

Mensch expanded her ideas about sexuality through the story of Hedi, Fanny's sister living at home. Hedi's same-sex passion functioned as the alternative to dangerous heterosexual free love. Hedi's crushes on other women were the source of hometown gossip, repeated by a scandalized Linda. But Fanny explained to her that platonic affairs were an acceptable outlet for feminine desire. While "average people" saw Hedi's affairs as "silly children's obsessions" and predicted that the "wondrous, fantastic creature will properly fall in love with a man," Fanny claimed that "people like Hedi never just 'fall in love', for them the word love has a stronger undertone" that is no longer "in the realm of the sensual…" Instead Hedi's love was "dematerialized" as the "intoxication of the born platonic."[19] Fanny celebrated platonic eroticism as superior to physical sensuality and compatible with moral standards essential to legitimate feminism. Denial of physical pleasure heightened and eroticized ideal love. "The more insight I gain into the deceitful and cruel play of love between the sexes," Fanny concluded, "the greater my admiration for the wonderfully tender poetry manifested in Hedi's homages and enthusiasms."[20]

Mensch addressed sexual desire and conservative state authority more directly in *Iconoclasts*. "If the state with its law tablets is an injustice to the individual," she insisted, "so the structure—family, marriage—from which it draws its main strength is mistaken and can be given up in favor of unbound life and love partnerships."[21] She rightly saw that liberal feminist aspirations could not be satisfied by enacting formal political equality. The patriarchal family itself was implicated. From her conservative standpoint, Mensch argued that both structures had to be maintained in order to control sexual desire. This thinking is quite at odds with her advocacy of independent unmarried women and with the circumstances of her life.

One clue to her contradictory arguments is found in her vehement criticism of the contemporary trend of women's poetry and novels that depicted sexual awakening. "Who would have believed that so many oppressed, tortured, love-starved females were sighing all around," she wrote sarcastically, "no, not even sighing anymore, but crying out [their] misery in prose and verse aloud for all the world."[22] She described the authors of trendy erotic literature as failing to "see the smirking, telling smiles that appear on the lips of the publishers and editors, when the doors of the editorial rooms close behind [them]." "It often hurts me to the depth of my soul," she continued, "when I'm the accidental witness to how these pseudo-heroines are hopelessly ridiculed" and "don't even notice."[23] Mensch took up the role that Fanny had played in the novel, warning emancipated women of the ridicule and humiliation that awaited women who claimed sexual subjectivity in public. Fanny's proud imposition of discipline returned here in the reversed form of shame. Well within the mainstream of the women's movement on sexual matters, Mensch's painful reproach reveals that women were still in a sexual bind in the first decades of the twentieth century. No doubt her caricature of the leering editor was an exaggerated product of her own sensitivity, but nevertheless it seems likely that women's assertion of desire did provoke male amusement as well as disapproval.[24] By wagging her finger at the few who explored sexual possibilities, perhaps Mensch hoped to draw moderate feminists in the direction of conservative politics.

Iconoclasts employed the modern disease metaphor to group members of the women's movement into categories of the "healthy" and the "sick." Those deemed "sick"—emancipated authors of erotic texts, along with movement radicals with international ties and utopian demands, and advocates for allowing married women to hold teaching positions—had in common a link between feminism and personal desire.[25] Since emancipation is at heart a claim to a better position for oneself—education, jobs, a voice in government, or sexual self-determination—it was immediately in conflict with middle-class women's socialization into ideals of sacrifice. Almost all feminists cloaked their demands in terms of the service they intended to render for the greater good, however they defined that nebulous concept. Mensch diagnosed as degenerate those who did not conform to this pattern.

The negative exposé form of *Iconoclasts* could not support a general feminist argument, but rather carved out a precarious space for sexually moralizing women like Mensch. *Iconoclasts* devoted a few of its pages to homosexuality, mainly to dismiss the accusation that feminists were lesbians by defining homosexuality as a debilitating perversion. She lumped medicalizing literature on the "third sex" with other regrettable sexually explicit literature. In contrast to her florid blasts at feminists claiming heterosexual subjectivity, *Iconoclasts* skirted the issue of love between two respectable women. Like many contemporary New Women, Mensch belonged to a circle of friends composed of educated unmarried women. Later biographers have speculated that she lived in close partnership with individual women.[26] While the novel provided a justification for same-sex passion, she could not find a way to address homosexuality as a category that might well apply to her own life.

In Mensch's ideology, the Prussian military state gave independent women the indispensable role of moralizing the masses through teaching children and reaching their mothers.[27] Yet her writing went beyond this feminine role to claim the masculine authority to explain history and society in the broader public sphere. In the process she scorned "emancipated" women who based their claims in individual desire, whether for personal autonomy or assertion of sexual subjectivity. To participate in masculine authority, she mimicked its apotheosis in conservative, authoritarian figures like Bismarck.

Anna Philipps—first-generation civil servant

Anna Philipps was one of the female teachers for whom Mensch advocated. She began teaching before the First World War and acquired the education necessary for a position at an academic high school. With the passage of the Weimar Constitution, promising gender equality, university-educated teachers received a civil service title, *Studienrätin*, equivalent to their male counterparts. *Rat/Rätin* titles entailed status in the state bureaucracy and considerable social prestige. Philipps's political subjectivity was closely linked to her bureaucratic status. Philipps's story depicts a transitional stage in women's emancipation and women's new political citizenship in the Weimar period.

The story was obscure except for Philipps's publication of *For Honor and Justice*, an account of her conflicts with the school bureaucracy.[28] In addition to a narrative of her life, it contained many documents from her voluminous personnel files creating an archive of her struggle to overturn disciplinary action taken against her by her school administration in 1923. The book invited the reading public to be her judge and advocate. It also described Philipps's interest in homosexuality, her close relationship with another teacher, and her attraction to one of her students.

The account began with a bold appropriation of sexual subjectivity. She reported having seen *Anders als die Anderen*, a 1919 melodramatic film about the blackmail of a homosexual. The film ended with homosexual rights activist Magnus Hirschfeld addressing the audience in a direct plea for decriminalization of male homosexuality.[29] Her interest in same-sex attraction piqued, Philipps sought out books by Hirschfeld and considered whether her relationships and desires might put her in the homosexual category.[30] As she read and thought more about homosexuality, she posed uncomfortable questions to her teacher colleagues and friends.

Eventually she developed a close relationship with one of her students. In addition to allowing the student to visit her in her living quarters at all hours, Philipps was reported to have told a fellow teacher that she (Philipps) and the student had "kissed each other senseless" and that she could not help her feelings toward the student.[31] Philipps's narrative presented these developments as normal and innocent. But the other teachers sensed danger in Philipps's insistence that her behavior, now defined as homosexuality, was no different from theirs. They approached the head of the school to accuse Philipps of having an inappropriate relationship with the student. In the course of the investigation, emotional attachments and bitter conflicts among the teachers came to be documented and circulated.

After the immediate investigation, Philipps was not found guilty of anything serious, since the evidence was ambiguous. Nevertheless, school administrators attempted to solve the problem of residual tension and conflict within the faculty by transferring Philipps to a school in a different town. They concluded that she was the instigator who had stirred up the sensitive and embarrassing issue of student–teacher same-sex desire. The education bureaucracy's support of this involuntary transfer only inflamed Philipps's outraged belief that she had been punished unjustly and that her honor had been damaged. Between 1923 and 1929, Philipps submitted petition after petition, working her way up the chain of bureaucratic authority, to demand that her case be reopened. Finally, the Prussian educational ministry ordered her to stop appealing or be fired.

Philipps's narrative of her early life explained her emancipated choices of education and career as a matter of necessity rather than feminist desire for autonomy. Yet her surprising admission of her earlier embrace of information about homosexuality demonstrates a firm and enthusiastic grasp of the new freedoms of the early Weimar period. Even in retrospect she saw no need to regret her right to access information about a stigmatized subject or to think and talk freely about her own sexual feelings and questions. Unlike Mensch, she had no intellectual goal or ideological scheme. Rather she described inhabiting an emancipated subjectivity through precarious opportunities and contingent choices and experiences.

Philipps framed her cause as a case of victimization through corruption and chicanery. She portrayed herself as an honorable citizen and bureaucrat standing up to a heartless, venal, politicized bureaucracy. In addition to mistreatment by systems and authority figures, her peers had betrayed the bonds of solidarity and honor expected between professional colleagues, especially those pioneering new opportunities for their gender. Like many tales of victimization, Phillips's incorporated a melodramatic plot of moral choice. Although the villainous bureaucrats tempted her by offering continued employment in exchange for dropping her claims, Philipps as heroine refused to become complicit in the cover-up of misdeeds by accepting this inducement.

Just as the early Weimar years provided an opening for Philipps's exploration of sexuality, its later conflicts became intertwined with her personal grievances. For example, the opening paragraph of the book directed readers' attention to the Prussian state that had come about as a result of the 1918–19 German Revolution and the Weimar Constitution.

> When I tell my story in the following pages, I don't do so in order to seem interesting or because I consider my fate so important, rather I do it in order to illuminate the conditions in the State of Prussia, founded in 1918, to urge others to come to their own judgment as to whether these conditions should continue or be changed, and, if they are convinced of the latter, to encourage them to take action to bring about these changes.[32]

In the increasingly politically polarized circumstances of 1931, foregrounding Prussia was neither straightforward nor innocent. Throughout the Weimar period, the reformist Social Democrats who led the Prussian provincial government sought to fulfill the liberalizing promises of the Weimar Constitution. In 1931, their hold on power was increasingly embattled and did not survive a right-wing coup the following year—a forerunner of the Nazi seizure of the national state in 1933. Philipps's mention of 1918 served as code for an anti-Weimar political stance, a position fostered by radical nationalists who had been determined to destroy the Republic since its founding. After the onset of economic depression and disillusionment in 1929, these political judgments became convenient explanations for individual fear and misery.

As Philipps appealed the case again and again, she became convinced that the failure of her accusations against her coworkers and superiors was evidence of a vast conspiracy against her. The unfavorable outcome of her petitions could not be seen as expedience or indifference of the establishment against an outsider's demands. She found it more plausible that her former friends, whom she accused of hiding their true homosexual nature, were in league with other homosexuals who pulled the strings of government for their own protection. Her aim in publishing the book was exposure of the "role the homosexuals and their helpers play today."[33] Her enemies were sexual criminals covering up their transgressions by smearing her: "The longer the fight for the rehabilitation of my professional honor lasts, the clearer the position of the government in this question becomes. Teachers who are prostitutes and homosexuals can do what they like—they are protected. Respectable teachers are subjected to the slander of these people... That is the new Germany!"[34] Disappointed by what she experienced as the false promises of the Weimar state, she implicated the whole of it as sexually as well as politically corrupt, implicitly aligning herself with the anti-Weimar forces gaining strength in the early thirties. Conflict with state authority provided the context for assertion of political subjectivity. Her experiences, she argued, gave her a privileged view of Weimar corruption.

After she was finally fired, Phillips sought supportive partners for her exposé of Weimar corruption. Rebuffed by the *Liga für Menschenrechte*, an advocacy organization for the defense of individual rights, and the right-wing DNVP, she finally won a promise of support and publicity from the local branch of the Nazi Party.[35] What most likely appealed to the NSDAP were her extravagant claims about the corruption of the Social Democratic Prussian authorities. But what about the Nazis appealed to Philipps? Their rhetoric of restoring purity to the state and defending the ordinary citizen against abuses by the powerful expressed a paranoia that harmonized well with Philipps's conspiracy theory.

Despite her convergence with stances taken by anti-republican forces of order and authority, Philipps presented her case in the language of rights and citizenship. She assumed that readers would understand and support the right of the injured autonomous individual to expect fair treatment from the authorities. The irony was that in her obsessive repetition of these claims, she began to appear increasingly irrational.[36]

Philipps's case presents some fascinating contradictions for gender history. Her dogged efforts to embody the new positions of civil servant and citizen ended in actions that matched gender stereotypes of hysteria and irrationality. The unspoken condition for her claims was the full citizenship and access to *Beamten* (civil service) status granted to women under the Weimar Constitution. Her confident entitlement belies the novelty and almost experimental nature of a woman asserting the authority to demand vindication and the right to confront high state officials with her judgments on their representation of state power. Philipps's displacement of her personal grievances onto a much broader struggle for a just and moral state was likely repeated among many of the new political subjects of the Weimar era. Philipps's developing political subjectivity gave her a mission to attack state power, even as she demanded the state's protection.

Single working women quickly assimilated the fruits of emancipation and turned them to their own purposes, sometimes, as with Philipps, completely repressing the conditions for their own claims. Those in public employment experienced the workings of the state up close for the first time. Philipps's claims to public standing had nothing to do with femininity or motherliness. Instead she tested the boundaries of new rights and positions formerly defined as exclusively masculine.

Philipps's case further extends understanding of the close connection between sexual and political subjectivity during the Weimar period. Philipps was not embarrassed to say that she was exploring her sexuality and the potential for sexual relationships among schoolteachers in the early 1920s. In the anger, betrayal, and shame she experienced when the others refused to admit to such feelings, she misread their panic and self-protective discretion as evidence of deception and perversion. Convinced of her own innocence, she revalued homosexuality from honest attraction to devious corruption. Sexual subjectivity had to be disavowed in order to assert political subjectivity based in preservation of innocence and honor.

Selli Engler—first-generation open homosexual activist

Selli Engler was a thoroughly political individual. Between 1924 and 1927, she published her own newspaper for the "ideal female friends" (a middle-class euphemism for lesbian couples) of Weimar Berlin, urging them to claim their identity and unite in a public movement to claim the respect they deserved.[37] She had moved to Berlin in 1914 following the death of her father, a provincial factory owner.[38] Engler's activist texts displayed a clear grasp of modern techniques for citizen politics and female entrepreneurialism.

She used publications as a platform for advertising her services as a social club and youth group leader, masseuse, café proprietor, and legal advisor. She also constructed an image of herself as a militant leader of the people. Song lyrics she wrote began, "I salute you, you beautiful, noble women/ Proud of your own kind/We will look each other in the eye/So that small-minded fearfulness will never separate us./We don't need to tremble/Or let life embitter us/Firm and true, we must follow our flag/And always stay on the high road."[39] In this musical version of "Liberty Leading the People," women were envisioned as politically active fighters.

In 1927, Engler joined a group of women producing a similar publication, *Frauenliebe*, supported by the then-flourishing mass male homosexual movement. The homosexual men's movement emerged soon after the war. Its organizations published several periodical titles, adding special titles aimed at recruiting more female members in the mid-1920s.[40] Engler was one of the very few individuals whose photograph appeared in print alongside her written texts, producing an embodied persona as a figure of identification and desire for the reading public of homosexual women.

Very suddenly in 1929, Engler moved from *Frauenliebe* to its apparently better-financed rival *Die Freundin*, where her visibility as a leader continued and expanded. No doubt she also understood the necessity of the funding male organizations could provide to keep her voice and image circulating among her public. A nasty public conflict between the Berlin affiliates of two national organizations precipitated Engler's move to *Die Freundin* and the *Bund für Menschenrecht*, headed by Friedrich Radszuweit. In a boxed item titled "Selli Engler Explains," she claimed the authority to assure readers that her move was justified by wrongdoing at the group affiliated with *Frauenliebe*.[41] Engler's appeals for members and the simultaneous defection to *Die Freundin* of Lotte Hahm, another leader with a prominent public profile, suggest that Radszuweit or his organization offered some advantages to lure these charismatic figures in hopes of bringing in additional dues from women as the economy contracted. If so, we may see Engler's actions as a canny move to parlay her status in Berlin into a position of greater stability and national visibility.

Engler used her authoritative stance to exhort women readers to greater political consciousness and activity, setting forth the justification, goals, and boundaries of the movement. She was uniquely outspoken in advocating a common front for homosexual men and women. Though she led the women, Engler deferred to the authority of male leaders of both organizations, addressing them in obsequious language. She reminded *Frauenliebe* readers, "Herr Bergmann has created *Frauenliebe* for us with persistent hard work, energy, and much sympathy."[42] Later at *Die Freundin*, she rallied the women to the support of Radszuweit. In an article calling on women to become more active, she addressed a poem to Radszuweit: "Thank you, our inspired leader/Never shrinking from thorns or from mockery./You lead us bravely to battle,/Take as your reward our loyalty."[43] Excessive public gratitude placed her in a subordinate position. Yet her personal style of leadership was not based on submissive femininity. Instead she followed male leaders' examples, employing female masculinity to legitimize her position.

As she claimed in one of her articles, "Most women of our outlook, predominantly with masculine sensibilities, have more business talent than normal men…" Engler criticized entrepreneurial homosexual women who put on "flowery hats and high heeled shoes" in order to use the mask of femininity to seek success. Engler also linked masculinity to support of the cause: "The independent woman is chosen, through her masculine mind, her competence, and precisely through her independence to march at the front in this struggle for the simplest human rights…"[44] Political subjectivity and aspiration were inextricably linked with the independence characteristic of homosexual women.

At *Die Freundin*, Engler aimed her leadership strategy at respectable middle-class women who identified themselves as homosexual. "Yes," she addressed them confidentially, "I know why you have not yet affiliated yourselves with any organization. In the existing circles and associations for women, one always encounters questionable elements." It was the "danger to [their] good reputation" that caused them to "avoid places where women of our kind meet," preferring "misery and loneliness." Engler promised to correct this deplorable state of same-sex socializing. She assured the "respectable and blameless women" that if they set the tone "certain women" would no longer choose to come to their events.[45] Using euphemistic language, Engler rejected women who openly acted out desire, and thus were suspected of promiscuity, prostitution, and lower-class gold digging.

Engler was the strongest of many female voices expressing their wish that homosexuality could be disassociated from sexual desire and physical sensuality. The movement periodicals in general tried to differentiate their readers from patrons of transgressive Weimar nightlife and from the perceived lack of sexual discretion they associated with the lower classes. The periodicals' obsessive return to this theme indicates that banishing visible desire from their ranks was a goal that remained unfulfilled and that many others among the new homosexual public enjoyed sexual display, flirting, and seduction. In this context, the goals expressed by Engler and other writers suggest that there was a very close connection between political aspirations and the work of policing the public face of homosexuality to rid it of the taint of uncontrolled desire.

Besides political exhortations, Engler's contributions to the periodicals included a number of serialized novels exploring the dangerous territory of same-sex desire. Desire caused anxiety among middle-class women precisely because it was experienced and acted on outside previous controls on female sexuality exercised by family, male partners, and ideologies of purity. Engler's stories staged the moral dilemmas of women's unregulated sexual relationships. The protagonists were usually women feminine in beauty and tenderness, but masculine in intelligence, assertiveness, and moral character. The leading character was often torn between desire for an undisciplined woman and her respectable homosexual identity.

A typical example was the serialized novella, "Bianca Torsten's Women."[46] From their first meeting, Johanna enflamed Bianca's desire: "Hot desire glowed in Johanna's eyes, and she pressed herself against Bianca with delicate seductiveness."[47] Bianca immediately responded in kind to Johanna's passion, but in the long run, she had to subordinate desire to ideal love. Visualizing love in religious terms as the gift of her heart placed on the altar of love and faithfulness, Bianca soon set out (unsuccessfully) to reform Johanna's unrestrained desire. Johanna's constant affairs with others just for the pleasure of it sparked a dialogue between the two about the meaning of love and sex. From Johanna's point of view, sex outside the relationship enhanced desire. "You don't have any idea how exciting cheating is," Johanna told her. "You hardly know a fraction of the sweetness of making up. Betray me once, Bianca. Quit being such a saint for once!" As Bianca pleaded with Johanna to "give up this obsession" she also tried to convince herself.[48]

Toward the end of the story, Bianca found a partner who shared her ideology of friendship instead of desire as the basis for lasting happiness and self-respect. The relationship with the aptly named Marry was associated with "a little house in the country, a little garden, and an un-made up face." Bianca and Marry's plan to devote their energies to shared artistic production stood in stark contrast to Johanna's obsessive pursuit of dance bars and one-night stands.[49] The didactic narrative guided readers in channeling their desires into respectable outlets. Another scene in the novella put Bianca and Johanna on the beach where Johanna acted out her desire for Bianca's unclad body. Bianca immediately flinched, stopped Johanna, and lectured her on avoiding the "unpleasant feeling of having the exquisite fineness of [their] love … exposed in broad daylight."[50] The shame behind this response along with the novella's religious theme and Bianca's progress toward an ideal relationship reveal that the story is more than just a model for finding female homosexual respectability. The temptations of sexual desire contended with women's desire to be a certain kind of person: a person who could claim authority and respect.

In another story, set in a fantasy Old Regime past, the protagonist Gisa was the unhappy daughter of the landlord of a great estate. Masculine Gisa longed for independence and resented family pressure to marry. Gisa's contrast in this scenario was her brother, whose pursuit of selfish desires made him unworthy of inheriting the estate. A love relationship with the orphaned daughter of a nearby aristocratic family solved the problem of restrictive gender roles, providing Gisa with an estate to manage. The story wove a fantasy of benevolent patriarchy open to the exceptional female, exemplified by Gisa's generosity toward the peasants on her father's estate.[51] The masculine daughter reconciled with her noble family and claimed patriarchal power guaranteed by her control of desire.

In 1931, Engler's image and writing completely vanished from the homosexual movement periodicals. Engler next appeared in the historical record in her dossier from the National Socialist period, which recorded that she wrote a play with the title "Heil Hitler!" and sent it to Hitler personally in 1933.[52] Was it the work of a true believer or an opportunist covering her tracks? Since we have neither the play nor Engler's commentary on it, it is impossible to say what motivated her to write it. A colleague of Engler's at *Die Freundin* went on to join the party and become active in the National Socialist Women's organization.[53] Both she and Engler later applied to join the National Socialist writers' organization. Whatever their motivations, passionate devotion of their time and energy to the cause of homosexual liberation was not a barrier to integration into the Nazi state, nor a cause for resistance and opposition. In Engler's case, it is possible to trace affinities that may have made sense in her enthusiasm for the leader ideal and her mission of enforcing class-specific norms of order, ideal love, cultivated personality, sexual self-control, and devotion to a cause. Engler's movement politics, based in an ideal of masculinity and the exclusion of those unable or unwilling to master dangerous desires, may have meshed seamlessly with aspects of National Socialist rhetoric.

Conclusion

The stories of these three women moving out of family roles and into independent lives and careers reveal some of the common dilemmas and dynamics that shaped women's emancipation strategies over the foundational period of German modernity. Occupying new social and public spaces and subject positions was not self-evident; it required construction of and identification with a model of the self. These are definitely not stories of awakening, self-discovery, and liberation. Instead they take the form of the *Bildungsroman*, the specialty of Goethe. The characters encounter tests and dilemmas and mature toward an accommodation to the social order that also allows for their individual autonomy. As the historical subjects matured, they drew on existing cultural materials, revising them to support occupation of new subject positions.

Those cultural materials can be identified from their writing. They included female socialization in feminine honor and fear of desire, the model of the autonomous male citizen as responsible head of household, ideals of service through public and private positions of leadership, and German patriotism. All of these cultural materials built on controlling and shaping desire through authority figures who have achieved such control of themselves. The German educated middle-class tradition laying stress on knowledge of the German classics and the cultivation of personality gave a particular shape and flavor to emerging subjectivities.[54] Mensch, Philipps, and Engler aspired to political citizenship as access to authority, not through feminine and motherly influence, but through embodiment of the same model and development as that of the male political subject: autonomy of thought and judgment, responsible community membership and leadership, and contributing to disciplining the unruly desires of the socially "weak."[55]

Because of their personal involvement with same-sex desires as represented in their writing, the struggle to understand and define desire is particularly visible in these sources. In three different ways, perhaps reflective of their generational positions, Mensch, Philipps, and Engler were impelled to situate same-sex desire within structures of authority. While women's movement rhetoric effaced desire, these subjects theorized it. Mensch championed sublimating desire as Platonic Eros, but Philipps initially considered desire as constituting a right as the early homosexual rights movement asserted. Encountering discipline and ostracism when she tried to assert that right, she revised her thinking to conceptualize homosexuality as a form of corrupting desire and herself as a crusader against it. Engler and many of the middle-class women in the homosexual movement emphasized that their personal and group identity conformed to the moral precept of love authorizing expression of desire. She preached the exclusion or discipline of openly desiring women. Although this essay touches on it only lightly, the conception of homosexuality as gender inversion also played a role in authorizing women to occupy a political subjectivity ordinarily gendered as male. Engler, embracing the homosexual label, is able to assert this connection most directly.[56]

For all three, the overlap between the desiring subject and the political subject created uneasy gaps that led individual subjects to anchor emancipation within imagined political frameworks of authority. Socialized to fear the sexual woman as a figure of disgust and ostracism, these and many other women seeking greater autonomy and influence pried open new subject positions by claiming the authority to police and denounce the perceived transgressions of other women. Seeking emancipated positions from which they could exercise their own authority while living autonomous lives meant modern self-fashioning. Yet pushing into modernity also required reframing elements of past models and socialization as the necessary condition for the kind of emancipation they desired.

Considering politics from the perspective of new political subjects in formation opens the possibility of a more nuanced analysis of political engagement generally. The methodology used here analyzes texts within the social historical contexts of individual authors. It is not necessary to accept these texts as transparent representations of actual experience to understand the importance to the writing subject of social relations and experiences. Politics and political loyalty are forged in just such intimate contexts where identification and self-making struggles intersect with intimacies of social life as well as new and received discourses. A new dimension to political history can be excavated by pairing political claims, rhetoric, and large-scale national dynamics with the self-making, desires, and social relations of individuals.

Notes

1   Anna Philipps, *Um Ehre und Recht: Mein Kampf gegen das Provinzial-Schulkollegium Hannover und das Ministerium für Wissenschaft, Kunst und Volksbildung* (Neuminster: unpublished printed manuscript, 1931?), pp. 4, 22. A version of the text with an added second section was published in Berlin in 1931. Unfortunately, I do not have a copy of the published version, cited in Kirsten Plötz, *Einsame Freundinnen? Lesbisches Leben während der zwanziger Jahre in der Provinz* (Hamburg: Männerschwarm Skript Verlag, 1999).

2   See Edward Ross Dickinson, "Dominion of the Spirit over the Flesh: Religion, Gender, and Sexual Morality in the German Women's Movement before World War I," *Gender & History* 17:2 (2005), pp. 378–9; Angelika Schaser, "Gertrud Bäumer—'eine der wildesten Demokratinnen' oder verhinderten Nationalsozialistin?" in Kirsten Heinsohn, Barbara Vogel, and Ulrike Weckel (eds.), *Zwischen Karriere und Verfolgung: Handlungsräume von Frauen in nationalsozialistischen Deutschland* (Frankfurt: Campus, 1997).

38 Heike Schader, *Virile, Vamps und wilde Veilchen: Sexualität, Begehren, und Erotik in der Zeitschriften homosexueller Frauen im Berlin der 1920er Jahre* (Königstein: Ulrike Helmer, 2004), p. 76.

39 Selli Engler, "Das Lied der Anderen," *Blätter für ideale Frauenfreundschaft: Monatshefte für weibliche Kultur* 2:2 (1927?), unpaginated sheet between pp. 18 and 19.

40 *Frauenliebe* was part of the German Friendship Association (Deutsche Freundschaftsverband), while *Die Freundin* was published by the Bund für Menschenrecht (Association for Human Rights). For more on these organizations, see Stefan Micheler, "Kampf, Kontakt, Kultur: Die Freundschaftsverbände gleichgeschlechtlich begehrende Männer und Frauen in der Weimarer Republik in Norddeutschland," in Paul M. Hahlbohm and Till Hurlin (eds.), *Querschnitt—Gender Studies: ein interdisziplinärer Blick nicht nur auf Homosexualität* (Kiel: Verlag Ludwig, 2001).

41 Selli Engler, "Selli Engler erklärt!" *Die Freundin* (September 18, 1929), p. 3.

42 Selli Engler, "Aufruf! Meine Damen!" *Frauenliebe* 4:13 (1929), p. 2.

43 Selli Engler, "Viele Stimmen und ein Ziel," *Die Freundin* (May 21, 1930), p. 2.

44 Selli Engler, "An die selbstständigen homosexuellen Frauen!" *Die Freundin* (April 8, 1931), p. 2.

45 Engler, "Viele Stimmen."

46 Selli Engler, "Die Frauen der Bianca Torsten," *Die Freundin*, October 16, 1929, and following.

47 Engler, "Bianca Torsten," *Die Freundin* (October 16, 1929), p. 3.

48 Engler, "Bianca Torsten," *Die Freundin* (December 18, 1929), p. 3.

49 Engler, "Bianca Torsten," *Die Freundin* (December 11, 1929), p. 5.

50 Engler, "Bianca Torsten," *Die Freundin* (November 6, 1929), p. 5.

51 Selli Engler, "Erkenntnis," *Frauenliebe* (1927), serialized in vol. 2, issues 32–50.

52 Schader, *Virile, Vamps und wilde Veilchen*, pp. 76–7.

53 The colleague was Elspeth Killmer. See Schader, *Virile, Vamps und wilde Veilchen*, pp. 80–1.

54 See Laura Tate, "The Culture of Literary *Bildung* in the Bourgeois Women's Movement in Imperial Germany," *German Studies Review* 24:2 (2001), pp. 267–81.

55 Jürgen Habermas, *The Structural Transformation of the Public Sphere: An Inquiry into a Category of Bourgeois Society*, trans. Thomas Berger (Boston: MIT Press, 1989), pp. 46–9; Carole Pateman, *The Sexual Contract* (Stanford: Stanford University Press, 1988).

56 This further suggests the utility of homosexual identities in first- and second-wave feminism. Embracing female masculinity could serve to authorize political claims different from those made by women's groups identifying more closely with the conventional female role. Such an interpretation suggests that rejection of heterosexuality was an essential part of the puzzle of constructing and performing new gender identities.

15

National Socialism and the Limits of "Modernity"

Mark Roseman

Introduction

Though this piece originally appeared in 2011 as part of a roundtable in the *American Historical Review*, it was in fact drafted in the context of the Rethinking Modernities workshops. It was reacting in part against a now standard, Peukertian reading of Nazism as somehow quintessentially modern. But beyond that it was also motivated by a sense that modernity, and even more the plural "modernities," were concepts that were being used too promiscuously to convey any kind of common standard or paradigm. Finally, it was written with a keen eye to the fact that the interwar era, the era which produced Nazism and the Holocaust, was in many ways so distinct from the years that preceded it and those which followed, even though all belonged to the modern epoch.

1

Nazism provides an interesting test case with which to evaluate modernity's utility as concept and historical lens. More than most other recent historical phenomena and issues, the Third Reich has provoked intense scrutiny of its relationship to the modern world.[1] Since the 1930s, analysts have wondered whether Nazism represented a throwback to a barbaric past or rather exemplified the worst of modernity, reflections that have continued up to the present, including a series of debates conducted since the 1980s in the wake of the loss of faith in modernization theory.[2] A well-established narrative, in vogue in the 1960s and 1970s, of Nazism as the product of uneven development and of its exponents as searchers for a mythical past gave way to a recognition that in its roots and impulses Nazism drew on and expressed recognizable and widespread modern developments. Ever since then, the disturbing evidence of the Nazis' contemporaneity has both reflected and influenced our thinking about modernity.[3] Yet while the Nazis cannot be explained away by reference to some kind of special departure from the modern world, the present essay argues that the concept of modernity has proven surprisingly unhelpful as diagnosis and explanation. The problem is partly our lack of clarity about what modernity means, partly that in rejecting older modernization theories' normative assumptions we have often produced a new moralizing counternarrative about modernity's "fatal potential," and partly that the Nazis were a product far more of their particular epoch than of a generic Modern.[4] This in turn is an indicator less of Nazi specialness per se than of the fact that the basic ingredients of modernity allow for such massively varying societal outcomes and such huge differences between successive epochs, as to give modernity very little explanatory power.

2

For the modernization theories of the 1950s, Nazism was something of a provocation, since it was industrially modern but neither pluralistic nor benign.[5] Whereas Stalinism and to a certain extent Italian Fascism could be explained as developmental dictatorships, Nazism—despite the efforts of some authors—did not easily fit into this pattern.[6] Instead, it proved easier to read it as development gone wrong, a sign that the interlocking mechanisms that made up the modernization syndrome could get horribly out of sync. In the model of the German special path or *Sonderweg*, feudal elites were seen as having manipulated the political system, substituting chauvinistic and radical ideologies for genuine representation and allowing an irrational and antimodern movement to emerge and eventually gain political power.[7] As this brief account implies, much of this theorizing related to German society before 1933; Nazi Germany was the vanishing point for accounts of Germany's special path rather than the principal site on which the application of modernization theory took place.[8] However, some authors used modernization theory to attribute the regime's dysfunctional character to its lack of pluralism and rational structures.[9] Because it was clear that the regime had nevertheless made substantial use of modern technology, it was seen as exemplifying a kind of reactionary modernism.[10]

As modernization theory in general became discredited, so the *Sonderweg* approach in German history came under attack—particularly in its view of the limits to bourgeois influence and its emphasis on the power and influence of feudal groups.[11] The spread of new kinds of right-wing politics in Wilhelmine Germany, for example, was now no longer attributed to continuing feudal influence, but rather seen as a bourgeois response to the challenge to its leadership posed by the emergence of mass politics at a time of rapid change.[12] This, in turn, encouraged new ways of thinking about Nazism's roots and goals. Since the appearance of Detlev Peukert's book *Volksgenossen und Gemeinschaftsfremde* in 1982,[13] most references to modernity in work on Nazism have underlined the ways in which Nazism exemplified features of modernity or was born of a thoroughly modern crisis. From being an aberration from modernization, Nazism had become the quintessential manifestation of modernity.

Once the lens of classical modernization theory was cast aside, it became clear that Nazi electoral support did not come from marginal, backwards oriented groups and that the Nazis were not promising or seeking to escape from the framework of an industrial society.[14] To be sure the Nazis, like their fascist counterparts in Italy, prized the racial value of yeoman rural stock, but this was a common trope of contemporary racial theory and certainly no effort to turn back the clock.[15] Hitler himself was impatient with attacks on big business for the sake of the small man.[16] Industrial strength, affluent consumers, rural racial virtues, a vast tame agricultural hinterland—all these belonged to his notion of the Germany of the future.[17] Moreover, it also became clear that the early post-1945 decades had seen the suppression of many aspects of other contemporary societies that would have suggested that Nazism was in tune with contemporary trends.[18] Nowhere was this more evident than in the way that knowledge of the global support for social Darwinism and eugenics was suppressed in the wake of revelations about Nazism.[19] In the era of classical modernization theory, Nazism had thus looked more like an aberration than it should have. Finally, though this remains more contentious, it was far from clear that Nazism had proven so dysfunctional, in the sense either that popular discontent had forced it into war or that the regime's trajectory was the product of uncontrolled radicalization.

3

If neither the Nazis nor many of their supporters were looking backwards (except in the sense that all nationalists call on past myths and symbols), what did it mean to say that they were modern? Did it mean that the regime very largely resembled its contemporaries and the Third Reich was following or mirroring trends of neighboring societies? Was the point rather that its profile was distinctive but nonetheless made of modern clay? Or was it recognizably modern only in its point of departure—a thoroughly modern crisis—but with a subsequent trajectory that was *sui generis*? The striking variation in answers to these questions is not surprising on one level, given the hideous juxtapositions the Nazi regime has to offer, but on another it reveals the very considerable uncertainties as to what exactly modernity is, and what it looks like.

We can see this uncertainty in the terminology itself. Although "modernity" and "the modern" have emerged as the most influential concepts, "modernization"—admittedly different in its implications from older theories—has nevertheless retained an important place.[20] A small number of influential pieces have tried on "modernism" for size as a substitute for both terms.[21] Should modernity be understood as a set of common processes, albeit ones without the benign political associations they used to have? If so, the concept of modernization continues to be useful. If modernity is better conceptualized as a set of potentials or propensities, then "modernity" itself may be the preferred term.[22] Or should we be thinking rather of a state of mind or a claim made at various points in history—the kind of claim that, as Frederick Cooper put it, justified colonization—or perhaps the kind of dream of the future that encouraged dazzling new city visions?[23] If so, we may be moving into the territory of modernism.[24] These different usages map onto different ways of conceptualizing Nazism's relationship to the modern world. For example, "modernization" tends to be deployed for arguments that Nazism responded to similar social problems or pursued policies that were similar to those of neighboring societies.[25] Modernity and modernism, by contrast, tend to be preferred in work that foregrounds the distinctiveness of Nazi goals and actions, but diagnoses some underlying potential in modern society to which Nazism gave disturbing expression.[26] In short, the conceptual terrain reveals the plasticity in conceptualizations both of the modern world and of the Nazis' connection to it.

A glance at recent work on the Nazis as modernizers also reveals how difficult it has proved to classify social change given that the signposts offered by the classical theories of modernization have been dismantled. The most sophisticated efforts have come from Michael Prinz and Rainer Zitelmann, who saw Nazism as responding to the same challenges of renewal and development facing other industrial societies at the time of the world economic crisis.[27] Alongside their work, other authors claimed that the Nazis were offering innovative solutions to the economic crisis as "Keynesians before Keynes," or noted, among other things, the moves by the German Labor Front to promote productivity and the rational use of labor, or to remove the status barriers between blue- and white-collar workers in pursuit of a mobile and motivated workforce.[28] In 1933, Germany clearly did not stop being part of a transatlantic conversation about rationalization and effective man-management. Even within the SS, the men of the Business Administration Main Office combined a strong belief in the regime's priorities with a commitment to efficiency and modern management.[29]

Yet given the obvious political differences between Nazi Germany and other major industrial powers, it is clear that Nazi modernization cannot be subsumed under the classic notion of an interlocking syndrome, in which a given set of economic, social, and political developments necessarily fit together in a standard pattern. Some authors tried to address this with talk of "partial modernization," but then there was no longer a coherent sense of which developments were necessary or how they were functionally interrelated.[30] Classical theories had a clear measure of successful modernization, namely the development of pluralism and democracy, but the measure of modernity for newer work was much less obvious. It was reasonable for Michael Prinz to claim that we should not write off the Nazis' deprofessionalization of welfare through the winter-help scheme as antimodern, given the cyclical nature of governmental initiatives in the modern era more generally or for other authors to identity the modern elements in Nazi agrarian and environmental policies.[31] As long as the claim that the Nazis were willing modernizers is merely reactive, offering a critique of earlier modernization theory, it has traction: we can agree that, say, pro-agricultural policies are not necessarily a sign of romantic antimodernism. But the challenge, then, is to identify—particularly in the short-to-medium term—what policy trend would definitively *not* count as modernization.

Then again, no one was claiming the Holocaust as modernization, or arguing that a Germany which had carried out the mass murder of part of its population had thereby been *modernized*. Unlike the older literature, the newer work thus had no ready-made way of explaining the Nazis' exceptionality. At times the foregrounding of consumer dreams and the forgetting of mass murder seemed almost distasteful.[32]

4

The most influential conclusions about Nazism and modernity thus have not come from studies that focused on modernization as a set of "secular" processes but can rather be found in work from the Frankfurt School through Detlev Peukert to Zygmunt Bauman and Georgio Agamben identifying essential connections between Nazism's most striking and disturbing features and "modernity," here understood as a set of potentials or inherent impulses.[33] Influenced by Michel Foucault, historians have been increasingly aware of the repertoire of biopolitics that emerged in the eighteenth and nineteenth centuries, and of eugenics' growing influence in twentieth-century Europe and the United States.[34] Within Germany, eugenics had by the 1920s become a staple element in much social and medical policy discourse.[35] This biopolitics involved not just state ambition, but the increasing role of scientific knowledge (or at least knowledge that claimed scientific status) and specialist elites in shaping policy and discourse.[36] A second related argument has been to link the Nazis' embrace of selective racial engineering to the crisis of the welfare state. For Detlev Peukert, Germany was particularly vulnerable to calls for selective engineering because its advanced welfare state created ambitions and expectations that were not likely to survive economic crisis.[37] While Nazi antisemitism cannot be subsumed under quite the same narrative of efficiency and selectivity, here too there have been important arguments about the function and logic of murder in the context of Nazi imperial expansion.[38] At the broadest level, Zygmunt Bauman has argued that the Holocaust continued in relatively pure form—since territory and national competition were not at stake—a modern "garden culture," in which the modern state seeks to weed out the unfit and create the pure society, and Georgio Agamben and Enzo Traverso have placed Nazi violence in a similarly comprehensive setting of modern bioengineering.[39]

Yet if we glance at the question of eugenics again for a moment, for example, it is clear that precedents and parallels are not so clear-cut. Eugenics before 1933 came in a variety of forms, all of them freighted with potentially dangerous notions of heredity, but linked to political solutions, many of which were strikingly ameliorative and progressive.[40] Edward Ross Dickinson has reminded us also of eugenics' striking lack of political clout in the Weimar years despite its discursive presence.[41] If it is true that there were professionals who advocated "mercy killing" of useless individuals well before Hitler was on the political scene, it is also true that the majority of the profession was still opposed to such measures.[42] Moreover, the Nazis' central concept of the ethnic-racial *Volksgemeinschaft* radically altered the balance between individual and collective rights contained in Weimar's version of the social contract.[43] Neither in Germany nor elsewhere can 1920s welfare policy be restricted to its disciplinary aspects. The impetus was as much about inclusion, protection, and rights.[44] Once we reflect on the open-ended character of Weimar's social policy, we see a more general problem with the way characterizations of modernity are overly narrowly tailored to explaining the Nazi case.[45] It is certainly easier for the Nazis to be seen as "modern" if we forget about all those elements of modernity they did not exemplify.[46]

If one weakness of the modernity argument is thus that lines of continuity have been established too hastily, another is the misplaced emphasis on the role and power of reason. The ideologies and energies on which the Nazis drew often had little to do with rationality. It is clear that they were inspired by and gained traction from the reaction against rationalization as much as they sought to implement social rationalization.[47] Again, if we remain with biopolitics for a moment we can say that certainly, many scientific disciplines adapted and prospered under Nazism, knowledge was gained and effectively deployed. But in the biosciences, political pressure and ambitious opportunism often allowed the agenda to be driven from outside the realm of scientific knowledge.[48] It was widely known within the ministries dealing with racial matters that there was little evidence for the regime's claims about race. Even core players like Walter Gross were, as Claudia Koonz has noted, unsure of race's real existence.[49] Moreover, antisemitism's power and centrality made little sense in conventional calculations of social welfare or economic efficiency. The instrumental arguments deployed were strikingly versatile and thus clearly secondary.[50] Hitler himself later acknowledged that the Jews were not a race, though this dismantling of the ostensible logic of extermination did not mean he had abandoned his belief in their world-destructive role.[51] Overall, whether we look at Hitler's dreams of expansionism, at the clear evidence to informed insiders from December 1941 onward that Germany could not win the war, or at the mayhem Germany unleashed on others and itself, we are tempted to follow Ronald Aronson in talking of societal madness at least as much as we are inclined to emphasize the Nazis' rationality.[52] It certainly seems inappropriate to seek the genesis of the Holocaust in the "spirit of science."[53] As Michael Mann, Donald Bloxham, and others have shown, murderous population policies in the modern period were often pursued by nations thinking nationally without any very clear biologization of their identity beyond, perhaps, some strong narrative of descent or diffuse organicist nationalism.[54] "As a legitimation for genocide," writes Donald Bloxham, "biological racism is only at the extreme of a continuum of exclusionary beliefs that have the potential to attribute malign characteristics to all members of another group."[55]

Another important part of Bauman's account of the "gardener state" concerned the rationality and purposefulness of the tools with which it sought to clear out the weeds. Yet looking at the power and energy of Nazi bureaucracy, we are struck less by the rational power of bureaucracy per se than by the distinctive forces that gave it energy.[56] The pressure and competition provided by the mass party was crucial. In the Jewish question above all, but also in other facets of racial policy, the civil service was repeatedly chivied and radicalized by grassroots pressure.[57] Meanwhile, at a higher level, and particularly once the Nazis began to create new organizations in the occupied East, the dynamizing effect of competition for power in unregulated institutional space, conjoined with the *völkisch* ethos of a generation of ambitious younger staff, unleashed new energy.[58] Nazi mass shootings in the East recall other, more primitive genocides rather than a hyper-efficient modern state.[59] Paradoxically, Bauman's argument about the distinctive efficiency and calculus of the gardener state is weakened by the fact that recent work has shown all modern genocides have relied on bureaucracy.[60] The basic ability of a central bureaucracy to communicate and delegate looks rather more removed from any kind of defining explanation for genocide, when the little local township offices of the Rwandan context will do as well. It suggests that what is really at stake in the Nazi case is once again our disenchantment that highly educated bureaucrats, often in organizations of well-established pedigree, could nevertheless be deployed to such horrific ends. That is a different proposition from the claim that such bureaucracy was the decisive enabler.[61]

5

Of course, it is possible to make claims about Nazism's modernity that leave greater space for sentiment and for irrationality. Indeed, as both Frederic Jameson and Frederick Cooper have pointed out, for many contemporary observers of the *fin de siècle* and interwar periods, modernity's distinctive characteristic was not its rationality, and what was seen as modern was the polar opposite of cold reason.[62] Modernity was "speed, shock and the spectacle of constant sensation."[63] In the 1920s, to be modern often meant eschewing reason in the name of future, seeking a deeper truth than the flat mandate of orderly thought.[64] The aim of recent work presenting the Nazis not as modernizers but as "modernists" has been to capture the ways in which Nazism drew on such powerful sentiments and sensibilities.[65] According to both Peter Fritzsche and Roger Griffin, the Nazis shared with other modernist movements a commitment to radical renewal and the rooting out of decadence. Nazi utopianism, Griffin argues, allowed for "dynamically changing, kaleidoscopic combinations of past with future" mythic with "scientistic," "archaism with technicism."[66] In effect, the story is very similar to Herf's tale of "reactionary modernism" except that for Griffin the qualifying adjective is inappropriate because it rests on the false assumption that authentic modernism is of necessity socially progressive.[67]

The Nazis' metaphysical revolt against the constraints of civilization and their claim to be at the forefront of a new time is certainly reminiscent of other modernist manifestos (although the standard of inhumanity they actually set was unrivaled). Yet what does it really mean to call them modernists? First, we should be clear that to be "modernist" was quite distinct both from subjectively embracing the "modern" and from pursuing modernization. Modernism arguably bore some relation to modernity (or at least a temporally localized version of it), in the sense that it had been the shock of the new in the latter part of the nineteenth century that had helped give rise to it. Yet to be modernist often meant rejecting much that was then modern.[68] That was certainly true of Hitler, for whom modernity, indeed, was not a regular term in his vocabulary. Hitler's Darwinistic account of races and struggles was no modernization narrative, much as he recognized the potent threat represented by the United States.[69] Moreover, the Nazis were modernists in only a particular, limited sense. Hitler was no friend of much of the modernist aesthetic; far more than under Italian Fascism, artistic modernism's place in the Third Reich would remain complex and contested.[70] Nor did the Nazis embrace the dictates of technology with the enthusiasm of radical technical modernists such as Ernst Jünger.[71] So what made Nazis modernists, if that is what they were (it was not a term they themselves used), is less any particular kind of solution or direction to their policies than a radical style. Looking at the transformation of German politics after the First World War, however, we may well wonder whether their style and outlook was not the product of a narrower interwar conjuncture.

6

For the Frankfurt School,[72] Zygmunt Bauman, and others, modernity begins somewhere around the Enlightenment, and its defining characteristic is the imposition of order on society—the ultimate expression of which can be seen in Nazi racial engineering. For Roger Griffin, among many writers however, the focus is more narrowly on what has been dubbed "high modernity"—on the shock of the new and the search for new political and cultural forms in a mass political environment in the last quarter of the nineteenth century and the beginning of the twentieth century. Thus more narrowly defined, it is easier to see Nazism as a product of high modernity.[73]

Or is it? Consider the many characteristics of the interwar period that were so crucial for Nazism's character, aims, and resonance. Some of these characteristics radically heightened features of the foregoing epoch, some of them actually reversed previous trends, and some were without precedent. The first, and in many ways the author of the others was the First World War, including the defeat and the postwar settlement. The war's legacies in the international and domestic sphere affected the whole globe, but hit Germany as nowhere else. The experience of mechanized murder unleashed a cultural shock that provided a profoundly new resource for interpretation in the interwar period (though one malleable enough to be plied in very different shapes—some pacifist, some martial). In the course of the 1920s, the juxtaposition of the new experience of total war, on the one hand, with a decidedly un-total resolution to the global balance of power, on the other, created a very specific context within which German, Japanese, and other military elites thought about preparing for the next war. The strains that all the participating societies had experienced during the war, and the collapses and civil wars in its aftermath, suggested that creating a new kind of internal unity would be essential to winning the next conflict. The war's global nature, particularly American and colonial involvement in Europe's war, suggested also that the next conflict would be truly world-shaping. Apocalyptic visions surfaced in the notebooks of Ishiwara Kanji and Ernst Jünger and not just in Hitler's "struggle."[74]

The new paramilitary political style that smashed through the elegant plate glass of an older *Honoratiorenpolitik* in the 1920s was as much the product of the second transformative event that so left its mark on the period, namely, the Russian Revolution, and the chain of smaller revolutions that broke out in Central and Eastern Europe in its wake. The revolution, and Russia's lurking presence as the external embodiment of potential domestic revolt, created an overlay of external and internal threat that had not existed since the Napoleonic wars, perhaps not since the Thirty Years' War. As Andreas Wirsching has shown for both Berlin and Paris in the interwar period, every aspect of fascist politics was shaped by its confrontation with the radical left.[75] A third decisive feature of the interwar period was economic. Partly by dint of the war, partly by dint of the admittedly preexisting pressures for protectionism the interwar period saw a major disruption to longer term growth trends in international trade. Labor migration was hugely constrained, most notably because of new immigration laws in the United States. The slump radically accelerated this trend, creating a world of limited bilateral exchange and closed borders. For many thinkers in a colony-deprived Germany, a captive hinterland, as grain reserve and market, seemed essential, particularly as they looked to the growing power of the United States. Even the most export-oriented branches of German business lost their faith in the world economy.[76] By the mid-1930s, certainly, this pessimism was beginning to fade, and if Hitler had not been gearing the economy up for war there undoubtedly would have been a slide back toward greater international engagement. But the mercantilist climate of the interwar years was nevertheless crucial in shaping Hitler's worldview and that of the elites who backed the party.[77]

By unleashing the war, the Nazis dragged Germany to the brink of destruction and exposed it to decades of division. They brought the United States back into Europe and facilitated a division of the world into US and Soviet spheres. The war made the other powers economically dependent on the United States, and thus gave America the ability to shape the postwar economic system. The hydrogen bomb rendered interwar military thinking obsolete. The militarization of politics in European capitals was replaced by its economization, under the umbrella of US nuclear power and the US military industrial complex. Nazism also undermined many of the ideas with which it had become associated, setting a slow fuse burning underneath the concepts of race and antisemitism, and instantly depriving eugenics of respectability.[78] The Christian churches moved toward the explicit rejection of antisemitism (even if anticommunism remained an important source of continuity for a while).[79] The biopolitics of "modernity" would now look very different. Thus the Nazi disaster transformed flows of power, wealth, and ideas in the post–Second World War period.

These few brief remarks on the interwar period of course barely scratch the surface.[80] But they serve to remind us of the distinctiveness of different eras within the modern world. They also show how decisive the international context in was shaping the Nazi project. The balance of power, the sense of external threats, the opportunities for enrichment, but also the flow of ideas across borders, were crucial. This may well always be the case—and it certainly was when the First World War had made so many peoples and parties so conscious of the global character of alliances and power. The increased interdependence of nations is, of course, a central feature of modernity. As Chris Bayly has reminded us, the nation's most central and crucial characteristic was not the organization of power at home, but the fact that it found itself cheek by jowl with other nations.[81] While capitalist development, intellectual and religious movements, and evolving views about the international system might create certain kinds of uniformity, the international sphere remained in the interwar period in many senses unregulated and thus contingent. This contingency may be one reason why so many attempts to prove Nazism's modernity, and indeed why so many theories of modernization, pay the international context so little heed.

A growing number of historians have sought to acknowledge such diversity and contingency while rescuing the underlying idea of modernity by talking of "modernities" in the plural. Yet as Frederick Cooper has pointed out, this merely buries the problem.[82] The "family resemblance" between "modernities" is often not clear enough to justify the term (and, we might add, its distinction from the pre-modern period is rarely defined tightly enough to be meaningful).[83] Nazism, certainly, showed what a modern society could do. Our resulting disenchantment with the trappings of advanced industrial societies has been profound and enduring, and has caused us to rethink concepts such as progress, civilization, and modernization. But the effort to link National Socialism to pervasive or generic elements of modernity has shown not only the peculiarities of that strange and awful dictatorship, but also the fatal limitations of modernity as a concept with which to explain change in the modern world.[84]

Notes

1 For earlier reviews of these debates, see Norbert Frei, "Wie modern war der Nationalsozialismus," *Geschichte und Gesellschaft* 19:3 (1993), pp. 367–87; Mark Roseman, "National Socialism and Modernisation," in Richard Bessel (ed.), *Fascist Italy and Nazi Germany: Comparisons and Contrasts* (Cambridge: Cambridge University Press, 1996); Riccardo Bavaj, *Die Ambivalenz Der Moderne Im Nationalsozialismus: Eine Bilanz Der Forschung* (Munich: Oldenbourg, 2003).

2 Earlier luminaries who made important statements about Nazism's modernity (or antimodernity) include Ernst Bloch, "Amusement Co., Grauen, Drittes Reich" (1930), in *Erbschaft dieser Zeit. Gesamtausgabe IV* (1935; Frankfurt: Suhrkamp, 1977); Eric Voegelin, *Die Politischen Religionen* (Vienna: Bermann-Fischer Verlag, 1938); Ernst Fraenkel et al., *The Dual State: A Contribution to the Theory of Dictatorship* (New York: Oxford University Press, 1941); Walter Benjamin, "Theses on the Philosophy of History [1940]," in Hannah Arendt (ed.), *Illuminations* (New York: Schocken Books, 1969); Max Horkheimer and Theodor W. Adorno, *Dialectic of Enlightenment* (New York: Herder and Herder, 1972). The most important recent study of Nazism and modernity is Roger Griffin, *Modernism and Fascism: The Sense of a Beginning under Mussolini and Hitler* (Basingstoke: Palgrave Macmillan, 2007).

3   For an intelligent account of the links between attitudes to Nazism and the Holocaust and views of modernity, see Eric L. Santner, *Stranded Objects: Mourning, Memory, and Film in Postwar Germany* (Ithaca: Cornell University Press, 1990).

4   On the reification of the modern period, see also Carol Symes' essay in this Forum "When We Talk about Modernity," *The American Historical Review* 116:3 (2011), pp. 715–26.

5   On the bewildering variety of modernization theories, see Dean C. Tipps, "Modernization Theory and the Comparative Study of Societies: A Critical Perspective," *Comparative Studies in Society and History* 15:2 (1973), pp. 199–226.

6   David Ernest Apter, *The Politics of Modernization* (Chicago: University of Chicago Press, 1965); Cyril Edwin Black and Woodrow Wilson School of Public and International Affairs, Center of International Studies, *The Dynamics of Modernization: A Study in Comparative History* (New York: Harper & Row, 1966); A.F.K. Organski, *The Stages of Political Development* (New York: Knopf, 1965).

7   Heinrich A. Winkler, "Hitler, German Society and the Illusion of Restoration," *Journal of Contemporary History* 11:1 (1976), p. 1ff.; Seymour Martin Lipset, *Political Man: The Social Bases of Politics* (Garden City, NY: Doubleday, 1960); Bernd Weisbrod, *Schwerindustrie in der Weimarer Republik—Interessenpolitik zwischen Stabilisierung und Krise* (Wuppertal: P. Hammer 1978). On the Nazis' antimodernity, Henry Ashby Turner, *Faschismus Und Kapitalismus in Deutschland; Studien Zum Verhältnis Zwischen Nationalsozialismus Und Wirtschaft* (Göttingen: Vandenhoeck & Ruprecht, 1972), p. 162.

8   Helmut Walser Smith has eloquently drawn our attention to the way the vanishing point of 1933 long absorbed historians' attention to the detriment of 1941. Helmut Walser Smith, *The Continuities of German History: Nation, Religion, and Race across the Long Nineteenth Century* (Cambridge: Cambridge University Press, 2008), p. 13. The focus of the *Sonderweg* theory on the period before 1933, rather than Nazi rule itself, can be explained above all by the fact that it seemed that Nazi Germany eventually alienated or abandoned many of those groups most interested in some kind of restoration; Nazi policy was thus seen as an irrational ideology that had detached itself from its societal roots and run amok. Thus while modernization theory provided the essential backbone for the arguments about German society before 1933, the big debates in the 1960s and 1970s about the Nazi period itself often only implicitly made reference to modernization. Both sides of the intentionalist-functionalist debate shared the view of the regime's essential irrationality, but they differed in their assessment of how it worked. For both, the role of the charismatic leader was important, but whereas the intentionalists emphasized Hitler's agency, and assumed that mechanisms of obedience and fear sufficed to ensure the implementation of his agenda, the functionalists saw charisma as the glue that held together an otherwise unstable and dynamic set of competing agencies, and attributed to the irrationality of this power structure the dynamic that drove the regime

forward to destruction. This kind of structural-functional analysis clearly operated with notions of the rationality of modern governance similar to modernization theorists, but it rested in this case not directly on a belief in the necessity of pluralism as a recipe for balanced modernization but rather on a Weberian analysis of the charismatic rule that was at the heart of the regime. By melding charismatic and bureaucratic rule, the Nazis both incorporated and opposed principles of rational government. But because this was not articulated in the context of modernization theory, it has to a certain extent survived despite very differing assumptions to other more recent work. See Hans Mommsen, "Die Realisierung Des Utopischen: Die 'Endlösung Der Judenfrage' Im 'Dritten Reich,' " *Geschichte und Gesellschaft* 9:3 (1983), pp. 381–420; Martin Broszat, *Der Staat Hitlers. Grundlegung Und Entwicklung Seiner Inneren Verfassung* (Munich: Deutscher Taschenbuch, 1969); Mark Roseman, "Beyond Conviction? Perpetrators, Ideas, and Action in the Holocaust in Historiographical Perspective," in Frank Biess, Mark Roseman, and Hanna Schissler (eds.), *Conflict, Catastrophe and Continuity: Essays on Modern German History* (New York: Berghahn, 2007).

9   Horst Matzerath and Heinrich Volkmann, "Modernisierungstheorie und Nationalsozialismus," in Jürgen Kocka (ed.), *Theorien in der Praxis des Historikers. Geschichte und Gesellschaft Sonderheft* 3 (Göttingen: Vandenhoeck & Ruprecht, 1977), pp. 86–102 (with discussion of the piece by other historians pp. 102–16).

10 Jeffrey Herf, *Reactionary Modernism: Technology, Culture, and Politics in Weimar and the Third Reich* (Cambridge: Cambridge University Press, 1984). Ralf Dahrendorf and David Schoenbaum argued that the contradiction between reactionary aims and modern means led in the end to the unwitting modernization of German society, as the Nazis' totalitarian aspirations led them to destroy their authoritarian roots. Ralf Dahrendorf, *Gesellschaft Und Demokratie in Deutschland* (Munich: R. Piper, 1965); David Schoenbaum, *Hitler's Social Revolution: Class and Status in Nazi Germany, 1933–1939* (Garden City, NY: Doubleday, 1966). On the differences between them, see Roseman, "National Socialism and Modernisation."

11 For the connections between modernization theory and German history, see Hans Ulrich Wehler, *Modernisierungstheorie Und Geschichte* (Göttingen: Vandenhoeck & Ruprecht, 1975), p. 18ff. For the *Sonderweg* critique, see David Blackbourn and Geoff Eley, *The Peculiarities of German History: Bourgeois Society and Politics in Nineteenth-Century Germany* (New York: Oxford University Press, 1984). Modernization theory has recently made a comeback in some branches of political science. It still has difficulty contending with Nazi Germany, however. See Ronald Inglehart and Christian Welzel, *Modernization, Cultural Change, and Democracy: The Human Development Sequence* (New York: Cambridge University Press, 2005), pp. 161–6.

12 Geoff Eley, *Reshaping the German Right: Radical Nationalism and Political Change after Bismarck* (New Haven: Yale University Press, 1980).

13 Detlev Peukert, *Volksgenossen Und Gemeinschaftsfremde: Anpassung, Ausmerze Und Aufbegehren Unter Dem Nationalsozialismus* (Cologne:

Bund, 1982). Published in English as Detlev Peukert, *Inside Nazi Germany: Conformity, Opposition, and Racism in Everyday Life* (New Haven: Yale University Press, 1987).

14 Jürgen W. Falter, *Hitlers Wähler* (Munich: Beck, 1991); Thomas Childers, *The Nazi Voter: The Social Foundations of Fascism in Germany, 1919–1933* (Chapel Hill: University of North Carolina Press, 1983); Peter Fritzsche, *Rehearsals for Fascism: Populism and Political Mobilization in Weimar Germany* (New York: Oxford University Press, 1990). Monika Renneberg and Mark Walker, "Scientists, Engineers and National Socialism," in Monika Renneberg and Mark Walker (eds.), *Science, Technology, and National Socialism* (Cambridge: Cambridge University Press, 1994), pp. 1–29.

15 Rainer Zitelmann, *Hitler, Selbstverständnis Eines Revolutionärs*, 3. Aufl. ed. (Stuttgart: Klett-Cotta, 1990).

16 For an outstanding account of Nazi economic thinking, see J. Adam Tooze, *The Wages of Destruction: The Making and Breaking of the Nazi Economy* (London: Allen Lane, 2006). See also Griffin, *Modernism and Fascism*, p. 314.

17 On this, see also Jill Stephenson, *Hitler's Home Front: Württemberg under the Nazis* (London: Hambledon Continuum, 2006).

18 Jean-François Lyotard argued that the forty-year postwar desire to safeguard the "modern project" had led to the reality of Nazism being hidden. Jean-François Lyotard, "Ticket to a New Decor," *Copywright* 1:10 (1987), pp. 14–15: http://www.egs.edu/faculty/jean-francois-lyotard/articles/ticket-to-a-new-decor/ [accessed 10 May 2010].

19 In 1945, the Encyclopedia Britannica quietly euthanized that entry for "Civilization" which since its 1910 edition had declared that the future of humanity would probably be ruled by the "biological improvement of the race" and by man applying "whatever laws of heredity he knows or may acquire in the interests of his own species, as he has long applied them in the case of domesticated animals." Enzo Traverso, *The Origins of Nazi Violence* (New York: New Press, 2003), pp. 122–3. The 1911 edition can be found on the website "Civilization—LoveToKnow 1911": http://www.1911encyclopedia.org/Civilization.

20 Thomas Mergel notes the shift from modernization to modernity, but wrote too early to see the more recent work on modernism. Thomas Mergel, "Geht Es Weiterhin Voran? Die Modernisierungstheorie Auf Dem Weg Zu Einer Theorie Der Moderne," in Thomas Mergel and Thomas Welskopp (eds), *Geschichte Zwischen Kultur Und Gesellschaft: Beiträge Zur Theoriedebatte* (Munich: CH Beck, 1997). On the extensive continued use of modernization as concept, see Bavaj, *Die Ambivalenz Der Moderne Im Nationalsozialismus*.

21 Most notably, Peter Fritzsche, "Nazi Modern," *Modernism/modernity* 3:1 (1996), pp. 1–22; Griffin, *Modernism and Fascism*.

22 Lyotard, "Ticket to a New Decor."

23 On the visions behind colonization, see Frederick Cooper, "Modernity," in Fredrick Cooper (ed.), *Colonialism in Question: Theory, Knowledge, History* (Berkeley: University of California Press, 2005), pp. 113–17. On city visions,

see Richard Dennis, *Cities in Modernity: Representations and Productions of Metropolitan Space, 1840–1930* (Cambridge: Cambridge University Press, 2008).

24 On the complex relationship between modernity and modernism, see Robin W. Winks and Joan Neuberger, *Europe and the Making of Modernity, 1815–1914* (Oxford: Oxford University Press, 2005), pp. 309–10.

25 See, for example, Michael Prinz and Rainer Zitelmann, *Nationalsozialismus Und Modernisierung* (Darmstadt: Wissenschaftliche Buchgesellschaft, 1991).

26 This work is explored in the following section.

27 Prinz and Zitelmann, *Nationalsozialismus Und Modernisierung*; Zitelmann, *Hitler, Selbstverständnis Eines Revolutionärs*; Uwe Backes, Eckhard Jesse and Rainer Zitelmann (eds.), *Die Schatten Der Vergangenheit: Impulse Zur Historisierung Des Nationalsozialismus* (Berlin: Propyläen, 1990).

28 Albrecht Ritschl, "Zum Verhaeltnis Von Markt Und Staat in Hitlers Weltbild. Überlegungen Zu Einer Forschungskontroverse," in Uwe Backes, Eckhard Jesse, and Rainer Zitelmann (eds.), *Die Schatten Der Vergangenheit: Impulse Zur Historisierung Des Nationalsozialismus* (Berlin: Propyläen, 1990); Werner Abelshauser and Anselm Faust, *Wirtschafts- Und Sozialpolitik: Eine Nationalsozialistische Sozialrevolution?* (Tübingen: Dt. Inst. für Fernstudien, 1983). Michael Prinz was influential here, too. Michael Prinz, *Vom Neuen Mittelstand Zum Volksgenossen: Die Entwicklung Des Sozialen Status Der Angestellten Von Der Weimarer Republik Bis Zum Ende Der Ns-Zeit*, Studien Zur Zeitgeschichte (Munich: R. Oldenbourg, 1986). See also Tilla Siegel, "Rationalisierung Statt Klassenkampf. Zur Rolle Der Deutschen Arbeitsfront in Der Nationalsozialistischen Ordnung Der Arbeit," in Hans Mommsen and Susanne Willems (eds.), *Herrschaftsalltag Im Dritten Reich: Studien Und Texte* (Düsseldorf: Schwann, 1988).

29 Michael Thad Allen, *The Business of Genocide: The SS, Slave Labor, and the Concentration Camps* (Chapel Hill: University of North Carolina Press, 2002).

30 Wolfgang Zollitsch, *Arbeiter Zwischen Weltwirtschaftskrise Und Nationalsozialismus: Ein Beitrag Zur Sozialgeschichte Der Jahre 1928 Bis 1936* (Göttingen: Vandenhoeck & Ruprecht, 1990), p. 241.

31 Michael Prinz, "Die Soziale Funktion Moderner Elemente in Der Gesellschaftspolitik Des Nationalsozialismus," in Michael Prinz and Rainer Zitelmann (eds.), *Nationalsozialismus Und Modernisierung* (Darmstadt: Wissenschaftliche Buchgesellschaft, 1991); Rainer Zitelmann, "Die Totalitäre Seite Der Moderne," in Prinz and Zitelmann, *Nationalsozialismus Und Modernisierung*.

32 See Norbert Frei's review of Zitelmann's work in Frei, "Wie Modern."

33 Horkheimer and Adorno, *Dialectic of Enlightenment*; Detlev Peukert, *Max Webers Diagnose Der Moderne*, Kleine Vandenhoeck-Reihe (Göttingen: Vandenhoeck & Ruprecht, 1989); Zygmunt Bauman, *Modernity and the Holocaust* (Ithaca: Cornell University Press, 1989); Giorgio Agamben, *Homo Sacer. Sovereign Power and Bare Life* (Stanford: Stanford University Press, 1998).

34   Michel Foucault, *History of Sexuality, Volume 1: An Introduction* (London: Allen Lane, 1979); Martin Shaw, "Sociology and Genocide," in Donald Bloxham and A. Dirk Moses (eds.), *The Oxford Handbook of Genocide Studies* (New York: Oxford University Press, 2010), p. 150.

35   Paul Weindling, *Health, Race, and German Politics between National Unification and Nazism, 1870–1945* (Cambridge: Cambridge University Press, 1993); Gisela Bock, *Zwangssterilisation Im Nationalsozialismus: Studien Zur Rassenpolitik Und Frauenpolitik* (Opladen: Westdeutscher Verlag, 1986); Cornelie Usborne, *The Politics of the Body in Weimar Germany: Women's Reproductive Rights and Duties* (Ann Arbor: University of Michigan Press, 1992).

36   Ernst Klee, *"Euthanasie" Im Ns-Staat: Die "Vernichtung Lebensunwerten Lebens"* (Frankfurt: S. Fischer, 1983).

37   Detlev Peukert, *The Weimar Republic: The Crisis of Classical Modernity* (London: Allen Lane, 1991).

38   Among many others Götz Aly and Susanne Heim, *Vordenker Der Vernichtung: Auschwitz Und Die Deutschen Pläne Für Eine Neue Europäische Ordnung* (Hamburg: Hoffmann und Campe, 1991); Christian Gerlach, *Kalkulierte Morde: Die Deutsche Wirtschafts- Und Vernichtungspolitik in Weissrussland 1941 Bis 1944*, 1. Aufl. ed. (Hamburg: Hamburger Edition, 1999); Christian Gerlach and Götz Aly, *Das Letzte Kapitel: Realpolitik, Ideologie Und Der Mord an Den Ungarischen Juden 1944/1945* (Stuttgart: Deutsche Verlags-Anstalt, 2002).

39   Bauman, *Modernity and the Holocaust*, p. 83; Agamben, *Homo Sacer*; Traverso, *The Origins of Nazi Violence*.

40   See, to take one example, the important recent work on Charlotte Perkins Gilman, which recognizes her eugenics for what it is—significant but shaped by a series of liberal and feminist assumptions. Judith A. Allen, *The Feminism of Charlotte Perkins Gilman: Sexualities, Histories, Progressivism* (Chicago: University of Chicago Press, 2009), esp. pp. 321–3.

41   E.R. Dickinson, "Biopolitics, Fascism, Democracy: Some Reflections on Our Discourse About 'Modernity,'" *Central European History* 37:1 (2004), pp. 1–48.

42   Michael Burleigh, *Death and Deliverance: "Euthanasia" In Germany c. 1900–1945* (Cambridge: Cambridge University Press, 1994), pp. 38–9.

43   A more empowering relationship between individual and collective had been at the heart of so much that was modern in Germany so the radical break from the process of individualization needs closer attention. Ute Daniel, "'Kultur' und Gesellschaft. Überlegungen zum Gegenstandsbereich der Sozialgeschichte," *Geschichte und Gesellschaft* 19:1 (1993), pp. 69–99.

44   Young-sun Hong, *Welfare, Modernity, and the Weimar State, 1919–1933* (Princeton: Princeton University Press, 1998).

45   Fritzsche, "Nazi Modern," p. 10.

46   For example, in so many other historical contexts, modernity as a concept is seen as integrally involving individualism, be it in cultural expression,

in discussion of political rights, or in the formation of public and private identities. See Winks and Neuberger, *Europe and the Making of Modernity, 1815–1914*, or the suggestive comments in Michael P. Steinberg, *Judaism Musical and Unmusical* (Chicago: University of Chicago Press, 2007), p. 6ff.

47 Mary Nolan, *Visions of Modernity: American Business and the Modernization of Germany* (New York: Oxford University Press, 1994).

48 Michael Burleigh is particularly good on the mixture of adaptation, opportunism, political pressure, and personnel change in Burleigh, *Death and Deliverance*, ch. 2.

49 Claudia Koonz, *The Nazi Conscience* (Cambridge: Belknap Press, 2005), pp. 115, 28, 175.

50 See Mark Roseman, "Ideas, Contexts and the Pursuit of Genocide," *Bulletin of the German Historical Institute* 25:1 (May 2003), pp. 64–87, reprinted in Jeremy Black (ed.), *The Second World War: Volume V, The Holocaust* (Aldershot: Ashgate, 2007), pp. 1–25.

51 See Adolf Hitler and Martin Bormann, *Hitler's politisches Testament*, pp. 68–9, cited in Richard Steigmann-Gall, "Aryan and Semite, Christ and Antichrist: Rethinking Religion and Modernity in Nazi Antisemitism," unpublished paper, "Rethinking German Modernity" conference, Toronto, 2005.

52 Tooze, *The Wages of Destruction*, pp. 506–08; Ronald Aronson, "Social Madness," *Violence and Abuse Abstracts* 6:3 (2000), pp. 125–41; Ronald Aronson, *Technological Madness: Towards a Theory of the Impending Nuclear Holocaust* (London: Menard, 1983).

53 Detlev Peukert, "The Genesis of the 'Final Solution' from the Spirit of Science," in David F. Crew (ed.), *Nazism and German Society, 1933–1945: Rewriting Histories* (London: Routledge, 1994).

54 Michael Mann, *The Dark Side of Democracy: Explaining Ethnic Cleansing* (Cambridge: Cambridge University Press, 2005), pp. 61–8.

55 Donald Bloxham, *The Final Solution: A Genocide* (Oxford: Oxford University Press, 2009), p. 6.

56 The argument that the division of labor enabled detachment from murderous decision-making, for example, is true only as a postwar legal defense. During the war itself, the protagonists claimed ownership—and indeed historians trying to unravel the chain of decision-making often face the reverse problem—namely, that participants in the final solution, be it a Heydrich, a Greiser, or an Eichmann, claimed more, not less authorship than was warranted. Moreover, these were not desk-murderers shielded from the reality of their actions. A staple element of SS leadership style was to visit the killing sites repeatedly. Himmler's key decisions were most often made after the latest visit to the bloodbath. Mid-ranking Gestapo and SD operatives circulated between desk job and field job throughout the war. See Roseman, "Beyond Conviction?"

57 On the role of popular forces in pushing the Jewish agenda, see Michael Wildt, *Volksgemeinschaft Als Selbstermächtigung: Gewalt Gegen Juden in Der Deutschen Provinz 1919 Bis 1939*, 1. Aufl. ed. (Hamburg: Hamburger Edition, 2007).

58 Michael Wildt, *Generation Des Unbedingten: Das Führungskorps Des Reichssicherheitshauptamtes* (Hamburg: Hamburger Edition, 2002).

59 See also Nancy Scheper-Hughes, "Coming to Our Senses: Anthropology and Genocide," in Alexander Laban Hinton (ed.), *Annihilating Difference: The Anthropology of Genocide* (Berkeley: University of California Press, 2002).

60 Donald Bloxham, "Organized Mass Murder: Structure, Participation, and Motivation in Comparative Perspective," *Holocaust and Genocide Studies* 22:2 (2008), pp. 203–45.

61 See also Shaw, "Sociology and Genocide."

62 Frederic Jameson, "Foreword" to Jean-François Lyotard, *The Postmodern Condition: A Report on Knowledge* (Minneapolis: University of Minnesota Press, 1984), p. xviii; Cooper, *Colonialism in Question*, p. 123. I am indebted to Donald Bloxham for the insight that Arnold Toynbee saw the 1870s as the beginning of postmodernity, because of the retreat from modern rationality. Arnold Joseph Toynbee, *A Study of History* (London: Oxford University Press, 1934).

63 Harry D. Harootunian, *Overcome by Modernity: History, Culture, and Community in Interwar Japan* (Princeton: Princeton University Press, 2000), p. 18.

64 Winks and Neuberger, *Europe and the Making of Modernity*, pp. 309–10.

65 Fritzsche, "Nazi Modern," p. 10.

66 Griffin, *Modernism and Fascism*, pp. 270, 332.

67 Herf, *Reactionary Modernism*.

68 Griffin, *Modernism and Fascism*.

69 Tooze, *The Wages of Destruction*, p. 11ff.

70 Ulrich Schmid, "Style versus Ideology: Towards a Conceptualisation of Fascist Aesthetics," *Totalitarian Movements and Political Religions* 6:1 (2005), pp. 127–40.

71 Thomas Rohrkrämer, "Antimodernism, Reactionary Modernism and National Socialism. Technocratic Tendencies in Germany," *Contemporary European History* 8:1 (1999), pp. 48–9.

72 Horkheimer and Adorno, *Dialectic of Enlightenment*.

73 Ulrich Herbert, "Europe in High Modernity. Reflections on a Theory of the 20th Century," *Journal of Modern European History* 5:1 (2007), pp. 5–21.

74 Mark R. Peattie, *Ishiwara Kanji and Japan's Confrontation with the West* (Princeton: Princeton University Press, 1975); Ernst Jünger, *Der Arbeiter* (Hamburg: Hanseatische Verlagsanstalt, 1932).

75 Andreas Wirsching, *Vom Weltkrieg Zum Bürgerkrieg?: Politischer Extremismus in Deutschland Und Frankreich 1918–1933/39: Berlin Und Paris Im Vergleich* (Munich: Oldenbourg, 1999).

76 Volker R. Berghahn, *Unternehmer Und Politik in Der Bundesrepublik* (Frankfurt: Suhrkamp, 1985), p. 29ff.

77   Though as Adam Tooze notes, the objective realities of the economy did not suffice to explain the kinds of risk Hitler was willing to take in order to create an empire to rival the United States. Tooze, *The Wages of Destruction*, p. xxv.

78   See above and note 19. On the secrecy surrounding Nazi eugenics after the war, see Burleigh, *Death and Deliverance*, p. 269ff.

79   Geoffrey Wigoder, *Jewish-Christian Relations since World War II* (Manchester: Manchester University Press/St. Martin's Press, 1988).

80   Just to make the obvious point, this is not to claim that Nazism is explicable solely in the context of the interwar period. There are many concentric or overlapping circles of explanation and connection, some of which tie Nazism to other movements in the twentieth century, some to roots in the high modern period, and some indeed to the whole of the period of what we call modernity.

81   C.A. Bayly, *The Birth of the Modern World, 1780–1914: Global Connections and Comparisons* (Malden, MA: Blackwell, 2004).

82   Cooper, "Modernity," p. 127.

83   See the use of the concept of family resemblances in relation to modernity in Michael L. Satlow, "Defining Judaism: Accounting for 'Religions' in the Study of Religion," *Journal of the American Academy of Religion* 74:4 (2006), pp. 837–60 and the discussion in Steinberg, *Judaism Musical and Unmusical*, p. 6.

84   I particularly welcome recent efforts to place Nazism and the Holocaust in their epochal context, most notably Bloxham, *Final Solution*.

INDEX

Note: Locators followed by the letter 'n' refer to notes.

.